EMIKO SUPERSTAR

Published by DC Comics,
1700 Broadway, New York, NY 10019.

Printed in Canada.
DC Comics, a Warner Bros.
Entertainment Company.

ISBN: 978-1-4012-1536-1

Cover by Steve Rolston

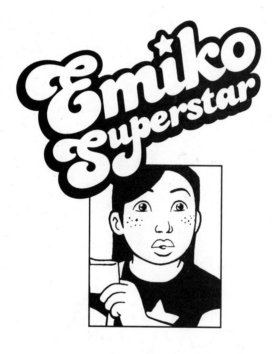

Emiko Superstar

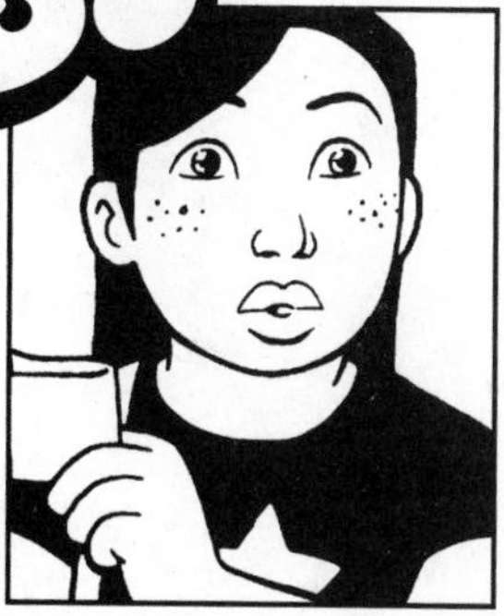

Written by Mariko Tamaki
Illustrated by Steve Rolston

Lettering by Jared K. Fletcher

minx

CHARACTER HEIGHTS
(barefoot height in brackets)

5'10"

5'0"

5'7" (5'4")

5'4" (5'1")

5'9" (5'8")

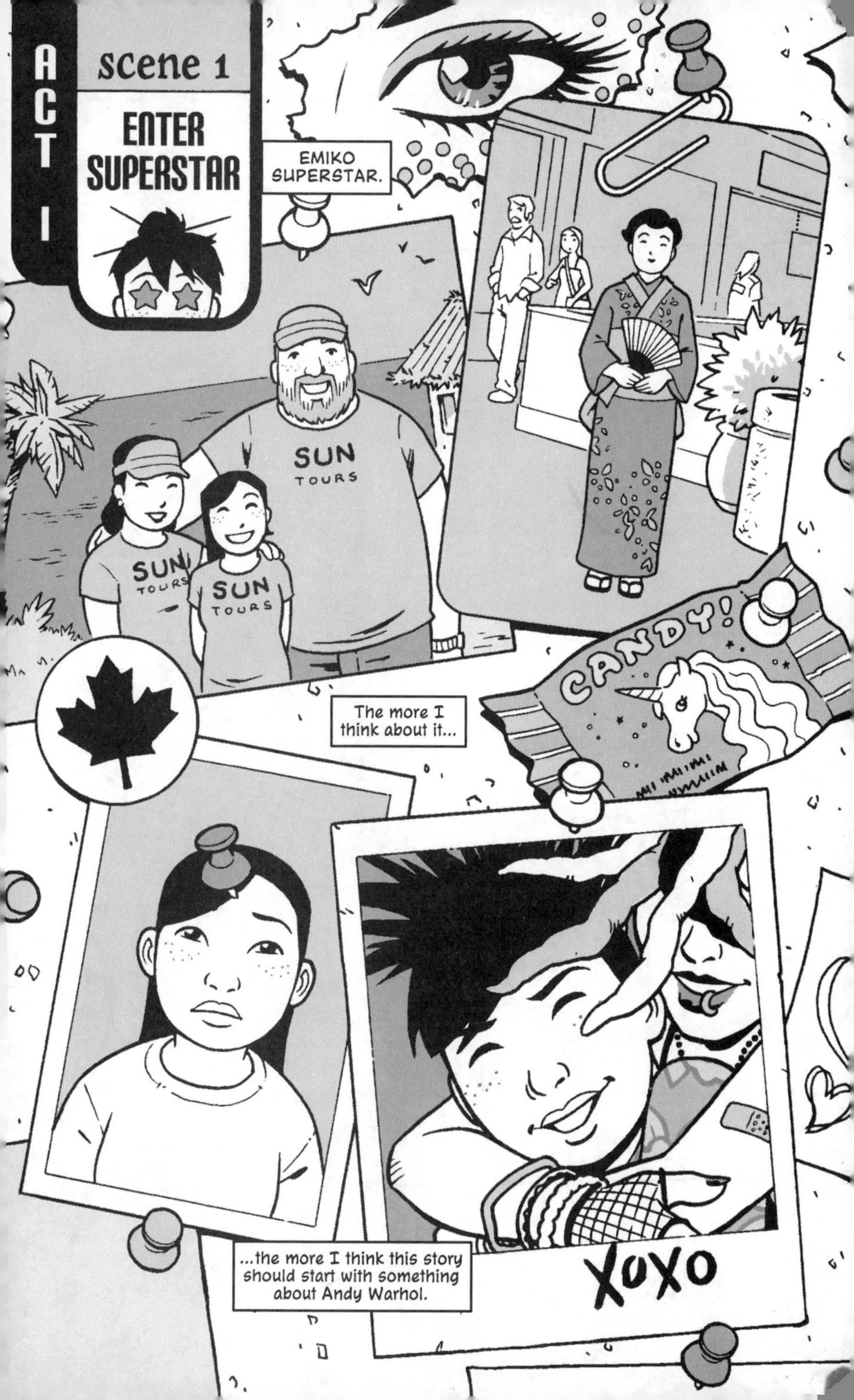
ACT I
scene 1
ENTER SUPERSTAR
EMIKO SUPERSTAR.
SUN TOURS
SUN TOURS
SUN TOURS
CANDY!
The more I think about it...
...the more I think this story should start with something about Andy Warhol.
XOXO

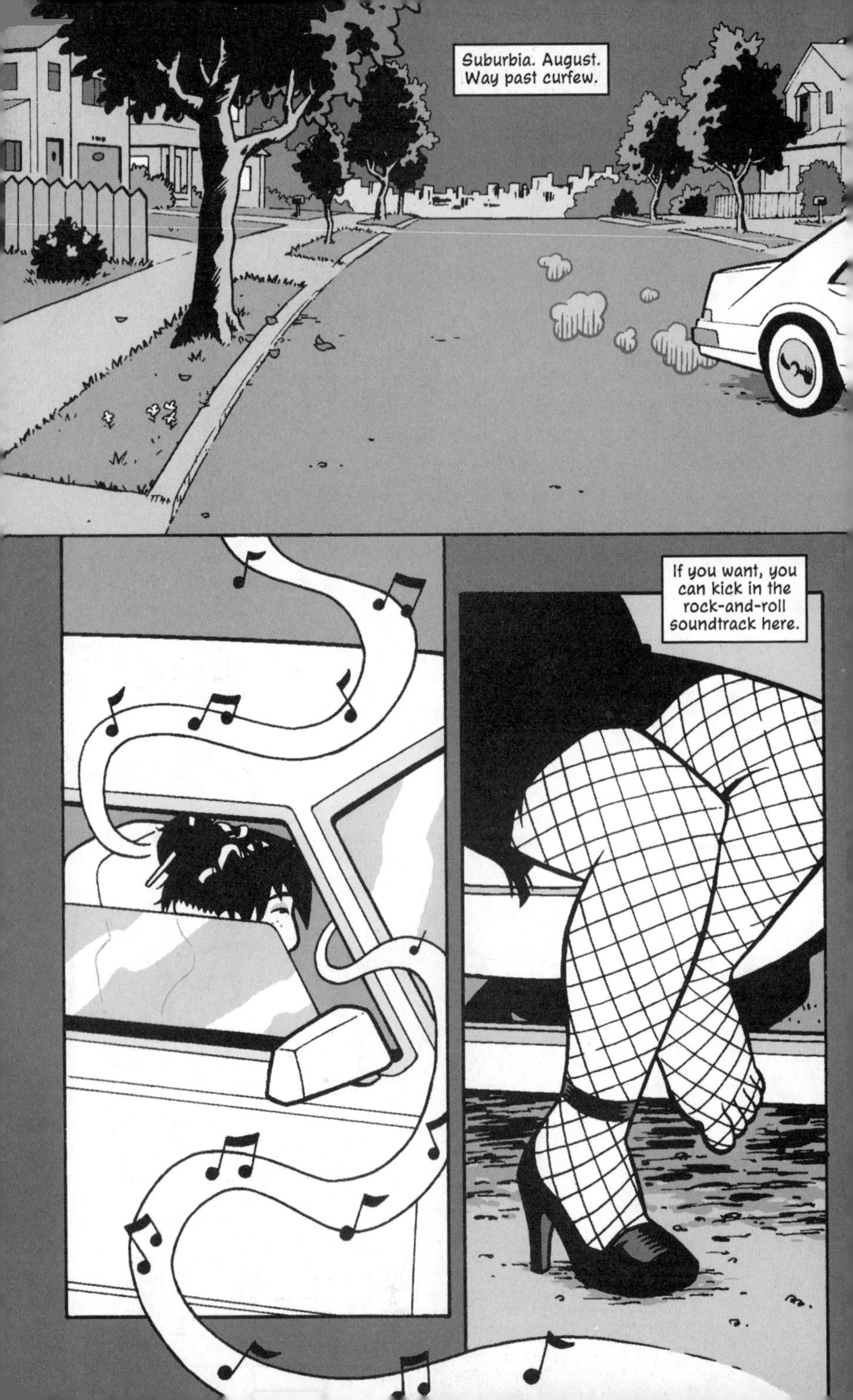

Suburbia. August. Way past curfew.
If you want, you can kick in the rock-and-roll soundtrack here.

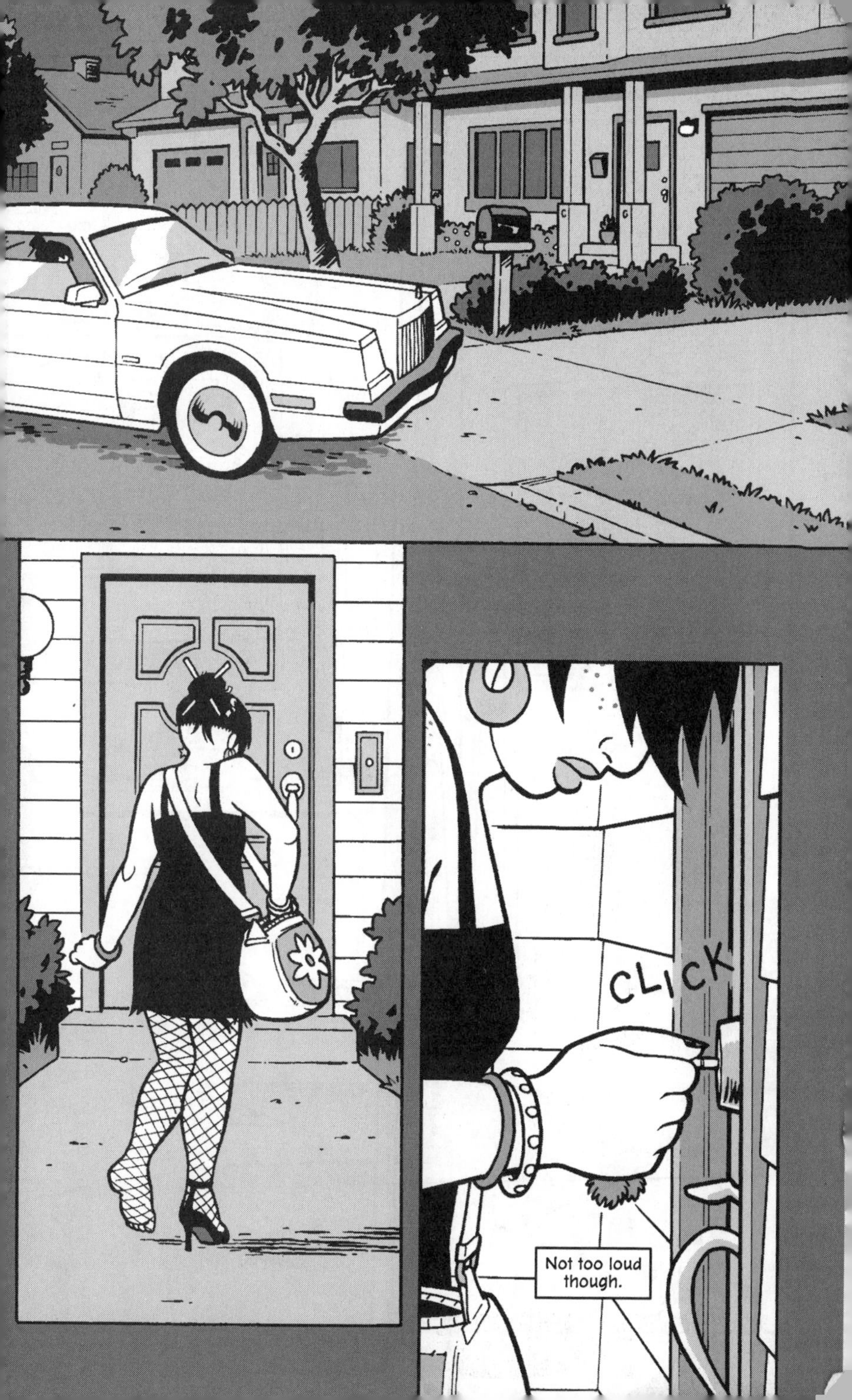
CLICK
Not too loud though.

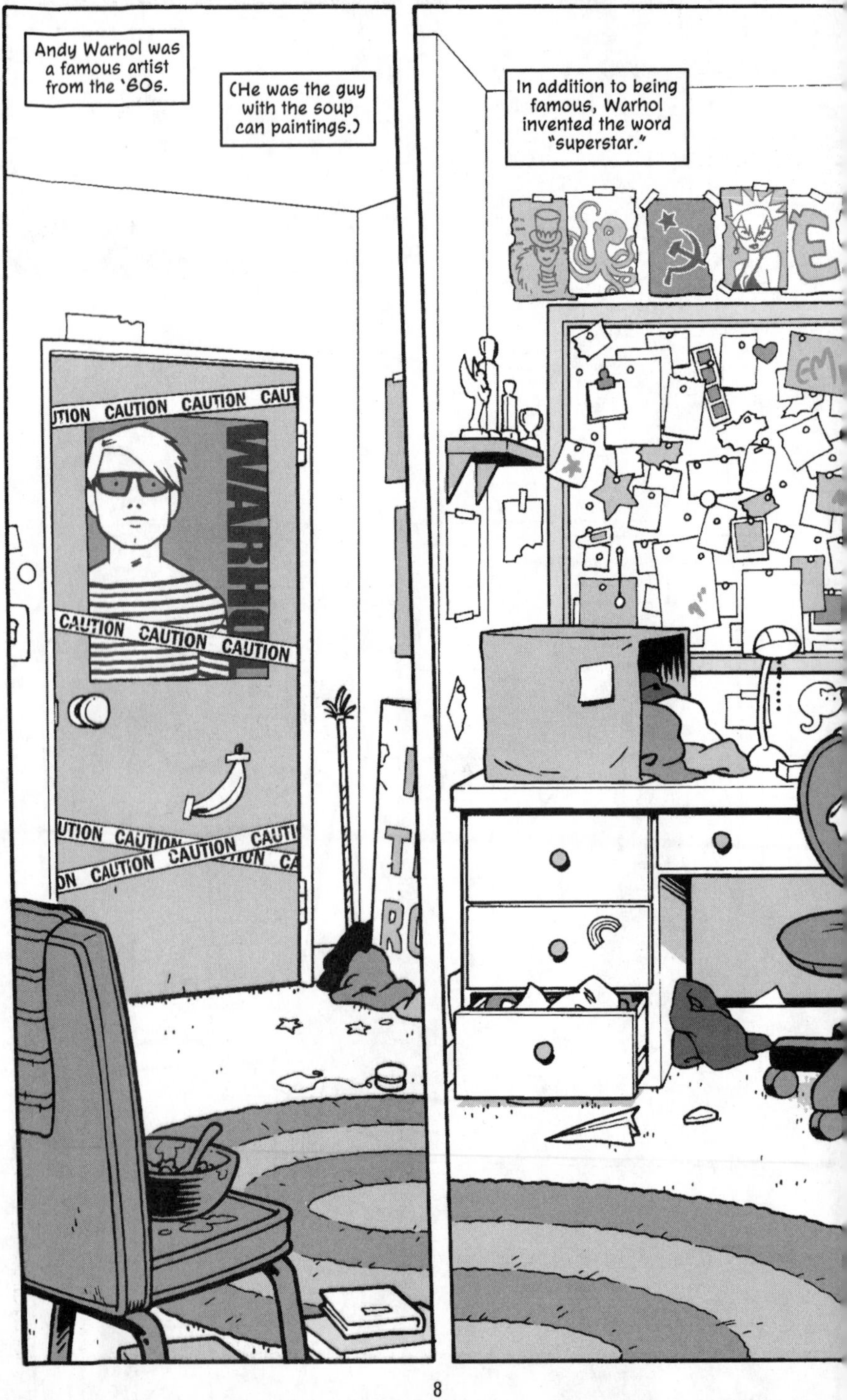
Andy Warhol was a famous artist from the '60s.
(He was the guy with the soup can paintings.)
In addition to being famous, Warhol invented the word "superstar."

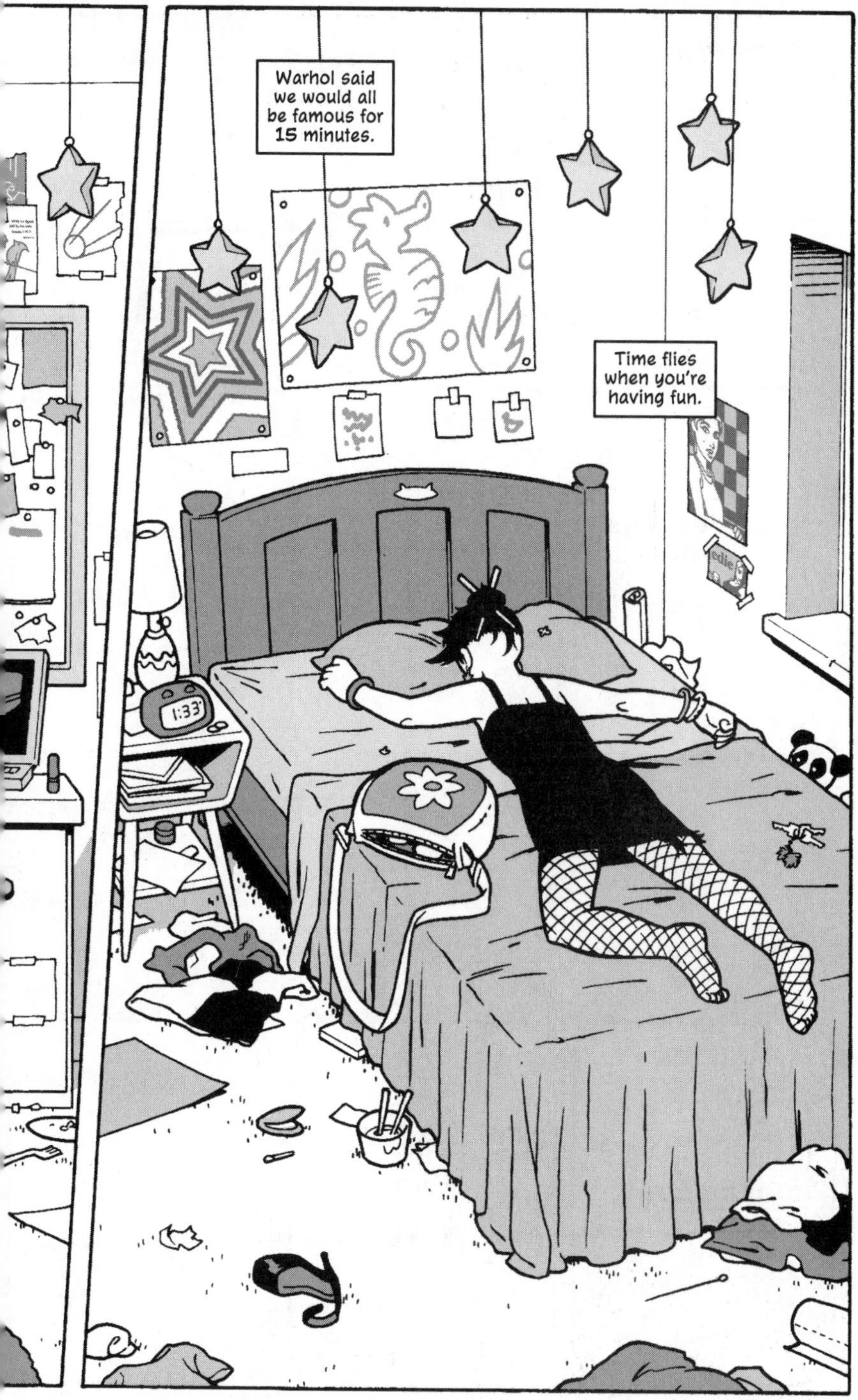
Warhol said we would all be famous for 15 minutes.
Time flies when you're having fun.

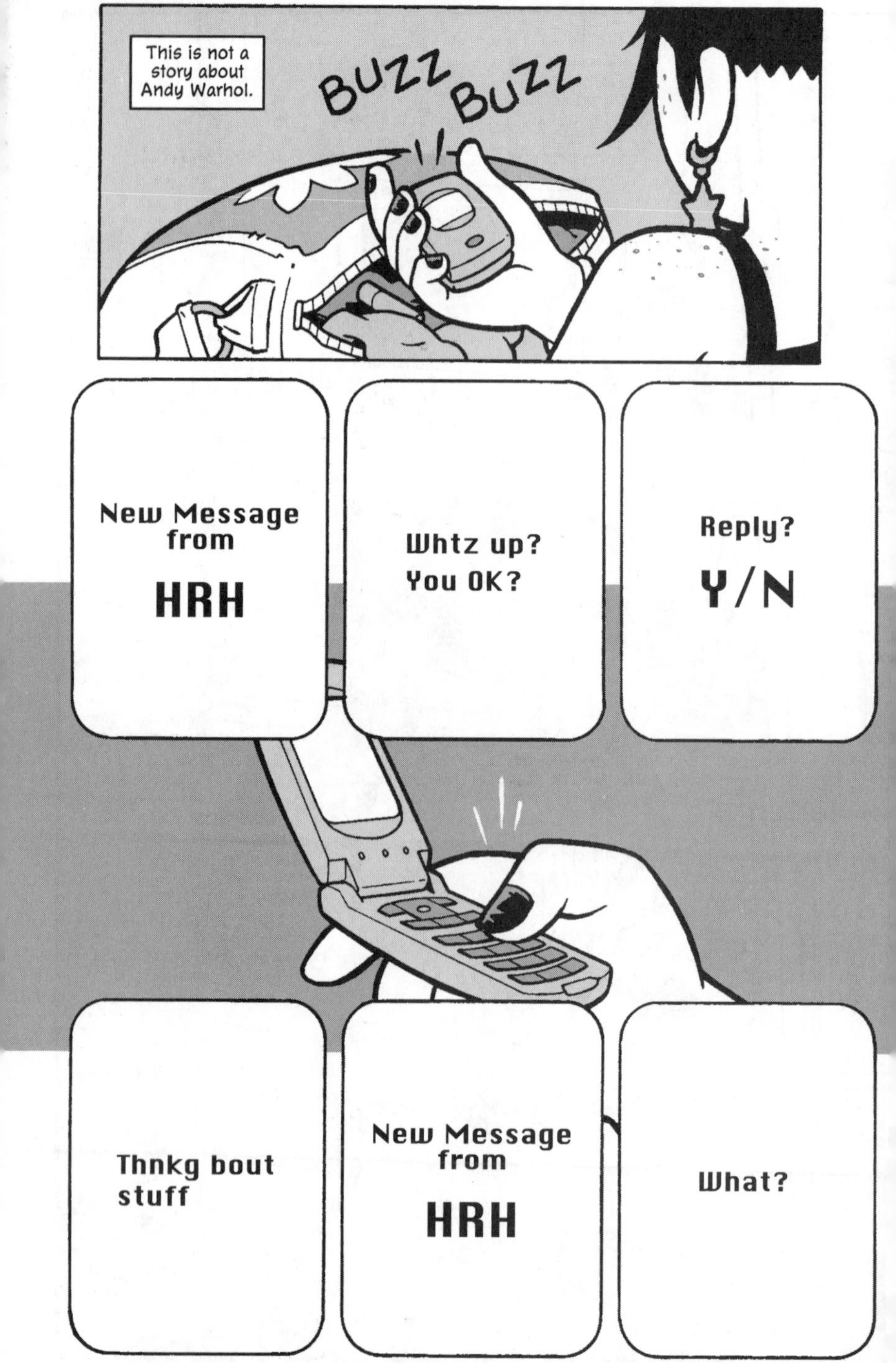
This is not a story about Andy Warhol.
BUZZ BUZZ
New Message from
HRH
Whtz up? You OK?
Reply?
Y/N
Thnkg bout stuff
New Message from
HRH
What?

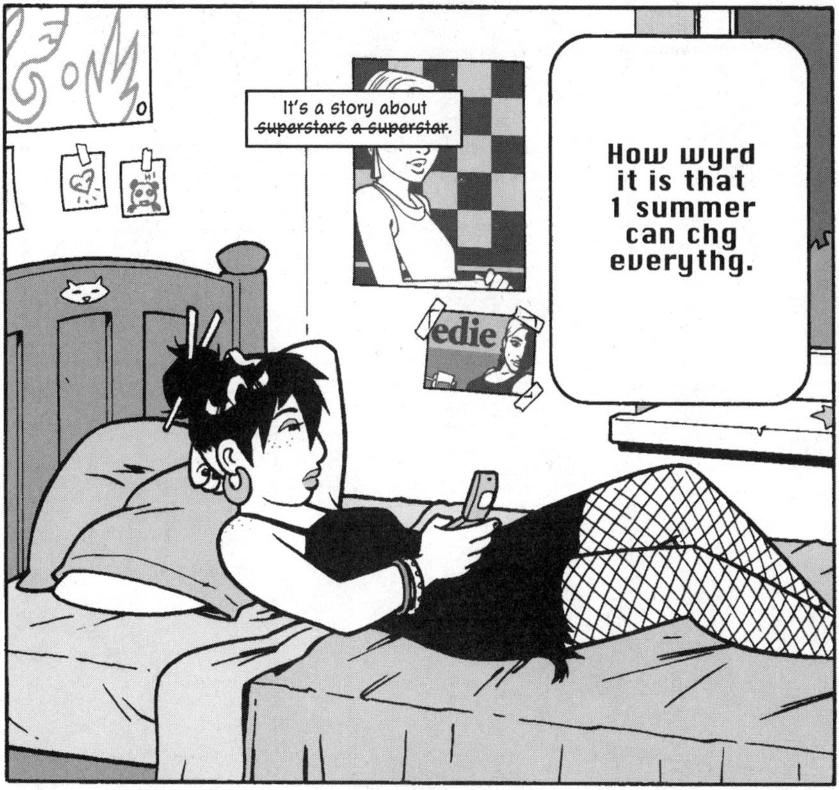
It's a story about ~~superstars a superstar~~.
How wyrd it is that 1 summer can chg everythg.
edie

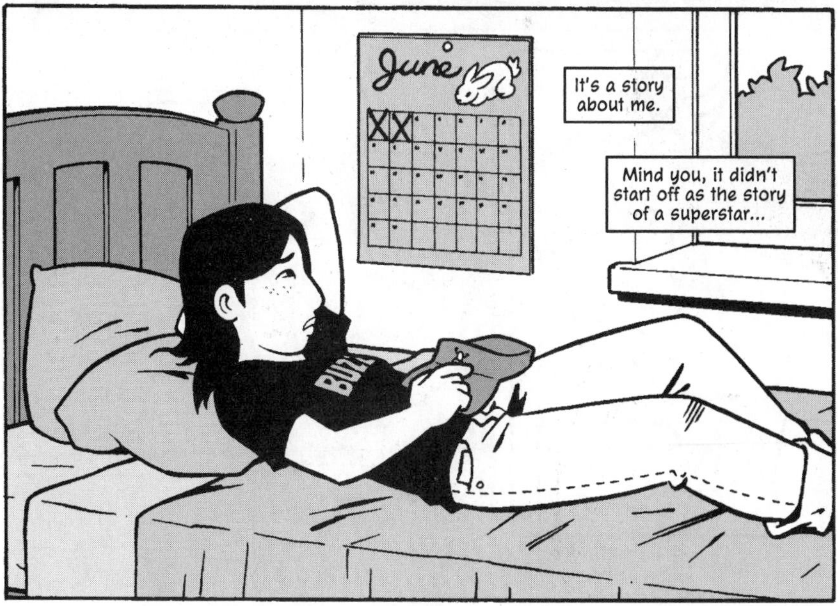
June
It's a story about me.
Mind you, it didn't start off as the story of a superstar...

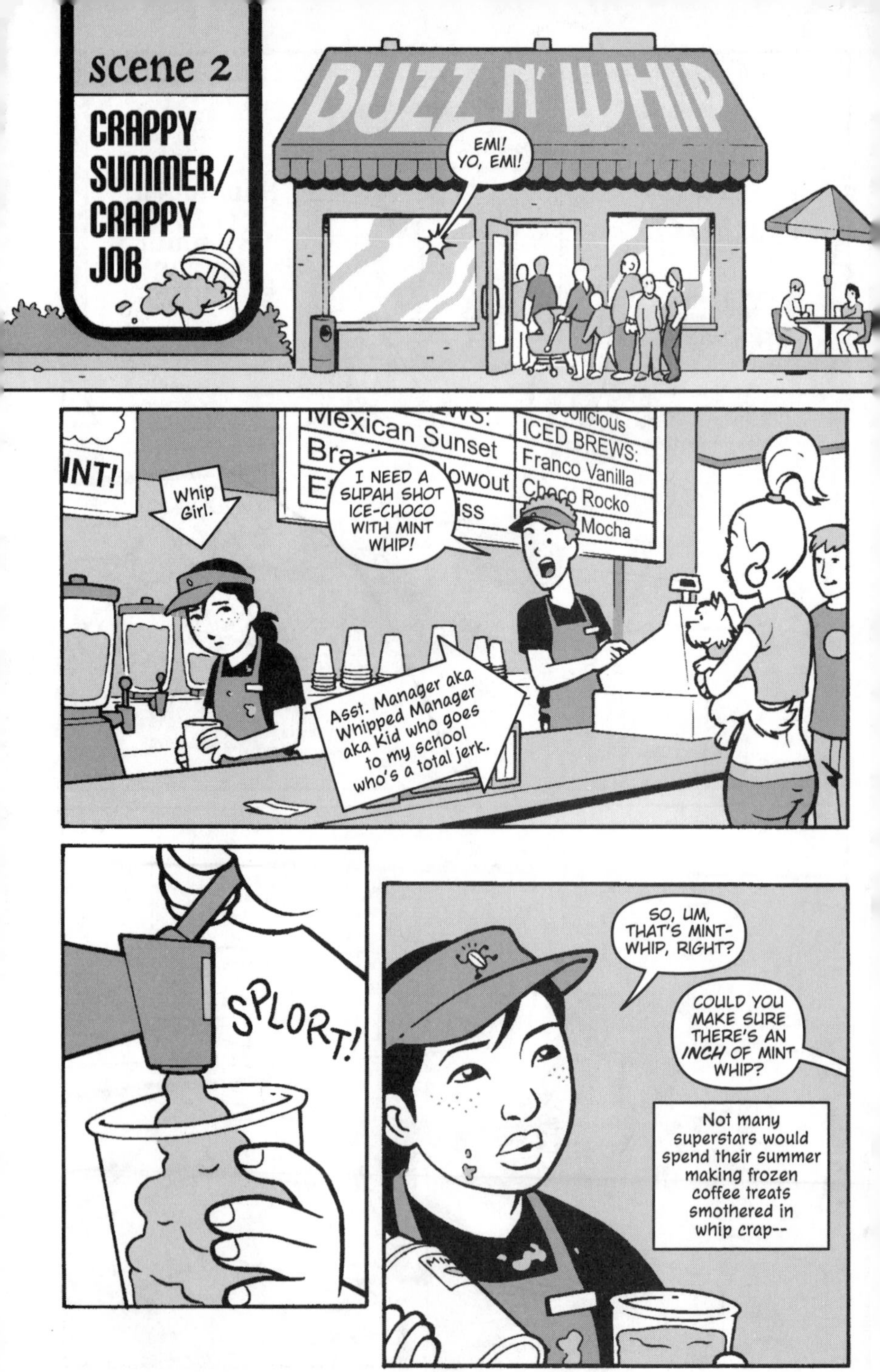
scene 2
CRAPPY SUMMER/ CRAPPY JOB
BUZZ N' WHIP
EMI! YO, EMI!
Mexican Sunset
ICED BREWS:
Franco Vanilla
Choco Rocko
Mocha
Whip Girl.
I NEED A SUPAH SHOT ICE-CHOCO WITH MINT WHIP!
Asst. Manager aka Whipped Manager aka Kid who goes to my school who's a total jerk.
SPLORT!
SO, UM, THAT'S MINT-WHIP, RIGHT?
COULD YOU MAKE SURE THERE'S AN *INCH* OF MINT WHIP?
Not many superstars would spend their summer making frozen coffee treats smothered in whip crap--

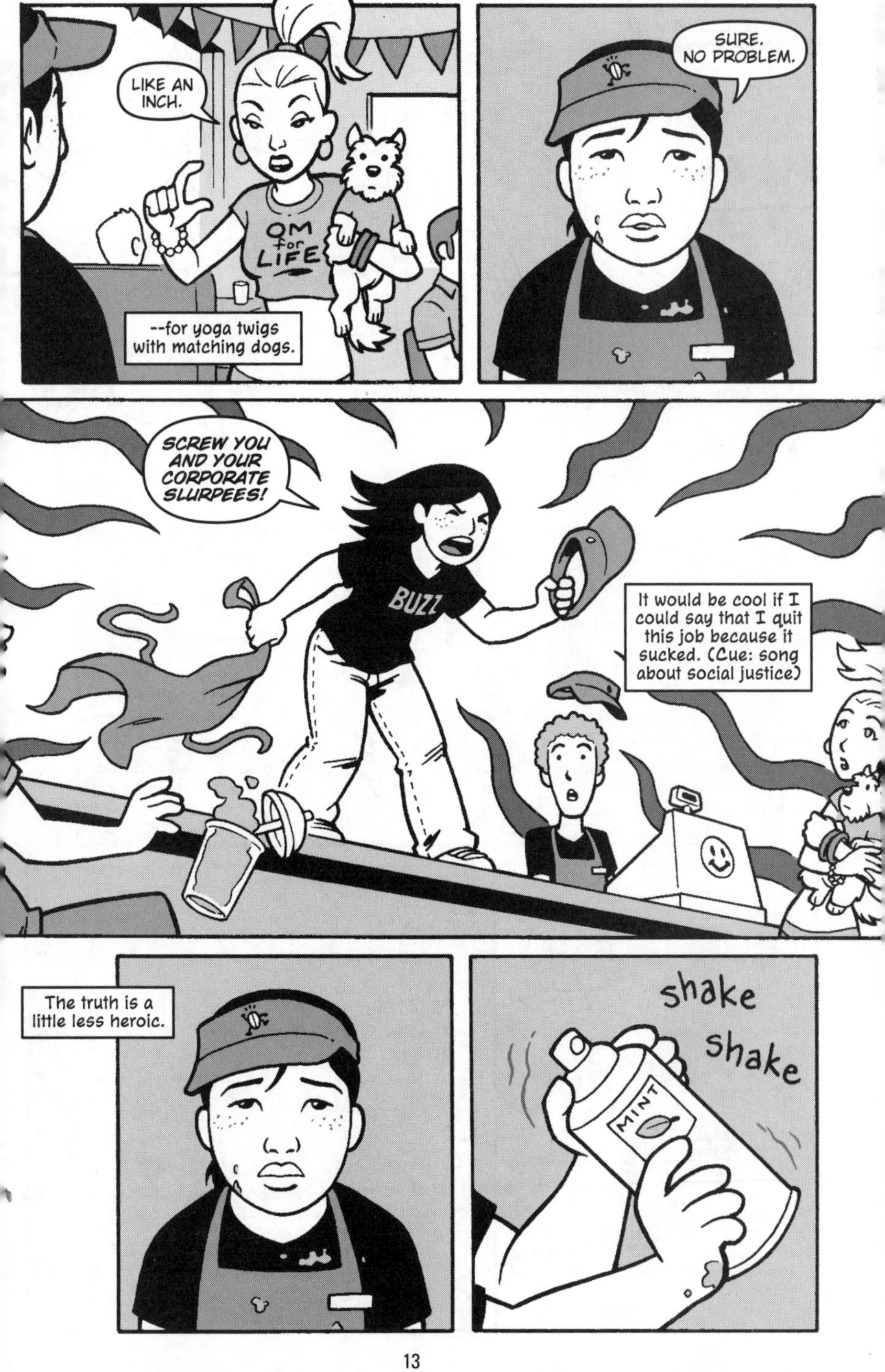
LIKE AN INCH.
OM for LIFE
--for yoga twigs with matching dogs.
SURE. NO PROBLEM.
SCREW YOU AND YOUR CORPORATE SLURPEES!
BUZZ
It would be cool if I could say that I quit this job because it sucked. (Cue: song about social justice)
The truth is a little less heroic.
shake
shake
MINT

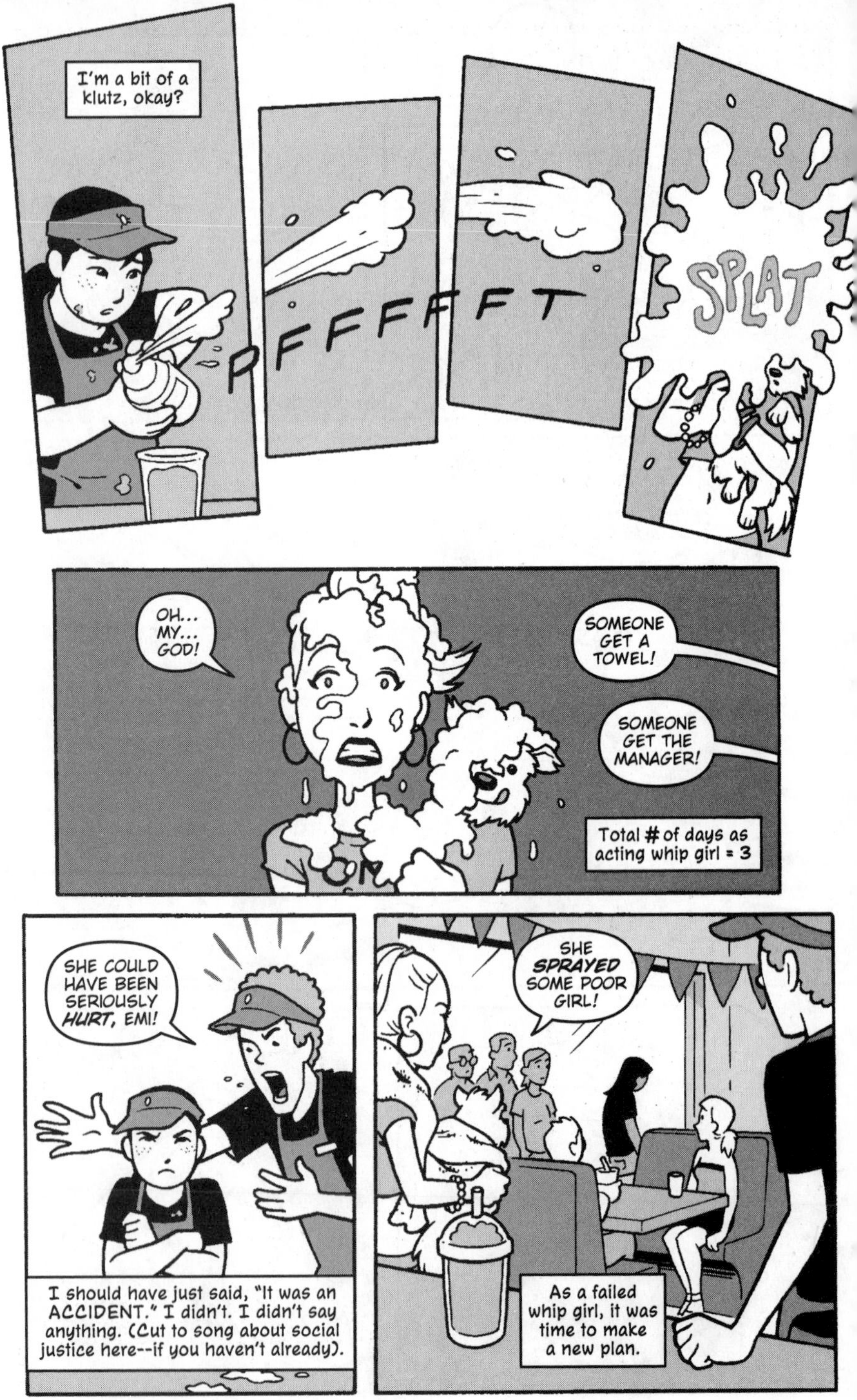
I'm a bit of a klutz, okay?
PFFFFFFT
SPLAT
OH... MY... GOD!
SOMEONE GET A TOWEL!
SOMEONE GET THE MANAGER!
Total # of days as acting whip girl = 3
SHE COULD HAVE BEEN SERIOUSLY HURT, EMI!
I should have just said, "It was an ACCIDENT." I didn't. I didn't say anything. (Cut to song about social justice here--if you haven't already).
SHE SPRAYED SOME POOR GIRL!
As a failed whip girl, it was time to make a new plan.

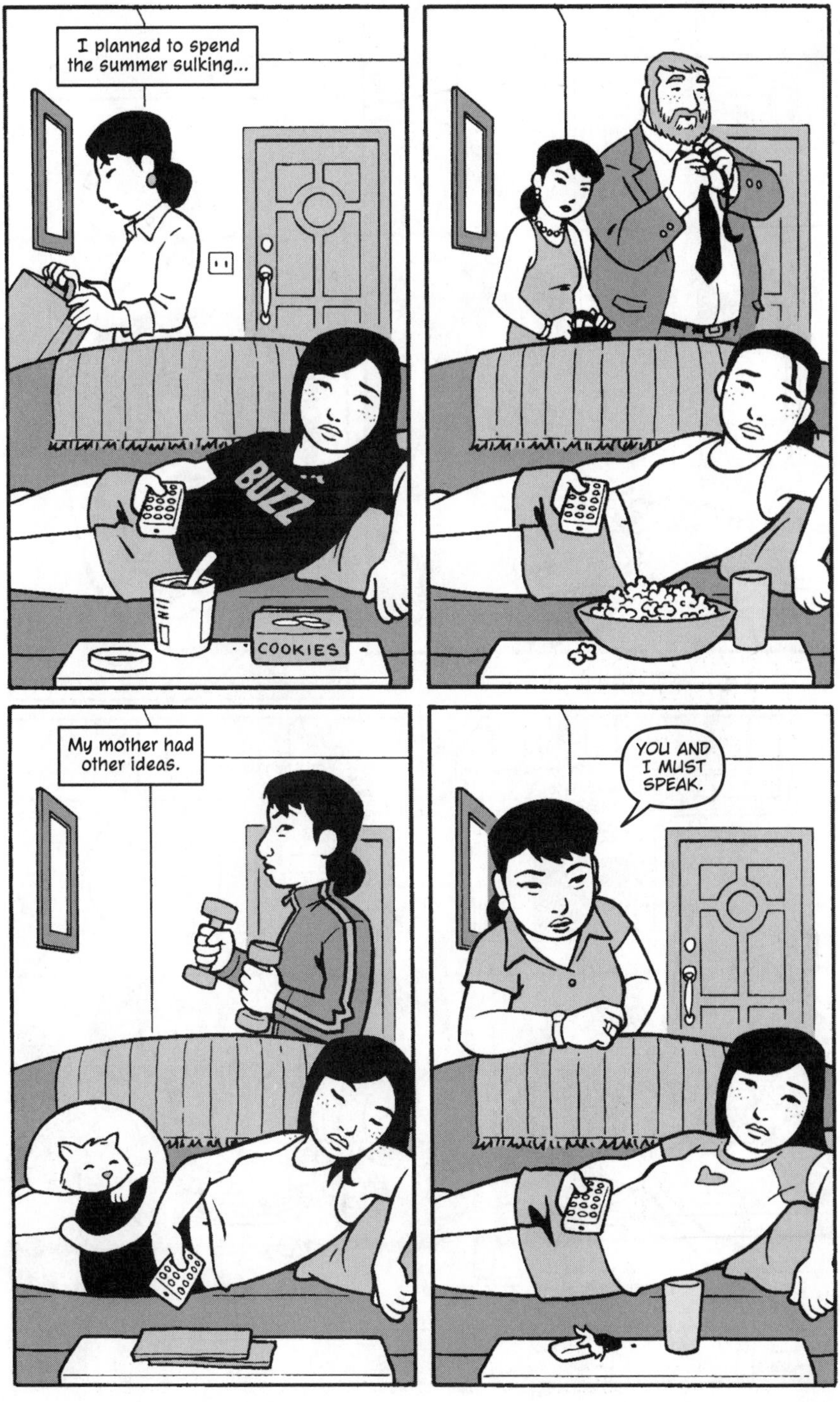
I planned to spend the summer sulking...
BUZZ
COOKIES
My mother had other ideas.
YOU AND I MUST SPEAK.

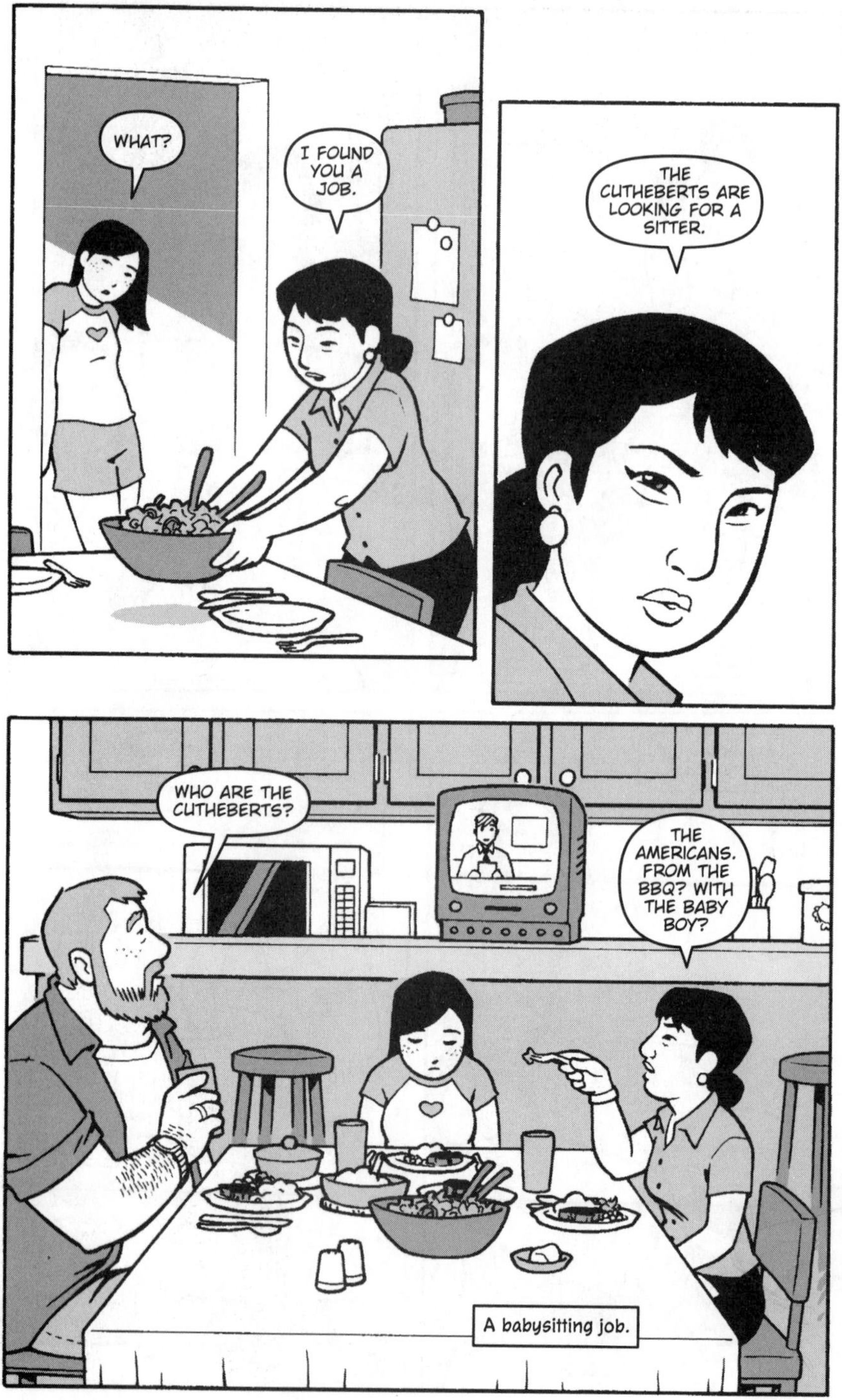
WHAT?
I FOUND YOU A JOB.
THE CUTHEBERTS ARE LOOKING FOR A SITTER.
WHO ARE THE CUTHEBERTS?
THE AMERICANS. FROM THE BBQ? WITH THE BABY BOY?
A babysitting job.

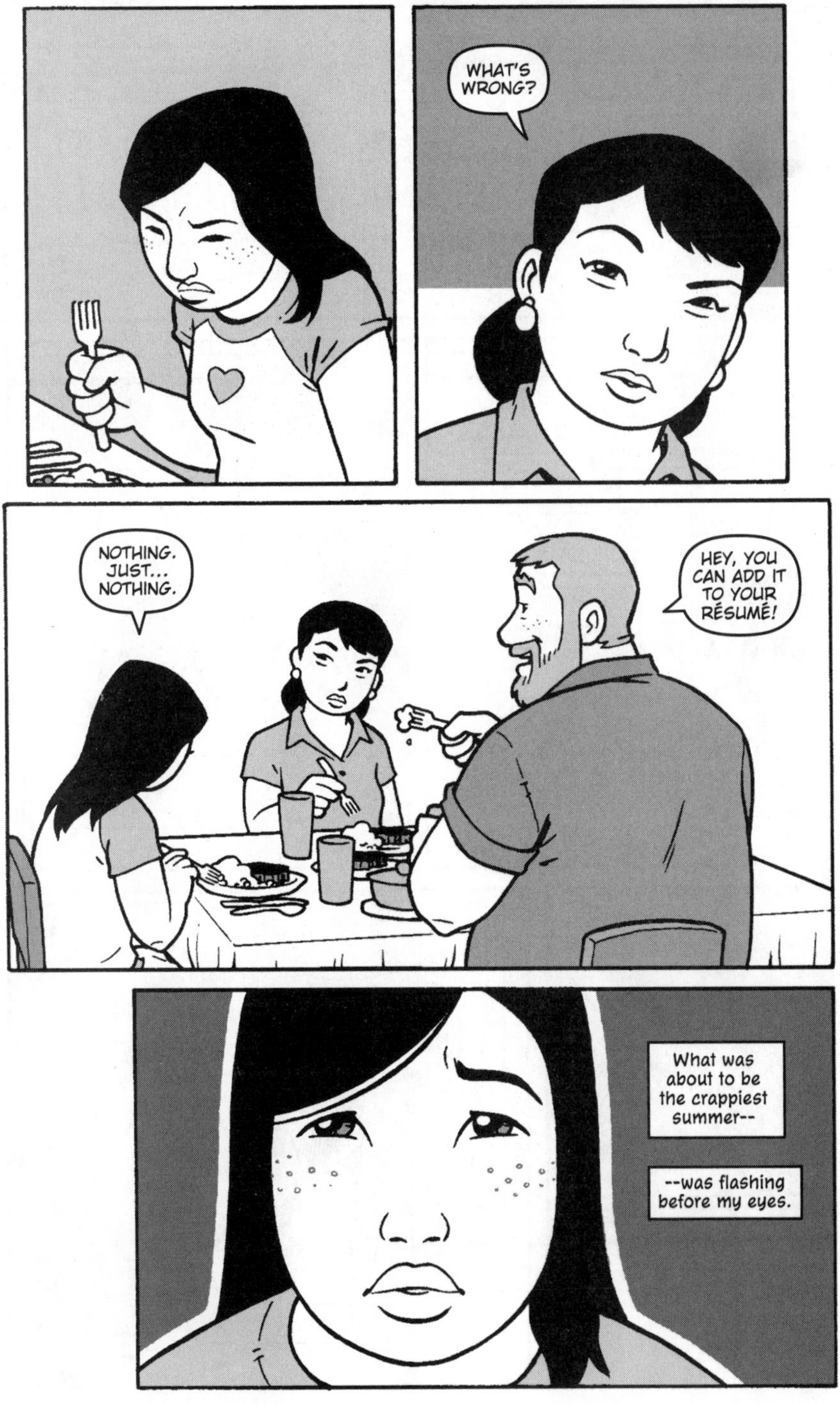
WHAT'S WRONG?
NOTHING. JUST... NOTHING.
HEY, YOU CAN ADD IT TO YOUR RÉSUMÉ!
What was about to be the crappiest summer--
--was flashing before my eyes.

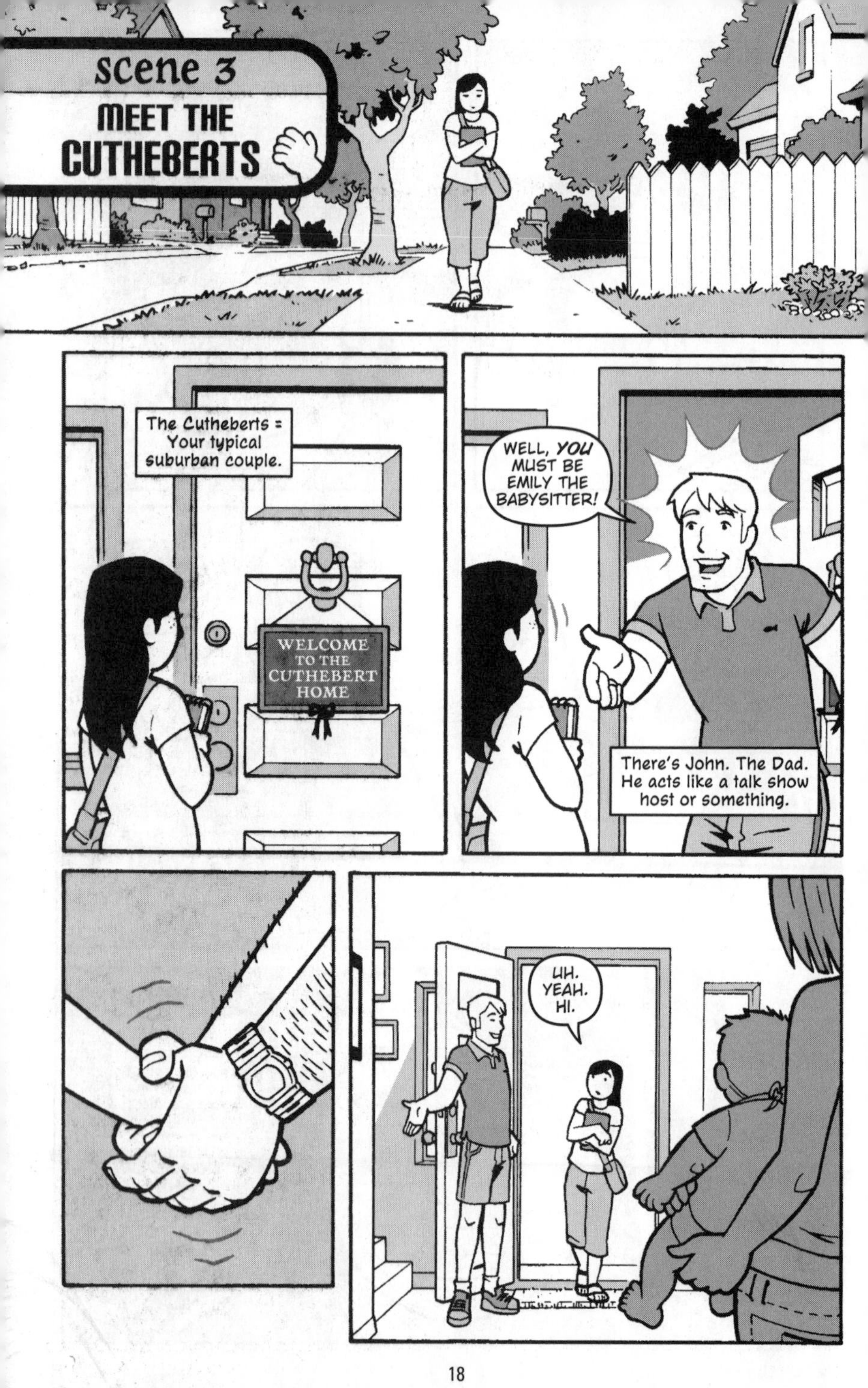
scene 3
MEET THE CUTHEBERTS
The Cutheberts = Your typical suburban couple.
WELCOME TO THE CUTHEBERT HOME
WELL, YOU MUST BE EMILY THE BABYSITTER!
There's John. The Dad. He acts like a talk show host or something.
UH. YEAH. HI.

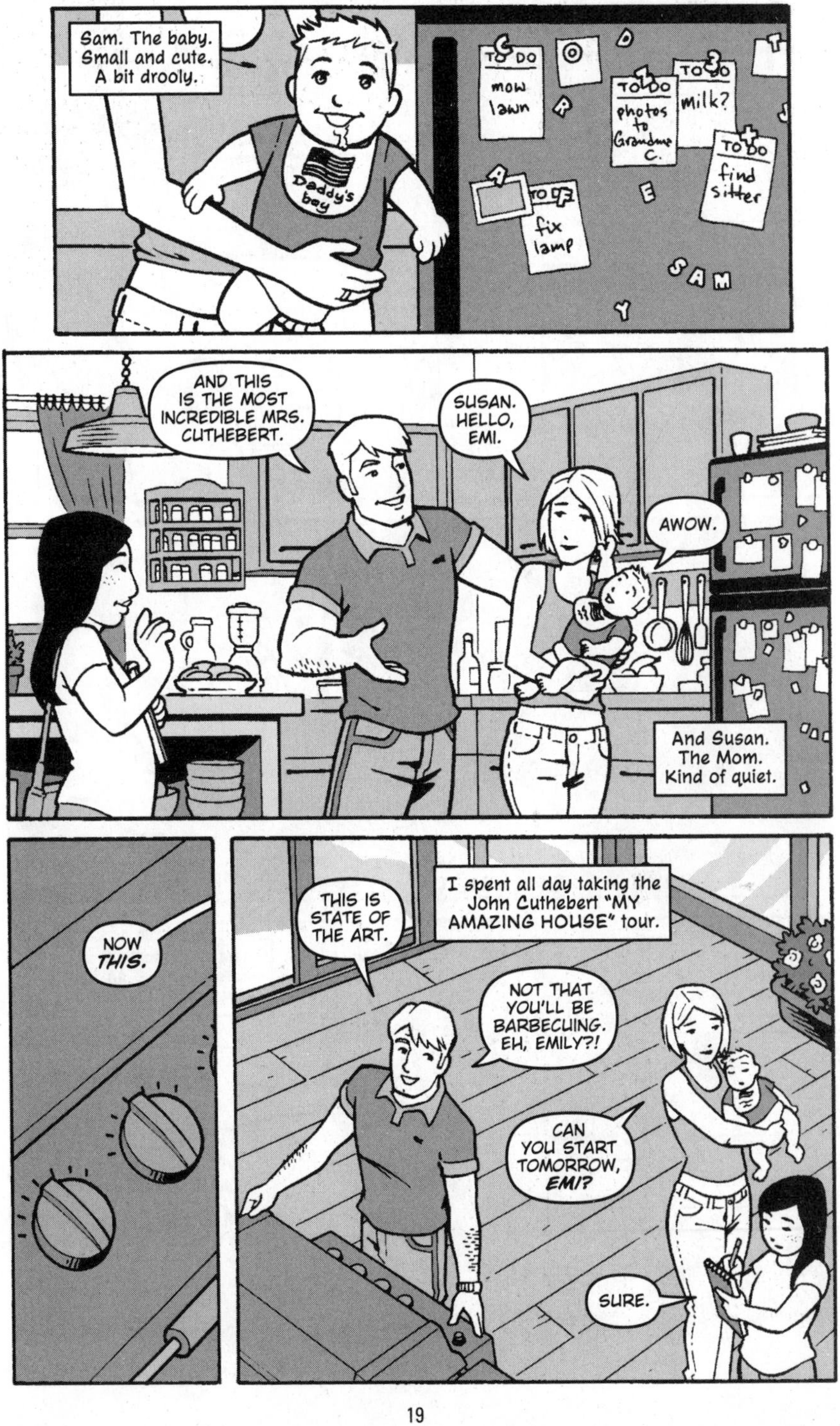

Sam. The baby. Small and cute. A bit drooly.
Daddy's boy
TO DO mow lawn
TO DO photos to Grandma C.
TO DO milk?
TO DO find sitter
TO DO fix lamp
SAM
AND THIS IS THE MOST INCREDIBLE MRS. CUTHEBERT.
SUSAN. HELLO, EMI.
AWOW.
And Susan. The Mom. Kind of quiet.
NOW *THIS.*
I spent all day taking the John Cuthebert "MY AMAZING HOUSE" tour.
THIS IS STATE OF THE ART.
NOT THAT YOU'LL BE BARBECUING. EH, EMILY?!
CAN YOU START TOMORROW, *EMI?*
SURE.

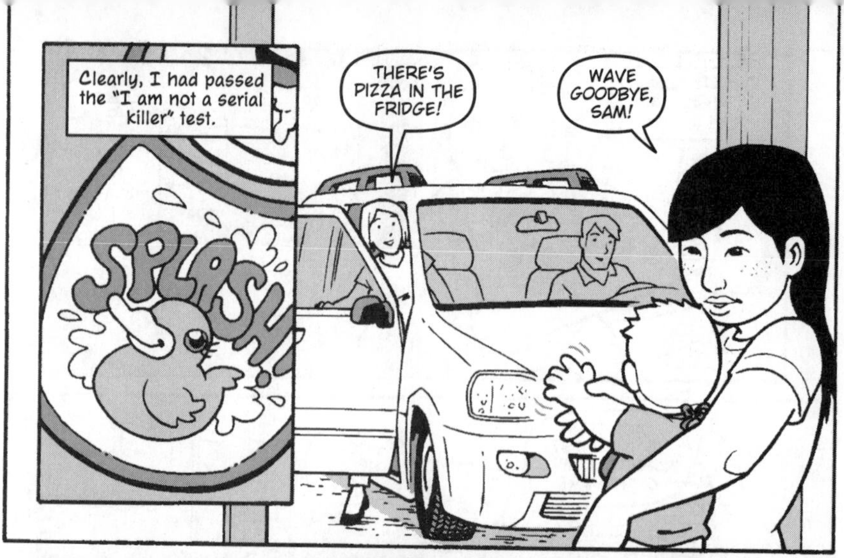
Clearly, I had passed the "I am not a serial killer" test.
THERE'S PIZZA IN THE FRIDGE!
WAVE GOODBYE, SAM!
SPLASH!

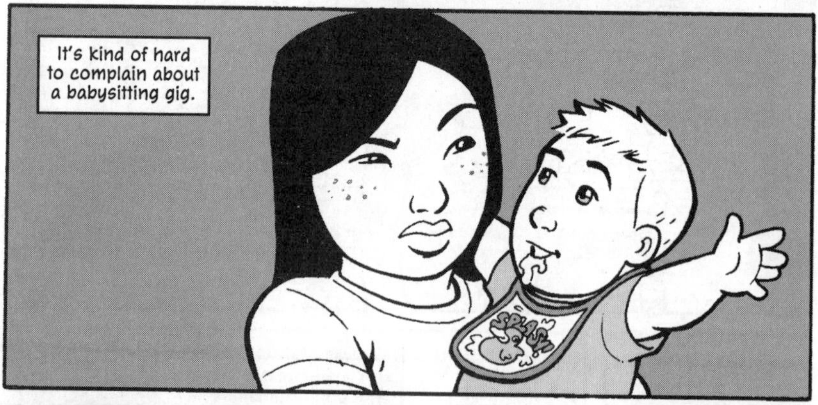
It's kind of hard to complain about a babysitting gig.

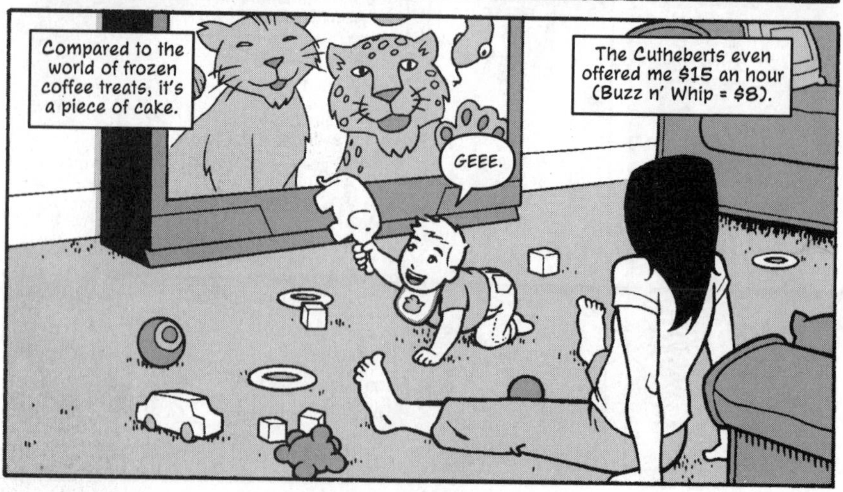
Compared to the world of frozen coffee treats, it's a piece of cake.
The Cutheberts even offered me $15 an hour (Buzz n' Whip = $8).
GEEE.

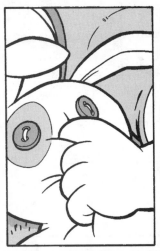

I had money, a cool new boyfriend, and pizza.

What more could a girl ask for?

A life.

NO OFFENSE, SAM, BUT THIS SUMMER IS KIND OF SUCKING THE BIG ONE RIGHT NOW.

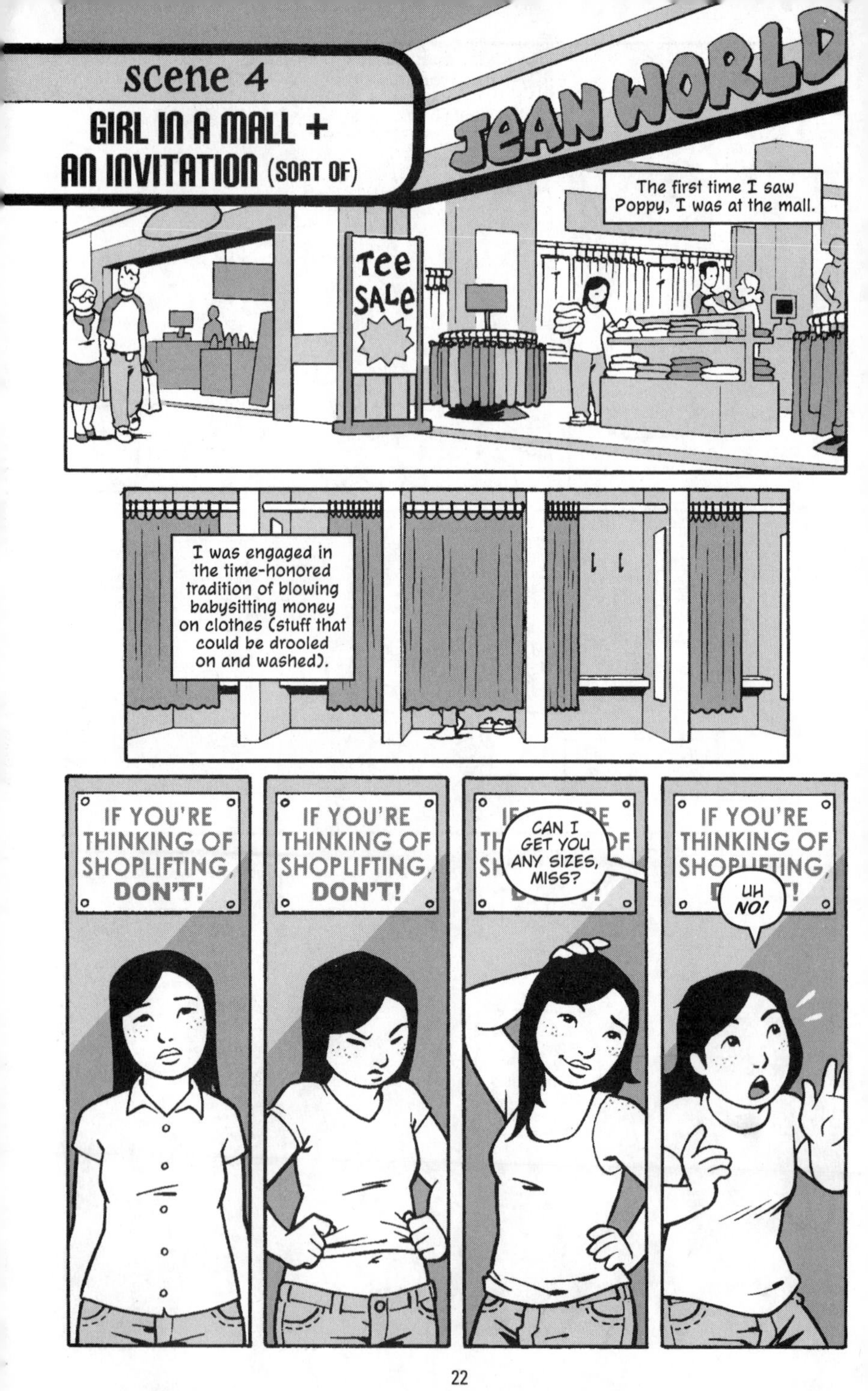
scene 4
GIRL IN A MALL + AN INVITATION (SORT OF)
JEAN WORLD
The first time I saw Poppy, I was at the mall.
TEE SALE
I was engaged in the time-honored tradition of blowing babysitting money on clothes (stuff that could be drooled on and washed).
IF YOU'RE THINKING OF SHOPLIFTING, DON'T!
IF YOU'RE THINKING OF SHOPLIFTING, DON'T!
CAN I GET YOU ANY SIZES, MISS?
IF YOU'RE THINKING OF
UH NO!

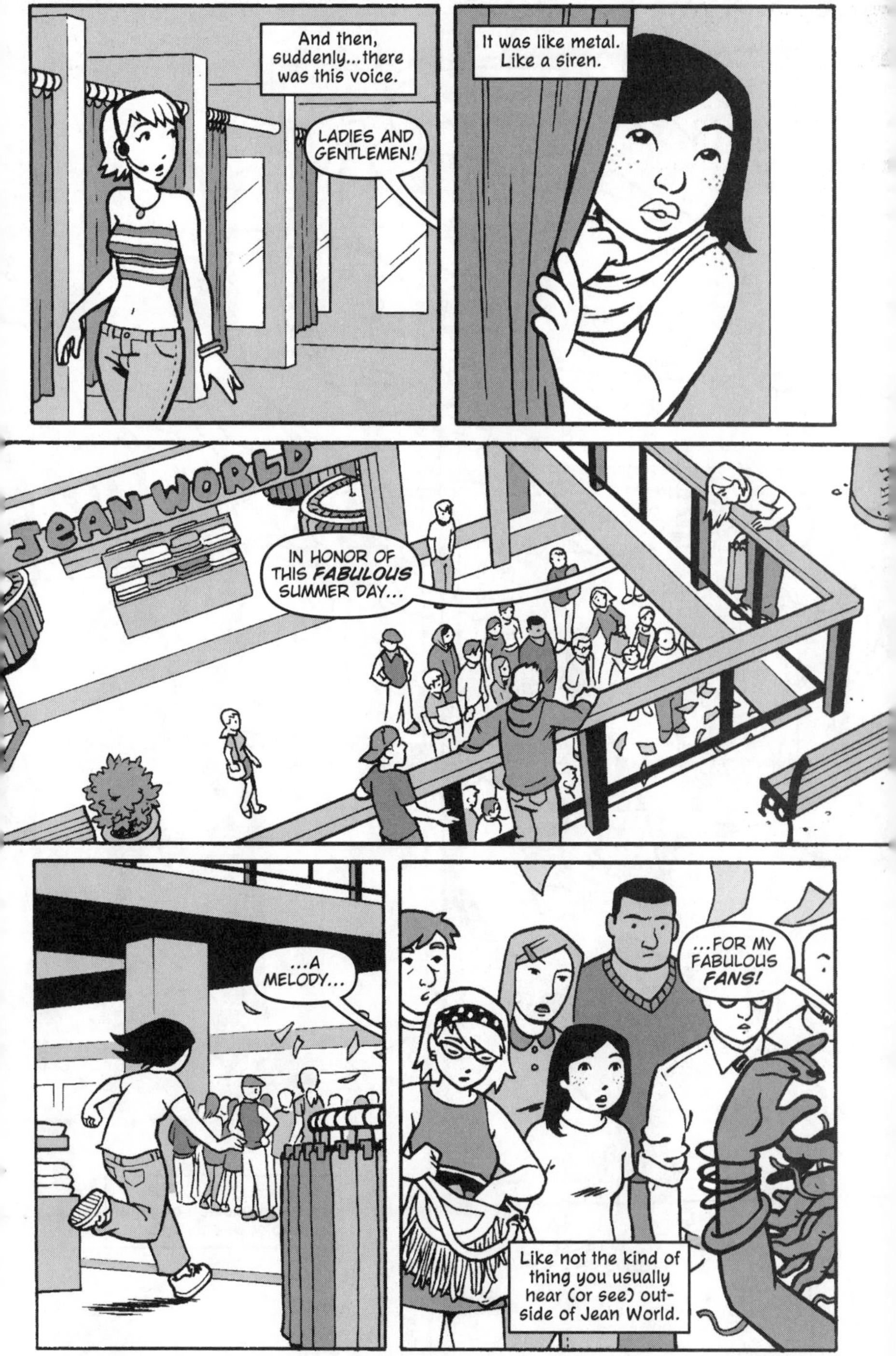
And then, suddenly...there was this voice.
LADIES AND GENTLEMEN!
It was like metal. Like a siren.
JEAN WORLD
IN HONOR OF THIS FABULOUS SUMMER DAY...
...A MELODY...
...FOR MY FABULOUS FANS!
Like not the kind of thing you usually hear (or see) outside of Jean World.

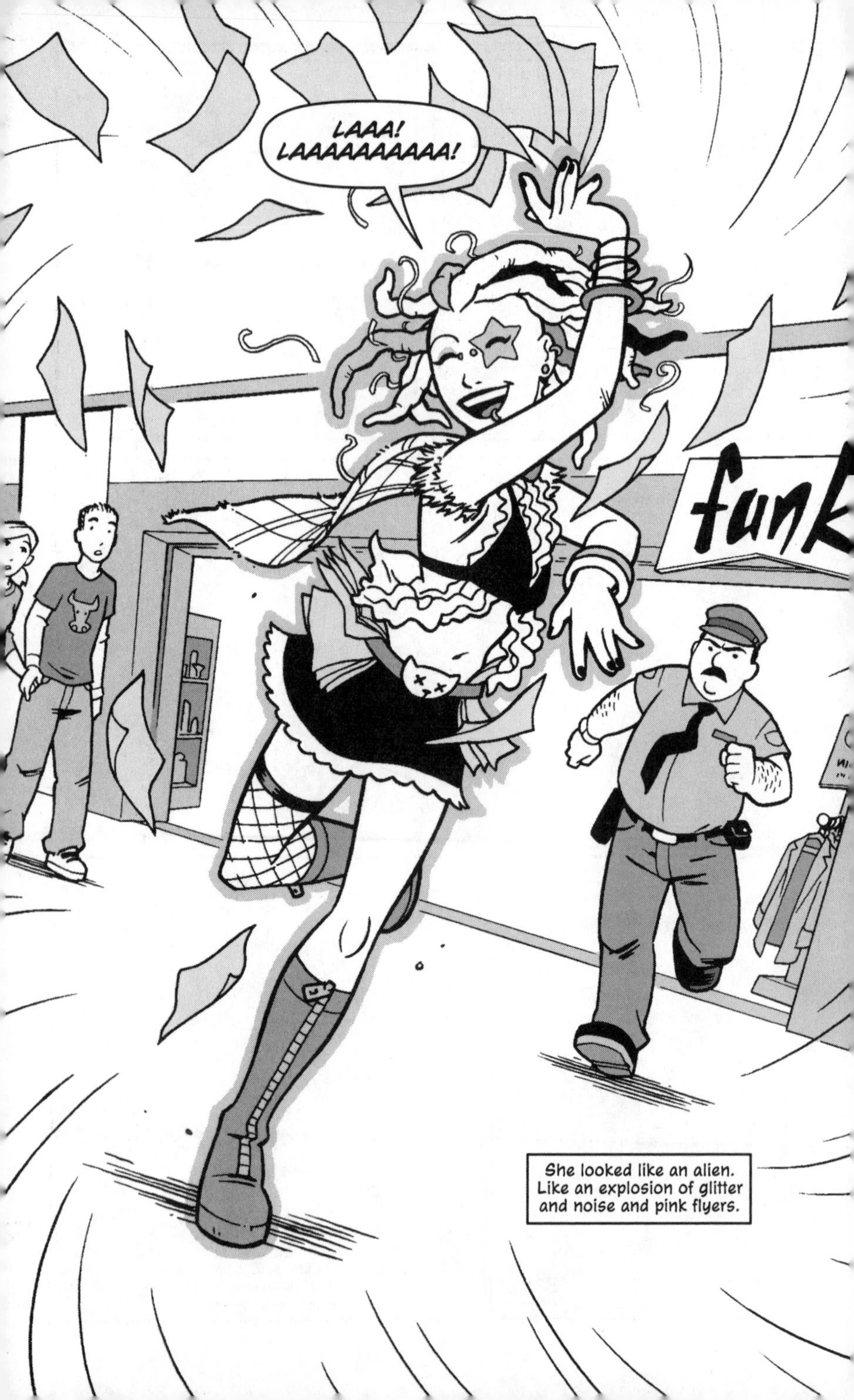
LAAA! LAAAAAAAAAAA!
funk
She looked like an alien. Like an explosion of glitter and noise and pink flyers.

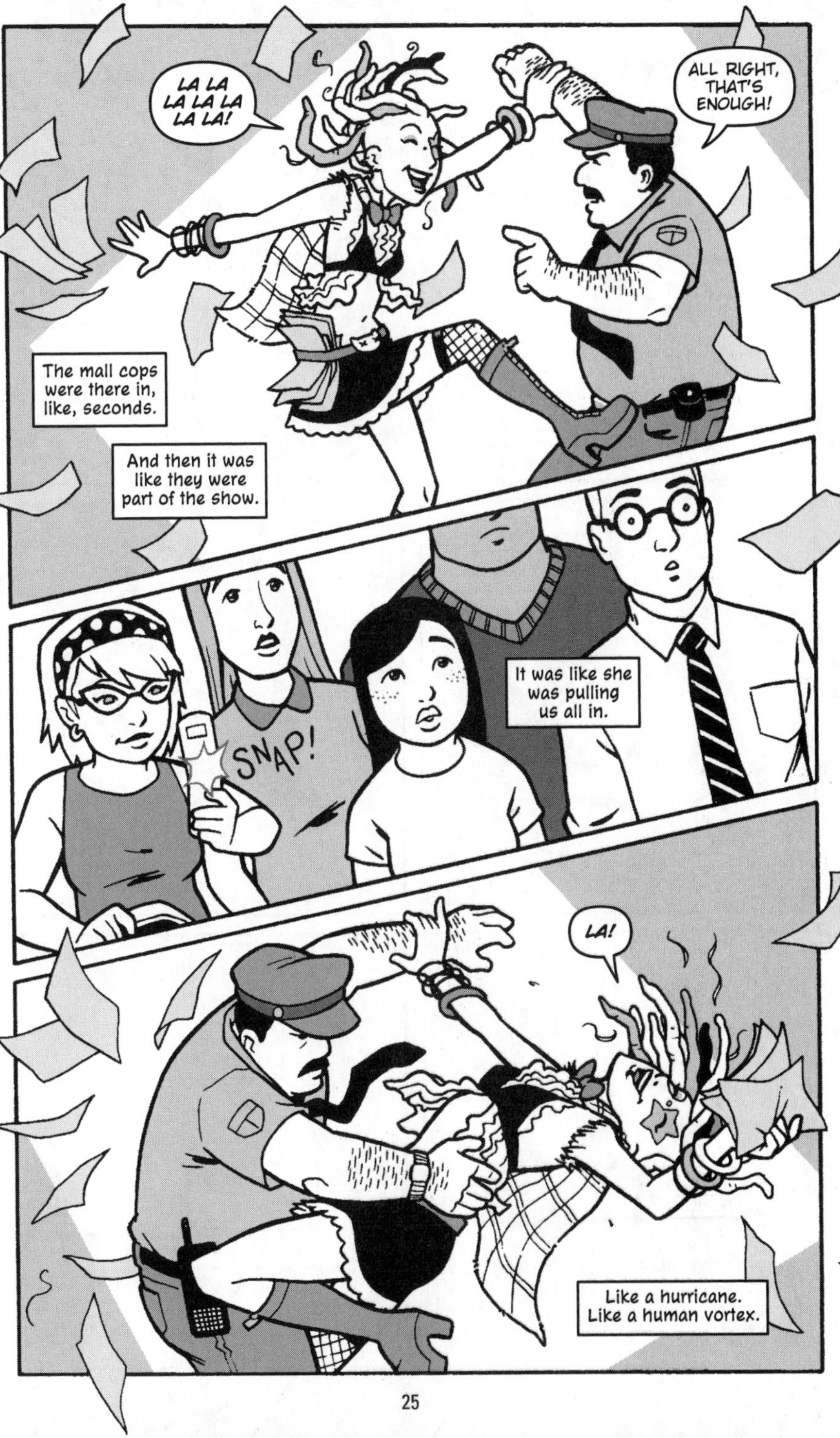
LA LA LA LA LA LA LA!
ALL RIGHT, THAT'S ENOUGH!
The mall cops were there in, like, seconds.
And then it was like they were part of the show.
It was like she was pulling us all in.
SNAP!
LA!
Like a hurricane. Like a human vortex.

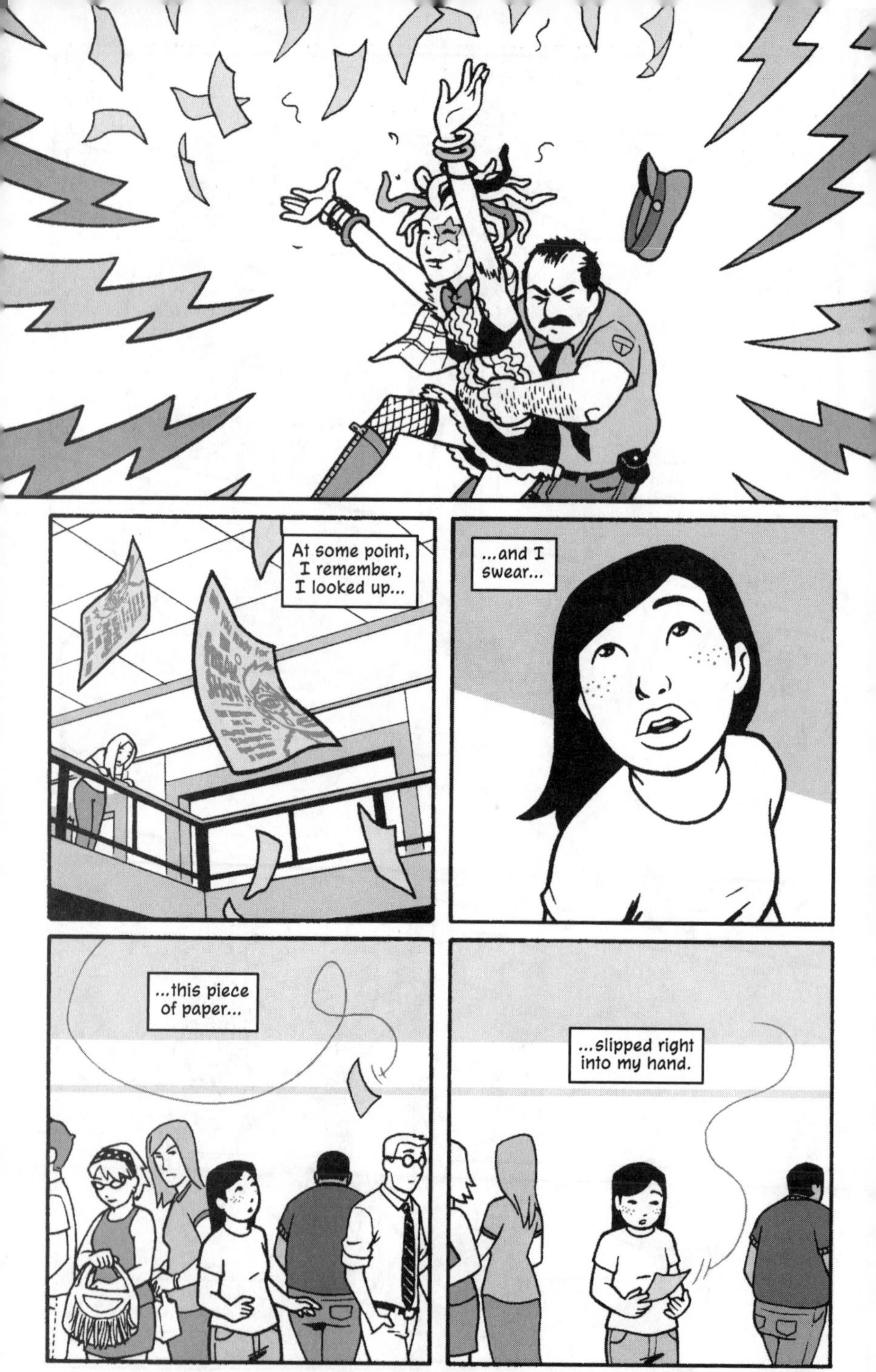
At some point, I remember, I looked up...
...and I swear...
...this piece of paper...
...slipped right into my hand.

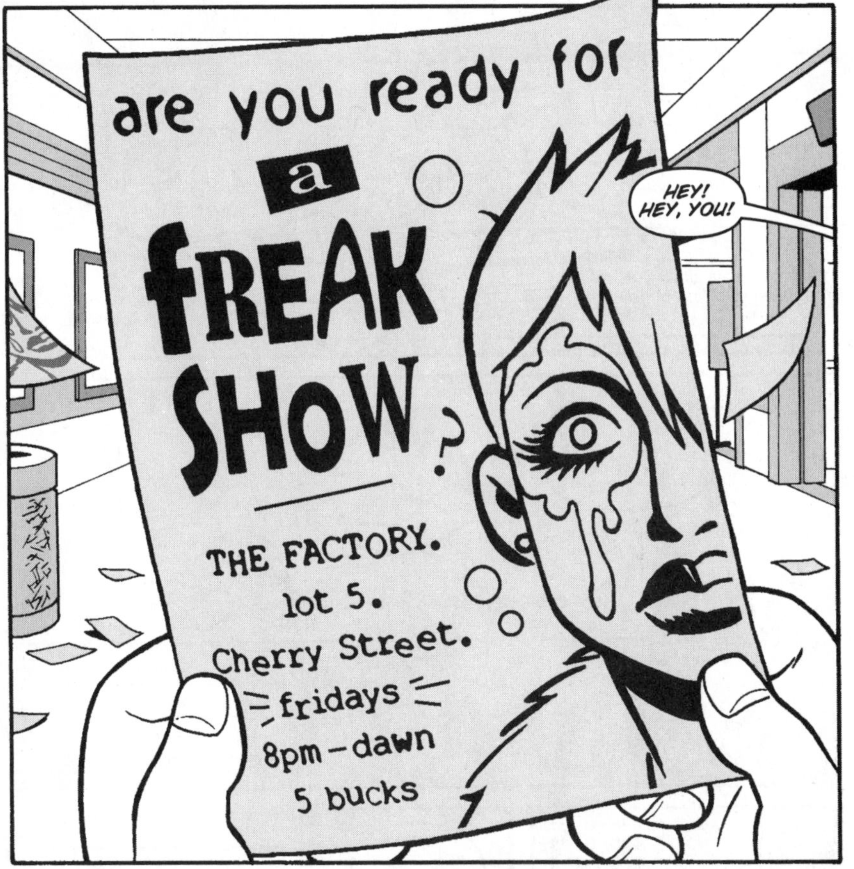
are you ready for
a
FREAK SHOW?
THE FACTORY.
lot 5.
Cherry Street.
fridays
8pm—dawn
5 bucks
HEY! HEY, YOU!

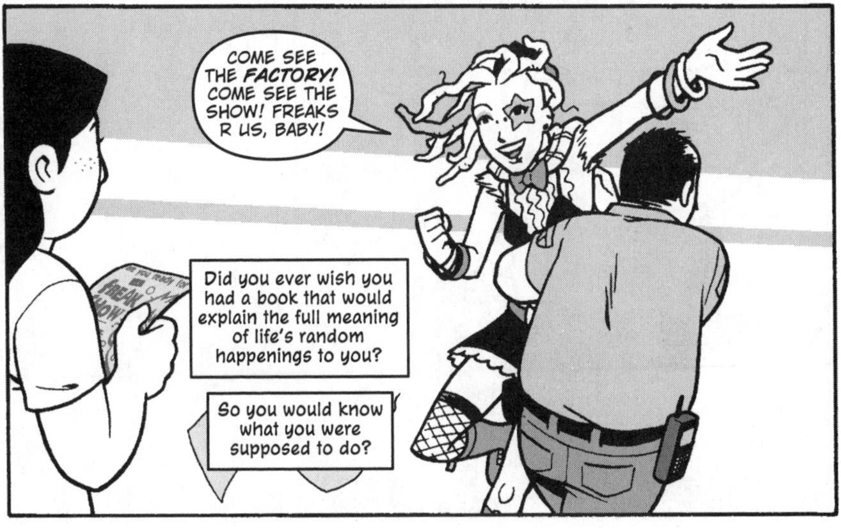
COME SEE THE FACTORY! COME SEE THE SHOW! FREAKS R US, BABY!
Did you ever wish you had a book that would explain the full meaning of life's random happenings to you?
So you would know what you were supposed to do?

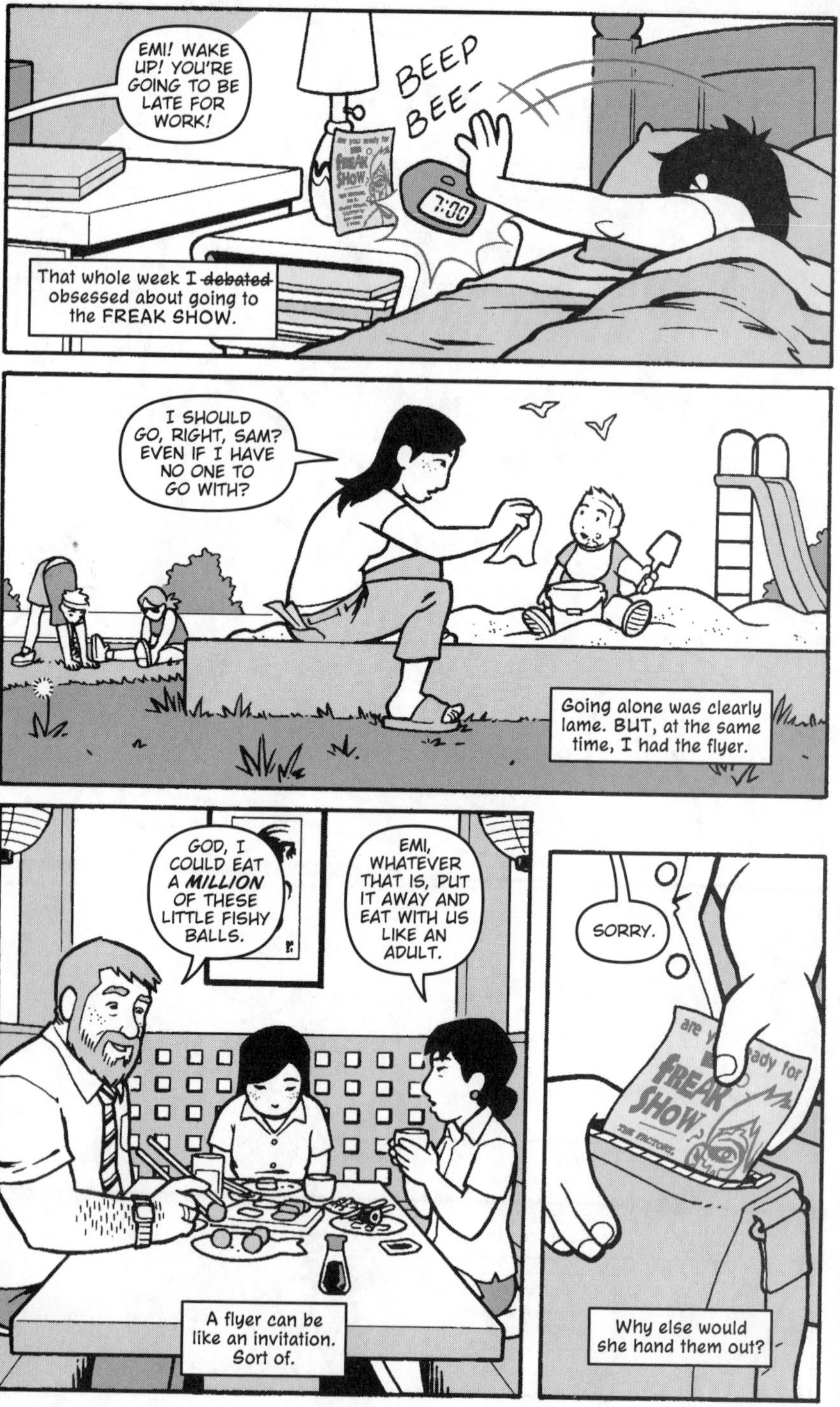
EMI! WAKE UP! YOU'RE GOING TO BE LATE FOR WORK!
BEEP BEE-
7:00
That whole week I ~~debated~~ obsessed about going to the FREAK SHOW.
I SHOULD GO, RIGHT, SAM? EVEN IF I HAVE NO ONE TO GO WITH?
Going alone was clearly lame. BUT, at the same time, I had the flyer.
GOD, I COULD EAT A *MILLION* OF THESE LITTLE FISHY BALLS.
EMI, WHATEVER THAT IS, PUT IT AWAY AND EAT WITH US LIKE AN ADULT.
A flyer can be like an invitation. Sort of.
SORRY.
FREAK SHOW
Why else would she hand them out?

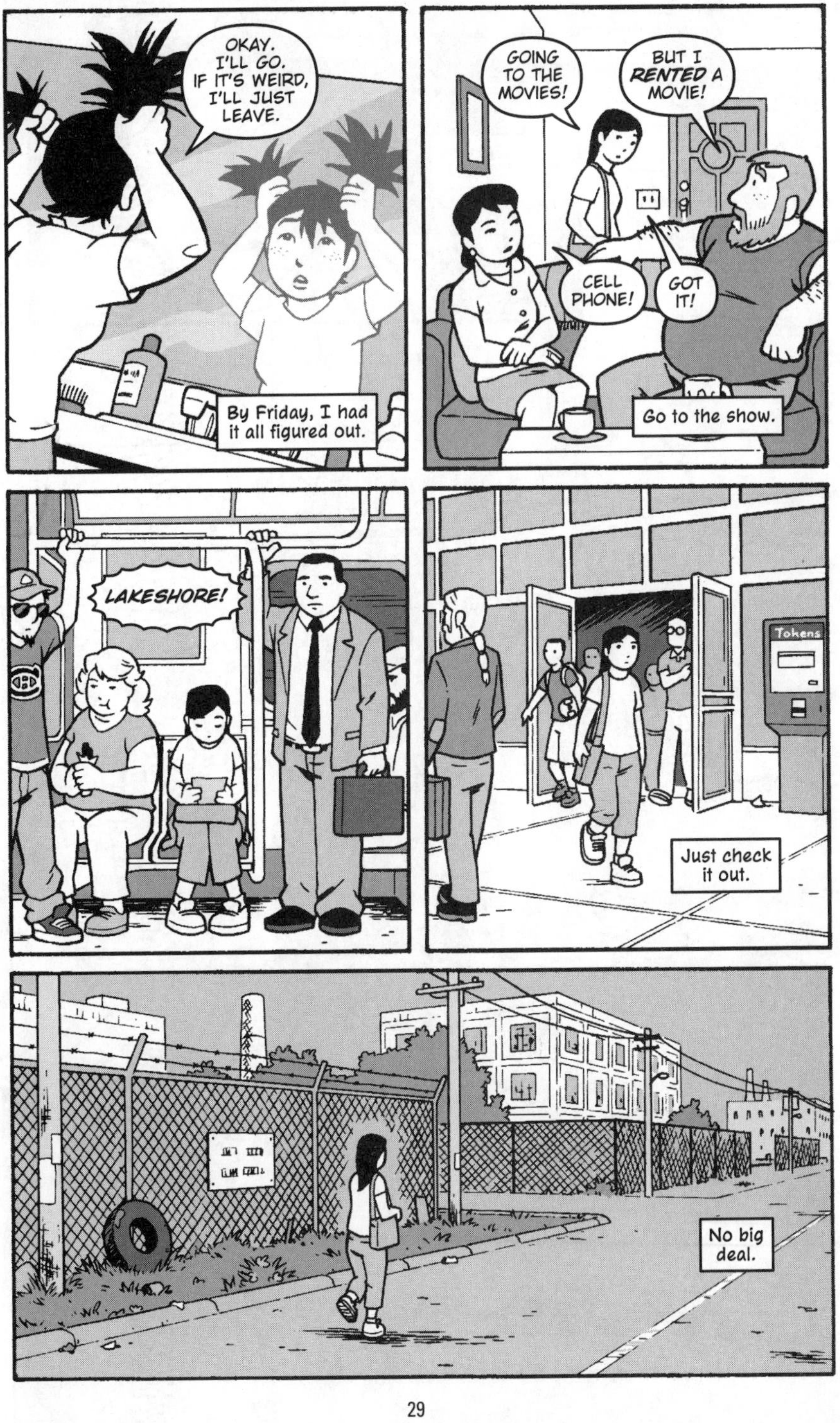
OKAY. I'LL GO. IF IT'S WEIRD, I'LL JUST LEAVE.
By Friday, I had it all figured out.
GOING TO THE MOVIES!
BUT I RENTED A MOVIE!
CELL PHONE!
GOT IT!
Go to the show.
LAKESHORE!
Tokens
Just check it out.
No big deal.

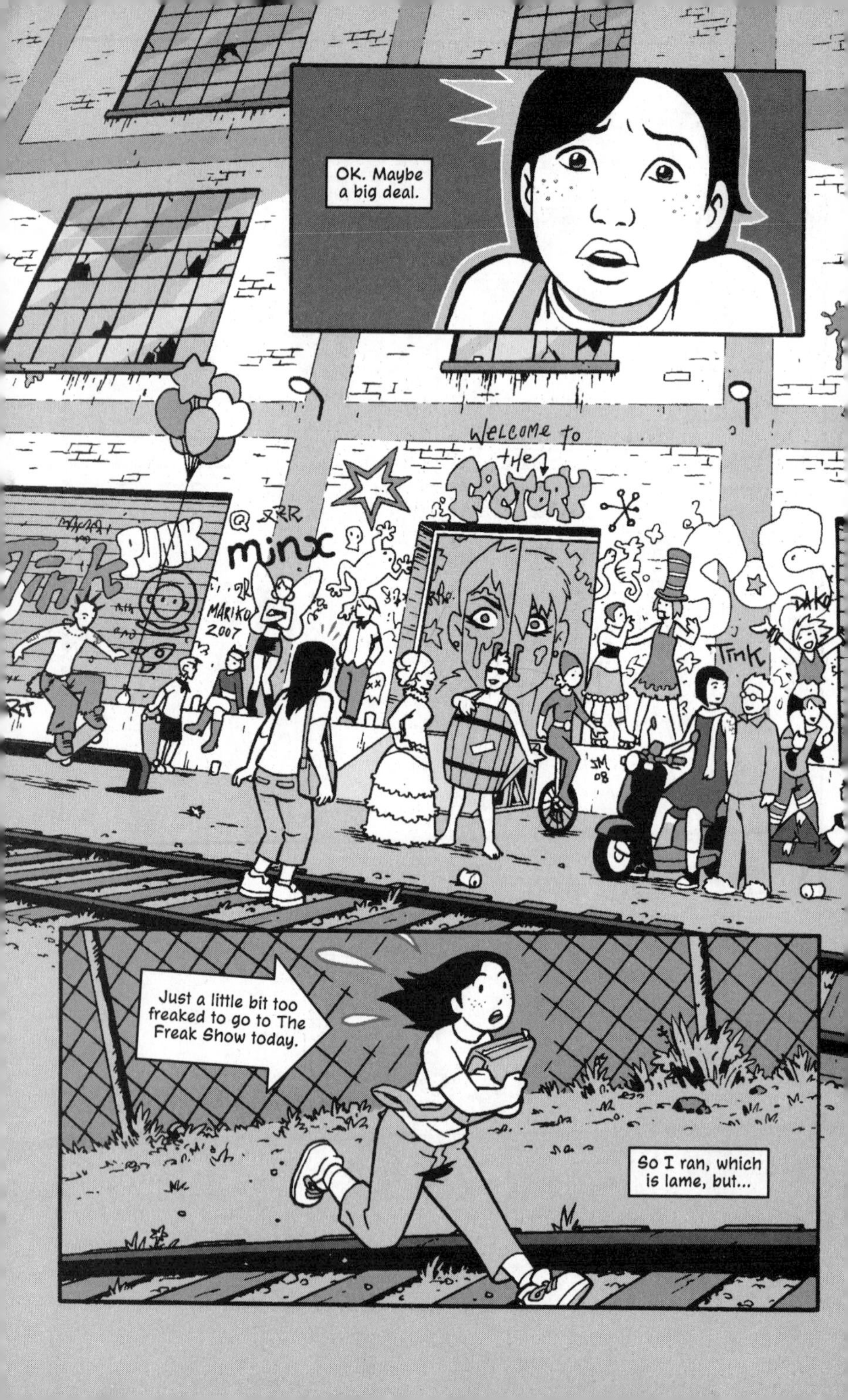
OK. Maybe a big deal.
Welcome to the Factory
Tink
Punk
minx
MARIKO 2007
TINK
Just a little bit too freaked to go to The Freak Show today.
So I ran, which is lame, but...

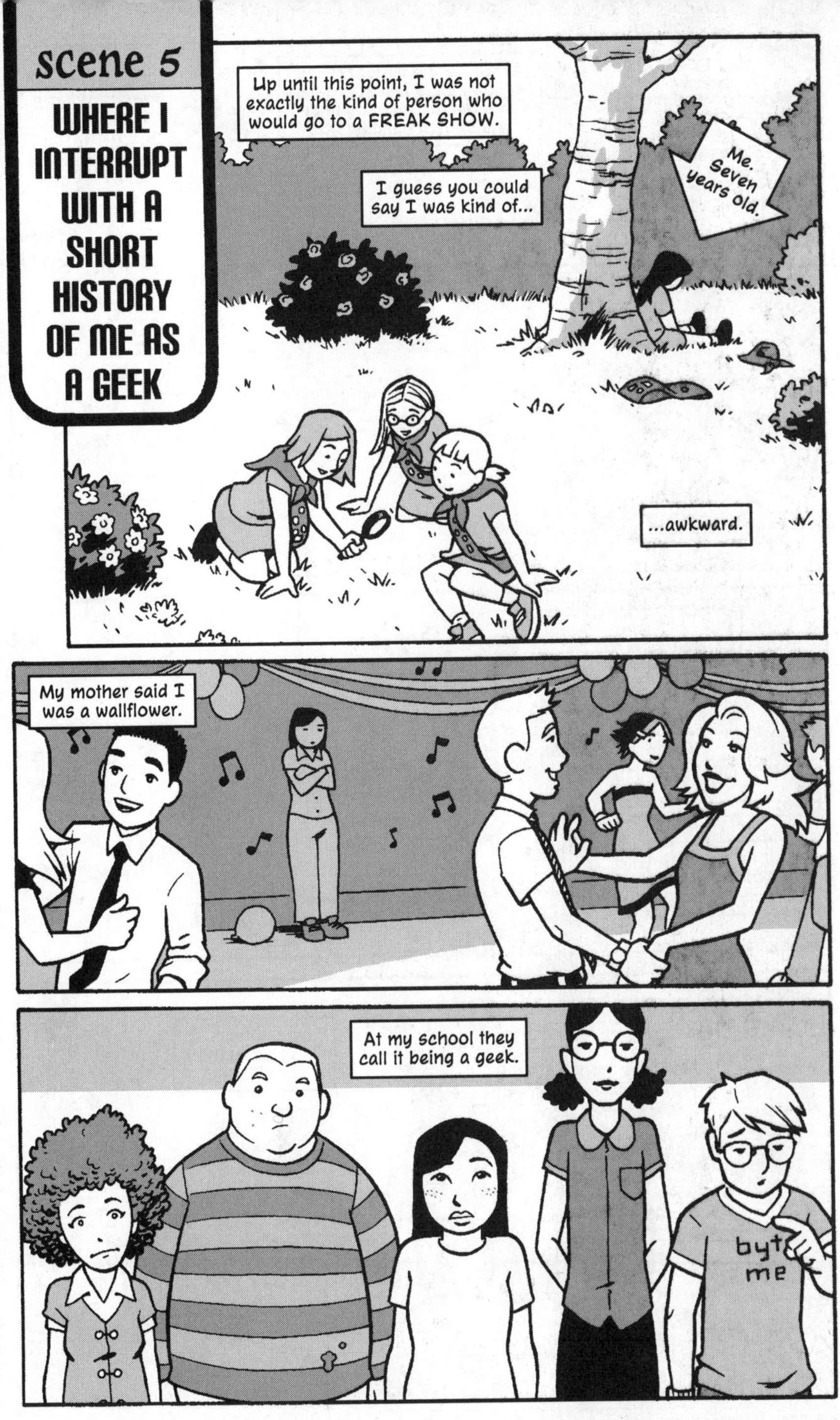
scene 5
WHERE I INTERRUPT WITH A SHORT HISTORY OF ME AS A GEEK
Up until this point, I was not exactly the kind of person who would go to a FREAK SHOW.
I guess you could say I was kind of...
Me. Seven years old.
...awkward.
My mother said I was a wallflower.
At my school they call it being a geek.

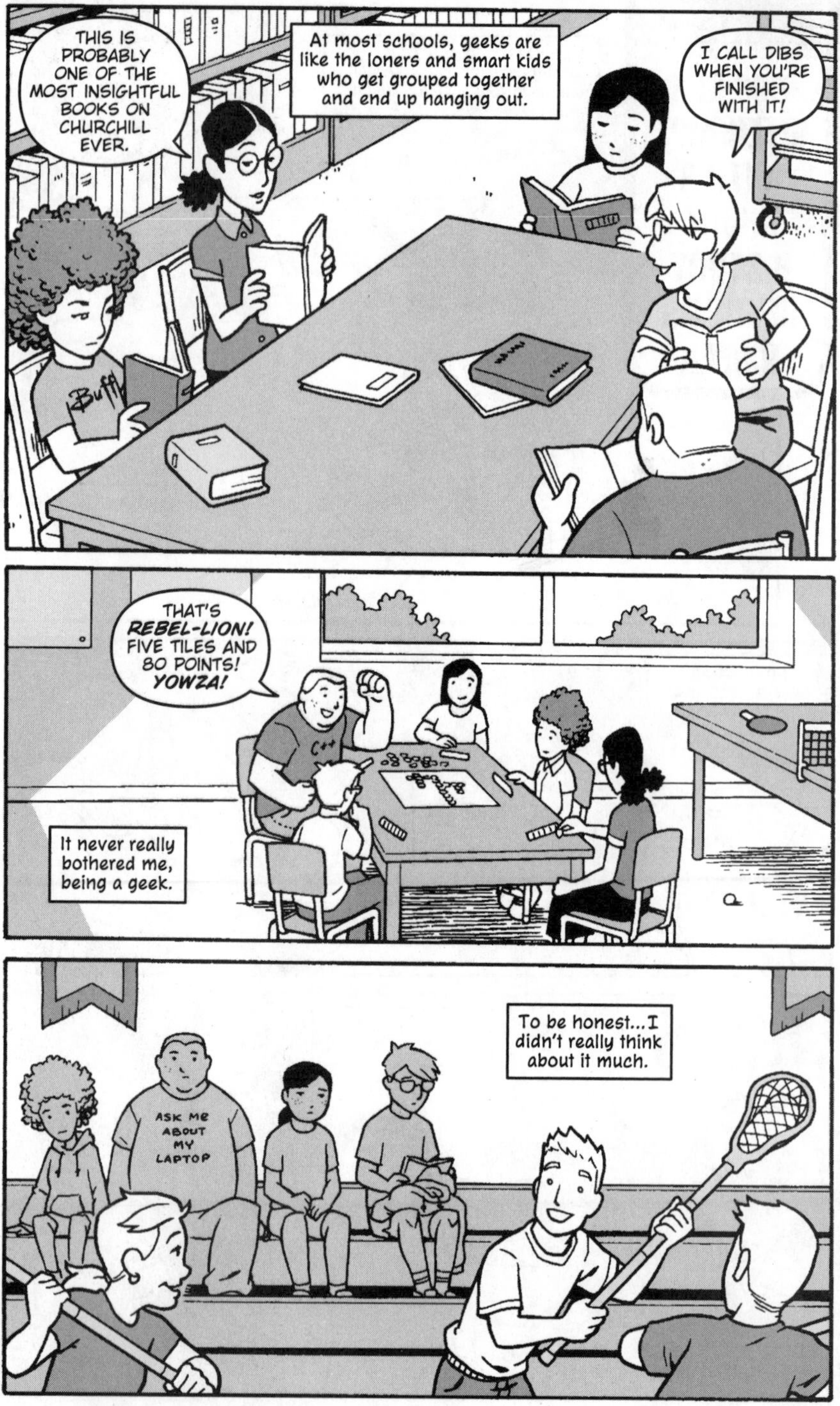
THIS IS PROBABLY ONE OF THE MOST INSIGHTFUL BOOKS ON CHURCHILL EVER.
At most schools, geeks are like the loners and smart kids who get grouped together and end up hanging out.
I CALL DIBS WHEN YOU'RE FINISHED WITH IT!
THAT'S ***REBEL-LION!*** FIVE TILES AND 80 POINTS! ***YOWZA!***
It never really bothered me, being a geek.
ASK ME ABOUT MY LAPTOP
To be honest...I didn't really think about it much.

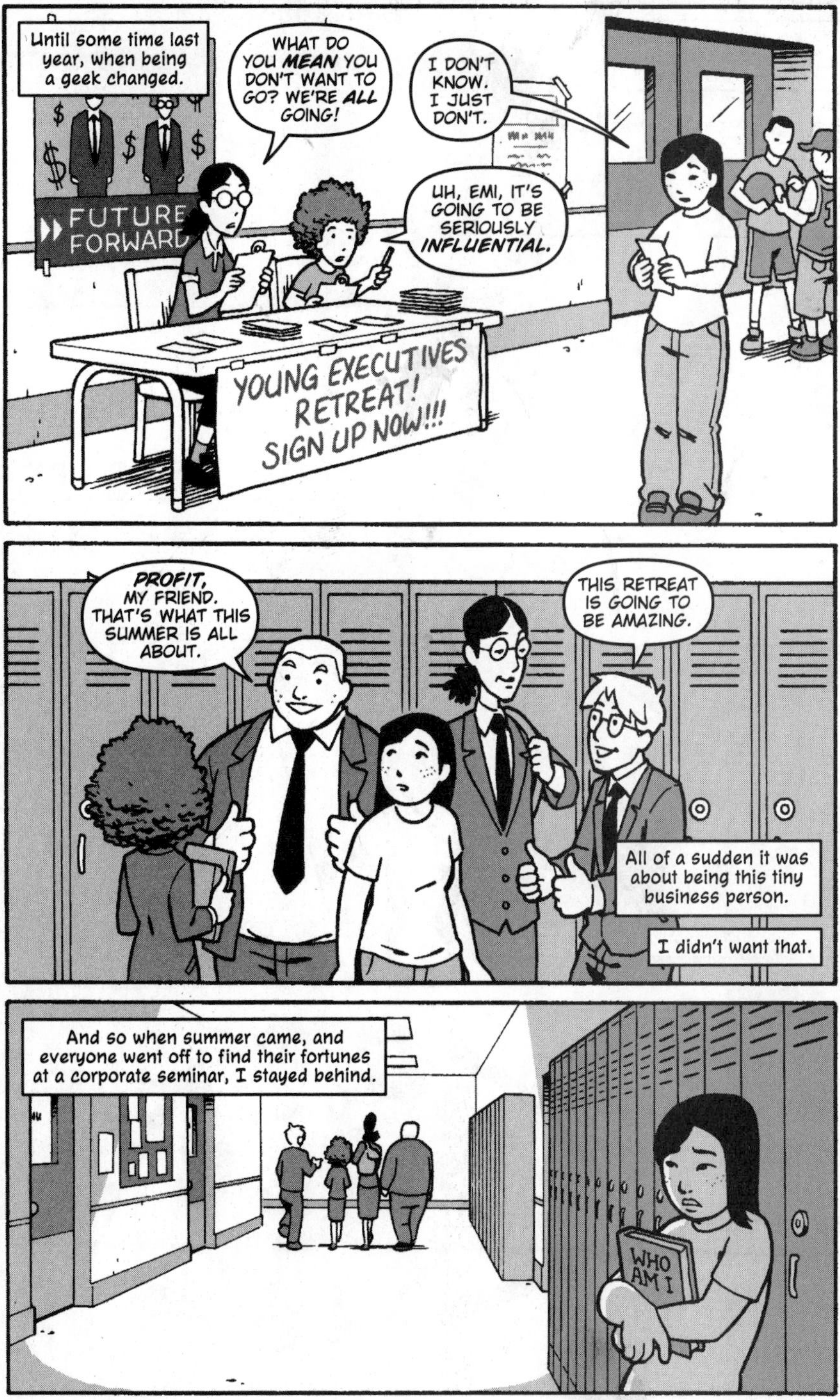

Until some time last year, when being a geek changed.
FUTURE FORWARD
WHAT DO YOU MEAN YOU DON'T WANT TO GO? WE'RE ALL GOING!
I DON'T KNOW. I JUST DON'T.
UH, EMI, IT'S GOING TO BE SERIOUSLY INFLUENTIAL.
YOUNG EXECUTIVES RETREAT! SIGN UP NOW!!!
PROFIT, MY FRIEND. THAT'S WHAT THIS SUMMER IS ALL ABOUT.
THIS RETREAT IS GOING TO BE AMAZING.
All of a sudden it was about being this tiny business person.
I didn't want that.
And so when summer came, and everyone went off to find their fortunes at a corporate seminar, I stayed behind.
WHO AM I

I was at what this book I found described as a "classic crossroads."

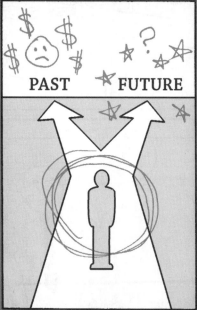

Where one thing gets left behind...

PAST   FUTURE

...and something else gets spotted in the distance.

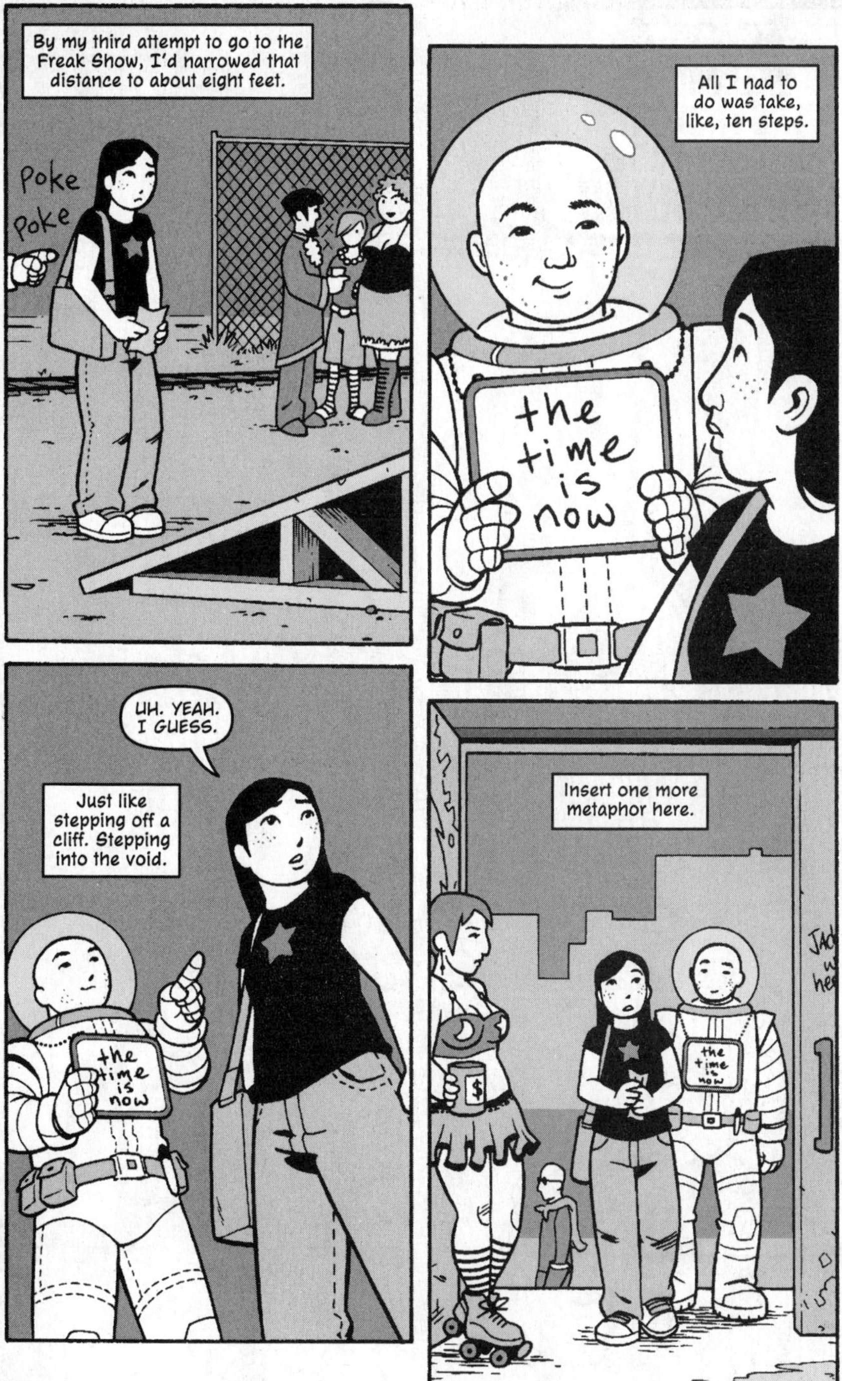
By my third attempt to go to the Freak Show, I'd narrowed that distance to about eight feet.
Poke
Poke
All I had to do was take, like, ten steps.
the time is now
UH. YEAH. I GUESS.
Just like stepping off a cliff. Stepping into the void.
the time is now
Insert one more metaphor here.
the time is now

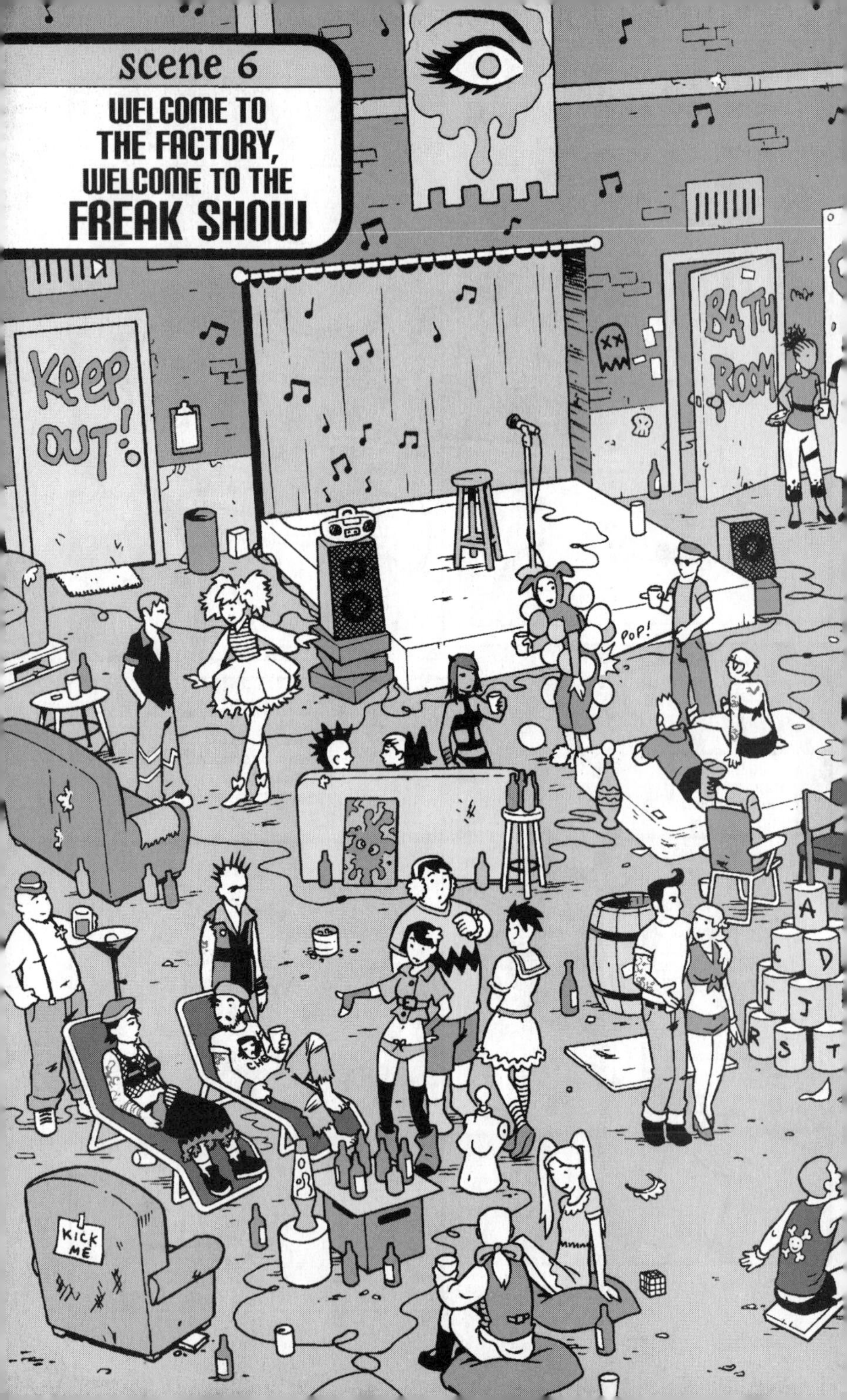
scene 6
WELCOME TO THE FACTORY, WELCOME TO THE FREAK SHOW
KEEP OUT!
BATH ROOM
POP!
CHE
A
C D
I J
R S T
KICK ME

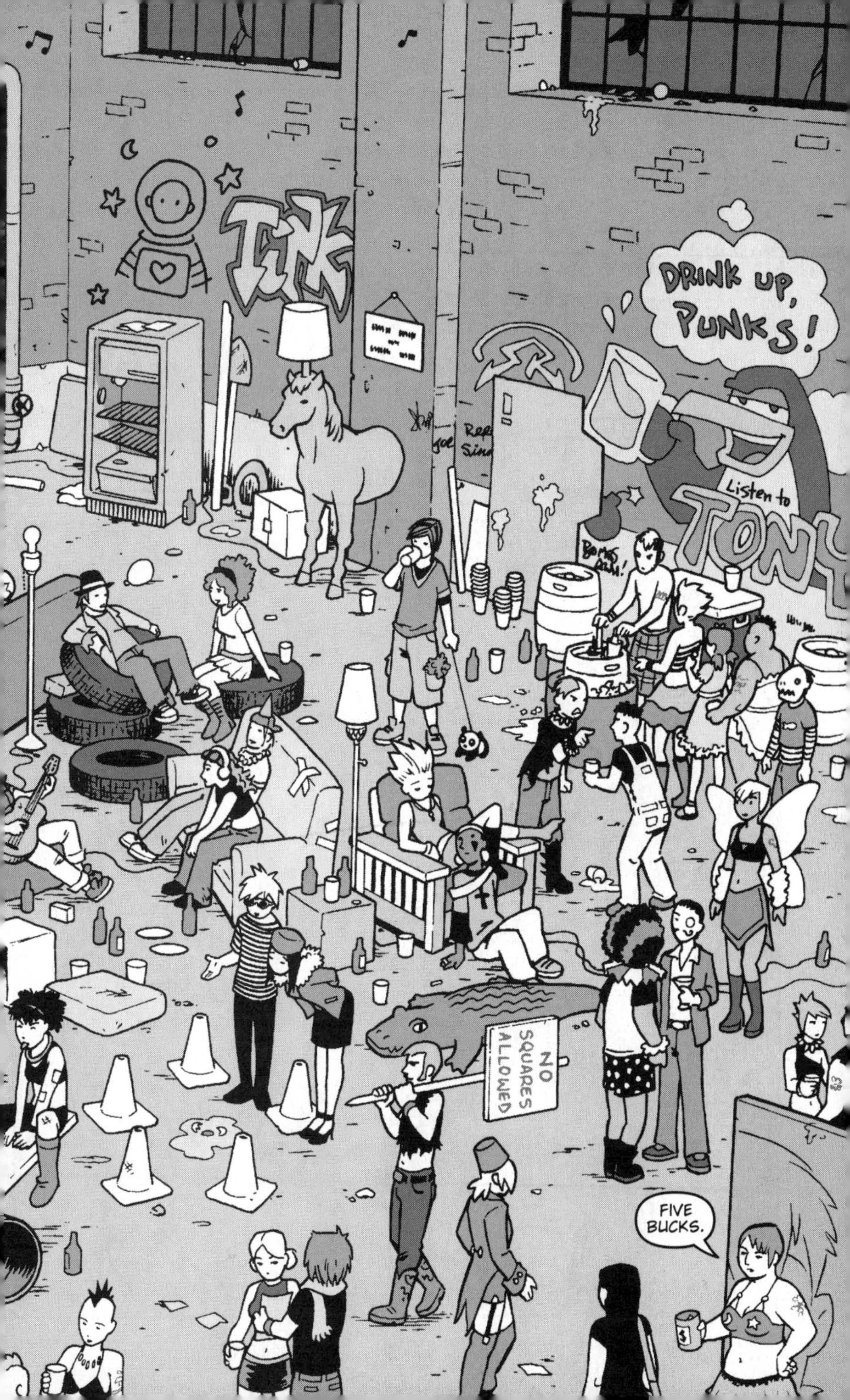

DRINK UP, PUNKS!
Listen to TONY
NO SQUARES ALLOWED
FIVE BUCKS.

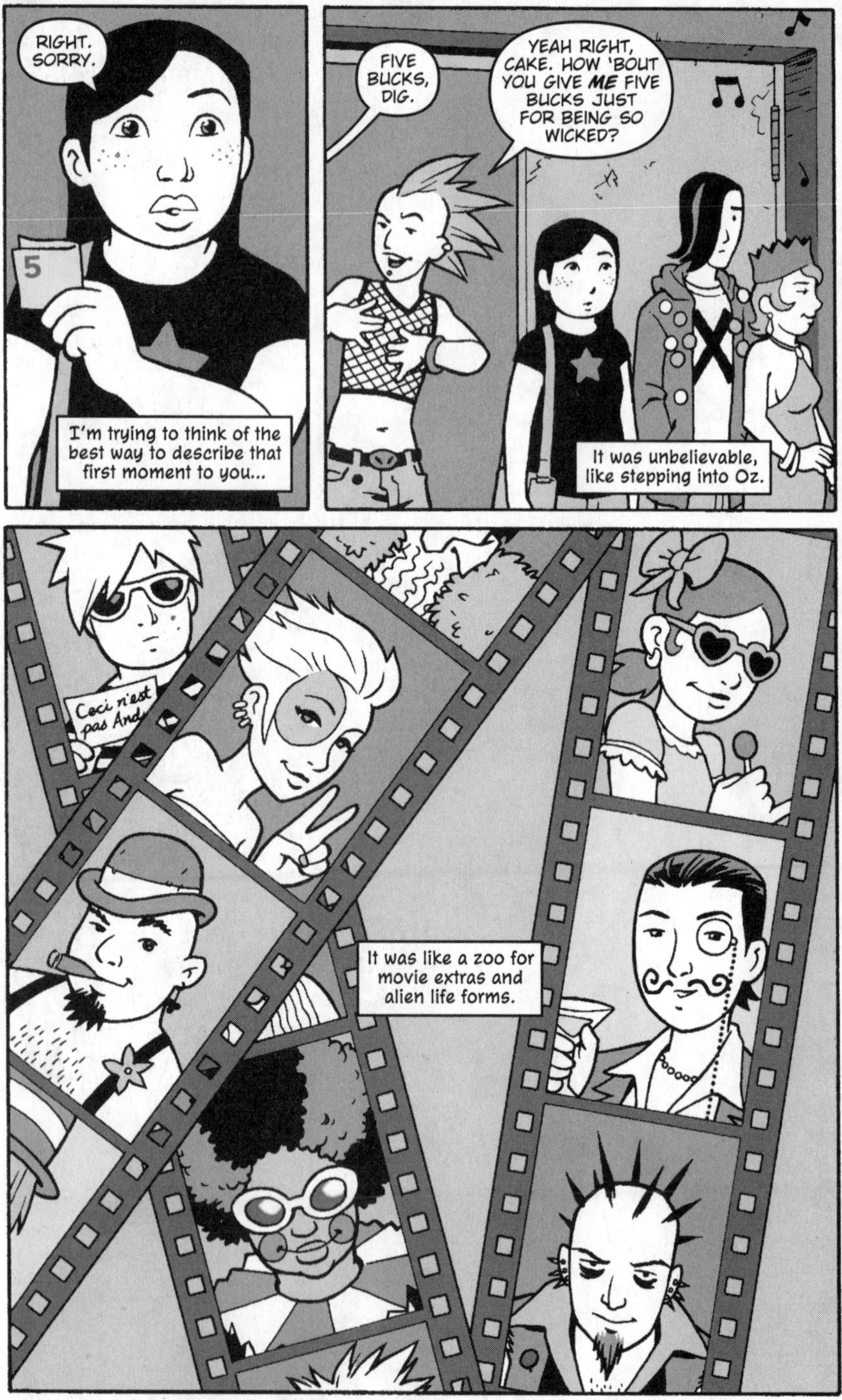
RIGHT. SORRY.
5
I'm trying to think of the best way to describe that first moment to you...
FIVE BUCKS, DIG.
YEAH RIGHT, CAKE. HOW 'BOUT YOU GIVE ME FIVE BUCKS JUST FOR BEING SO WICKED?
It was unbelievable, like stepping into Oz.
It was like a zoo for movie extras and alien life forms.

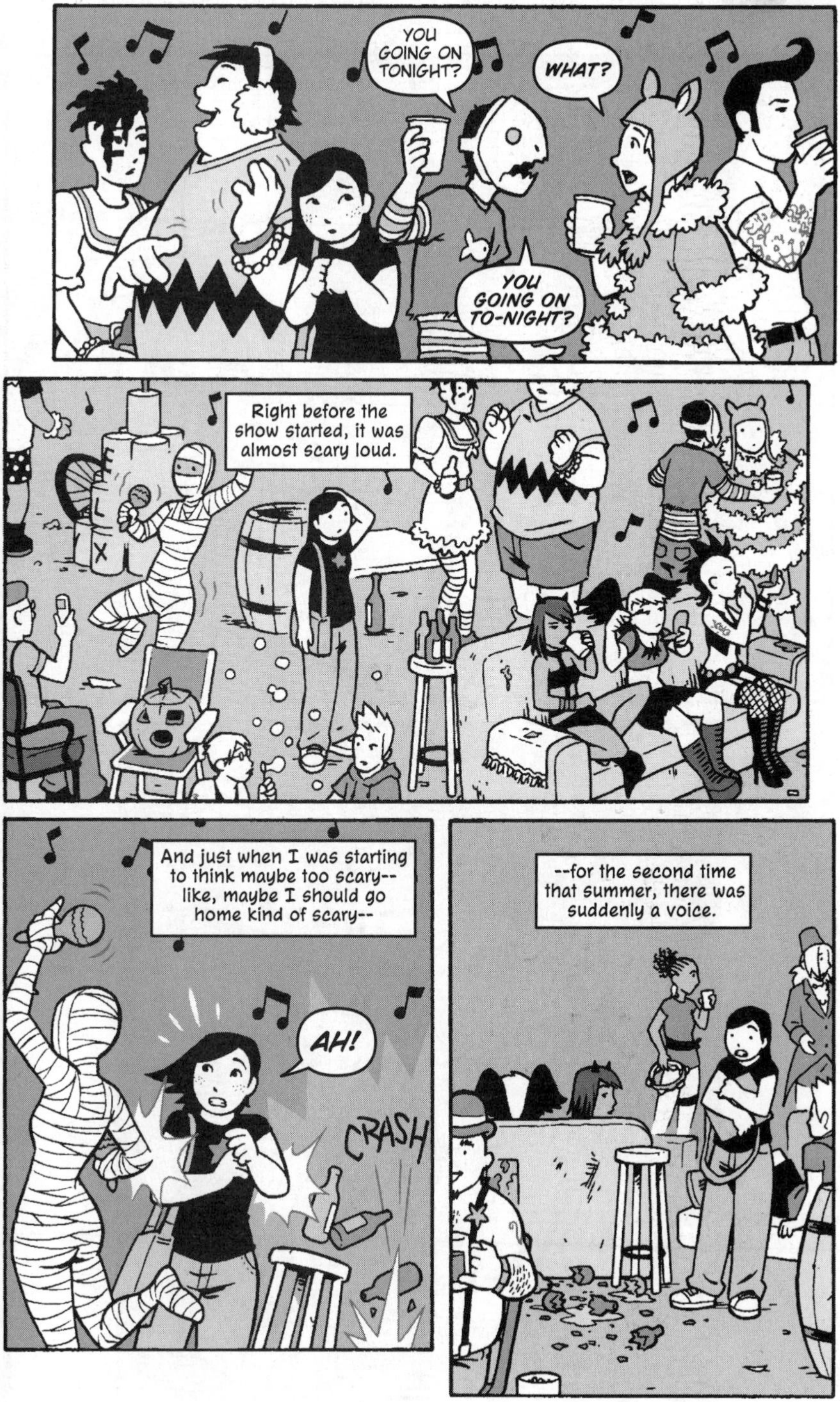
YOU GOING ON TONIGHT?
WHAT?
YOU GOING ON TO-NIGHT?
Right before the show started, it was almost scary loud.
And just when I was starting to think maybe too scary-- like, maybe I should go home kind of scary--
AH!
CRASH
--for the second time that summer, there was suddenly a voice.

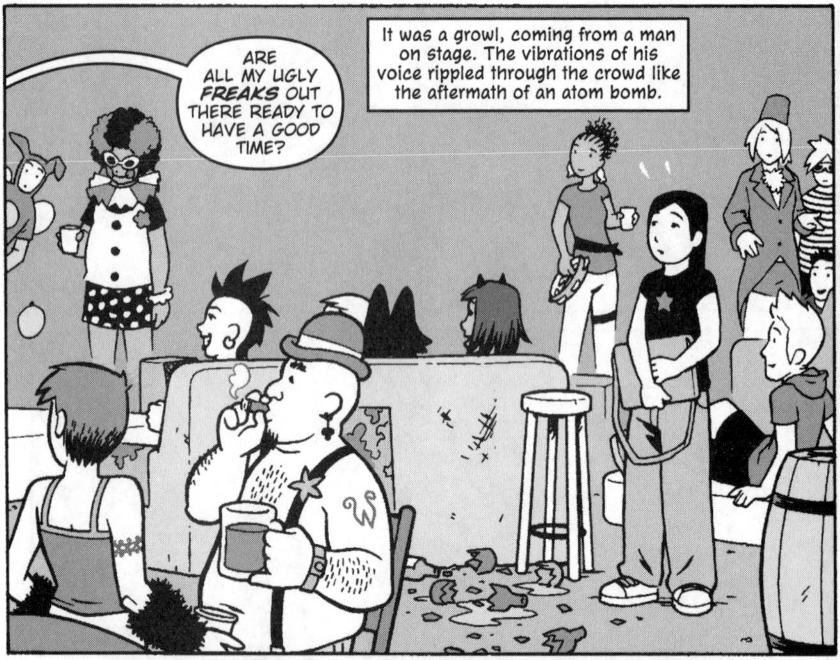
ARE ALL MY UGLY FREAKS OUT THERE READY TO HAVE A GOOD TIME?
It was a growl, coming from a man on stage. The vibrations of his voice rippled through the crowd like the aftermath of an atom bomb.

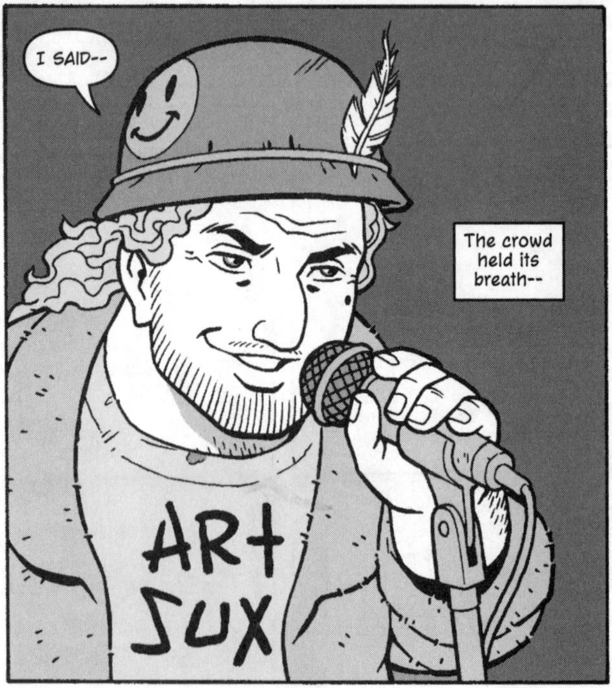
I SAID--
The crowd held its breath--
ART SUX

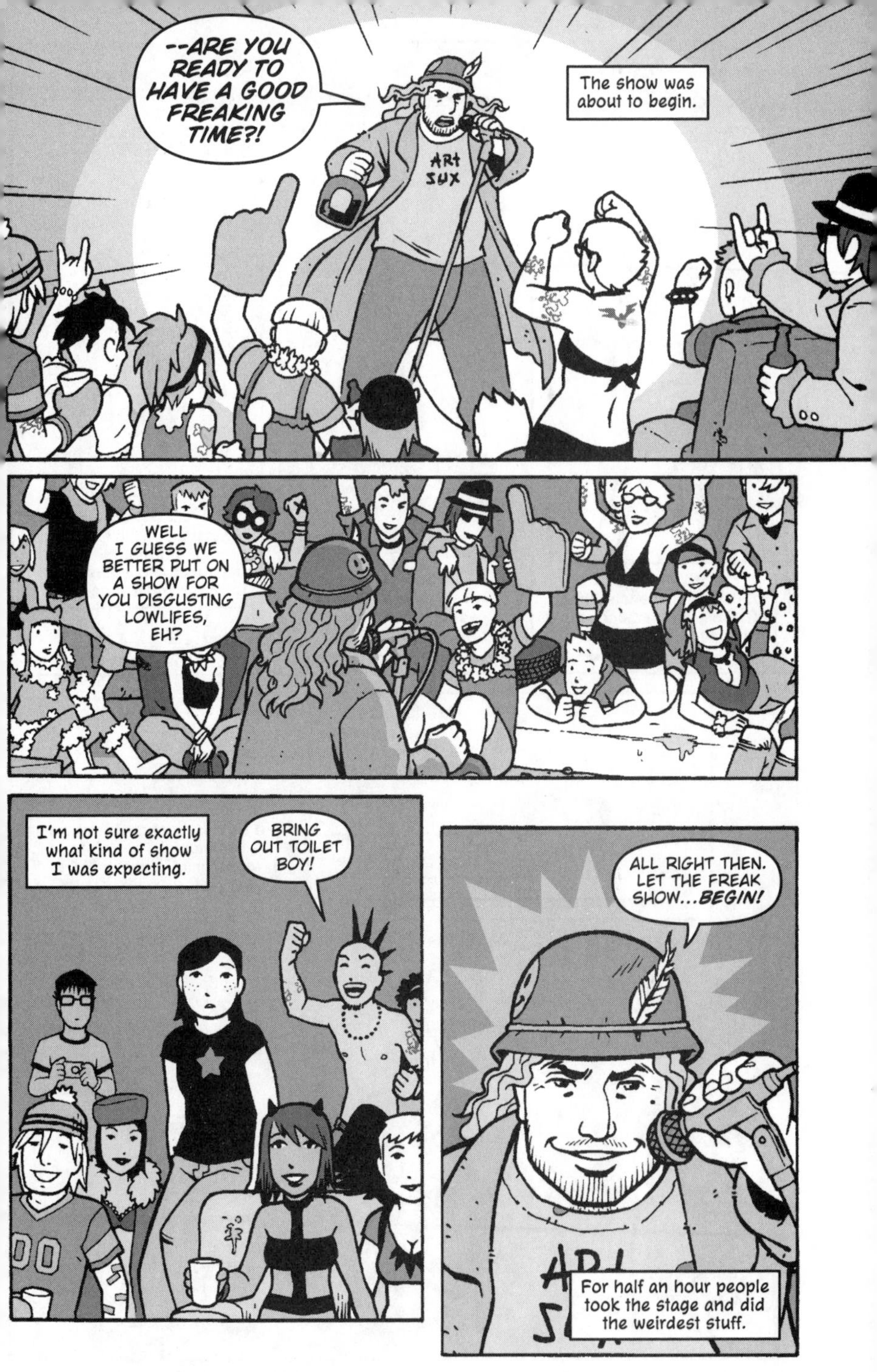
--ARE YOU READY TO HAVE A GOOD FREAKING TIME?!
The show was about to begin.
ART SUX
WELL I GUESS WE BETTER PUT ON A SHOW FOR YOU DISGUSTING LOWLIFES, EH?
I'm not sure exactly what kind of show I was expecting.
BRING OUT TOILET BOY!
ALL RIGHT THEN. LET THE FREAK SHOW...BEGIN!
For half an hour people took the stage and did the weirdest stuff.

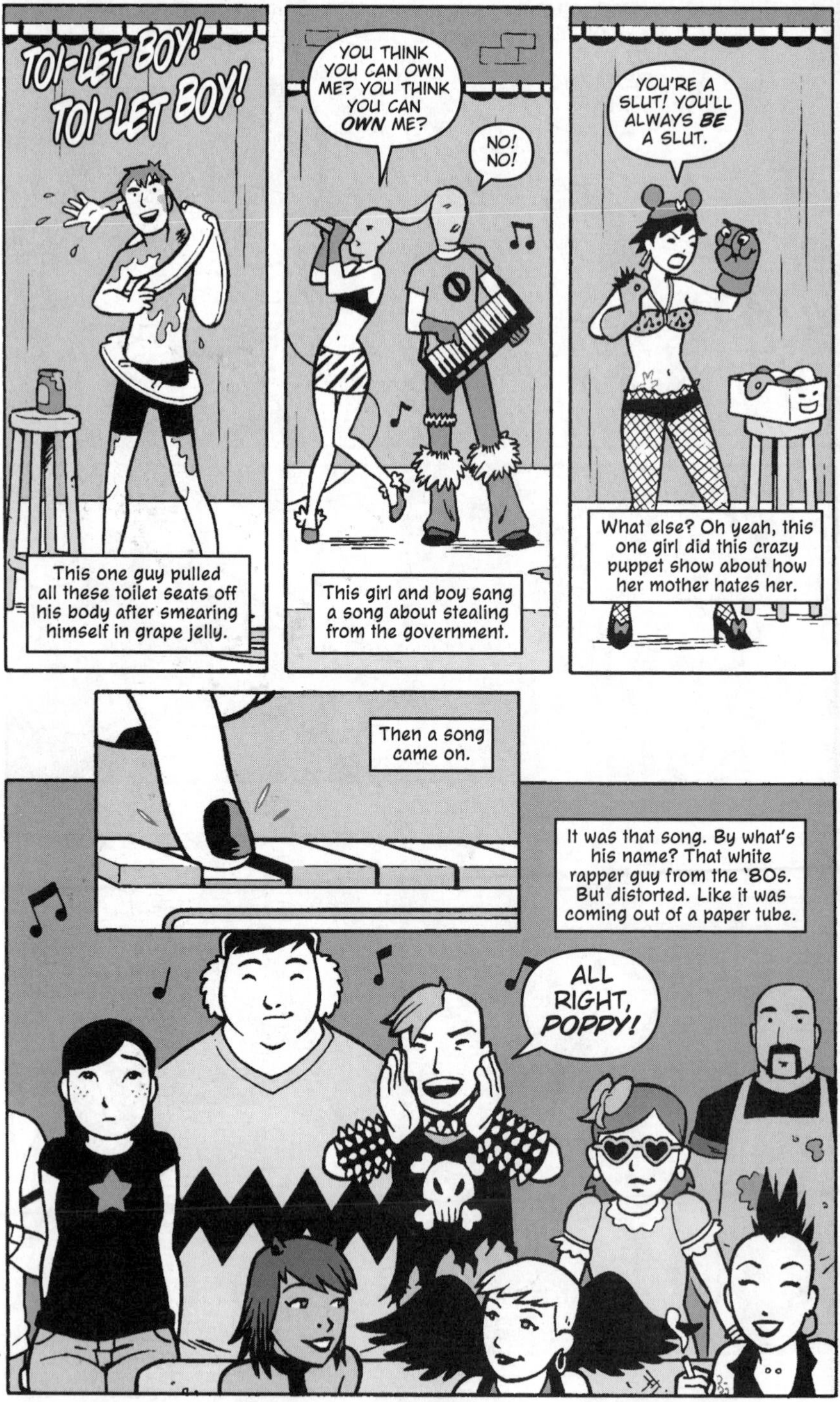
TOI-LET BOY! TOI-LET BOY!
This one guy pulled all these toilet seats off his body after smearing himself in grape jelly.
YOU THINK YOU CAN OWN ME? YOU THINK YOU CAN OWN ME?
NO! NO!
This girl and boy sang a song about stealing from the government.
YOU'RE A SLUT! YOU'LL ALWAYS BE A SLUT.
What else? Oh yeah, this one girl did this crazy puppet show about how her mother hates her.
Then a song came on.
It was that song. By what's his name? That white rapper guy from the '80s. But distorted. Like it was coming out of a paper tube.
ALL RIGHT, POPPY!

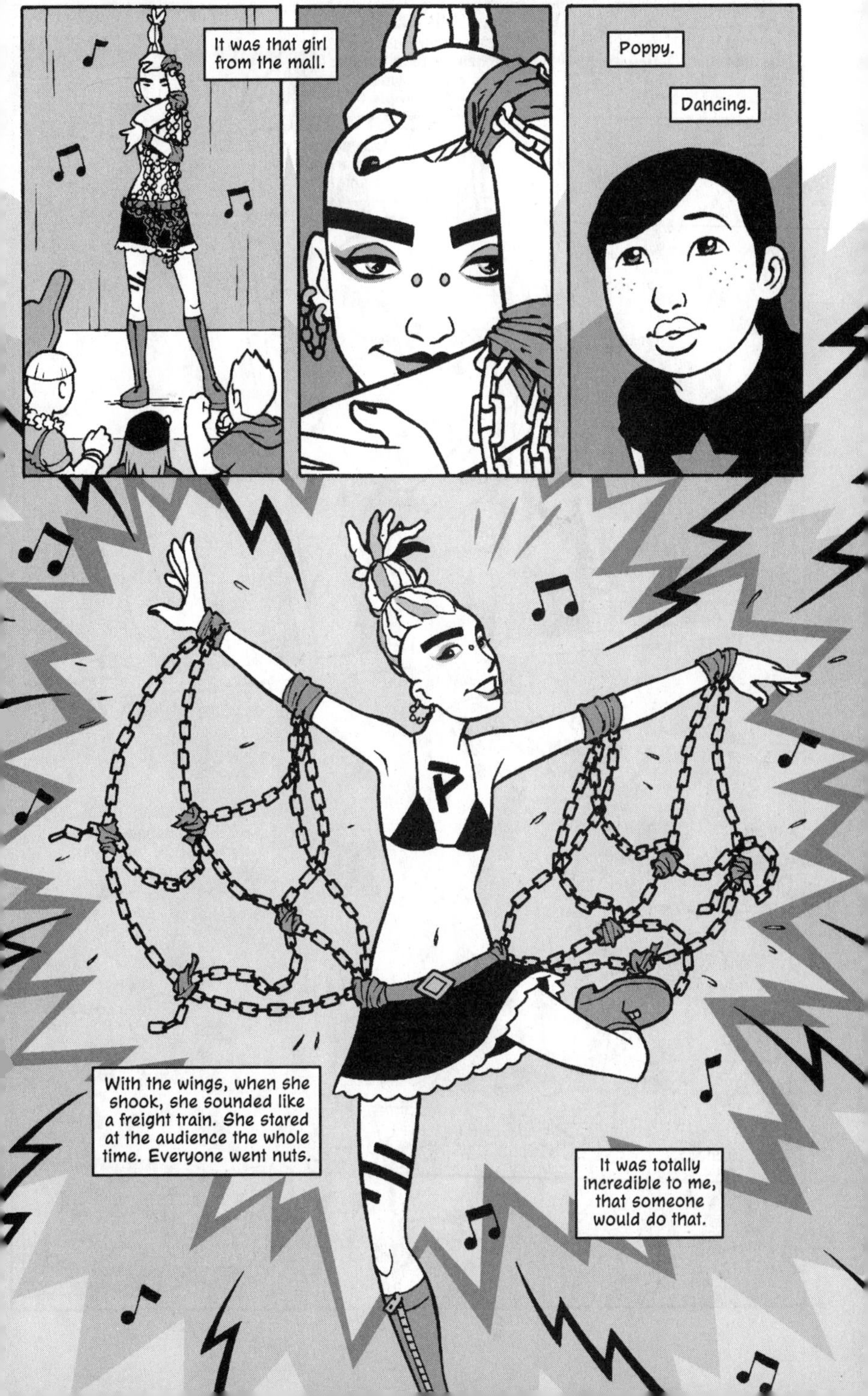
It was that girl from the mall.
Poppy.
Dancing.
With the wings, when she shook, she sounded like a freight train. She stared at the audience the whole time. Everyone went nuts.
It was totally incredible to me, that someone would do that.

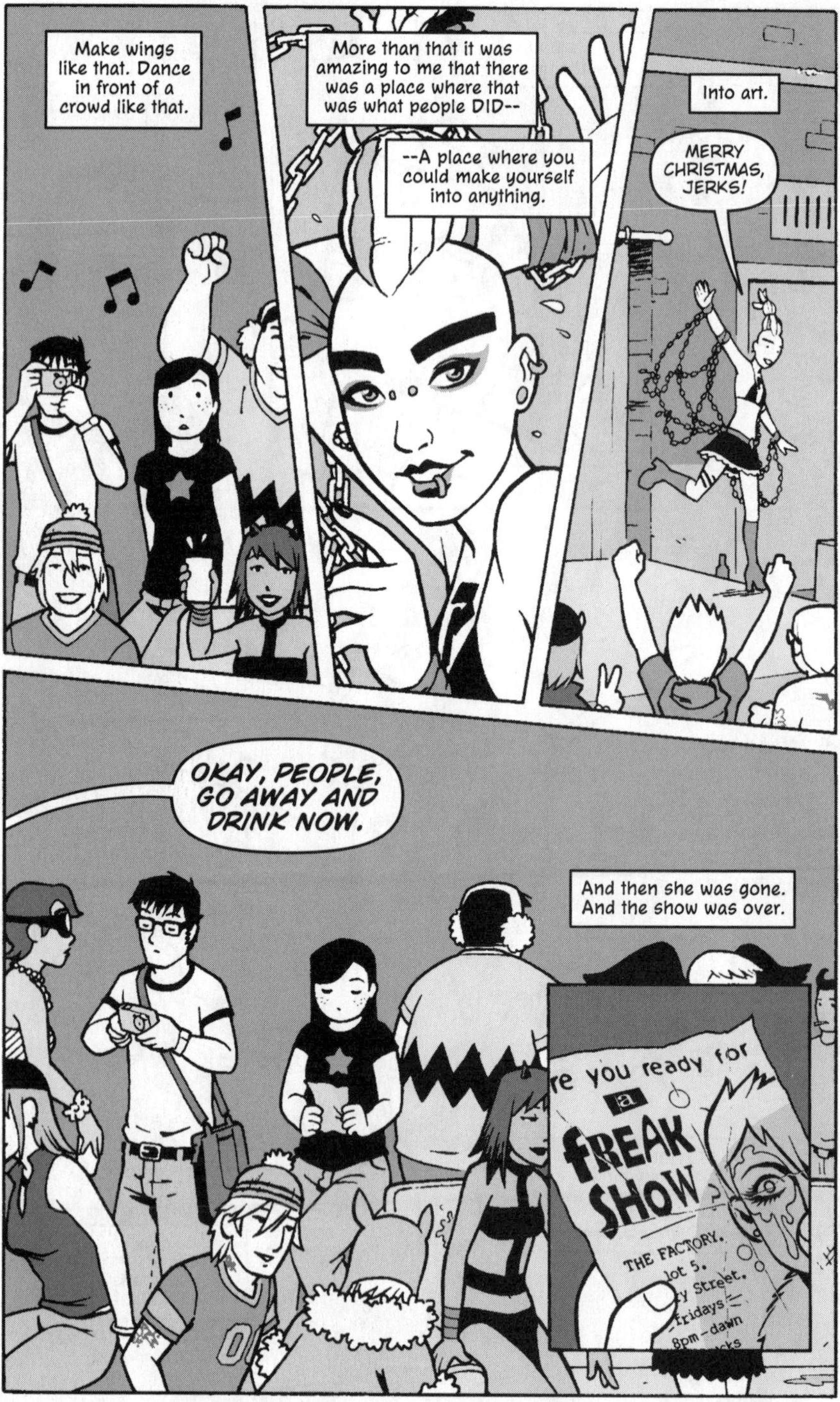
Make wings like that. Dance in front of a crowd like that.
More than that it was amazing to me that there was a place where that was what people DID--
--A place where you could make yourself into anything.
Into art.
MERRY CHRISTMAS, JERKS!
OKAY, PEOPLE, GO AWAY AND DRINK NOW.
And then she was gone. And the show was over.
you ready for
a
FREAK SHOW
THE FACTORY.
lot 5.
Street.
Fridays
8pm-dawn

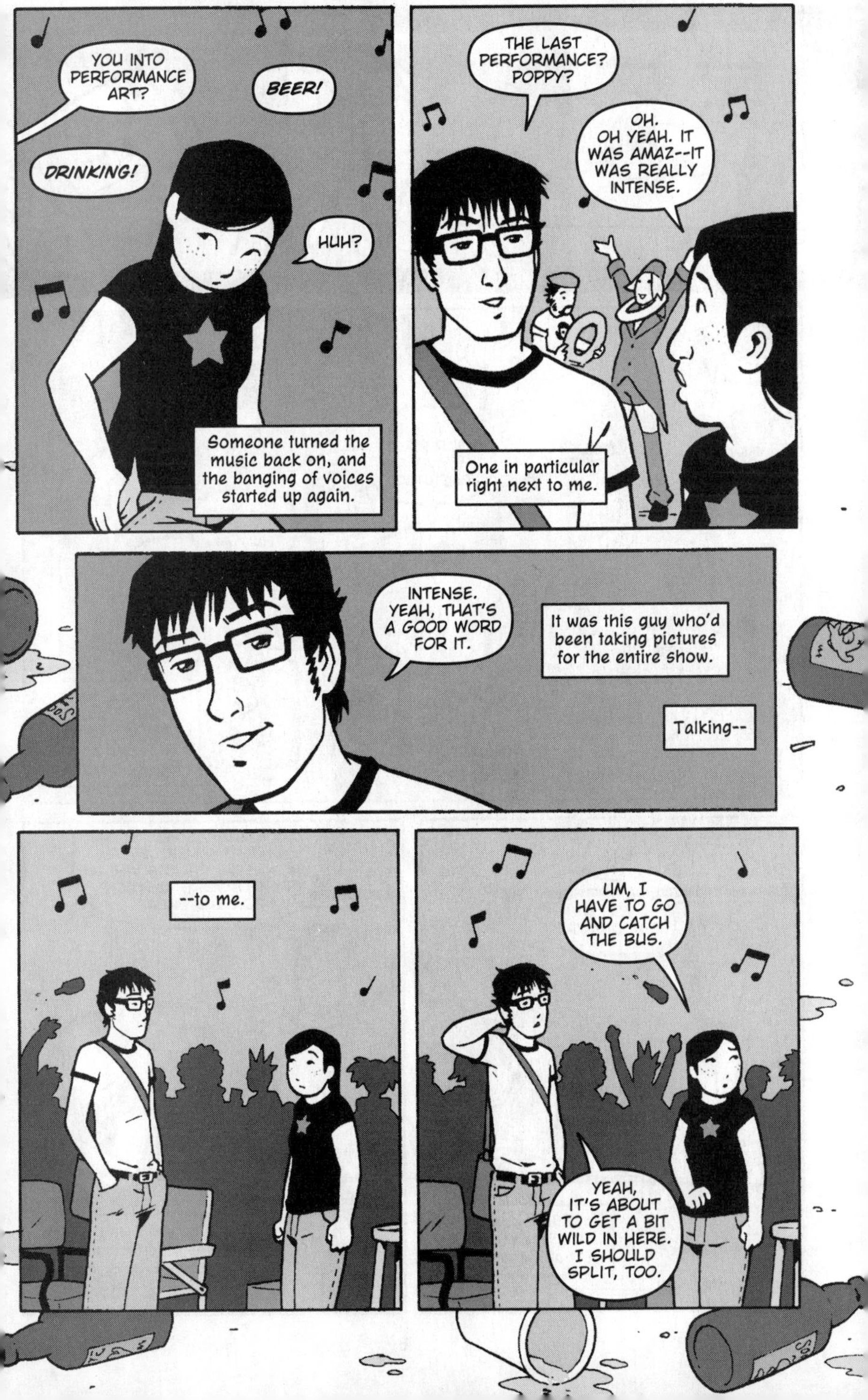
YOU INTO PERFORMANCE ART?
BEER!
DRINKING!
HUH?
Someone turned the music back on, and the banging of voices started up again.
THE LAST PERFORMANCE? POPPY?
OH. OH YEAH. IT WAS AMAZ--IT WAS REALLY INTENSE.
One in particular right next to me.
INTENSE. YEAH, THAT'S A GOOD WORD FOR IT.
It was this guy who'd been taking pictures for the entire show.
Talking--
--to me.
UM, I HAVE TO GO AND CATCH THE BUS.
YEAH, IT'S ABOUT TO GET A BIT WILD IN HERE. I SHOULD SPLIT, TOO.

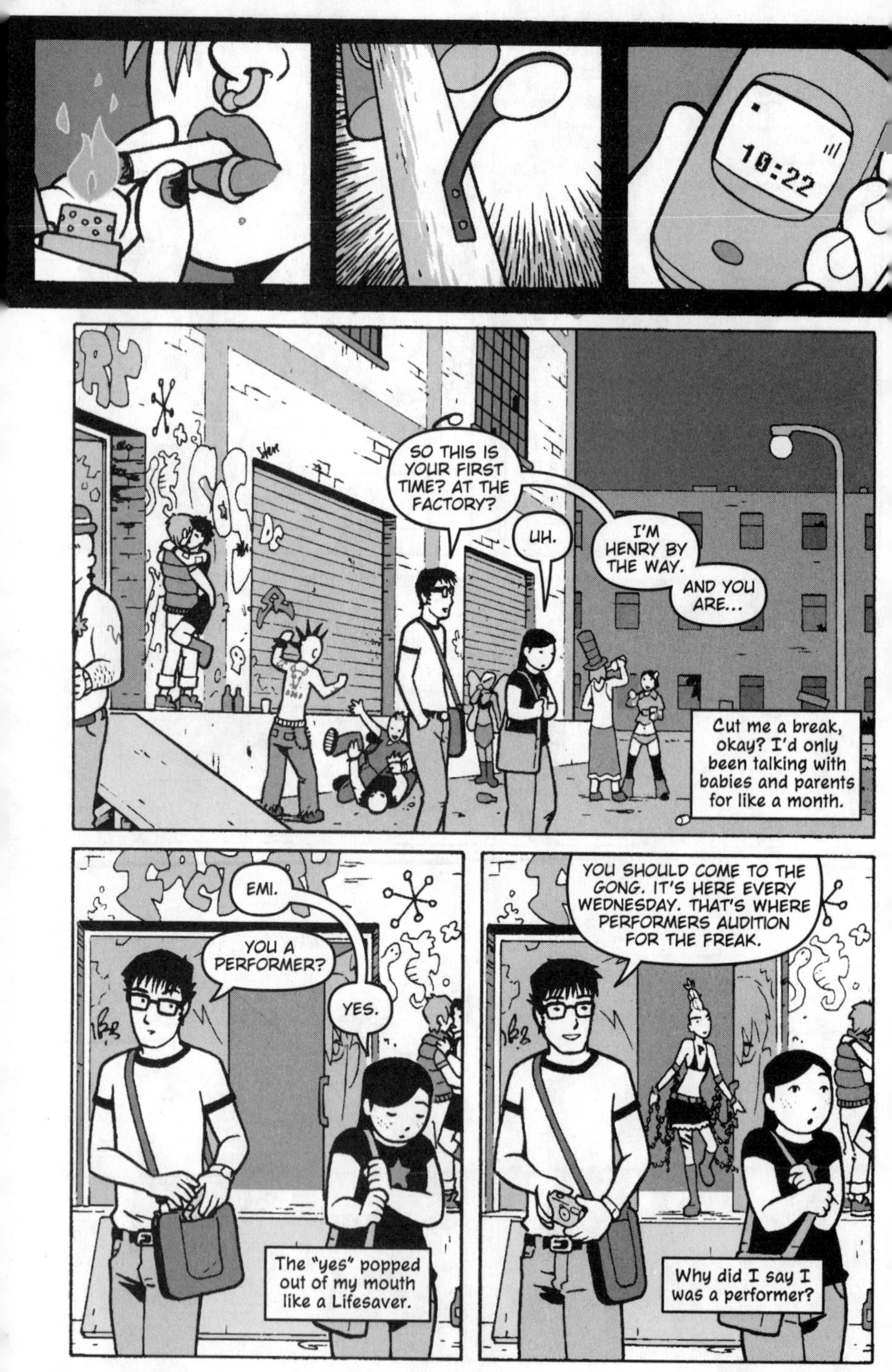
10:22
SO THIS IS YOUR FIRST TIME? AT THE FACTORY?
UH.
I'M HENRY BY THE WAY.
AND YOU ARE...
Cut me a break, okay? I'd only been talking with babies and parents for like a month.
EMI.
YOU A PERFORMER?
YES.
The "yes" popped out of my mouth like a Lifesaver.
YOU SHOULD COME TO THE GONG. IT'S HERE EVERY WEDNESDAY. THAT'S WHERE PERFORMERS AUDITION FOR THE FREAK.
Why did I say I was a performer?

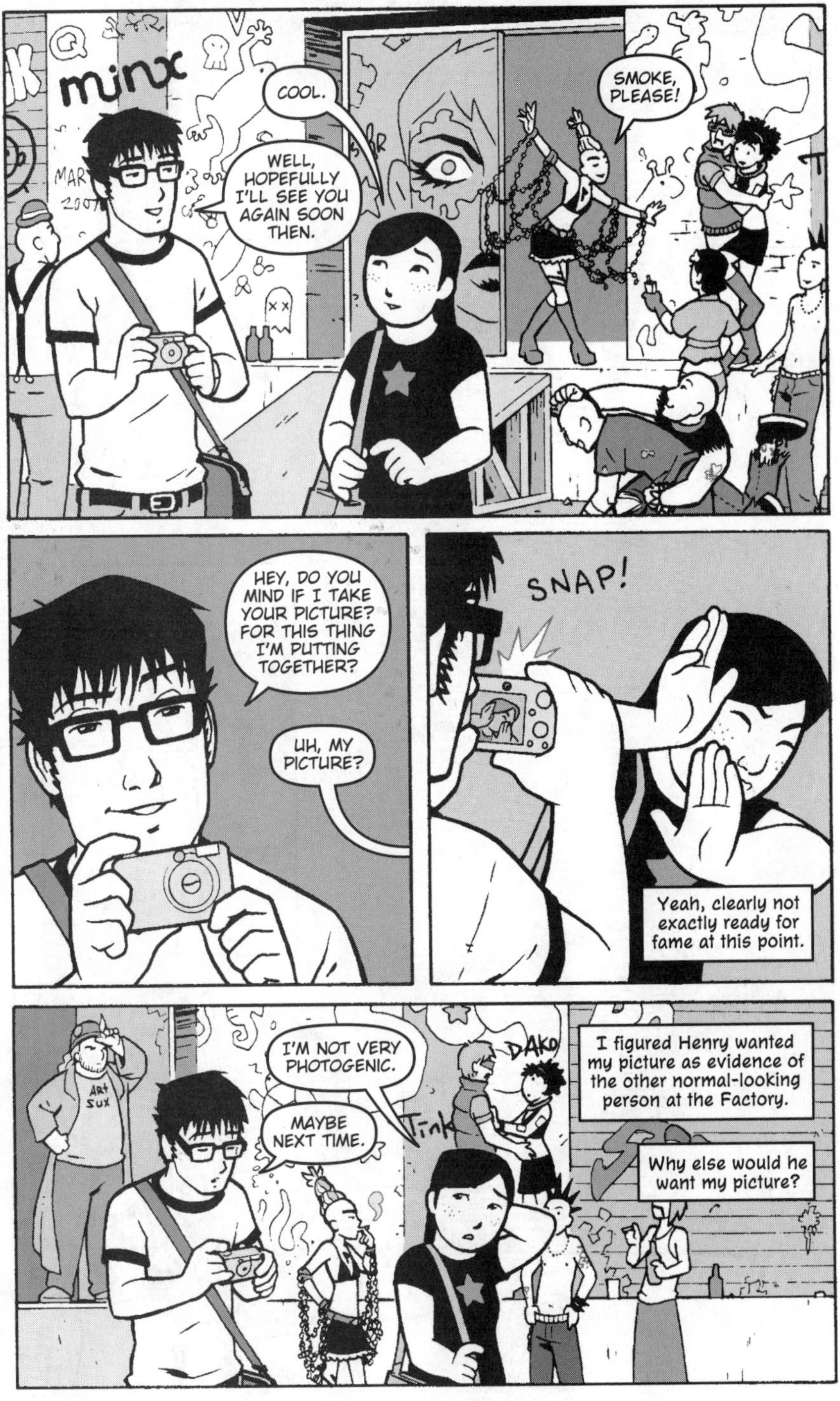
minx
COOL.
SMOKE, PLEASE!
WELL, HOPEFULLY I'LL SEE YOU AGAIN SOON THEN.
HEY, DO YOU MIND IF I TAKE YOUR PICTURE? FOR THIS THING I'M PUTTING TOGETHER?
UH, MY PICTURE?
SNAP!
Yeah, clearly not exactly ready for fame at this point.
ART SUX
I'M NOT VERY PHOTOGENIC.
MAYBE NEXT TIME.
DAKO
TINK
I figured Henry wanted my picture as evidence of the other normal-looking person at the Factory.
Why else would he want my picture?

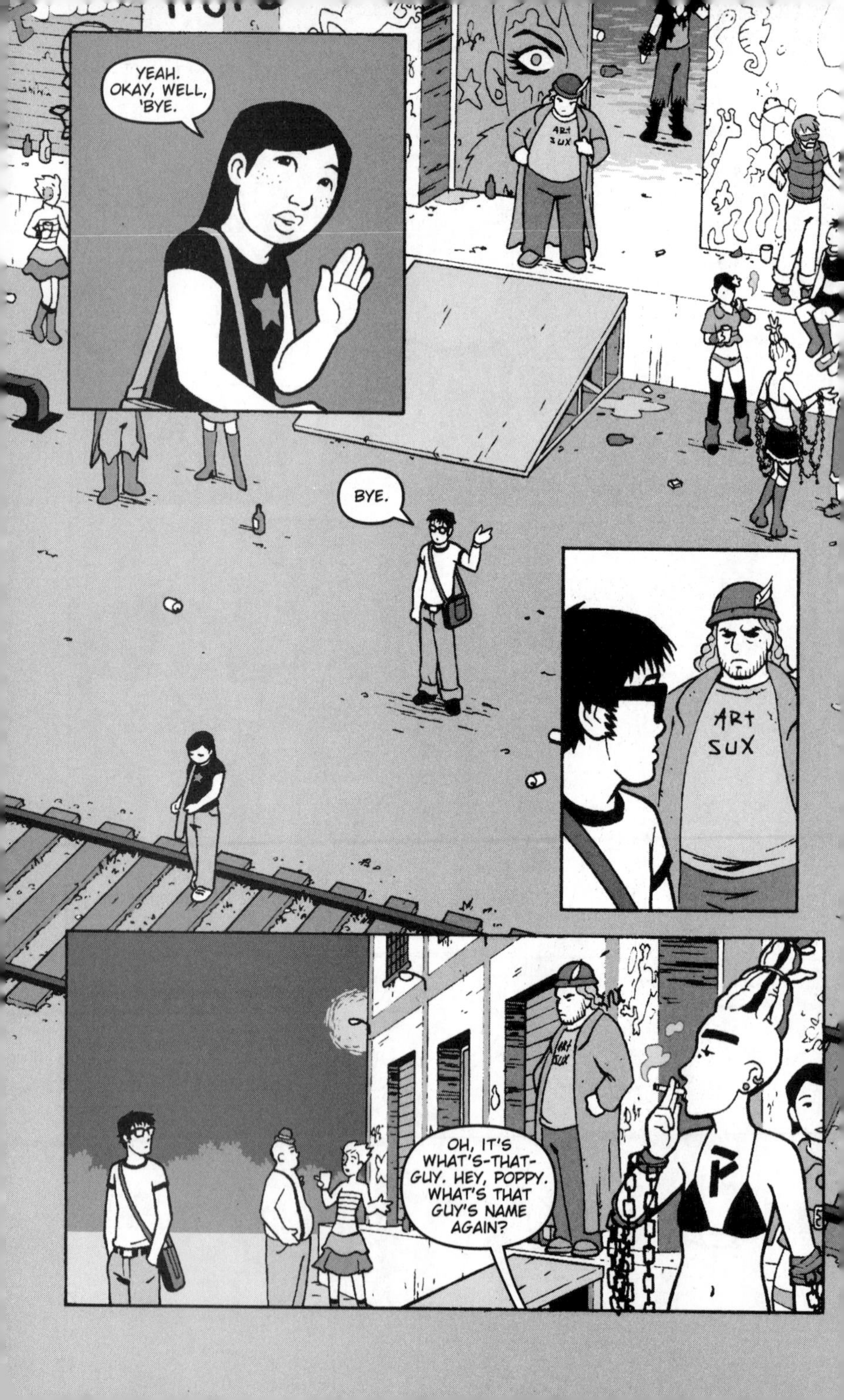
YEAH. OKAY, WELL, 'BYE.
BYE.
ART SUX
OH, IT'S WHAT'S-THAT-GUY. HEY, POPPY. WHAT'S THAT GUY'S NAME AGAIN?

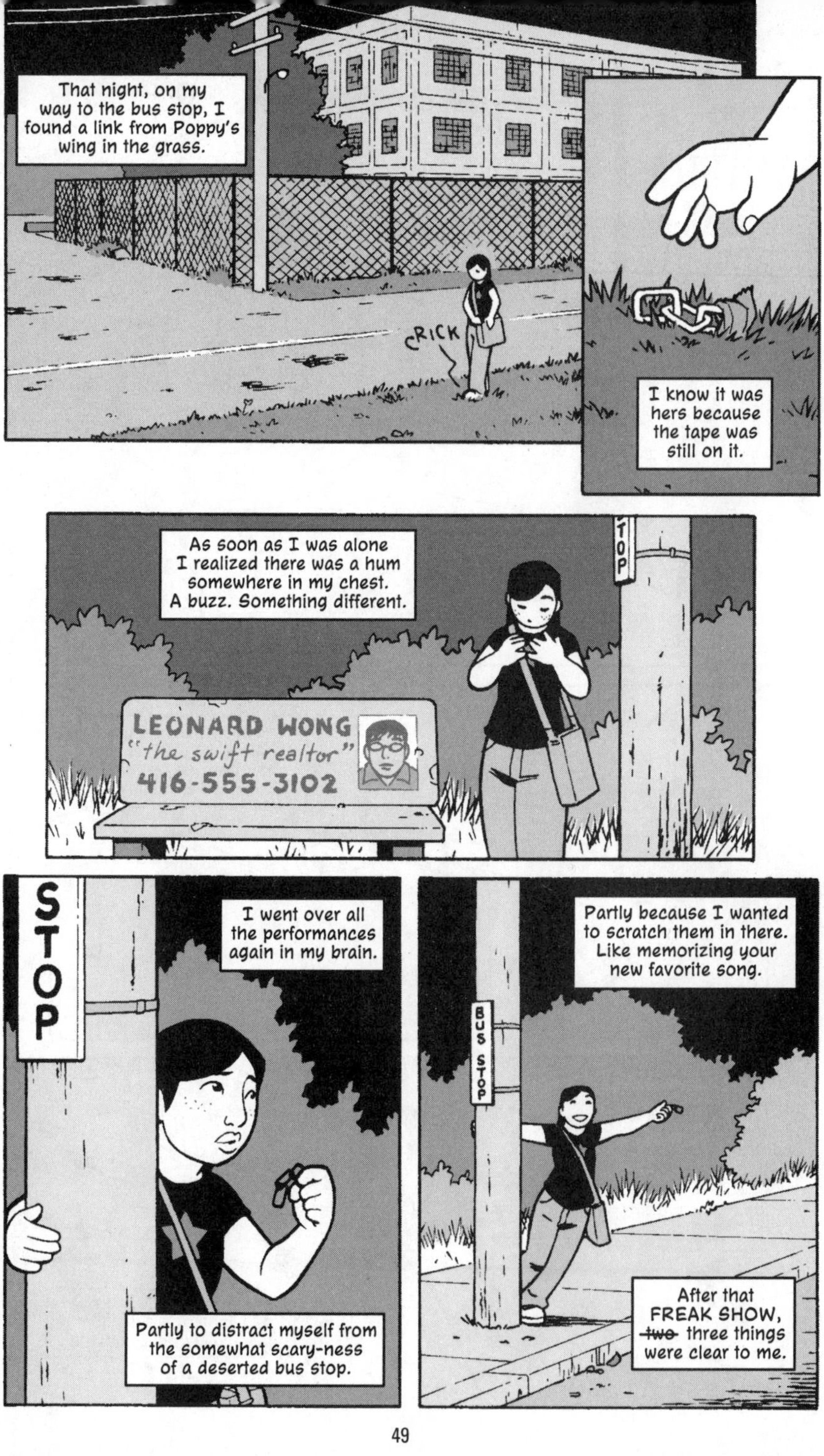
That night, on my way to the bus stop, I found a link from Poppy's wing in the grass.
CRICK
I know it was hers because the tape was still on it.
As soon as I was alone I realized there was a hum somewhere in my chest. A buzz. Something different.
STOP
LEONARD WONG
"the swift realtor"
416-555-3102
STOP
I went over all the performances again in my brain.
Partly to distract myself from the somewhat scary-ness of a deserted bus stop.
Partly because I wanted to scratch them in there. Like memorizing your new favorite song.
BUS STOP
After that FREAK SHOW, ~~two~~ three things were clear to me.

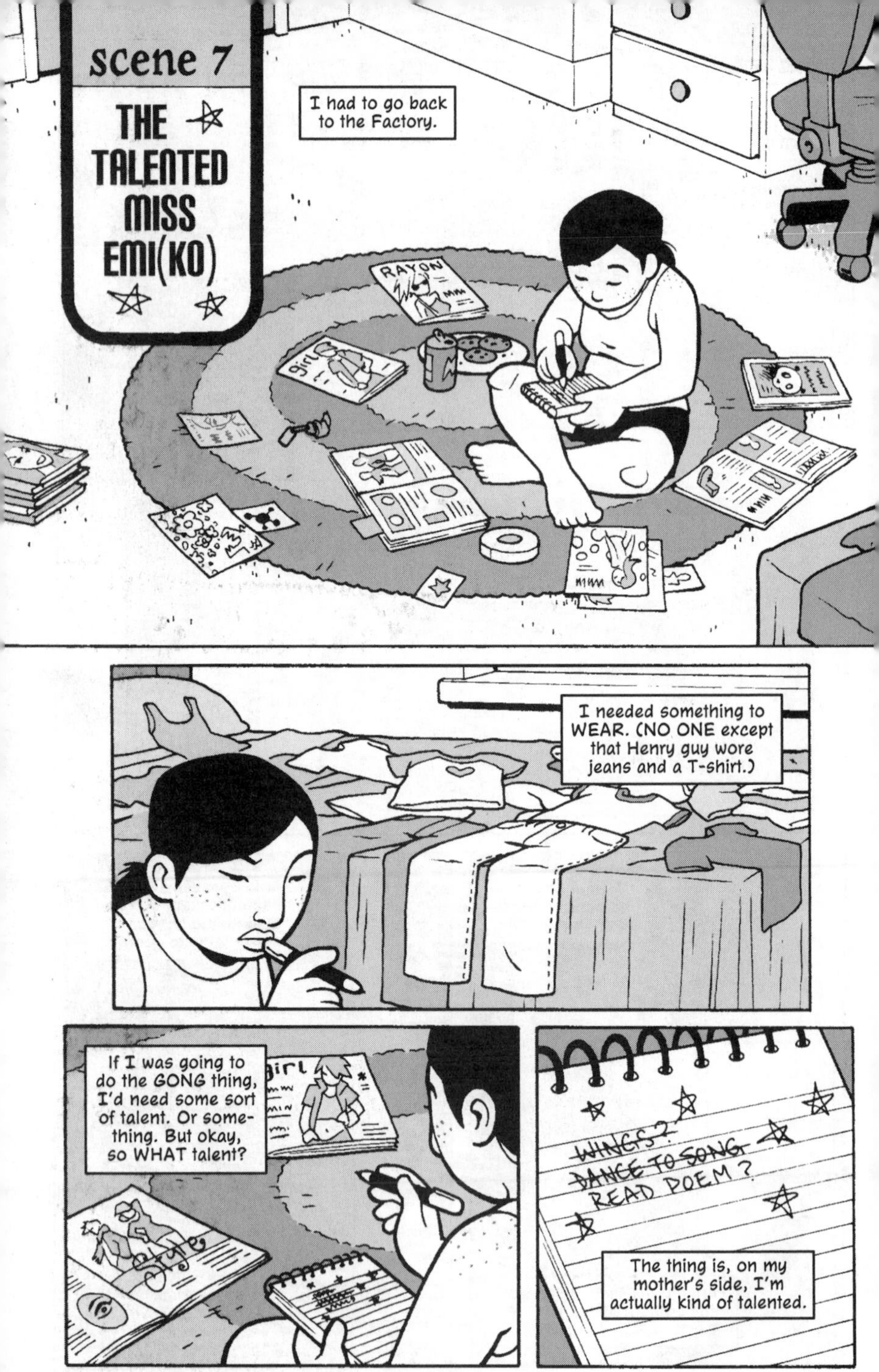
scene 7
THE TALENTED MISS EMI(KO)
I had to go back to the Factory.
RAYON
girl
I needed something to WEAR. (NO ONE except that Henry guy wore jeans and a T-shirt.)
If I was going to do the GONG thing, I'd need some sort of talent. Or something. But okay, so WHAT talent?
girl
WINGS?
DANCE TO SONG
READ POEM?
The thing is, on my mother's side, I'm actually kind of talented.

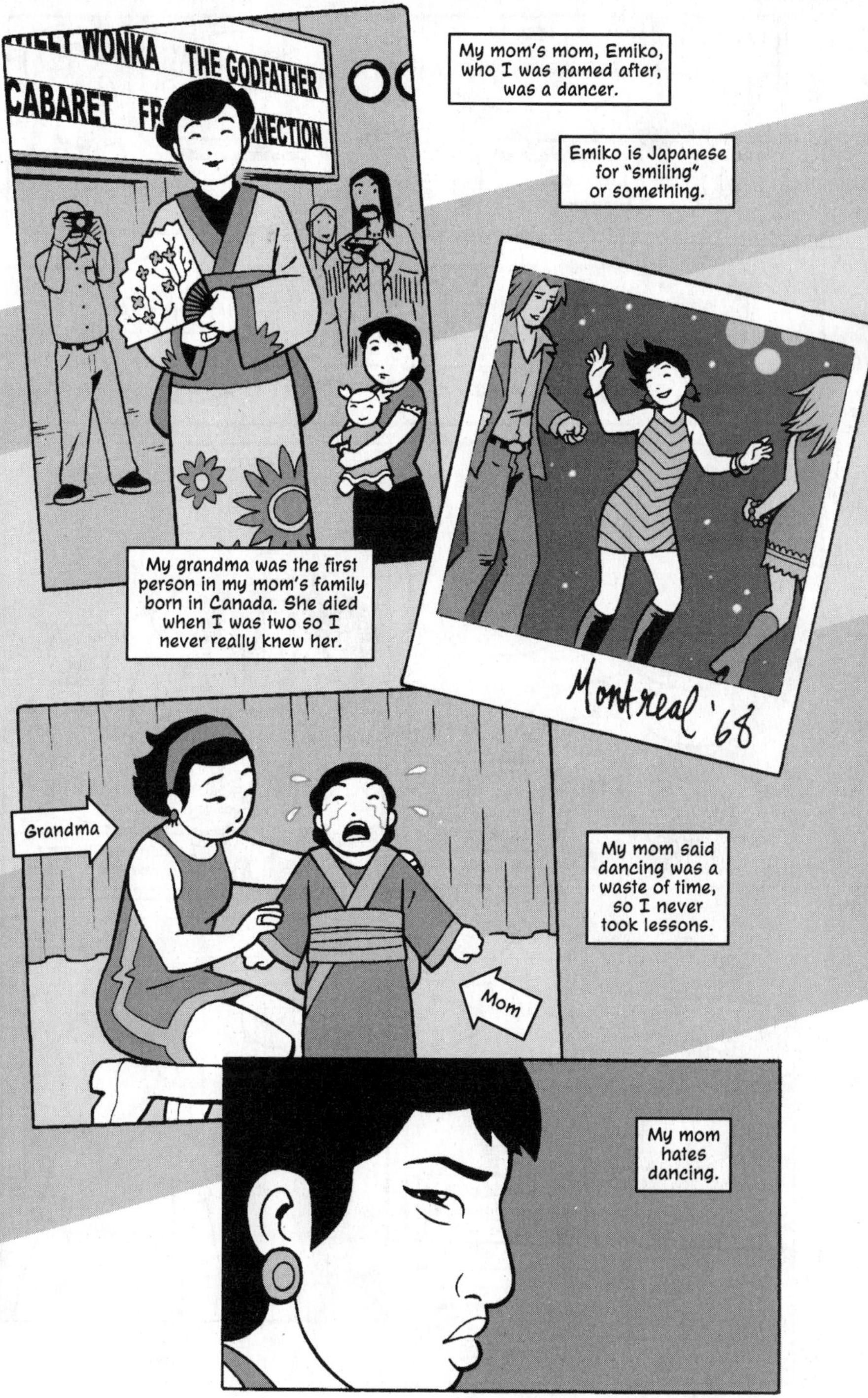
WILLY WONKA THE GODFATHER
CABARET FR NECTION
My mom's mom, Emiko, who I was named after, was a dancer.
Emiko is Japanese for "smiling" or something.
My grandma was the first person in my mom's family born in Canada. She died when I was two so I never really knew her.
Montreal '68
Grandma
Mom
My mom said dancing was a waste of time, so I never took lessons.
My mom hates dancing.

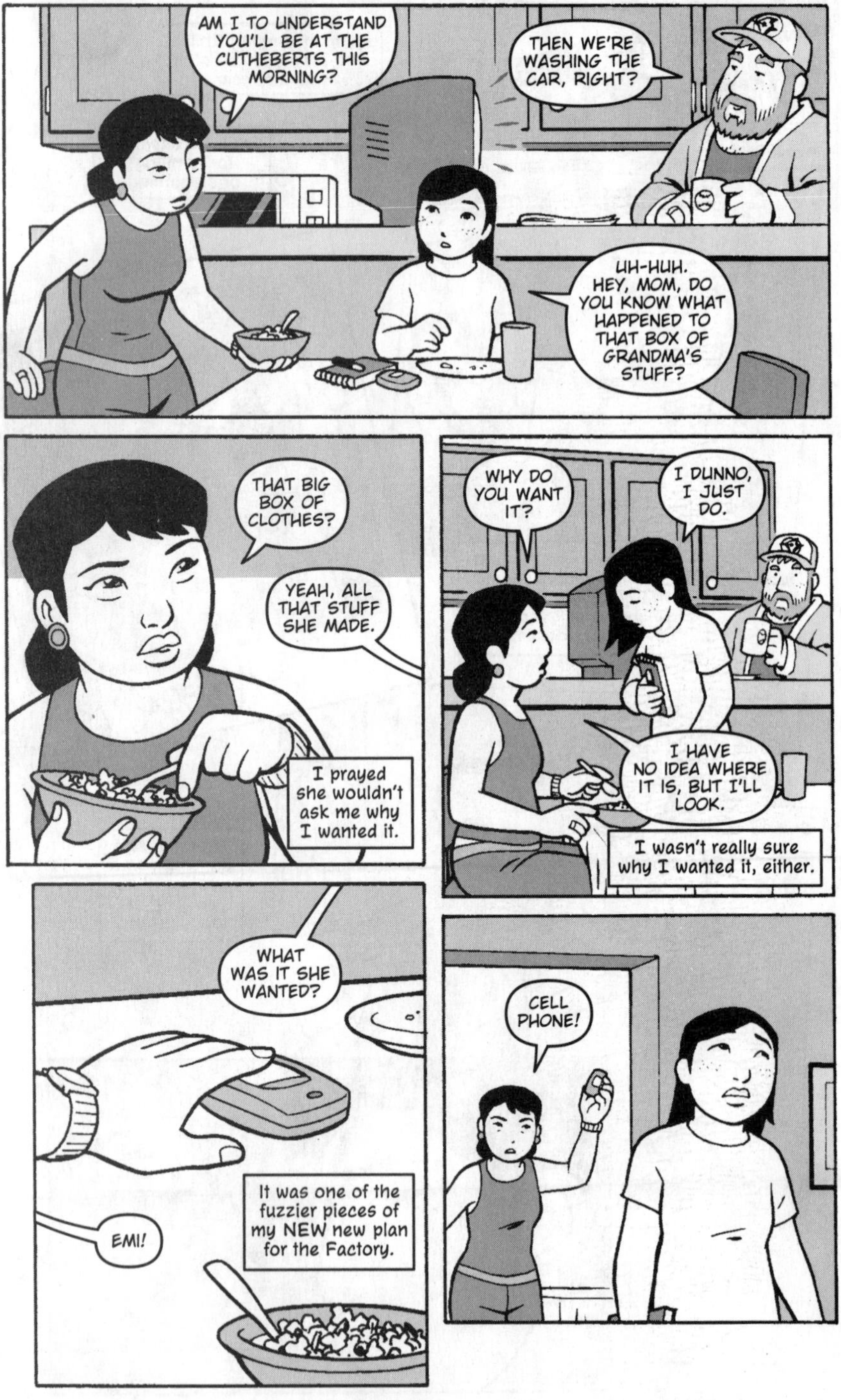
AM I TO UNDERSTAND YOU'LL BE AT THE CUTHEBERTS THIS MORNING?
THEN WE'RE WASHING THE CAR, RIGHT?
UH-HUH. HEY, MOM, DO YOU KNOW WHAT HAPPENED TO THAT BOX OF GRANDMA'S STUFF?
THAT BIG BOX OF CLOTHES?
YEAH, ALL THAT STUFF SHE MADE.
I prayed she wouldn't ask me why I wanted it.
WHY DO YOU WANT IT?
I DUNNO, I JUST DO.
I HAVE NO IDEA WHERE IT IS, BUT I'LL LOOK.
I wasn't really sure why I wanted it, either.
WHAT WAS IT SHE WANTED?
It was one of the fuzzier pieces of my NEW new plan for the Factory.
EMI!
CELL PHONE!

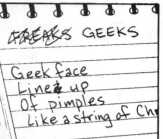

FREAKS GEEKS

Geek face
Line of up
Of pimples
Like a string of Chr

The clearest part of the plan involved me writing a poem to read at the GONG.

YAP!

YAP!

YAP!

BACK PROBABLY CLOSER TO TWO O'CLOCK, EMI, IF THAT'S OKAY.

TC

TEAM CUTHEBERT

NO PROBLEM.

I wrote a couple of poems for English class, and I figured: I listen to The Cure. I listen to Death Cab for Cutie. That's basically poetry.

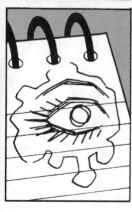

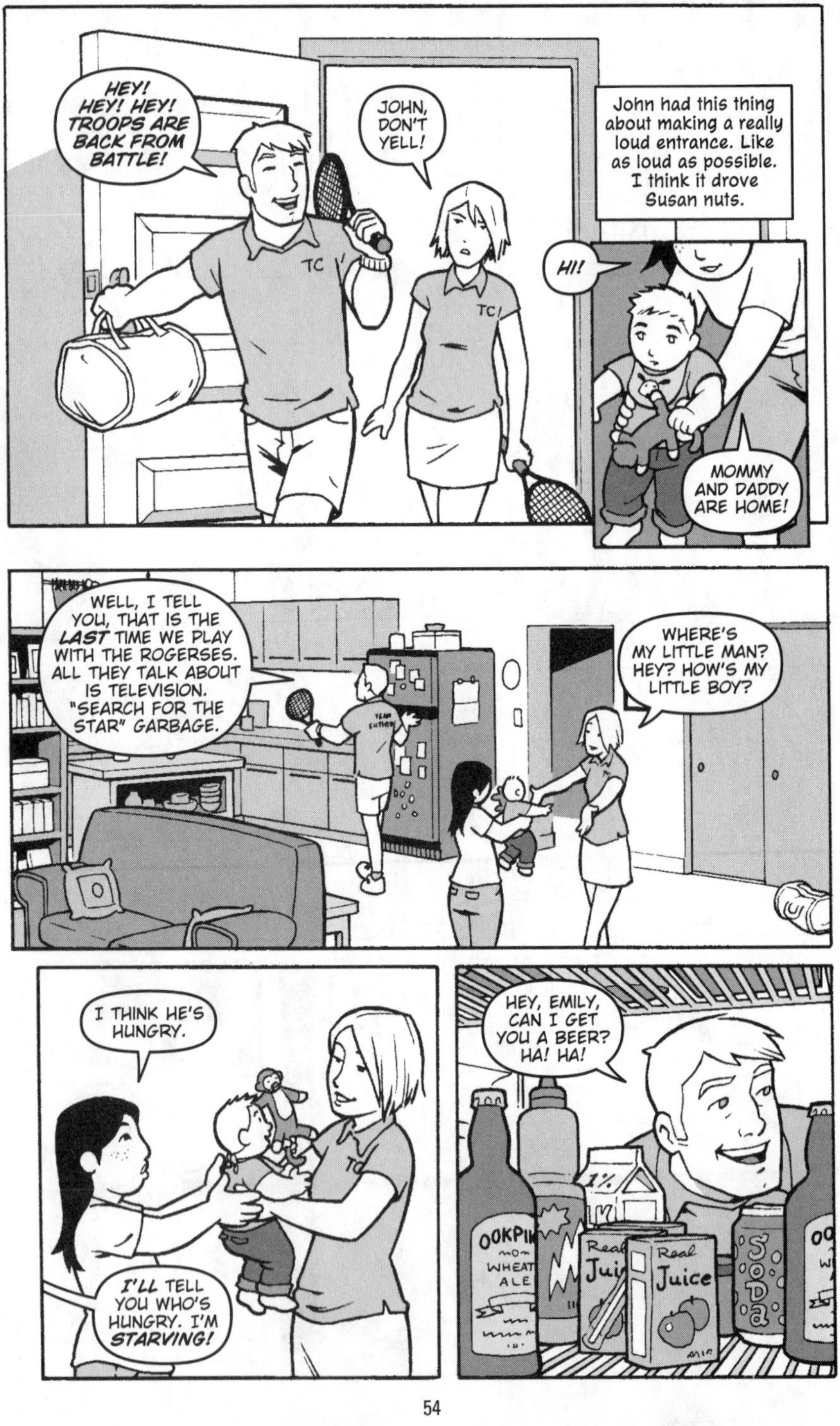
HEY! HEY! HEY! TROOPS ARE BACK FROM BATTLE!
JOHN, DON'T YELL!
John had this thing about making a really loud entrance. Like as loud as possible. I think it drove Susan nuts.
HI!
MOMMY AND DADDY ARE HOME!
WELL, I TELL YOU, THAT IS THE LAST TIME WE PLAY WITH THE ROGERSES. ALL THEY TALK ABOUT IS TELEVISION. "SEARCH FOR THE STAR" GARBAGE.
WHERE'S MY LITTLE MAN? HEY? HOW'S MY LITTLE BOY?
I THINK HE'S HUNGRY.
I'LL TELL YOU WHO'S HUNGRY. I'M STARVING!
HEY, EMILY, CAN I GET YOU A BEER? HA! HA!
1%
Real Juice
Real Juice
Soda
WHEAT ALE

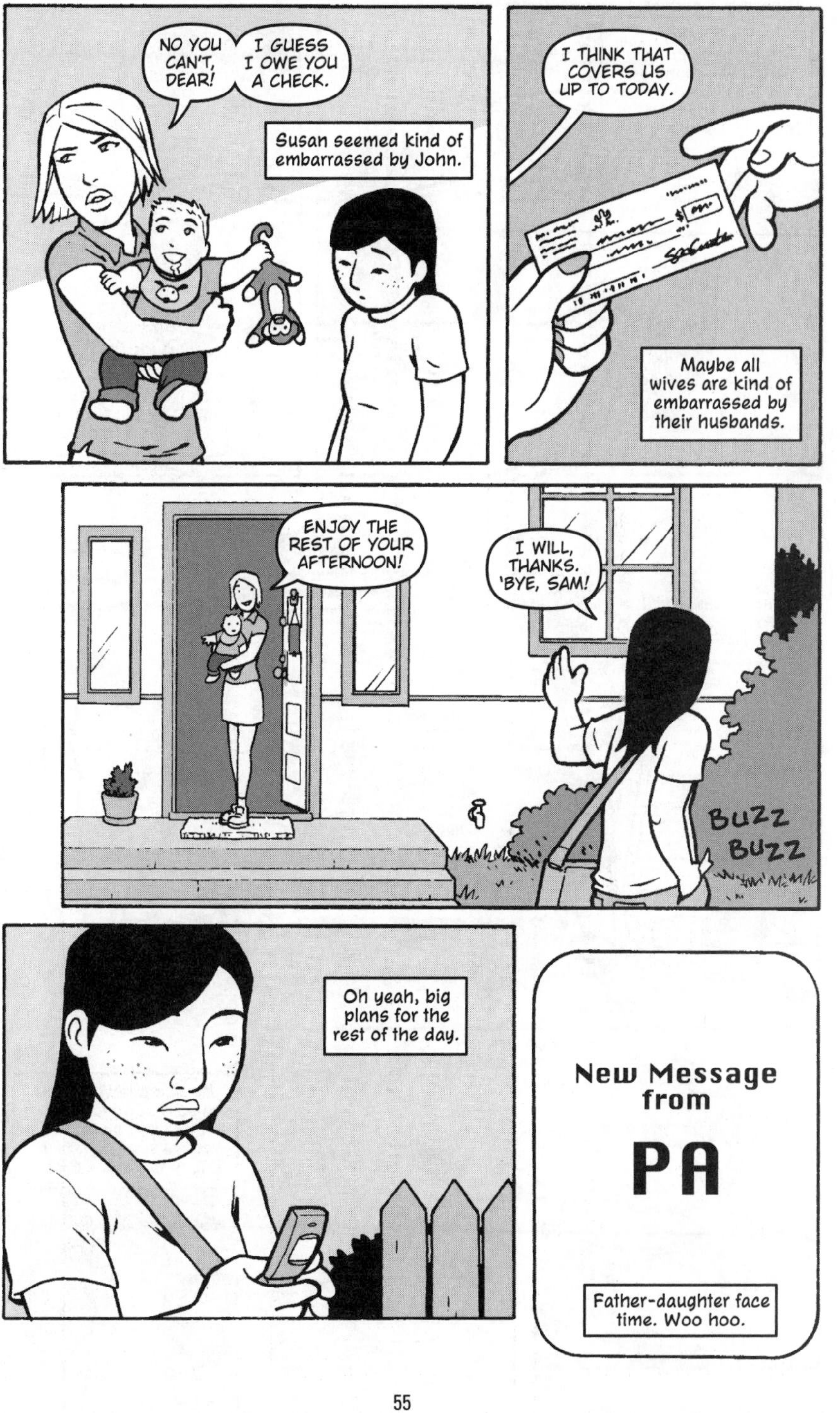
NO YOU CAN'T, DEAR!
I GUESS I OWE YOU A CHECK.
Susan seemed kind of embarrassed by John.
I THINK THAT COVERS US UP TO TODAY.
Maybe all wives are kind of embarrassed by their husbands.
ENJOY THE REST OF YOUR AFTERNOON!
I WILL, THANKS. 'BYE, SAM!
BUZZ BUZZ
Oh yeah, big plans for the rest of the day.
New Message from
PA
Father-daughter face time. Woo hoo.

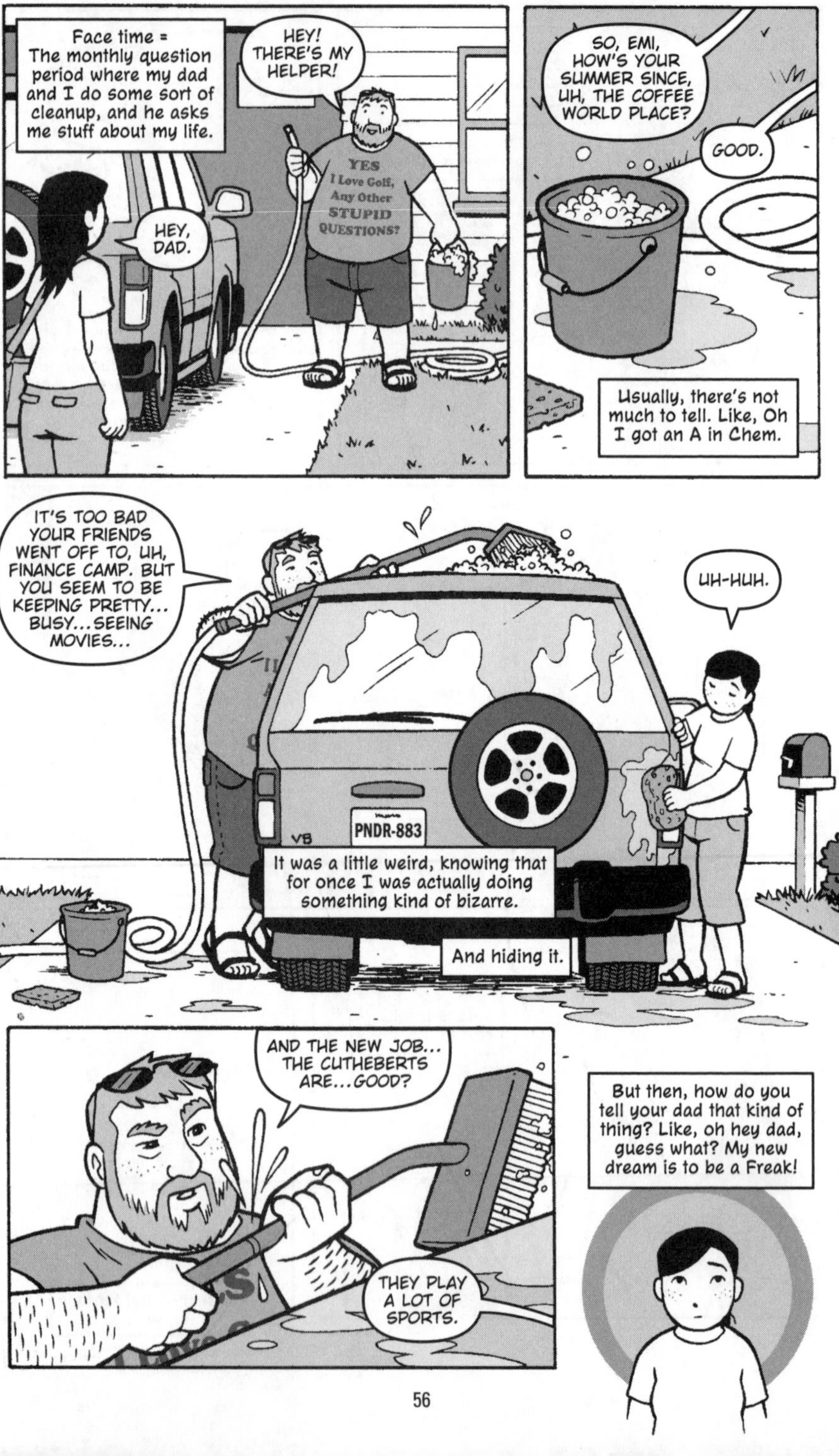
Face time = The monthly question period where my dad and I do some sort of cleanup, and he asks me stuff about my life.
HEY! THERE'S MY HELPER!
YES I Love Golf, Any Other STUPID QUESTIONS?
HEY, DAD.
SO, EMI, HOW'S YOUR SUMMER SINCE, UH, THE COFFEE WORLD PLACE?
GOOD.
Usually, there's not much to tell. Like, Oh I got an A in Chem.
IT'S TOO BAD YOUR FRIENDS WENT OFF TO, UH, FINANCE CAMP. BUT YOU SEEM TO BE KEEPING PRETTY... BUSY...SEEING MOVIES...
UH-HUH.
PNDR-883
It was a little weird, knowing that for once I was actually doing something kind of bizarre.
And hiding it.
AND THE NEW JOB... THE CUTHEBERTS ARE...GOOD?
THEY PLAY A LOT OF SPORTS.
But then, how do you tell your dad that kind of thing? Like, oh hey dad, guess what? My new dream is to be a Freak!

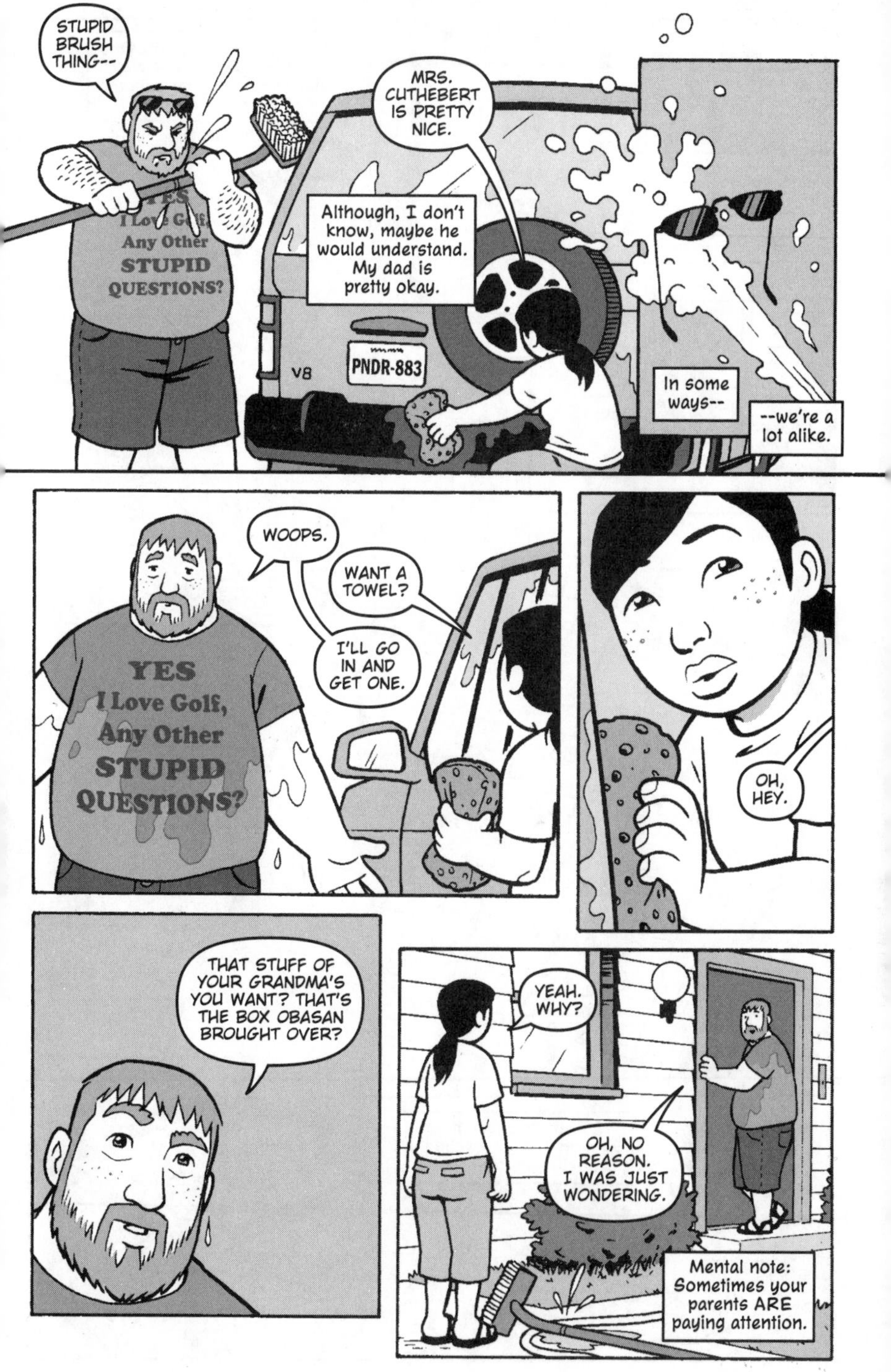
STUPID BRUSH THING--
MRS. CUTHEBERT IS PRETTY NICE.
Although, I don't know, maybe he would understand. My dad is pretty okay.
YES I Love Golf, Any Other STUPID QUESTIONS?
V8
PNDR-883
In some ways--
--we're a lot alike.
WOOPS.
WANT A TOWEL?
I'LL GO IN AND GET ONE.
YES I Love Golf, Any Other STUPID QUESTIONS?
OH, HEY.
THAT STUFF OF YOUR GRANDMA'S YOU WANT? THAT'S THE BOX OBASAN BROUGHT OVER?
YEAH. WHY?
OH, NO REASON. I WAS JUST WONDERING.
Mental note: Sometimes your parents ARE paying attention.

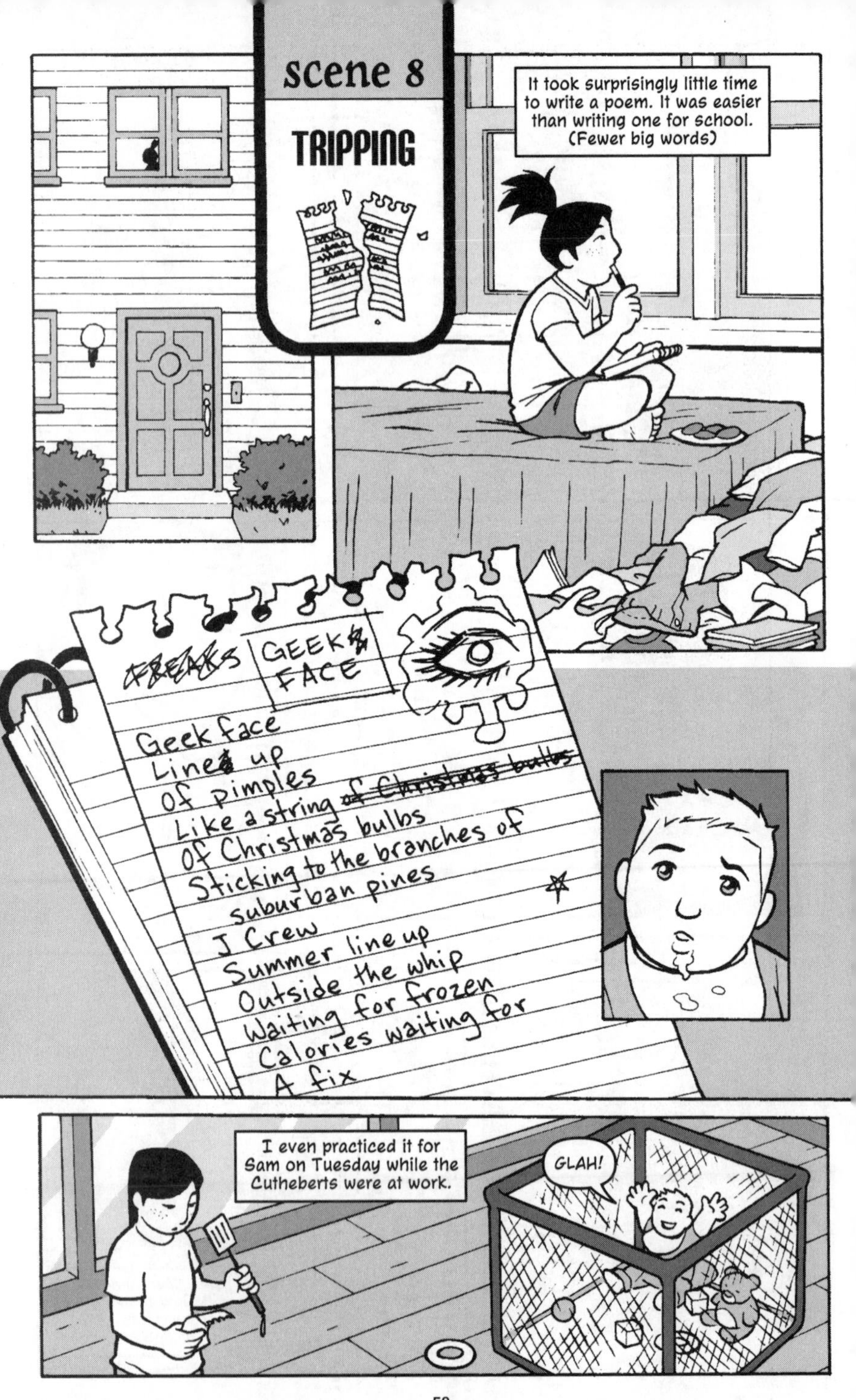

scene 8
TRIPPING
It took surprisingly little time to write a poem. It was easier than writing one for school. (Fewer big words)
~~FREAKS~~ GEEK~~S~~ FACE
Geek face
Line~~s~~ up
Of pimples
Like a string ~~of Christmas bulbs~~
Of Christmas bulbs
Sticking to the branches of
suburban pines
J Crew
Summer line up
Outside the whip
Waiting for frozen
Calories waiting for
A fix
I even practiced it for Sam on Tuesday while the Cutheberts were at work.
GLAH!

It was like everything came together on the night of the Gong. I even found what seemed like a sufficiently weird top in my closet (from an old Halloween costume).

I felt strangely cool about the whole thing.

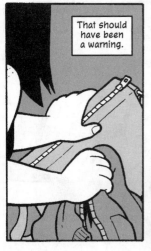

That should have been a warning.

MOVIE AGAIN! BACK BY ELEVEN!

CELL PHONE!

YEP!

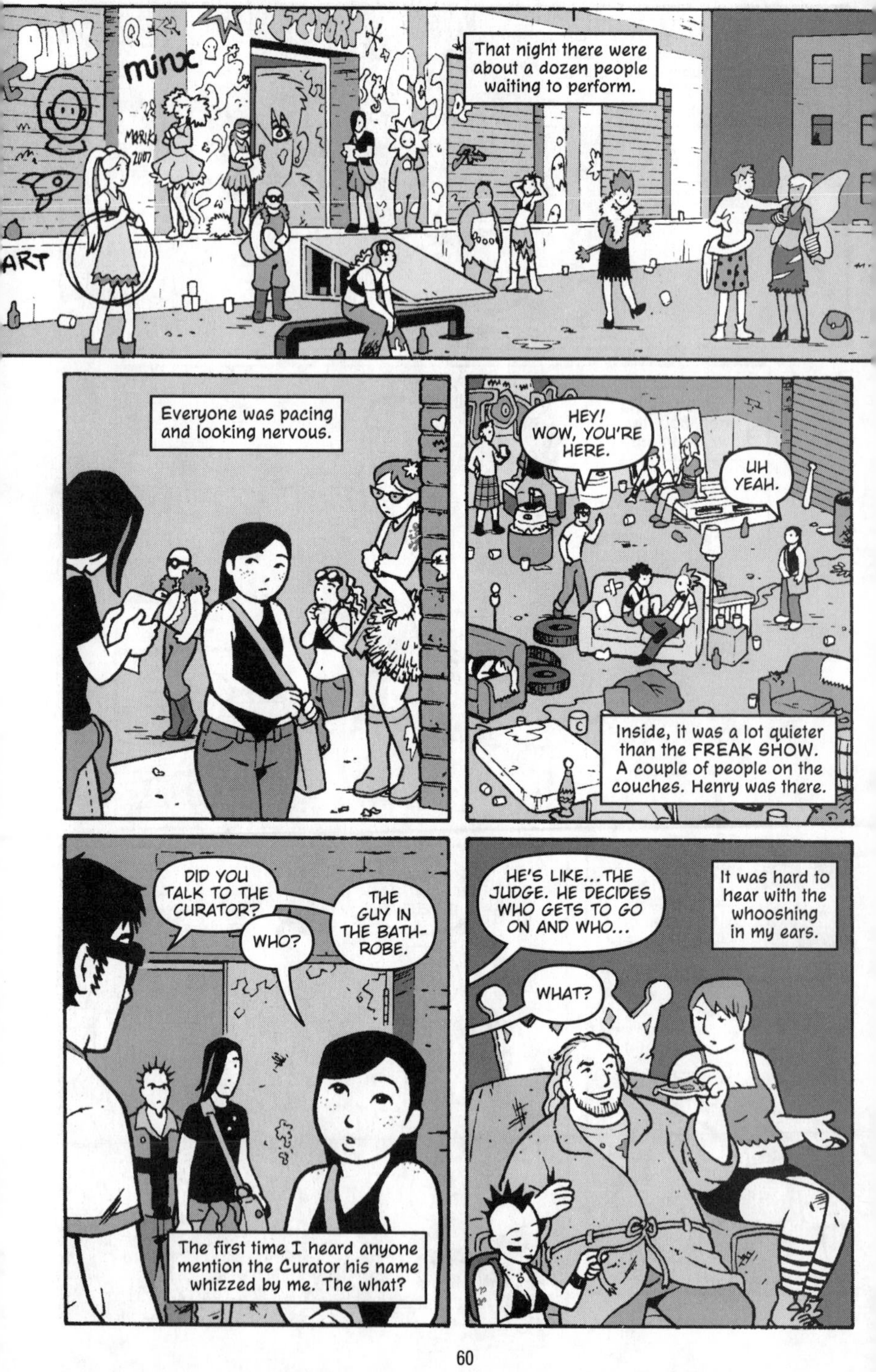
PUNK
minx
ART
That night there were about a dozen people waiting to perform.
Everyone was pacing and looking nervous.
HEY! WOW, YOU'RE HERE.
UH YEAH.
Inside, it was a lot quieter than the FREAK SHOW. A couple of people on the couches. Henry was there.
DID YOU TALK TO THE CURATOR?
WHO?
THE GUY IN THE BATH-ROBE.
The first time I heard anyone mention the Curator his name whizzed by me. The what?
HE'S LIKE...THE JUDGE. HE DECIDES WHO GETS TO GO ON AND WHO...
It was hard to hear with the whooshing in my ears.
WHAT?

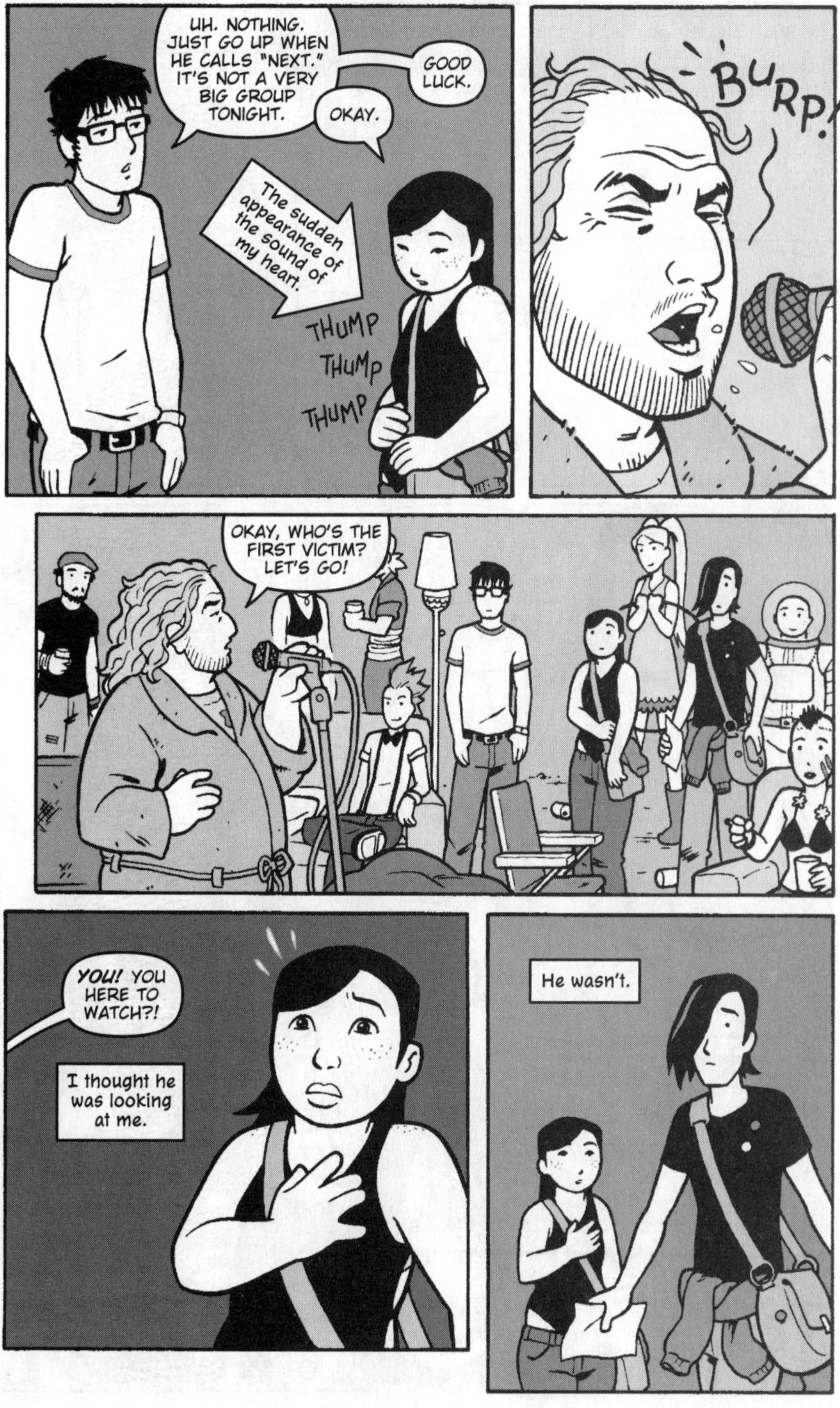
UH. NOTHING. JUST GO UP WHEN HE CALLS "NEXT." IT'S NOT A VERY BIG GROUP TONIGHT.
GOOD LUCK.
OKAY.
The sudden appearance of the sound of my heart.
THUMP
THUMP
THUMP
BURP!
OKAY, WHO'S THE FIRST VICTIM? LET'S GO!
YOU! YOU HERE TO WATCH?!
I thought he was looking at me.
He wasn't.

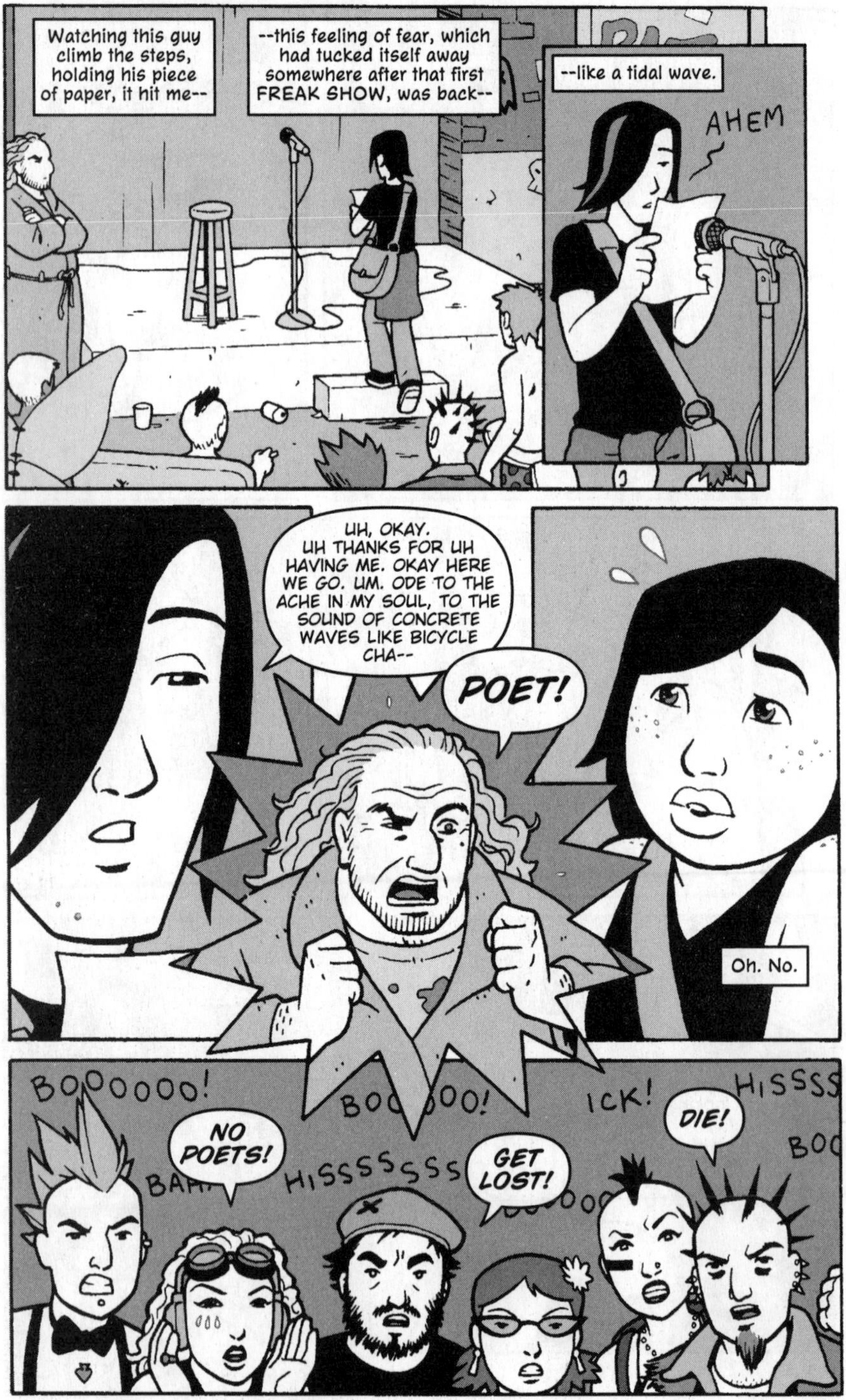
Watching this guy climb the steps, holding his piece of paper, it hit me--
--this feeling of fear, which had tucked itself away somewhere after that first FREAK SHOW, was back--
--like a tidal wave.
AHEM
UH, OKAY. UH THANKS FOR UH HAVING ME. OKAY HERE WE GO. UM. ODE TO THE ACHE IN MY SOUL, TO THE SOUND OF CONCRETE WAVES LIKE BICYCLE CHA--
POET!
Oh. No.
BOOOOOO!
NO POETS!
BOOOOO!
HISSSSSSS
GET LOST!
ICK!
DIE!
HISSSS

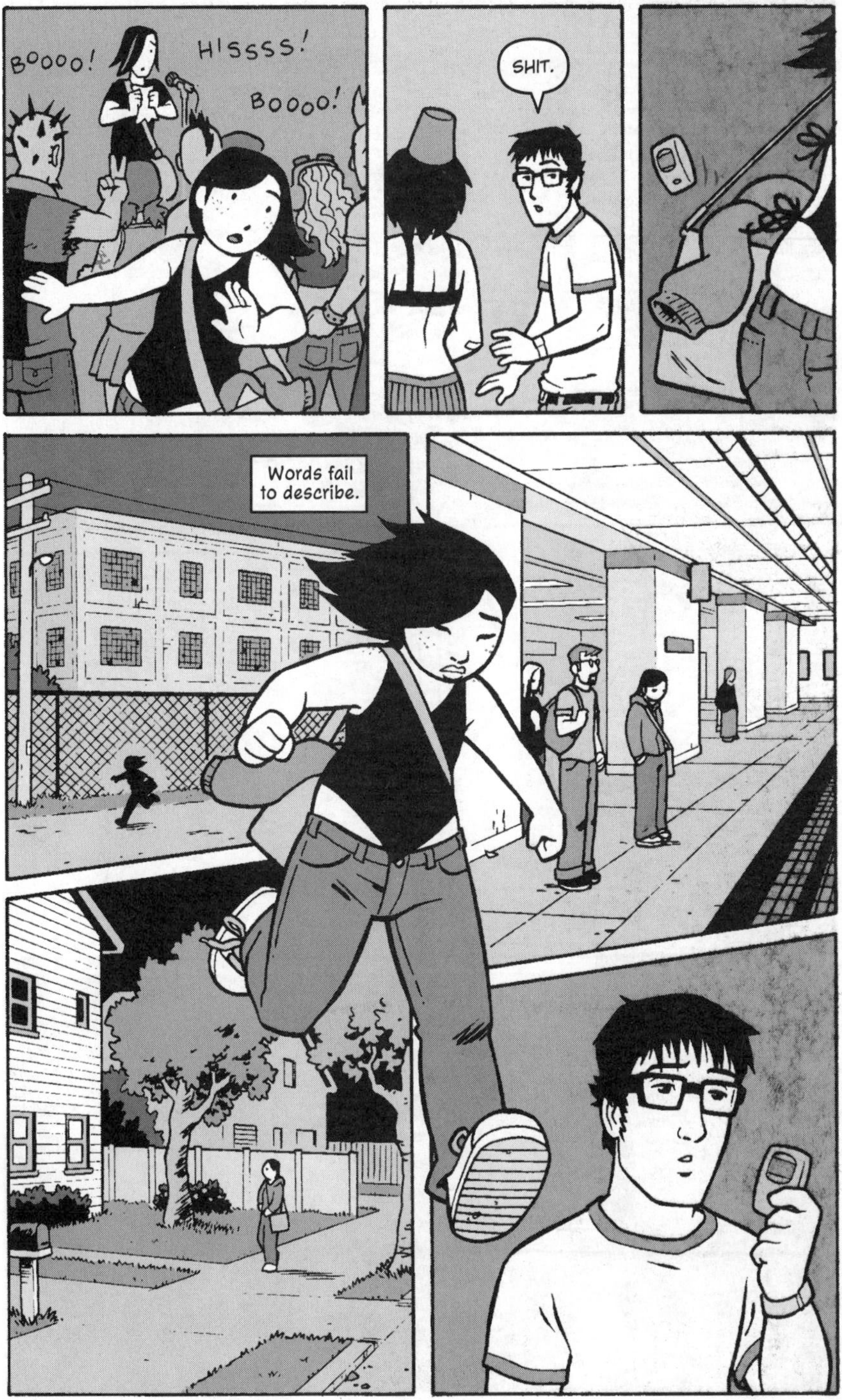
BOOOO!
HISSSS!
BOOOO!
SHIT.
Words fail to describe.

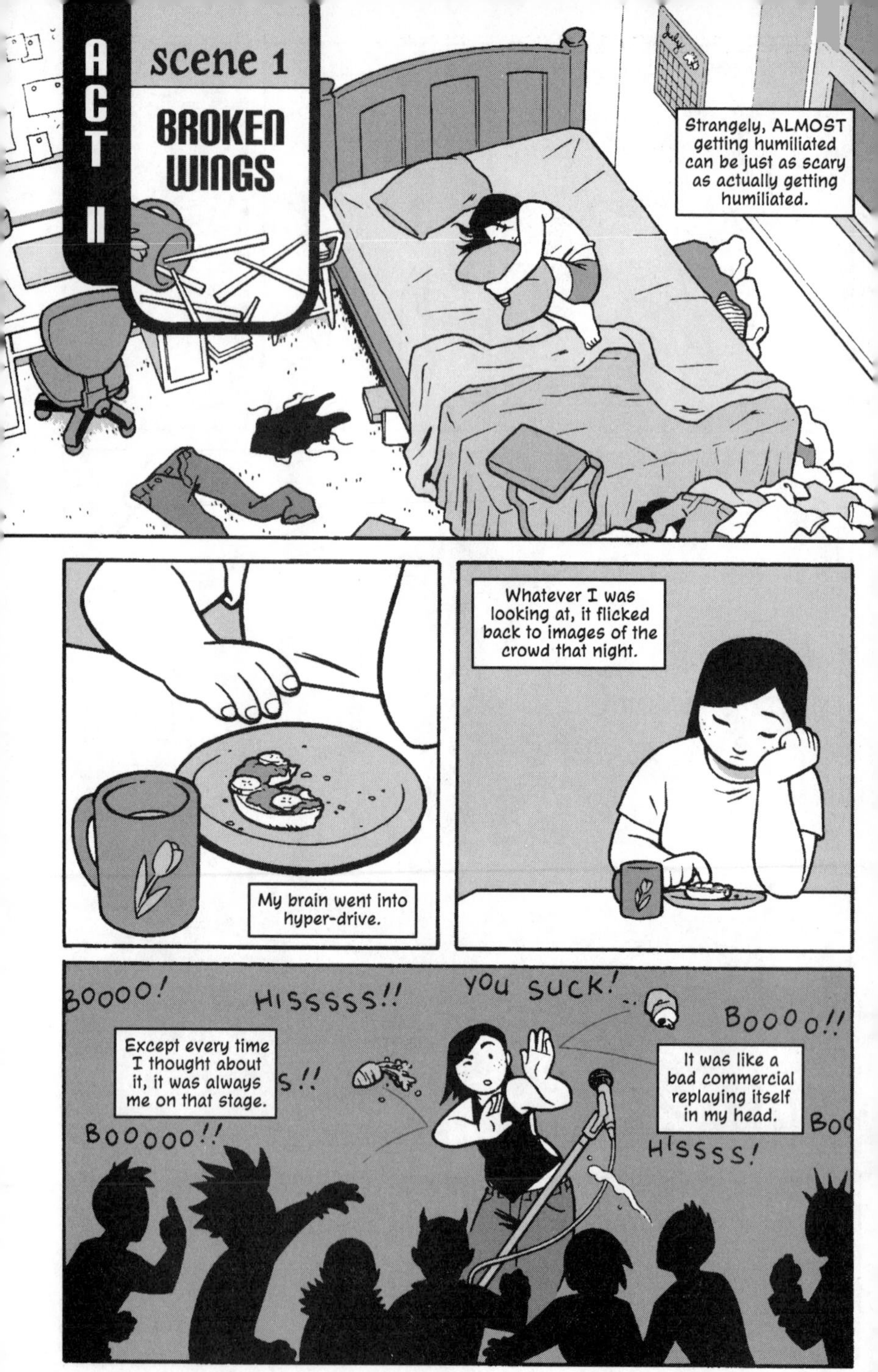
ACT II
scene 1
BROKEN WINGS
Strangely, ALMOST getting humiliated can be just as scary as actually getting humiliated.
My brain went into hyper-drive.
Whatever I was looking at, it flicked back to images of the crowd that night.
BOOOO!
HISSSSS!!
YOU SUCK!
BOOOO!!
Except every time I thought about it, it was always me on that stage.
S!!
It was like a bad commercial replaying itself in my head.
BOOOOO!!
HISSSS!

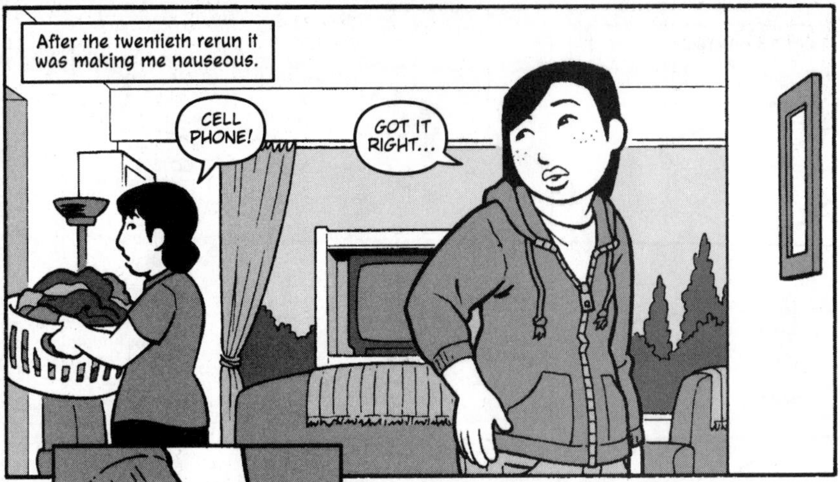
After the twentieth rerun it was making me nauseous.
CELL PHONE!
GOT IT RIGHT...

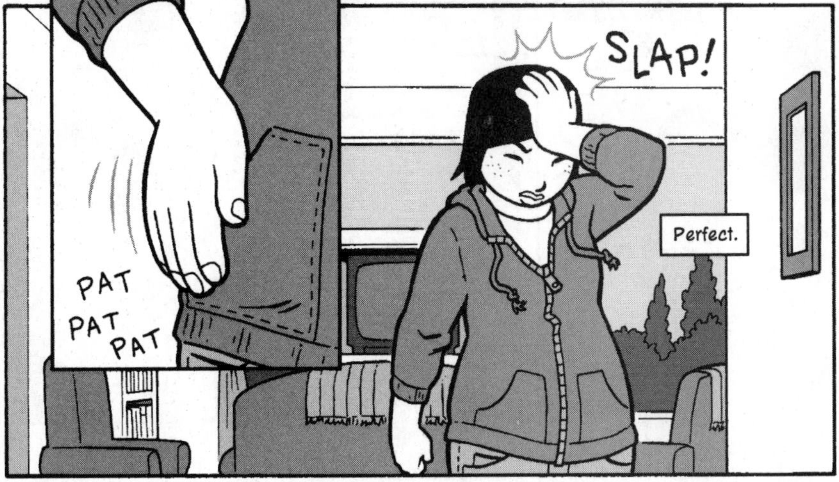
PAT
PAT
PAT
SLAP!
Perfect.

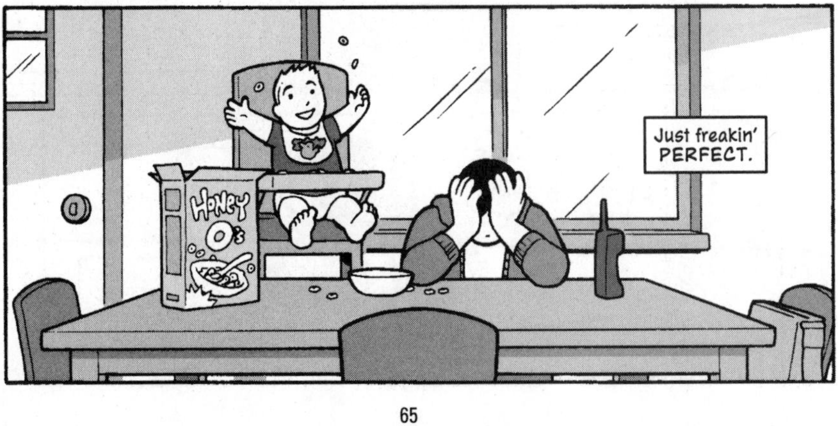
HONEY O's
Just freakin' PERFECT.

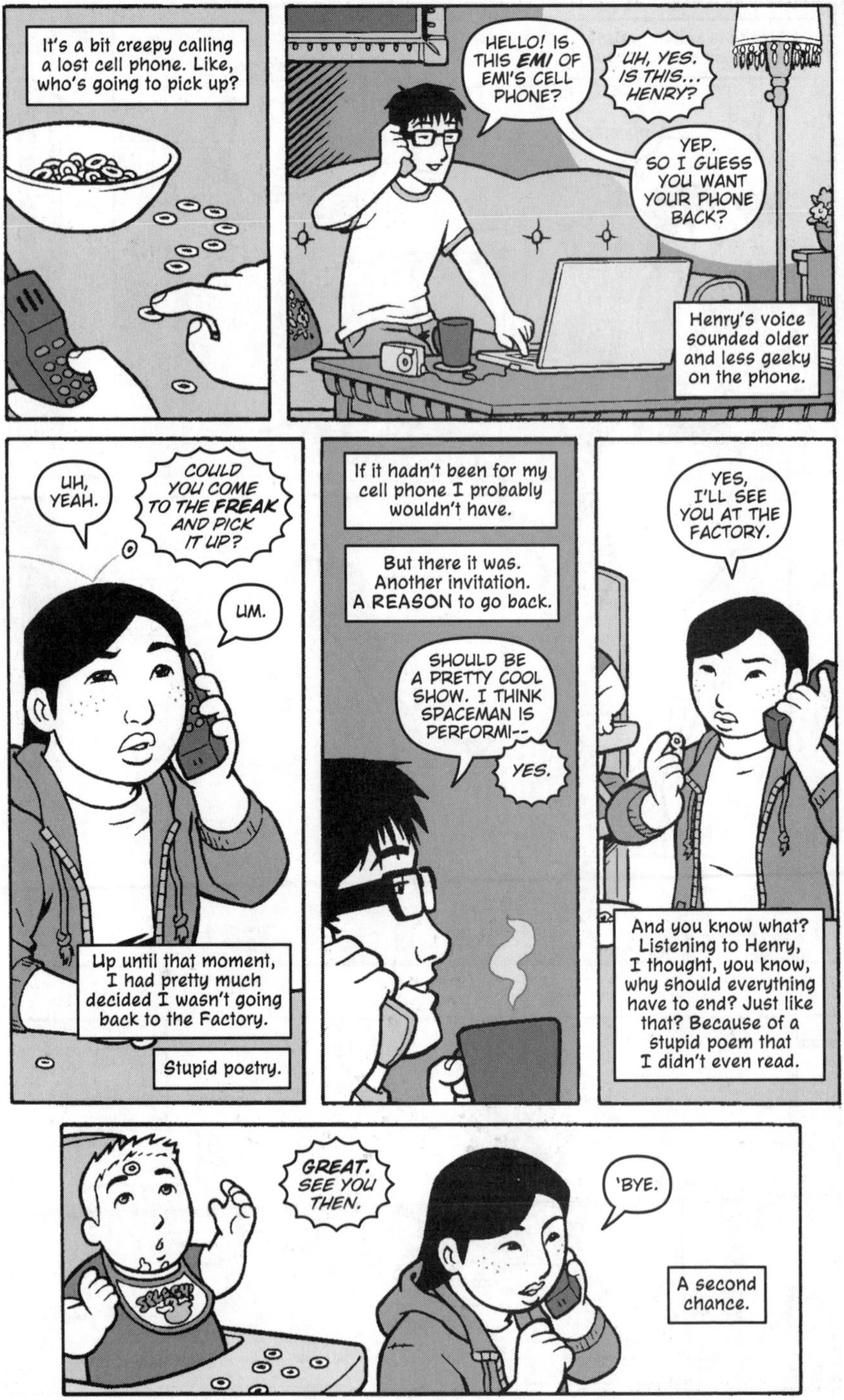
It's a bit creepy calling a lost cell phone. Like, who's going to pick up?
HELLO! IS THIS EMI OF EMI'S CELL PHONE?
UH, YES. IS THIS... HENRY?
YEP. SO I GUESS YOU WANT YOUR PHONE BACK?
Henry's voice sounded older and less geeky on the phone.
UH, YEAH.
COULD YOU COME TO THE FREAK AND PICK IT UP?
UM.
Up until that moment, I had pretty much decided I wasn't going back to the Factory.
Stupid poetry.
If it hadn't been for my cell phone I probably wouldn't have.
But there it was. Another invitation. A REASON to go back.
SHOULD BE A PRETTY COOL SHOW. I THINK SPACEMAN IS PERFORMI--
YES.
YES, I'LL SEE YOU AT THE FACTORY.
And you know what? Listening to Henry, I thought, you know, why should everything have to end? Just like that? Because of a stupid poem that I didn't even read.
GREAT. SEE YOU THEN.
'BYE.
A second chance.

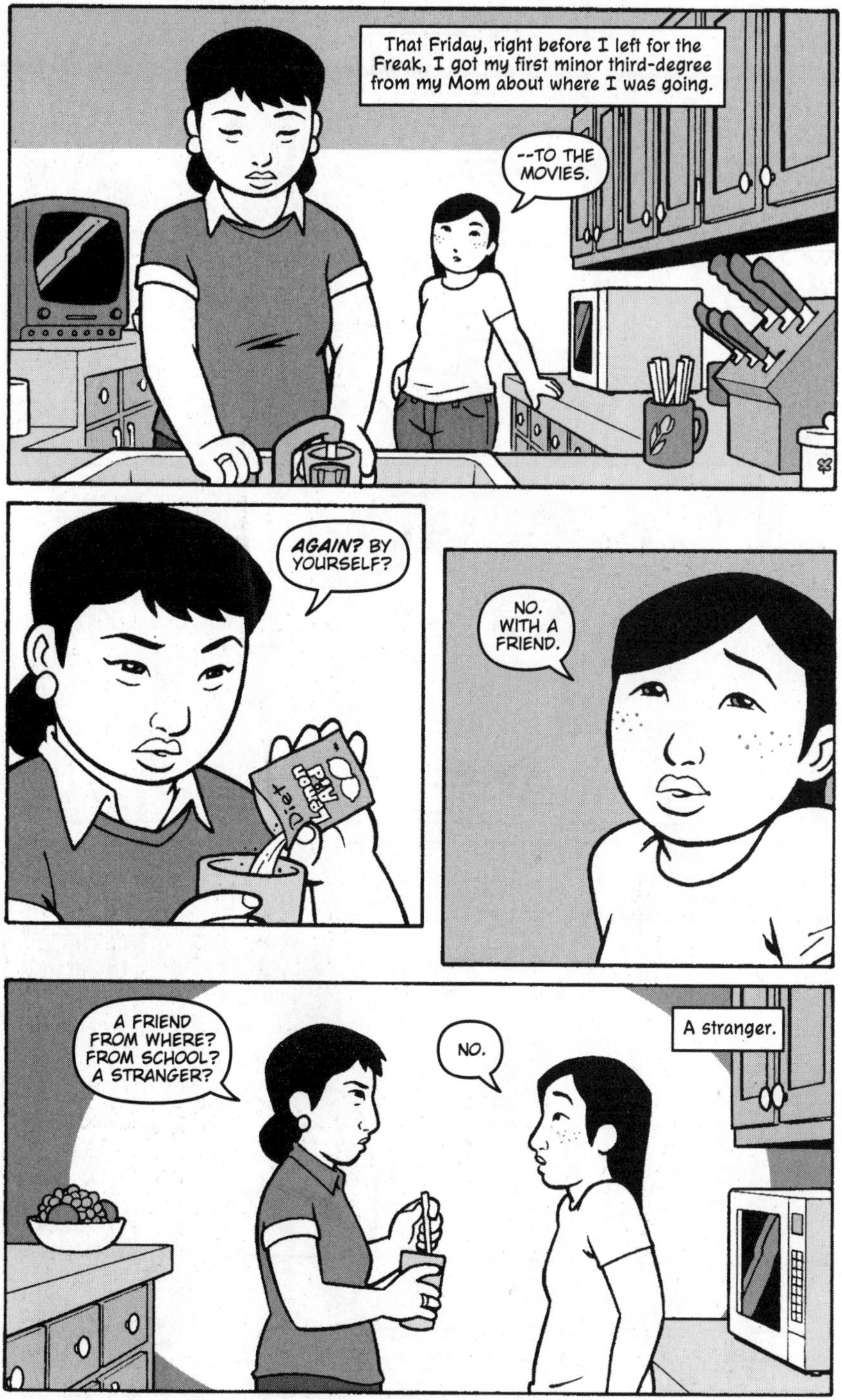
That Friday, right before I left for the Freak, I got my first minor third-degree from my Mom about where I was going.
--TO THE MOVIES.
AGAIN? BY YOURSELF?
Diet Lemon Aid
NO. WITH A FRIEND.
A FRIEND FROM WHERE? FROM SCHOOL? A STRANGER?
NO.
A stranger.

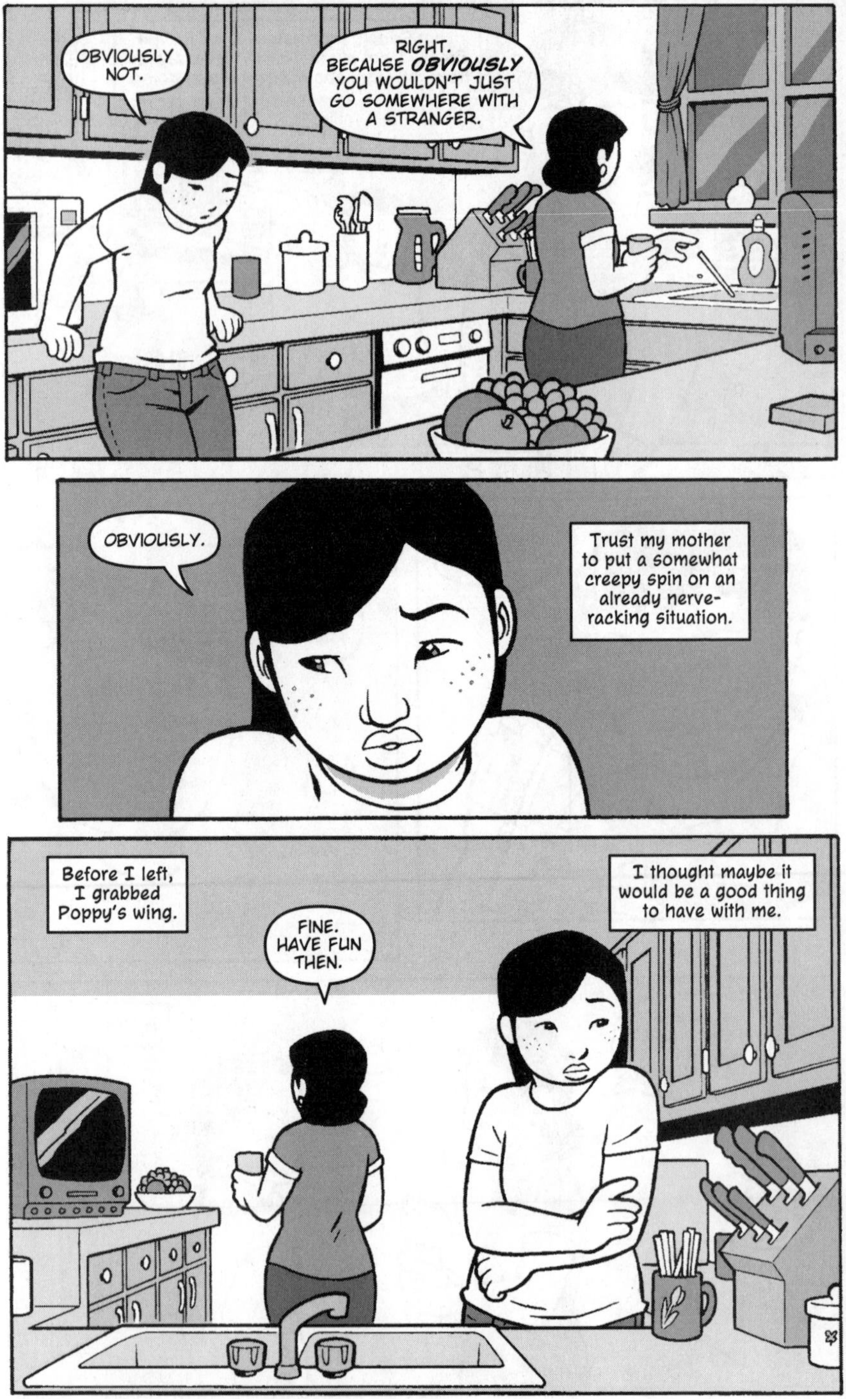
OBVIOUSLY NOT.
RIGHT. BECAUSE OBVIOUSLY YOU WOULDN'T JUST GO SOMEWHERE WITH A STRANGER.
OBVIOUSLY.
Trust my mother to put a somewhat creepy spin on an already nerve-racking situation.
Before I left, I grabbed Poppy's wing.
FINE. HAVE FUN THEN.
I thought maybe it would be a good thing to have with me.

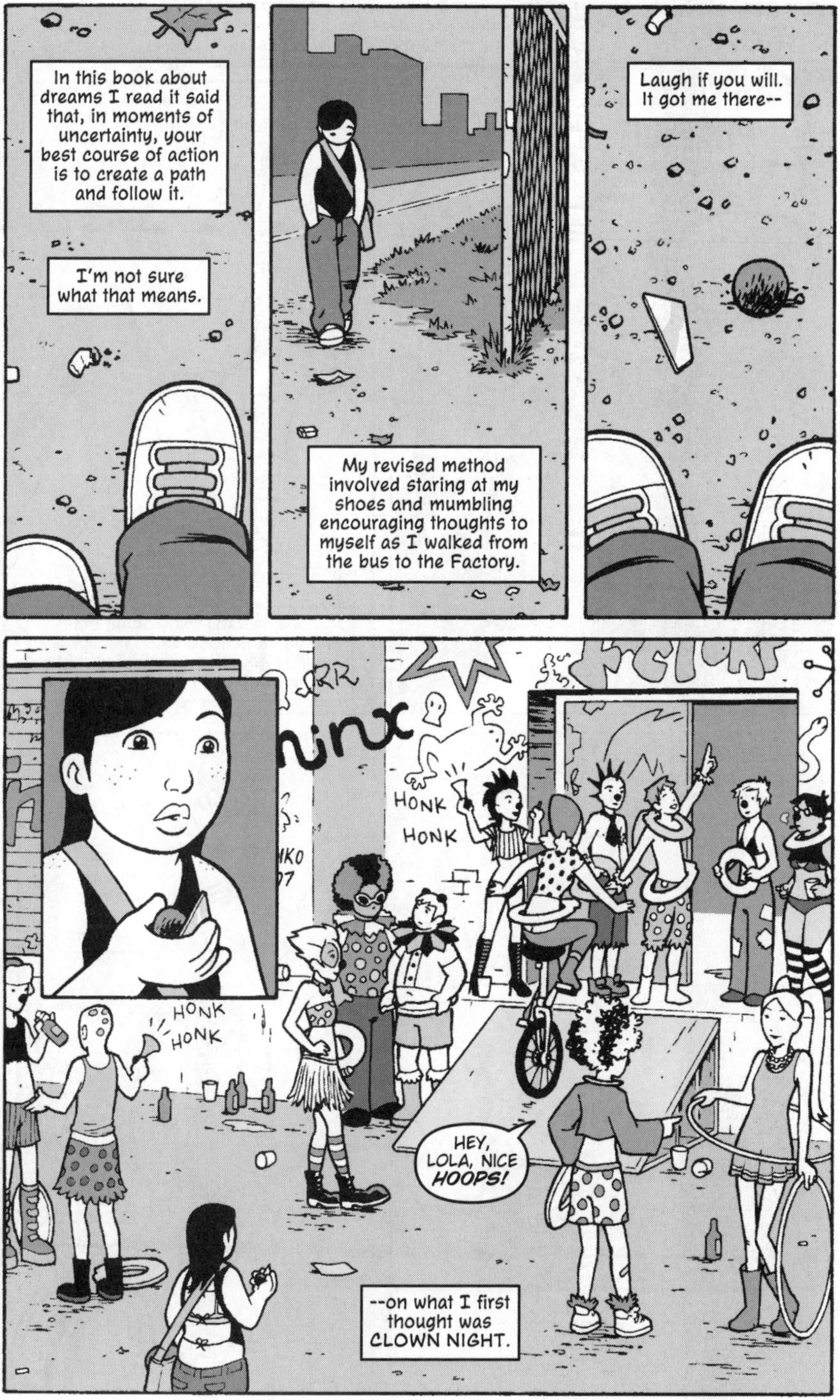
In this book about dreams I read it said that, in moments of uncertainty, your best course of action is to create a path and follow it.
I'm not sure what that means.
My revised method involved staring at my shoes and mumbling encouraging thoughts to myself as I walked from the bus to the Factory.
Laugh if you will. It got me there--
HONK
HONK
HONK
HONK
HEY, LOLA, NICE HOOPS!
--on what I first thought was CLOWN NIGHT.

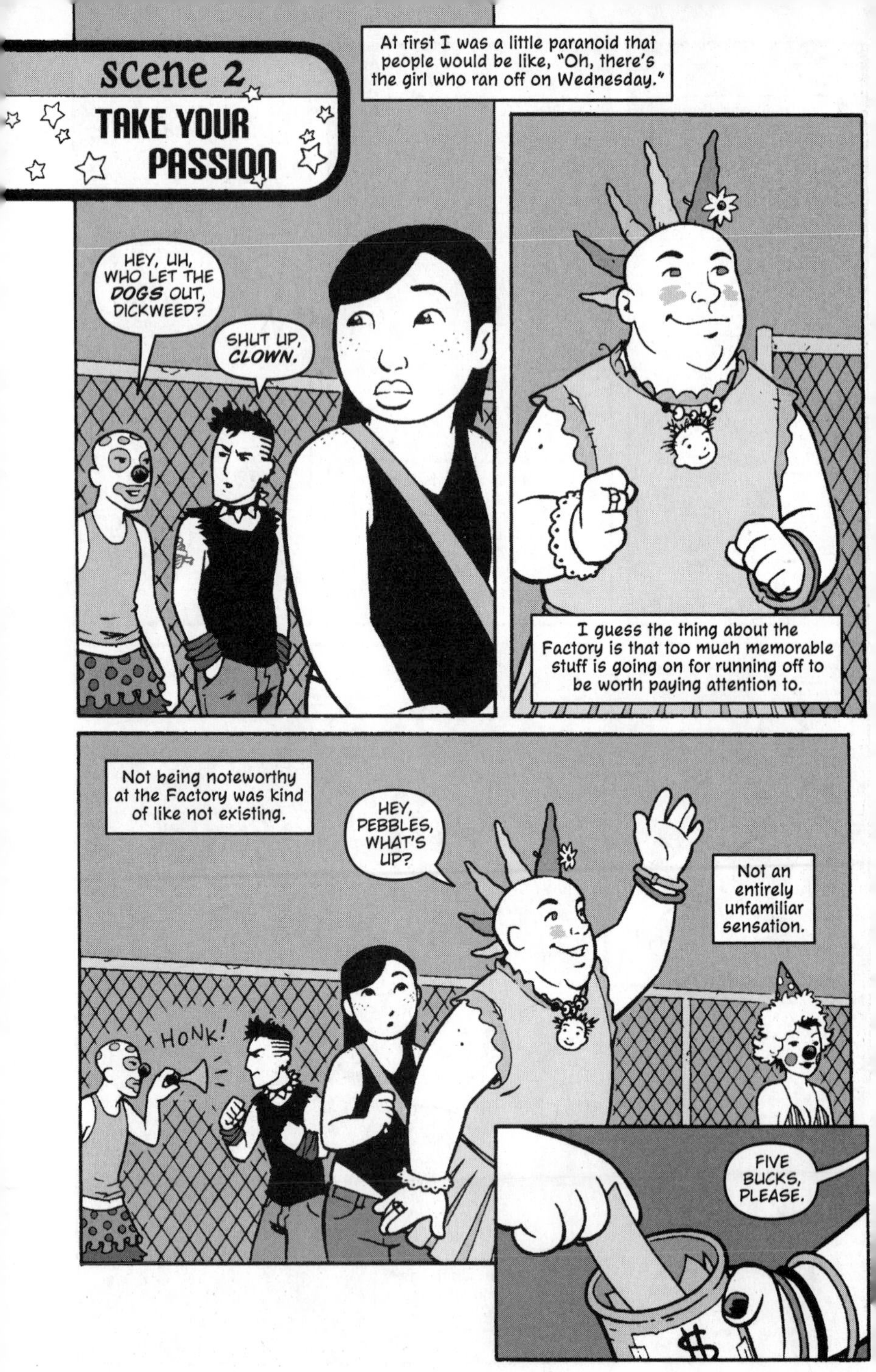
scene 2
TAKE YOUR PASSION
At first I was a little paranoid that people would be like, "Oh, there's the girl who ran off on Wednesday."
HEY, UH, WHO LET THE DOGS OUT, DICKWEED?
SHUT UP, CLOWN.
I guess the thing about the Factory is that too much memorable stuff is going on for running off to be worth paying attention to.
Not being noteworthy at the Factory was kind of like not existing.
HEY, PEBBLES, WHAT'S UP?
Not an entirely unfamiliar sensation.
HONK!
FIVE BUCKS, PLEASE.

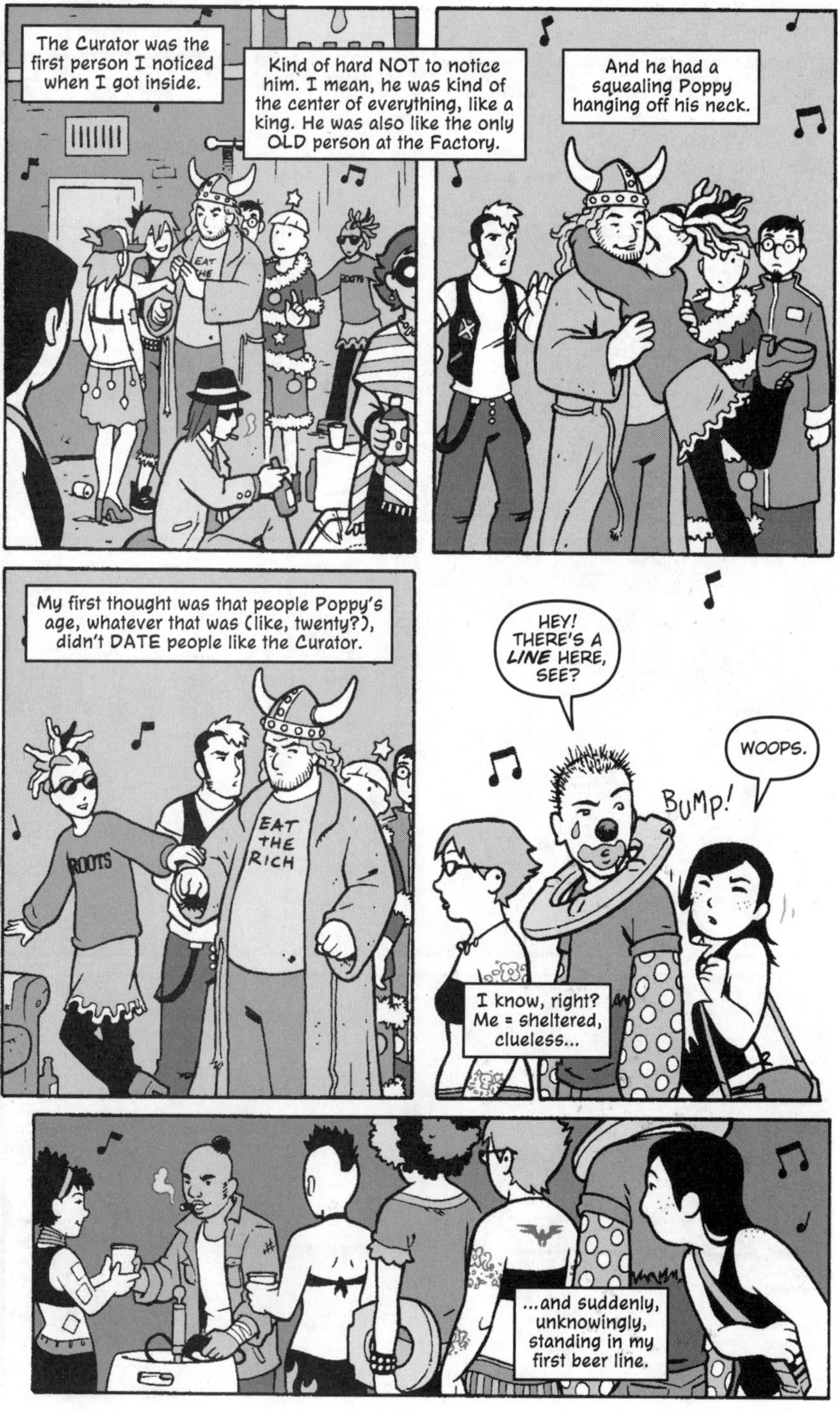

The Curator was the first person I noticed when I got inside.
Kind of hard NOT to notice him. I mean, he was kind of the center of everything, like a king. He was also like the only OLD person at the Factory.
EAT THE
ROOTS
And he had a squealing Poppy hanging off his neck.
My first thought was that people Poppy's age, whatever that was (like, twenty?), didn't DATE people like the Curator.
ROOTS
EAT THE RICH
HEY! THERE'S A LINE HERE, SEE?
BUMP!
WOOPS.
I know, right? Me = sheltered, clueless...
...and suddenly, unknowingly, standing in my first beer line.

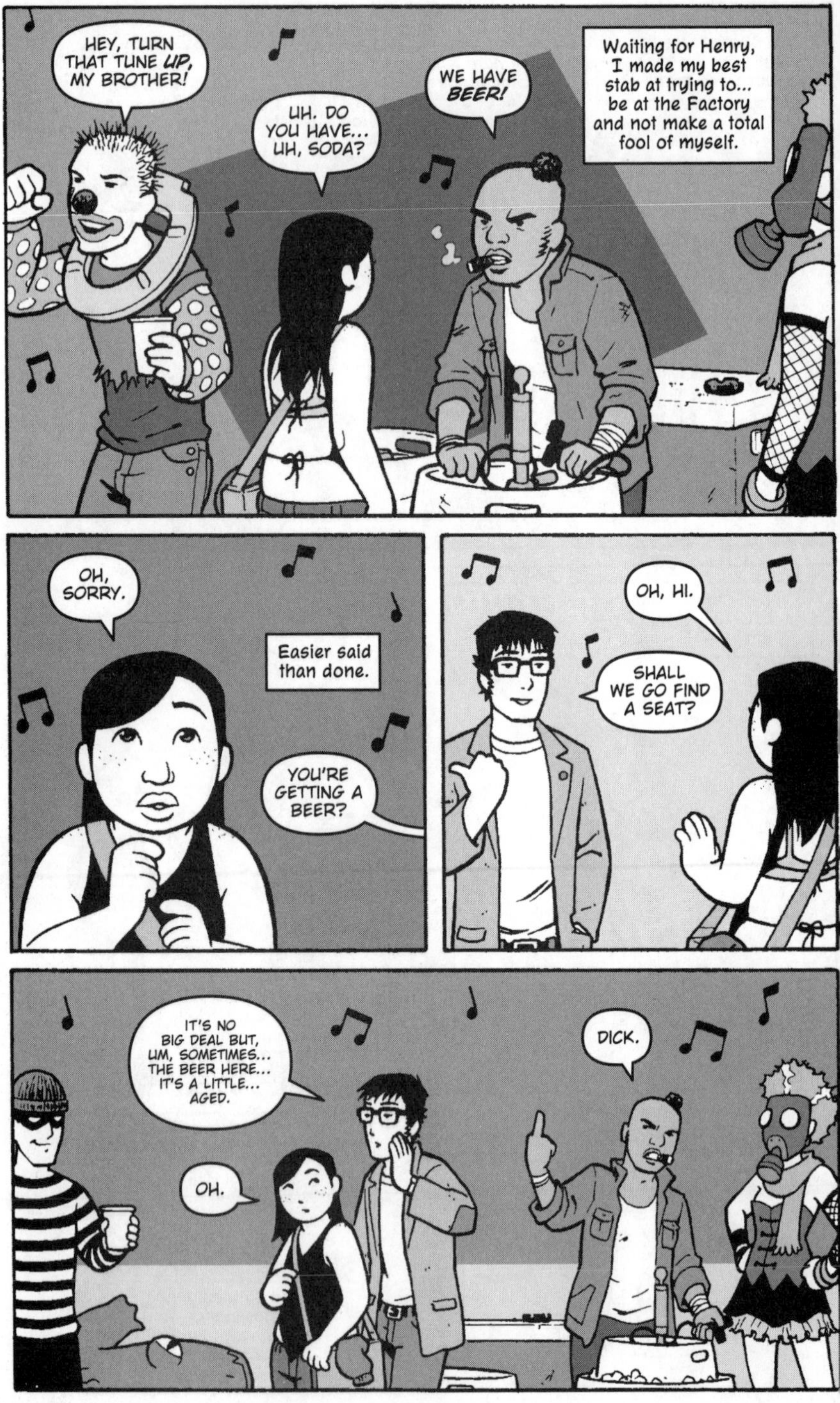
HEY, TURN THAT TUNE *UP*, MY BROTHER!
UH. DO YOU HAVE... UH, SODA?
WE HAVE *BEER!*
Waiting for Henry, I made my best stab at trying to... be at the Factory and not make a total fool of myself.
OH, SORRY.
Easier said than done.
YOU'RE GETTING A BEER?
OH, HI.
SHALL WE GO FIND A SEAT?
IT'S NO BIG DEAL BUT, UM, SOMETIMES... THE BEER HERE... IT'S A LITTLE... AGED.
OH.
DICK.

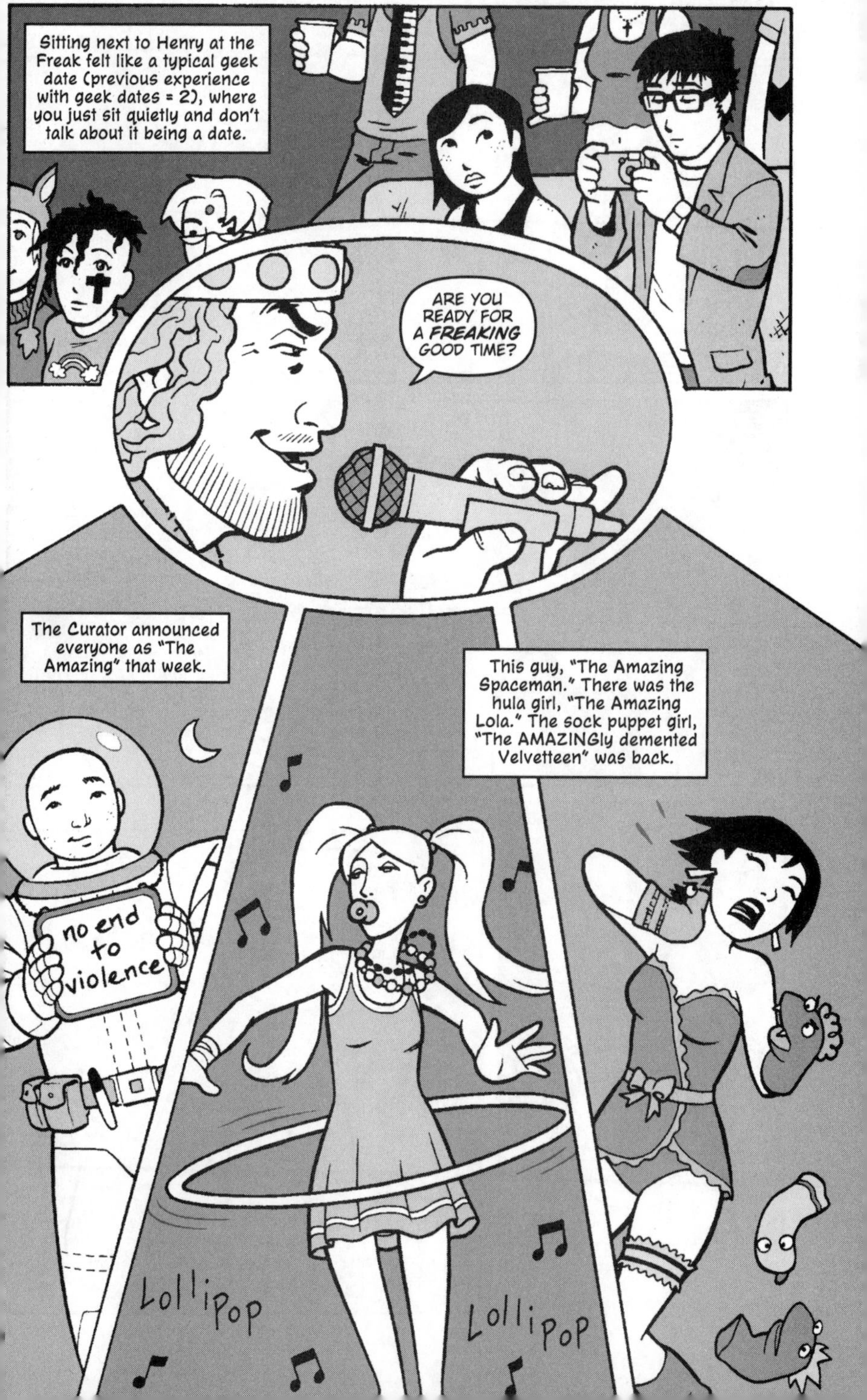

Sitting next to Henry at the Freak felt like a typical geek date (previous experience with geek dates = 2), where you just sit quietly and don't talk about it being a date.
ARE YOU READY FOR A FREAKING GOOD TIME?
The Curator announced everyone as "The Amazing" that week.
This guy, "The Amazing Spaceman." There was the hula girl, "The Amazing Lola." The sock puppet girl, "The AMAZINGly demented Velvetteen" was back.
no end to violence
Lollipop
Lollipop

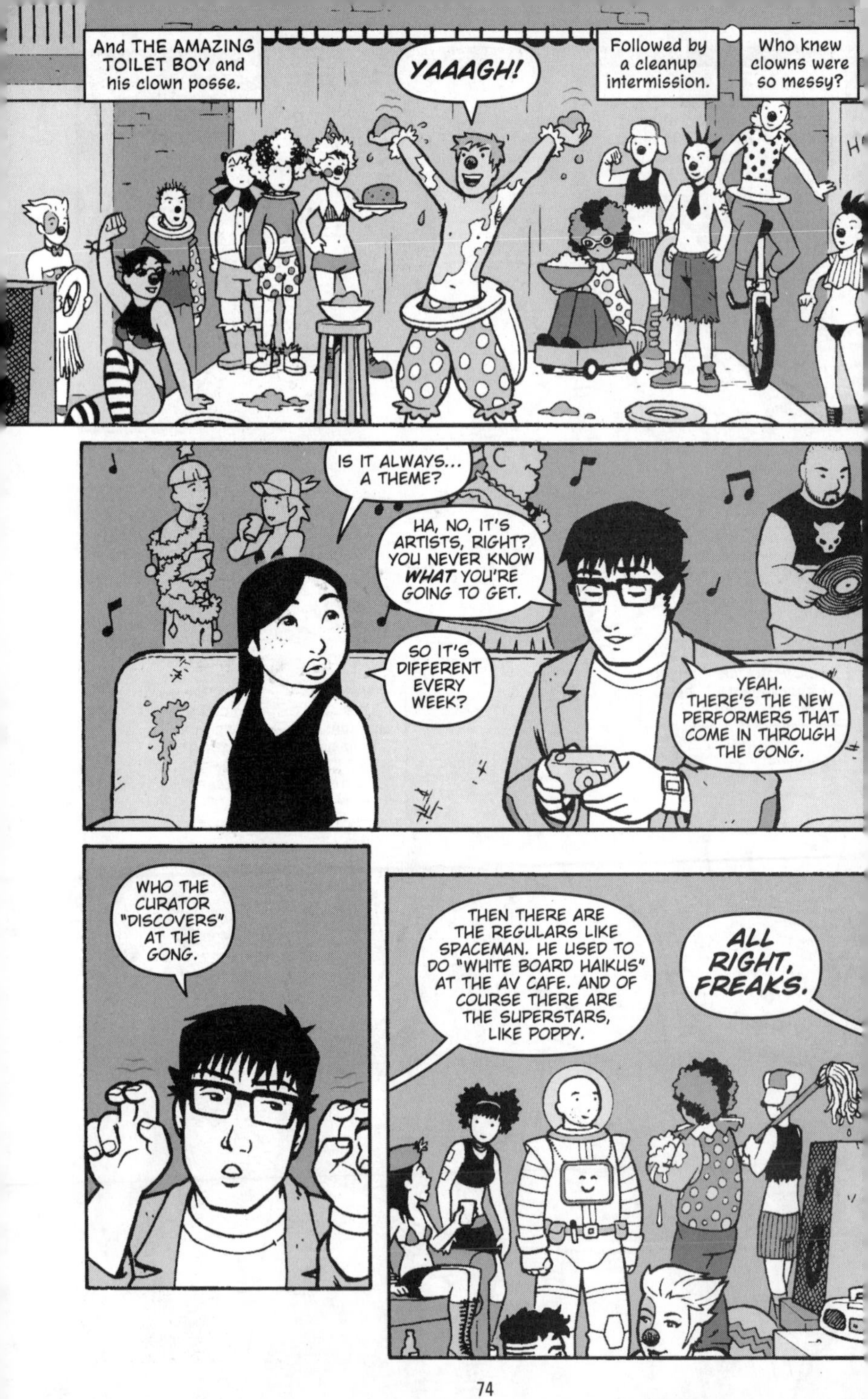
And THE AMAZING TOILET BOY and his clown posse.
YAAAGH!
Followed by a cleanup intermission.
Who knew clowns were so messy?
IS IT ALWAYS... A THEME?
HA, NO, IT'S ARTISTS, RIGHT? YOU NEVER KNOW WHAT YOU'RE GOING TO GET.
SO IT'S DIFFERENT EVERY WEEK?
YEAH. THERE'S THE NEW PERFORMERS THAT COME IN THROUGH THE GONG.
WHO THE CURATOR "DISCOVERS" AT THE GONG.
THEN THERE ARE THE REGULARS LIKE SPACEMAN. HE USED TO DO "WHITE BOARD HAIKUS" AT THE AV CAFE. AND OF COURSE THERE ARE THE SUPERSTARS, LIKE POPPY.
ALL RIGHT, FREAKS.

I THINK WE'RE ALL SCRAPED UP.

POPPY *ALWAYS* GETS THE LAST SPOT OF THE NIGHT.

OUR LAST ACT, LADIES AND UNDERLINGS!

THE *AMAZING* POPPY GALORE!

She was covered in silver and pieces of mirror. Like a disco ball. There was no music this time. We all sat in silence catching little pieces of our reflection in her skin.

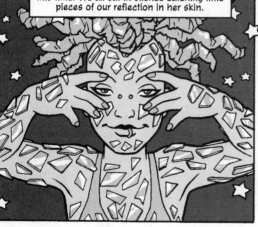

Superstar. That was the perfect word for it.

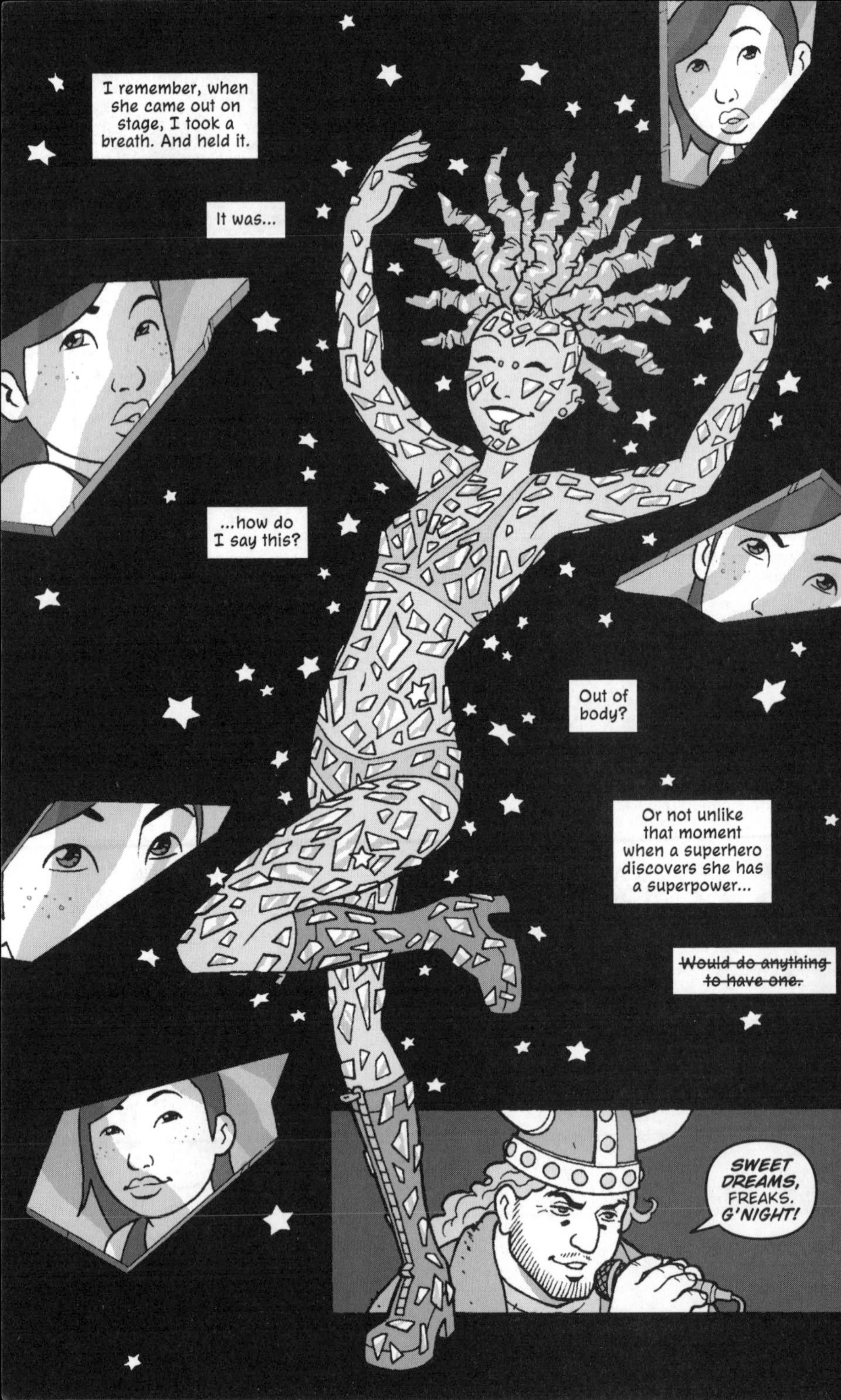
I remember, when she came out on stage, I took a breath. And held it.
It was...
...how do I say this?
Out of body?
Or not unlike that moment when a superhero discovers she has a superpower...
~~Would do anything to have one.~~
SWEET DREAMS, FREAKS. G'NIGHT!

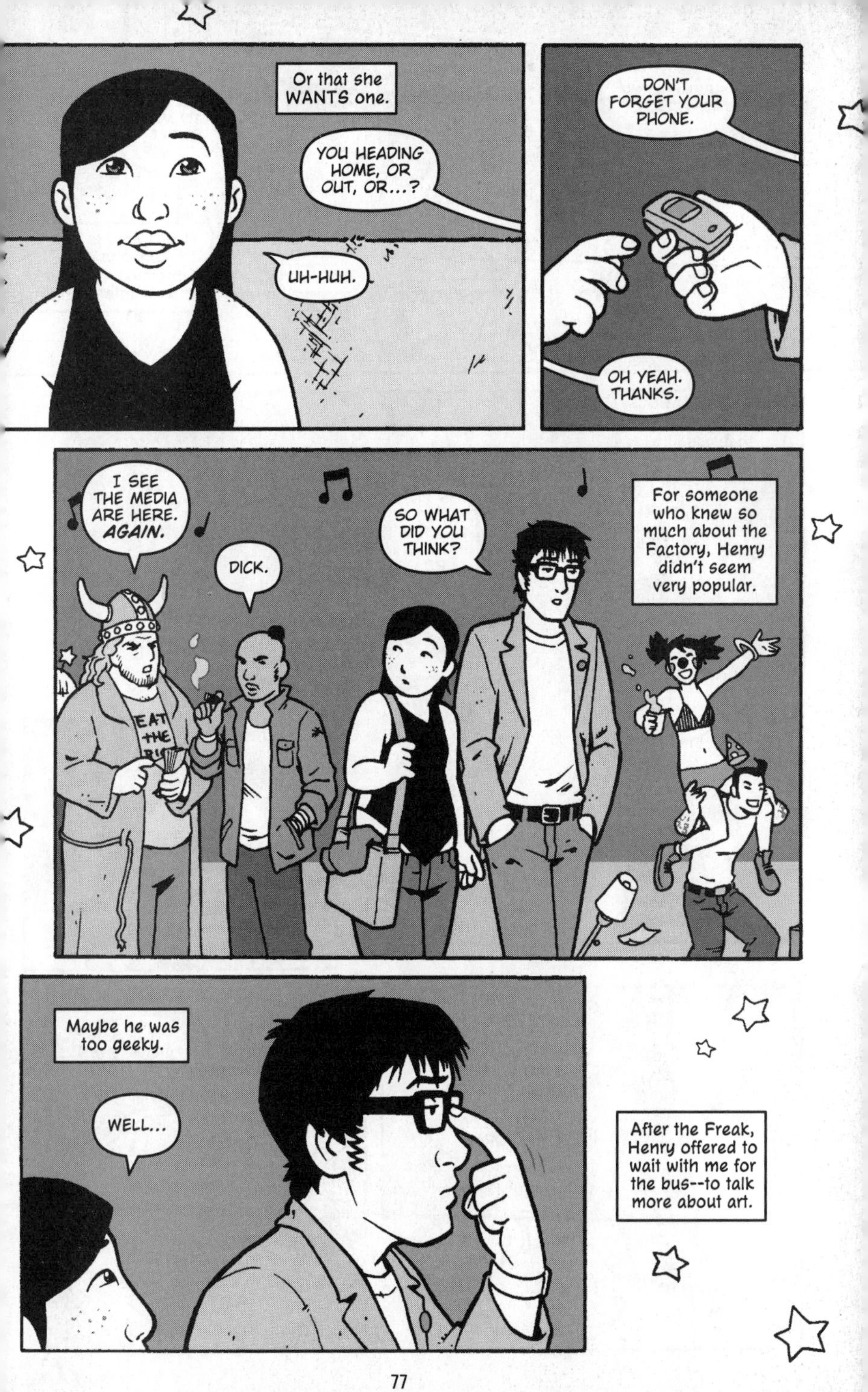

Or that she WANTS one.
YOU HEADING HOME, OR OUT, OR...?
UH-HUH.
DON'T FORGET YOUR PHONE.
OH YEAH. THANKS.
I SEE THE MEDIA ARE HERE. AGAIN.
DICK.
SO WHAT DID YOU THINK?
For someone who knew so much about the Factory, Henry didn't seem very popular.
Maybe he was too geeky.
WELL...
After the Freak, Henry offered to wait with me for the bus--to talk more about art.

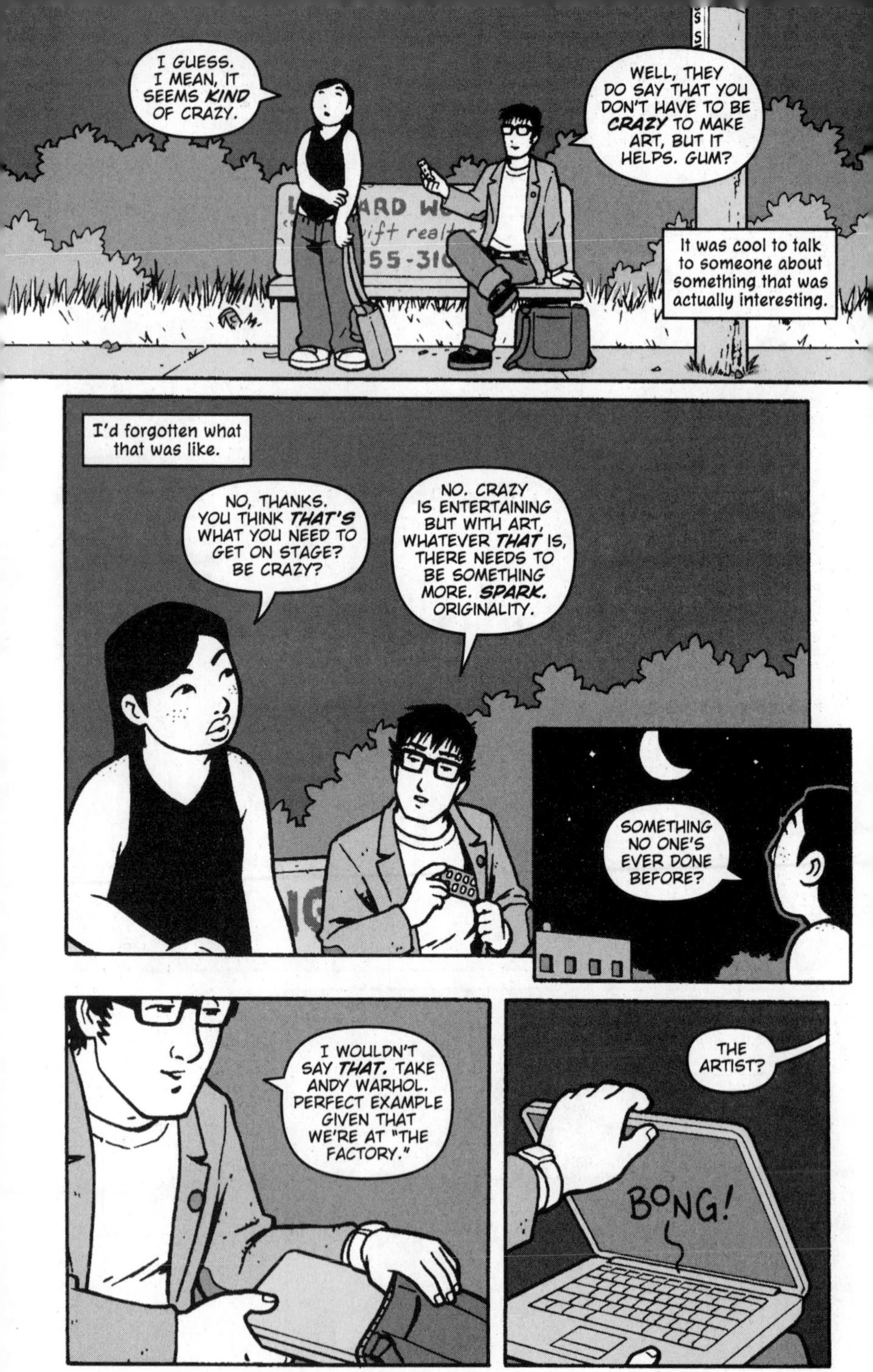
I GUESS. I MEAN, IT SEEMS KIND OF CRAZY.
WELL, THEY DO SAY THAT YOU DON'T HAVE TO BE CRAZY TO MAKE ART, BUT IT HELPS. GUM?
It was cool to talk to someone about something that was actually interesting.
I'd forgotten what that was like.
NO, THANKS. YOU THINK THAT'S WHAT YOU NEED TO GET ON STAGE? BE CRAZY?
NO. CRAZY IS ENTERTAINING BUT WITH ART, WHATEVER THAT IS, THERE NEEDS TO BE SOMETHING MORE. SPARK. ORIGINALITY.
SOMETHING NO ONE'S EVER DONE BEFORE?
I WOULDN'T SAY THAT. TAKE ANDY WARHOL. PERFECT EXAMPLE GIVEN THAT WE'RE AT "THE FACTORY."
THE ARTIST?
BONG!

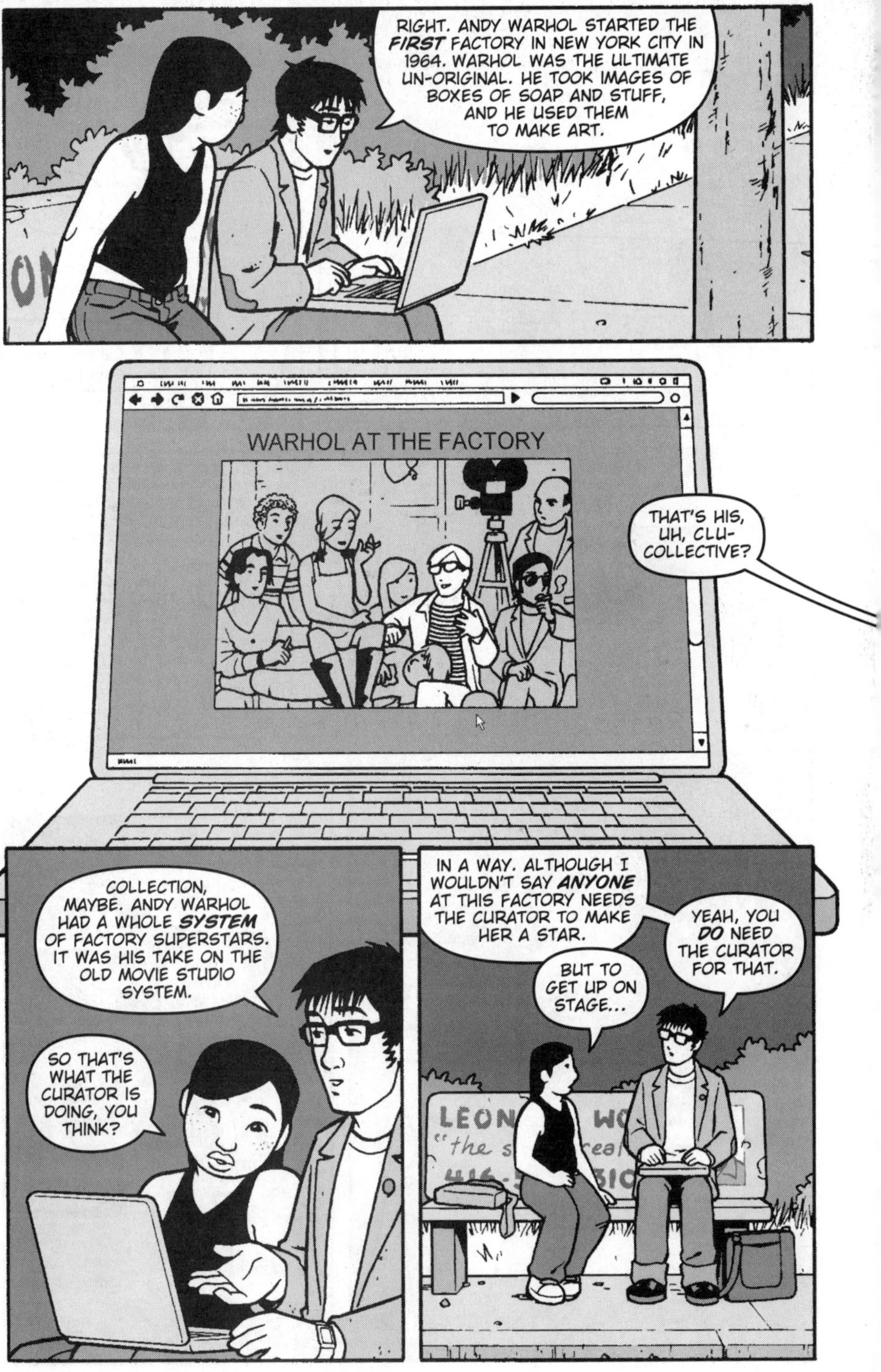
RIGHT. ANDY WARHOL STARTED THE FIRST FACTORY IN NEW YORK CITY IN 1964. WARHOL WAS THE ULTIMATE UN-ORIGINAL. HE TOOK IMAGES OF BOXES OF SOAP AND STUFF, AND HE USED THEM TO MAKE ART.
WARHOL AT THE FACTORY
THAT'S HIS, UH, CLU- COLLECTIVE?
COLLECTION, MAYBE. ANDY WARHOL HAD A WHOLE SYSTEM OF FACTORY SUPERSTARS. IT WAS HIS TAKE ON THE OLD MOVIE STUDIO SYSTEM.
SO THAT'S WHAT THE CURATOR IS DOING, YOU THINK?
IN A WAY. ALTHOUGH I WOULDN'T SAY ANYONE AT THIS FACTORY NEEDS THE CURATOR TO MAKE HER A STAR.
BUT TO GET UP ON STAGE...
YEAH, YOU DO NEED THE CURATOR FOR THAT.

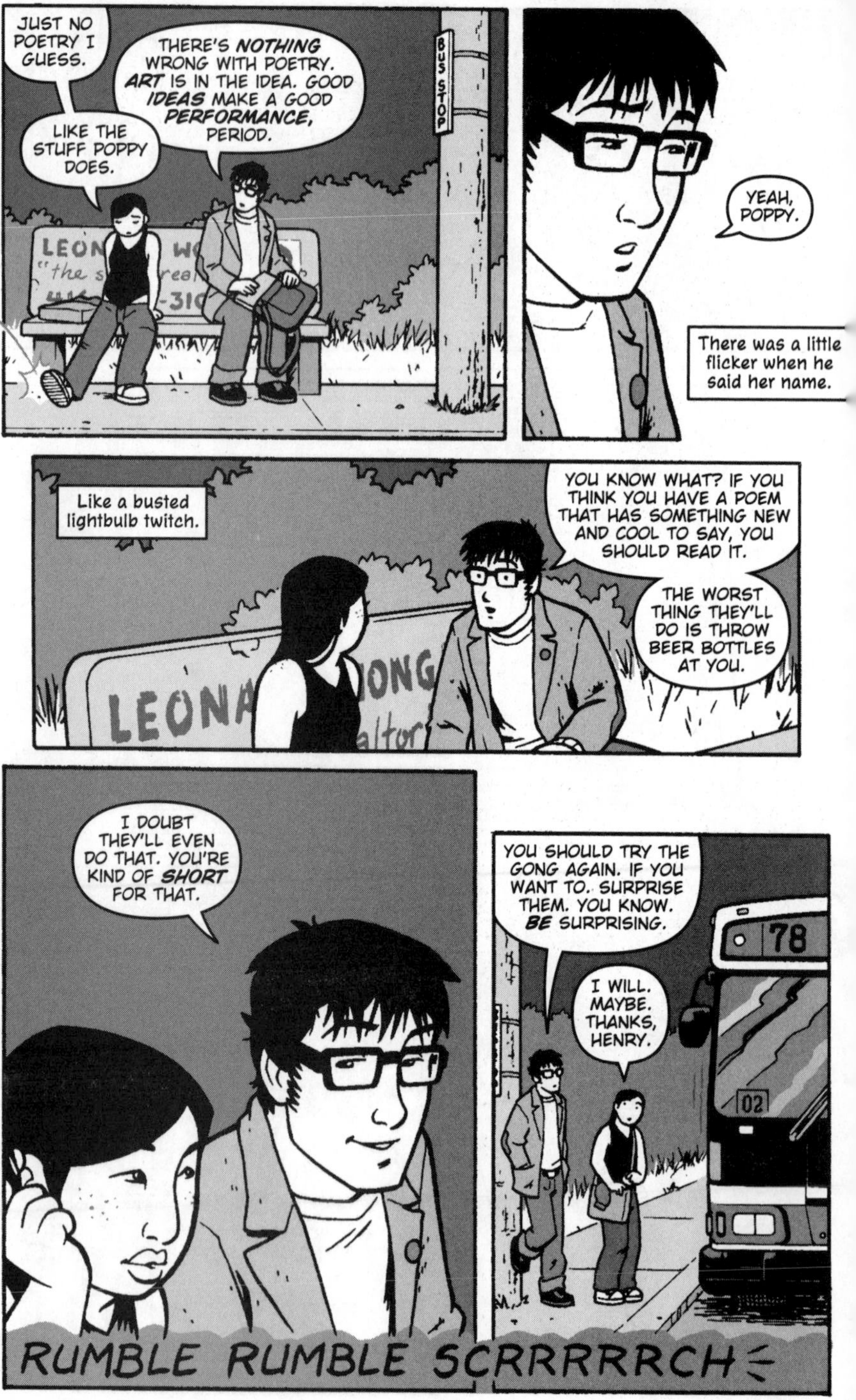

JUST NO POETRY I GUESS.
LIKE THE STUFF POPPY DOES.
THERE'S NOTHING WRONG WITH POETRY. ART IS IN THE IDEA. GOOD IDEAS MAKE A GOOD PERFORMANCE, PERIOD.
BUS STOP
YEAH, POPPY.
There was a little flicker when he said her name.
Like a busted lightbulb twitch.
YOU KNOW WHAT? IF YOU THINK YOU HAVE A POEM THAT HAS SOMETHING NEW AND COOL TO SAY, YOU SHOULD READ IT.
THE WORST THING THEY'LL DO IS THROW BEER BOTTLES AT YOU.
I DOUBT THEY'LL EVEN DO THAT. YOU'RE KIND OF SHORT FOR THAT.
YOU SHOULD TRY THE GONG AGAIN. IF YOU WANT TO. SURPRISE THEM. YOU KNOW. BE SURPRISING.
I WILL. MAYBE. THANKS, HENRY.
78
02
RUMBLE RUMBLE SCRRRRRRCH

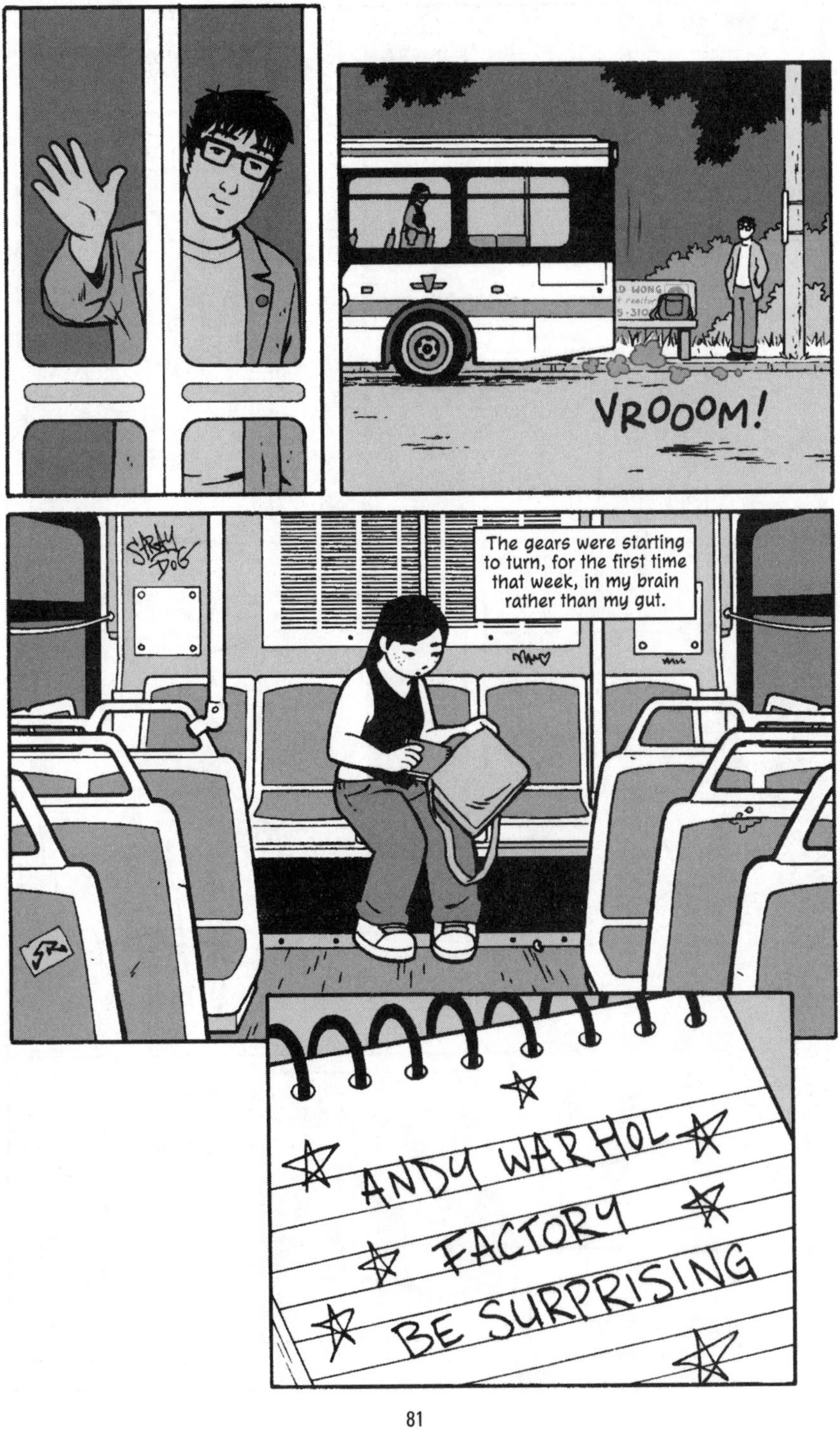
VROOOM!
The gears were starting to turn, for the first time that week, in my brain rather than my gut.
ANDY WARHOL
FACTORY
BE SURPRISING

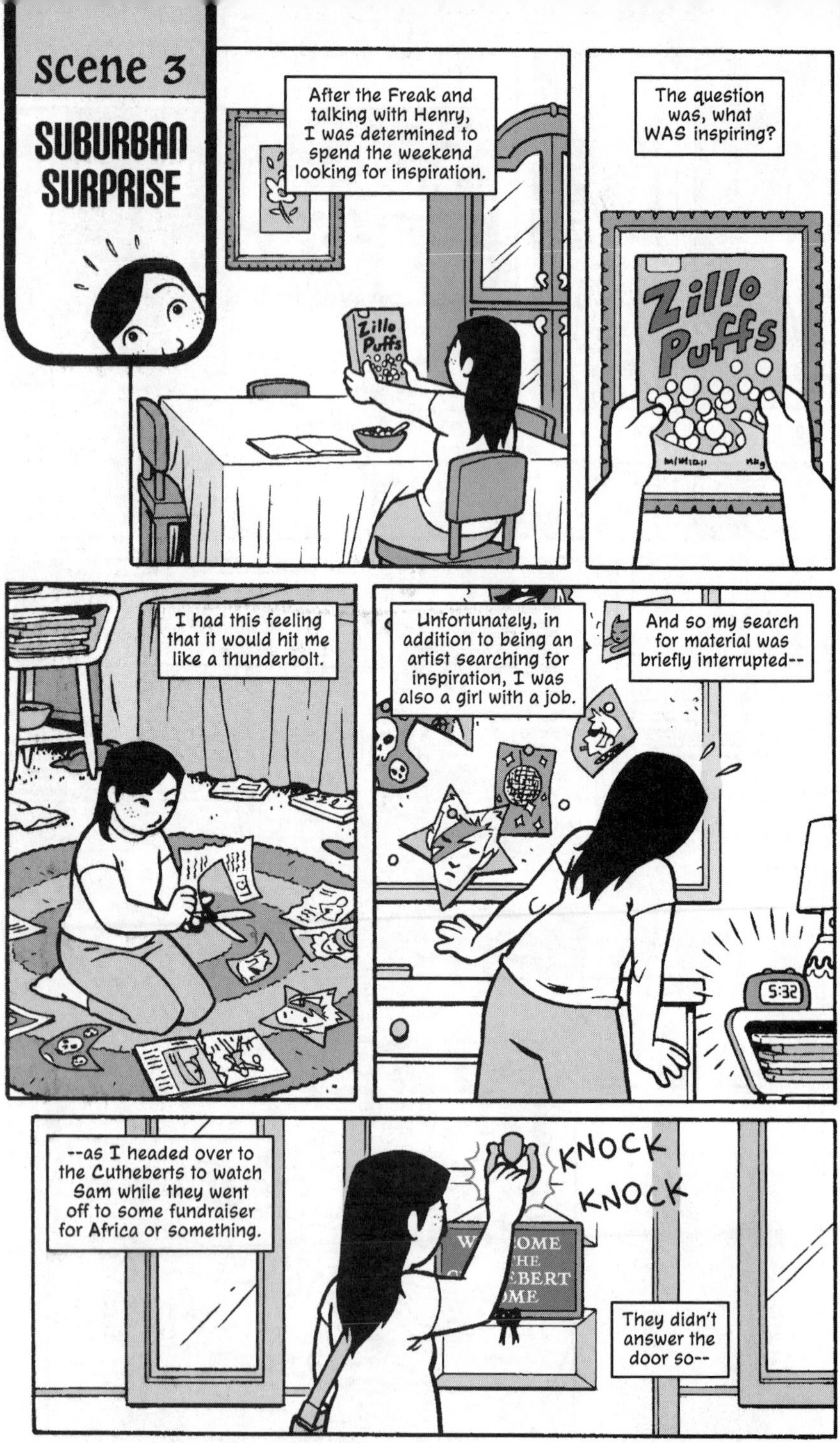
scene 3
SUBURBAN SURPRISE
After the Freak and talking with Henry, I was determined to spend the weekend looking for inspiration.
Zillo Puffs
The question was, what WAS inspiring?
Zillo Puffs
I had this feeling that it would hit me like a thunderbolt.
Unfortunately, in addition to being an artist searching for inspiration, I was also a girl with a job.
And so my search for material was briefly interrupted--
5:32
--as I headed over to the Cutheberts to watch Sam while they went off to some fundraiser for Africa or something.
KNOCK
KNOCK
They didn't answer the door so--

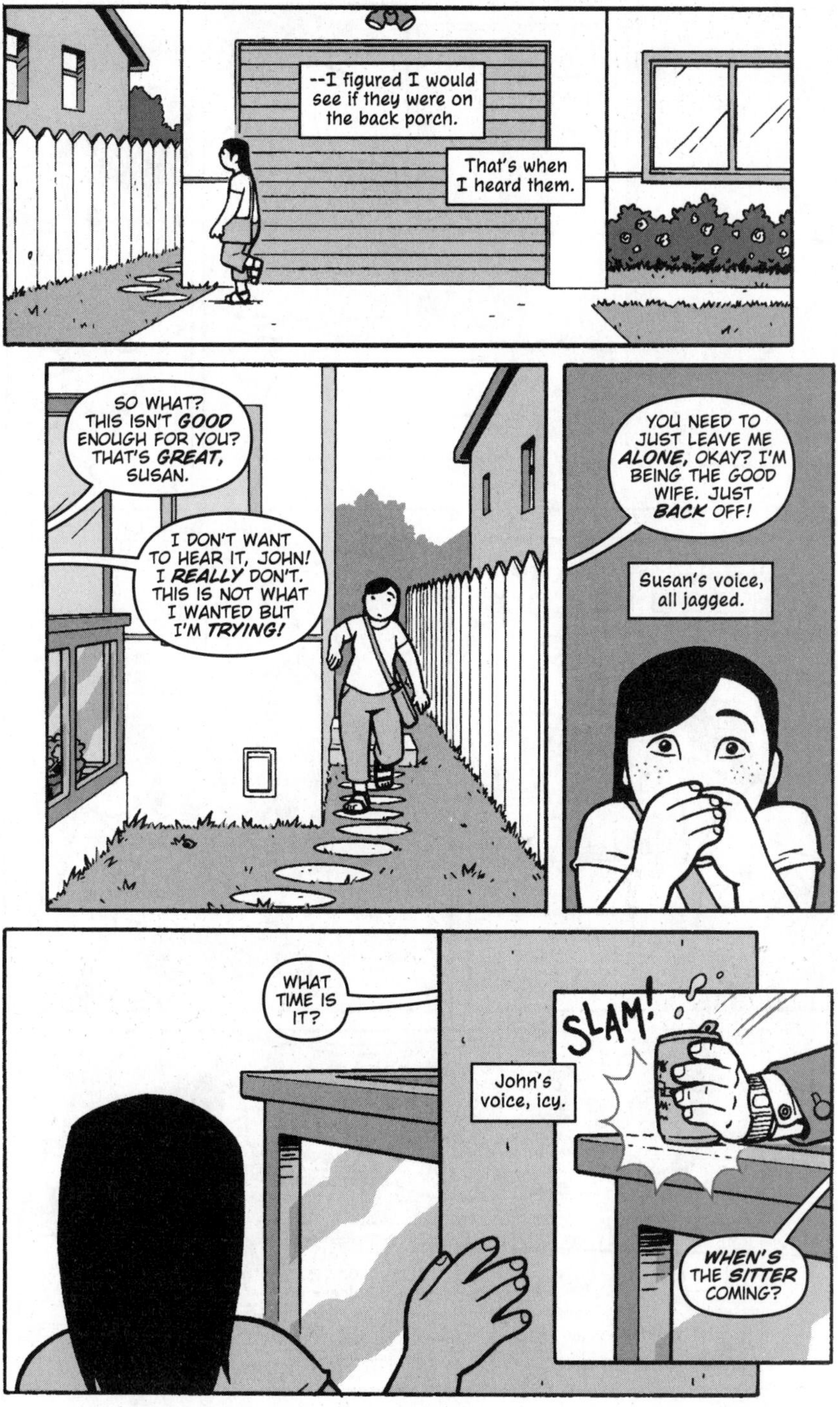
--I figured I would see if they were on the back porch.
That's when I heard them.
SO WHAT? THIS ISN'T GOOD ENOUGH FOR YOU? THAT'S GREAT, SUSAN.
I DON'T WANT TO HEAR IT, JOHN! I REALLY DON'T. THIS IS NOT WHAT I WANTED BUT I'M TRYING!
YOU NEED TO JUST LEAVE ME ALONE, OKAY? I'M BEING THE GOOD WIFE. JUST BACK OFF!
Susan's voice, all jagged.
WHAT TIME IS IT?
SLAM!
John's voice, icy.
WHEN'S THE SITTER COMING?

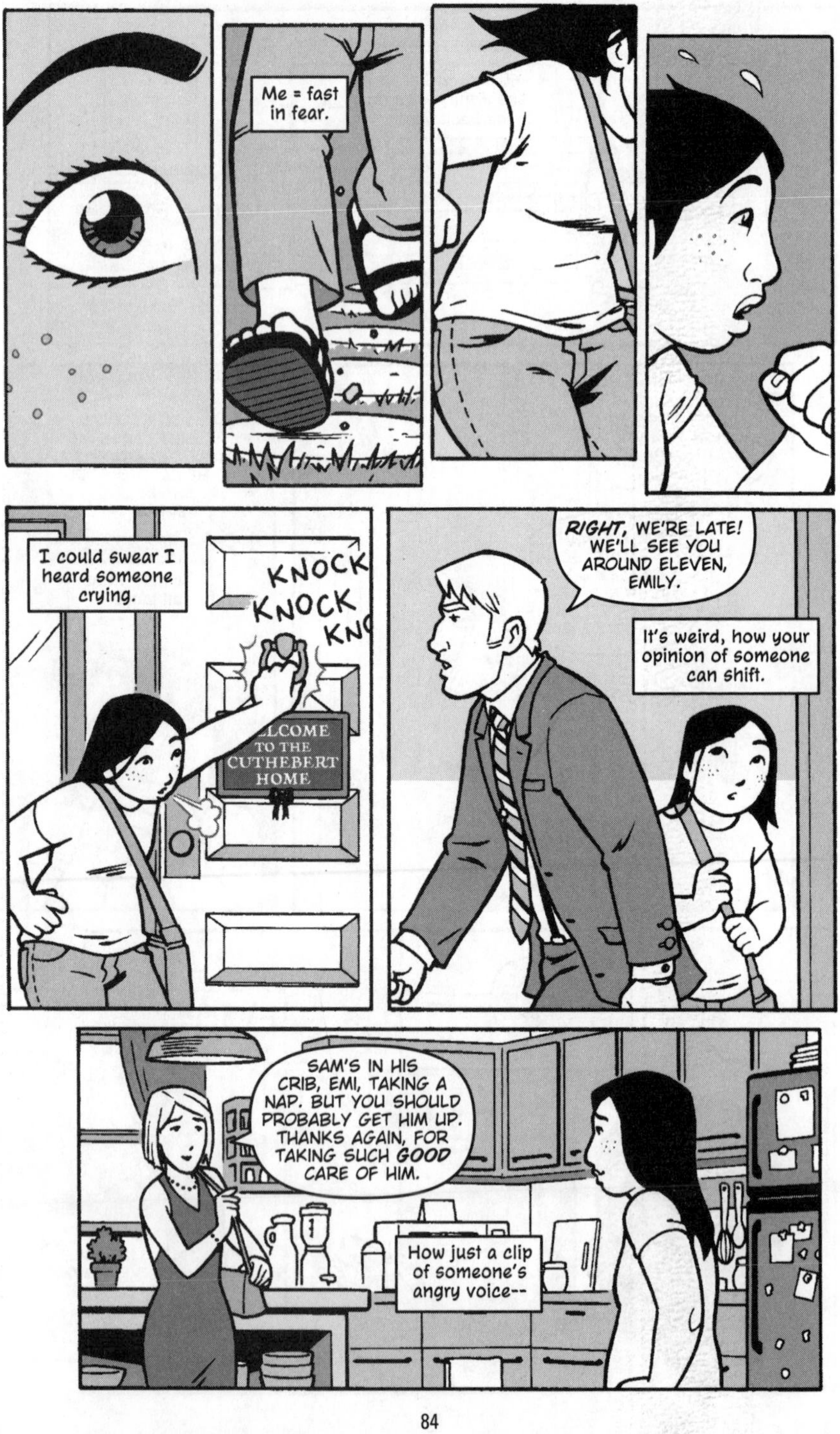
Me = fast in fear.
I could swear I heard someone crying.
KNOCK KNOCK KNO
WELCOME TO THE CUTHEBERT HOME
RIGHT, WE'RE LATE! WE'LL SEE YOU AROUND ELEVEN, EMILY.
It's weird, how your opinion of someone can shift.
SAM'S IN HIS CRIB, EMI, TAKING A NAP. BUT YOU SHOULD PROBABLY GET HIM UP. THANKS AGAIN, FOR TAKING SUCH GOOD CARE OF HIM.
How just a clip of someone's angry voice--

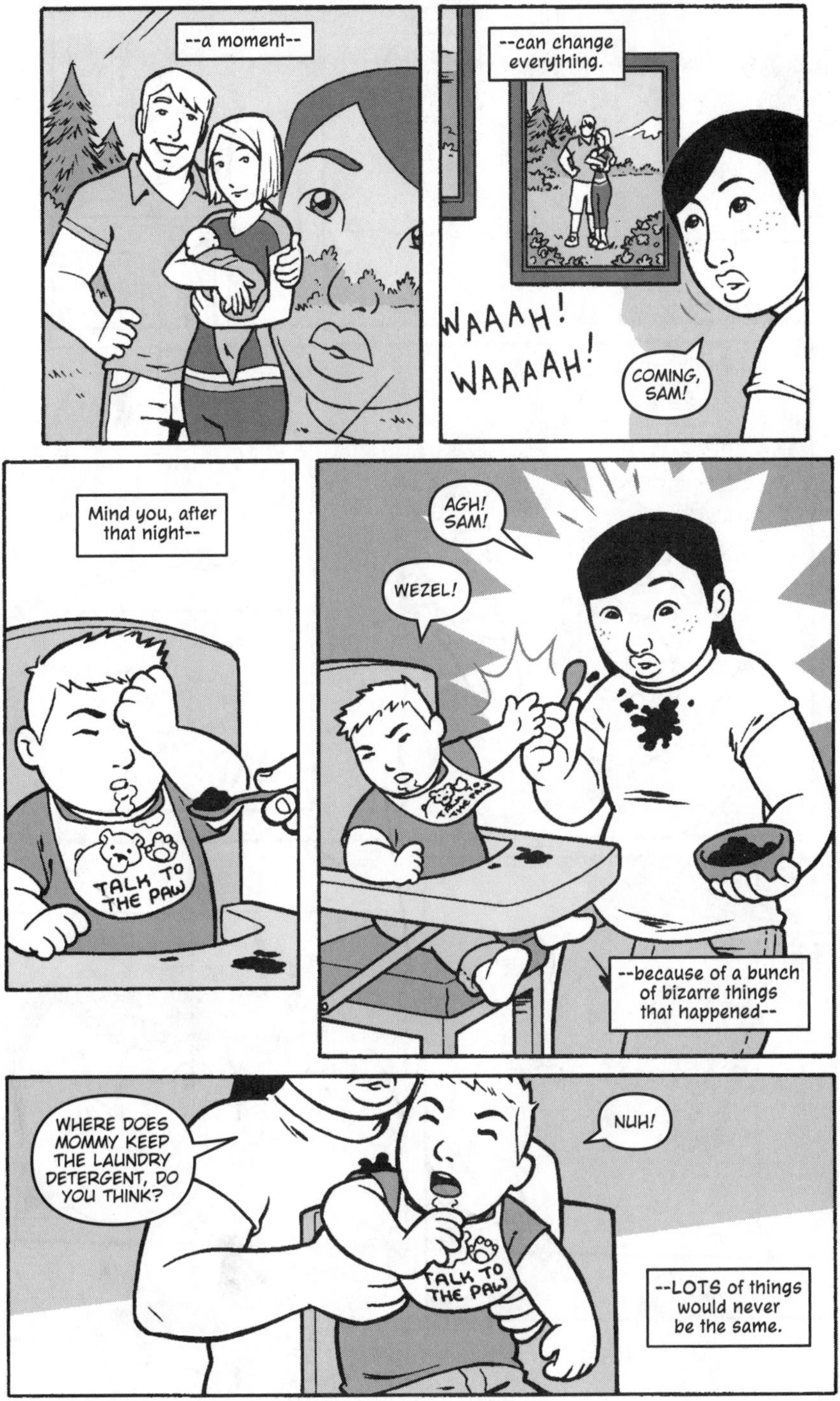
--a moment--
--can change everything.
WAAAH! WAAAAH!
COMING, SAM!
Mind you, after that night--
AGH! SAM!
WEZEL!
TALK TO THE PAW
--because of a bunch of bizarre things that happened--
WHERE DOES MOMMY KEEP THE LAUNDRY DETERGENT, DO YOU THINK?
NUH!
TALK TO THE PAW
--LOTS of things would never be the same.

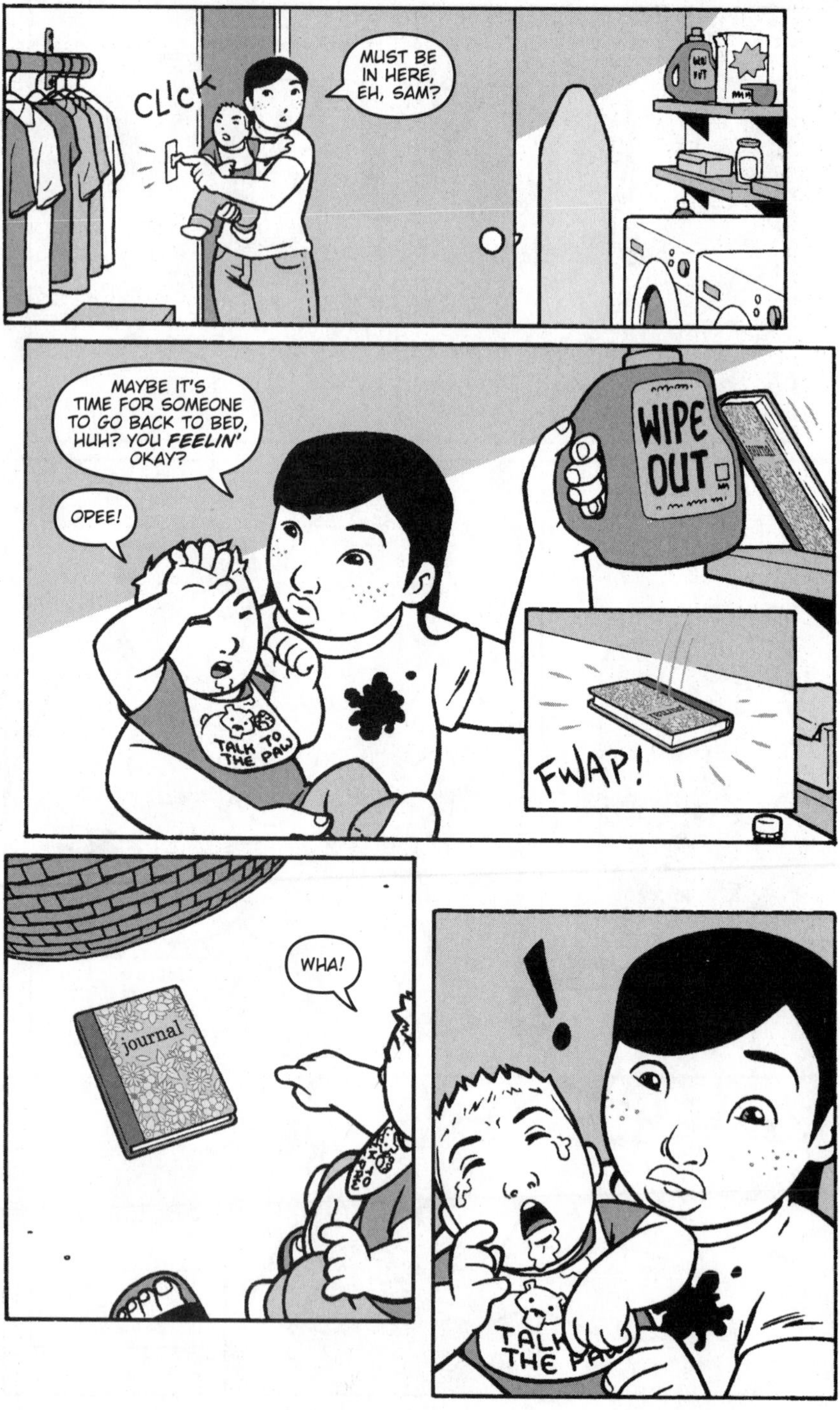
CLICK
MUST BE IN HERE, EH, SAM?
MAYBE IT'S TIME FOR SOMEONE TO GO BACK TO BED, HUH? YOU FEELIN' OKAY?
OPEE!
WIPE OUT
TALK TO THE PAW
FWAP!
journal
WHA!
!

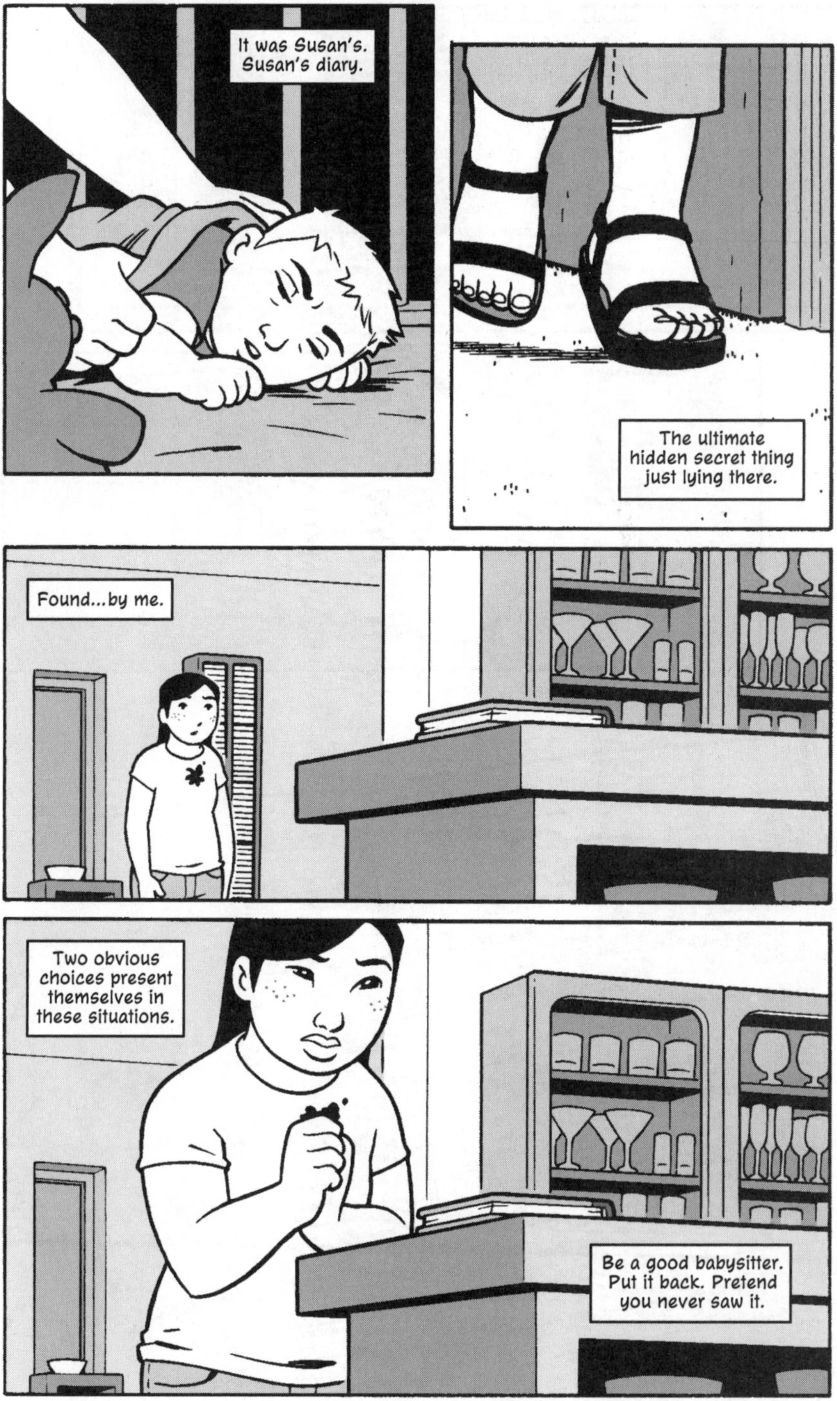

It was Susan's. Susan's diary.
The ultimate hidden secret thing just lying there.
Found...by me.
Two obvious choices present themselves in these situations.
Be a good babysitter. Put it back. Pretend you never saw it.

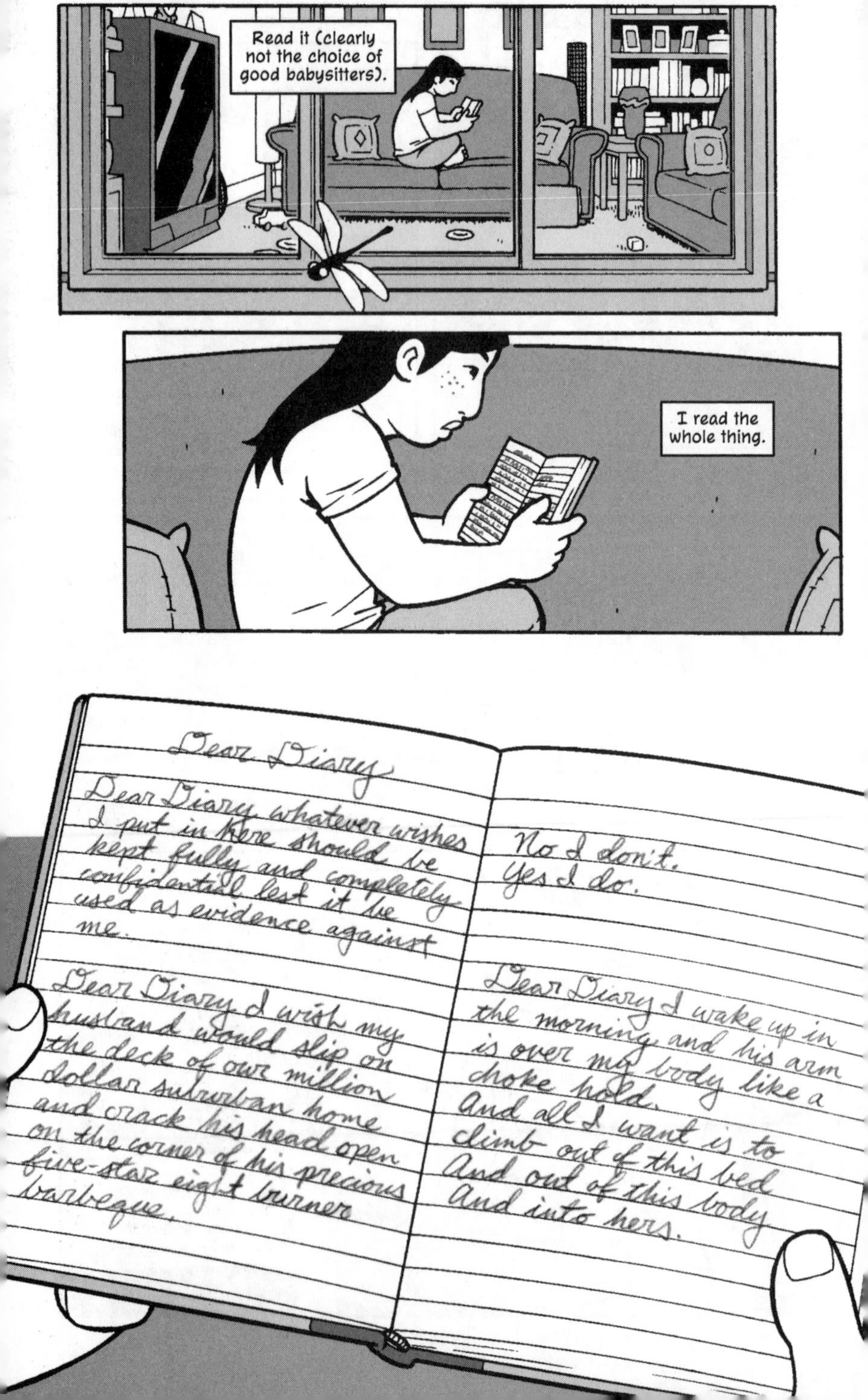
Read it (clearly not the choice of good babysitters).
I read the whole thing.
Dear Diary
Dear Diary whatever wishes I put in here should be kept fully and completely confidantill lest it be used as evidence against me.
Dear Diary I wish my husband would slip on the deck of our million dollar suburban home and crack his head open on the corner of his precious five-star eight burner barbeque.
No I don't.
Yes I do.
Dear Diary I wake up in the morning and his arm is over my body like a choke hold.
And all I want is to climb out of this bed
And out of this body
And into hers.

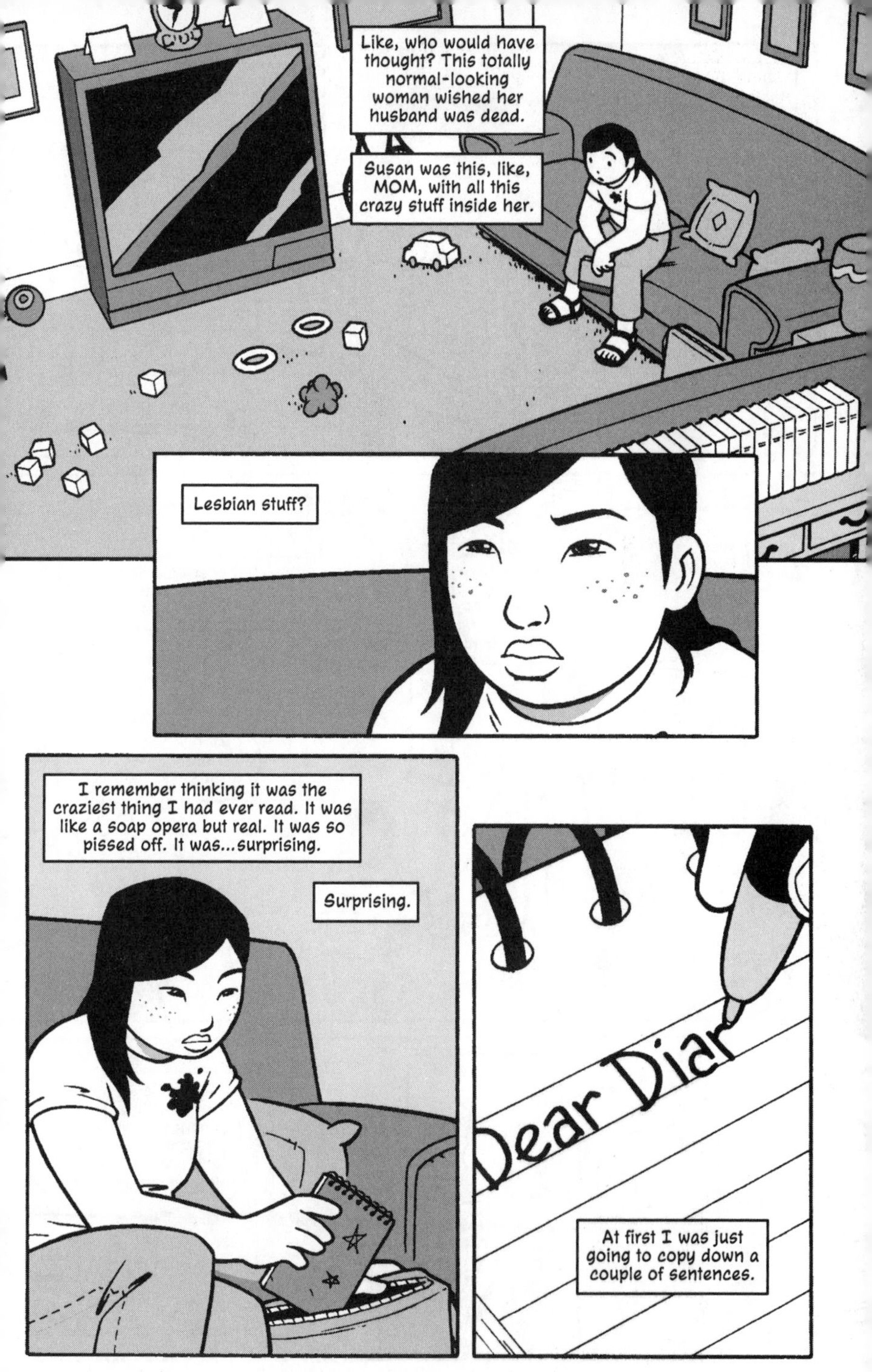
Like, who would have thought? This totally normal-looking woman wished her husband was dead.
Susan was this, like, MOM, with all this crazy stuff inside her.
Lesbian stuff?
I remember thinking it was the craziest thing I had ever read. It was like a soap opera but real. It was so pissed off. It was...surprising.
Surprising.
Dear Diar
At first I was just going to copy down a couple of sentences.

But in the end, I ~~took it all~~ copied the whole thing.

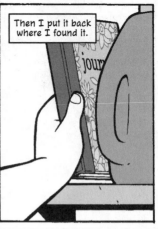

Then I put it back where I found it.

WE'RE HOME!

HEY, FANCY CHOCOLATES! THEY WERE *FREE!* YOUR DAD WILL EAT THEM!

When the Cutheberts came home that night, it was strange. Looking at John and Susan.

Not able to look at them, really.

EMI, DO YOU NEED A RIDE?

NO, I'LL WALK. THANKS.

BE SAFE, EMI. SEE YOU MONDAY.

Guilt, like a thousand tiny punches to all your joints and organs.

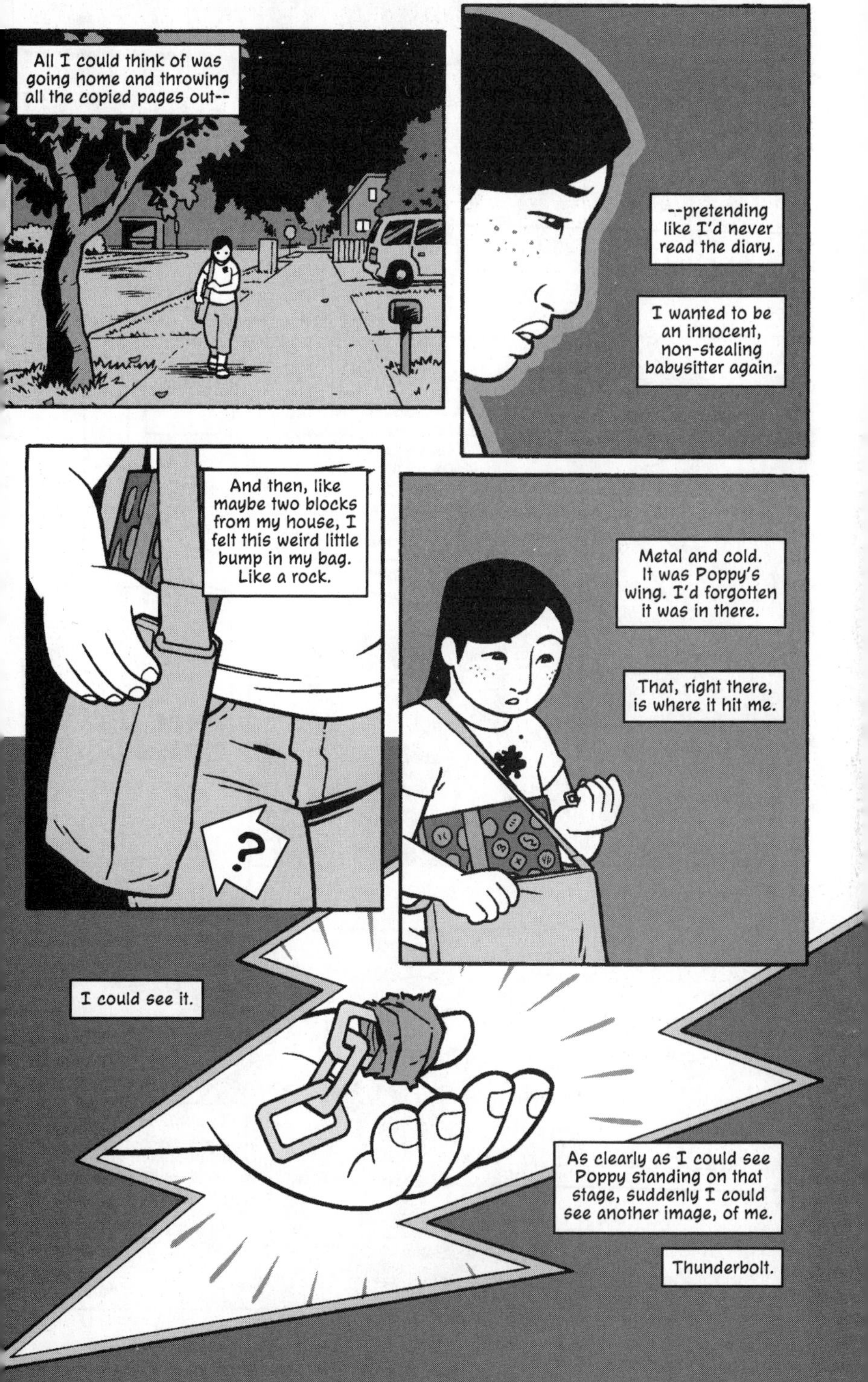
All I could think of was going home and throwing all the copied pages out--
--pretending like I'd never read the diary.
I wanted to be an innocent, non-stealing babysitter again.
And then, like maybe two blocks from my house, I felt this weird little bump in my bag. Like a rock.
?
Metal and cold. It was Poppy's wing. I'd forgotten it was in there.
That, right there, is where it hit me.
I could see it.
As clearly as I could see Poppy standing on that stage, suddenly I could see another image, of me.
Thunderbolt.

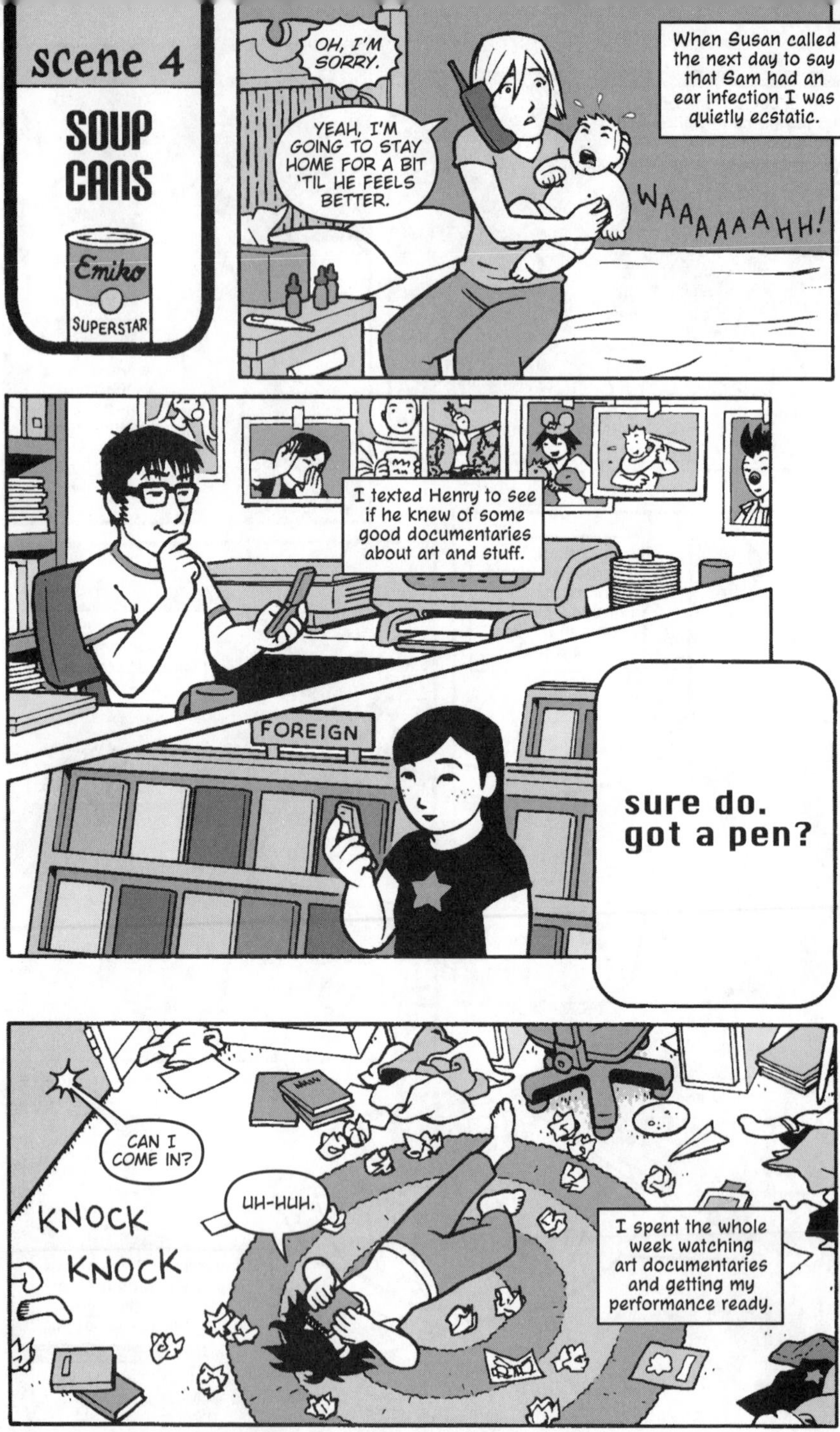
scene 4
SOUP CANS
Emiko
SUPERSTAR
When Susan called the next day to say that Sam had an ear infection I was quietly ecstatic.
OH, I'M SORRY.
YEAH, I'M GOING TO STAY HOME FOR A BIT 'TIL HE FEELS BETTER.
WAAAAAAHH!
I texted Henry to see if he knew of some good documentaries about art and stuff.
FOREIGN
sure do. got a pen?
CAN I COME IN?
KNOCK KNOCK
UH-HUH.
I spent the whole week watching art documentaries and getting my performance ready.

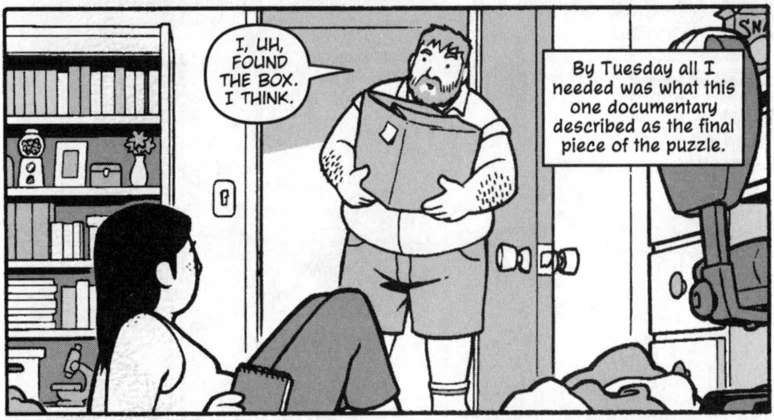
I, UH, FOUND THE BOX. I THINK.
By Tuesday all I needed was what this one documentary described as the final piece of the puzzle.

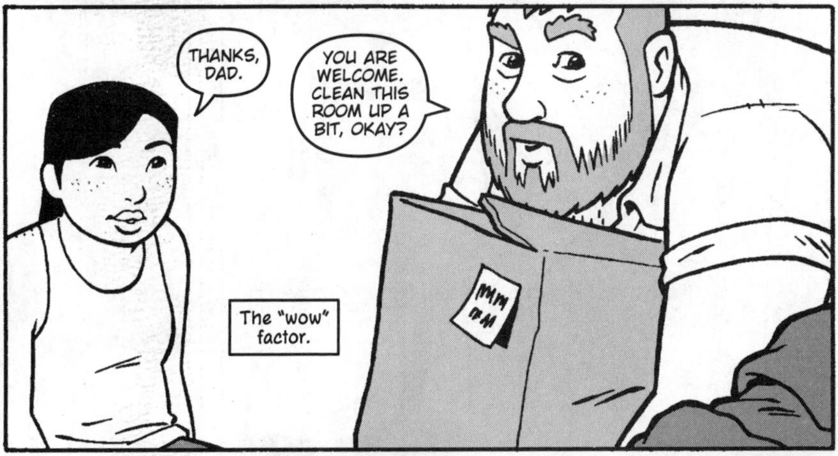
THANKS, DAD.
YOU ARE WELCOME. CLEAN THIS ROOM UP A BIT, OKAY?
The "wow" factor.

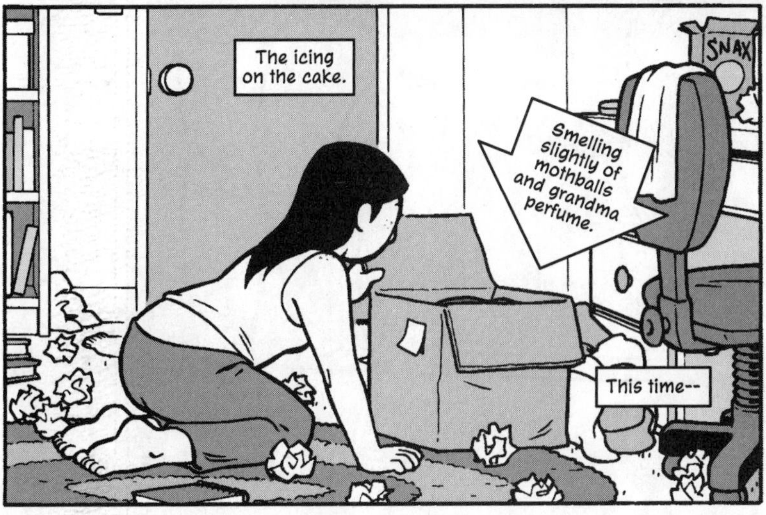
The icing on the cake.
SNAX
Smelling slightly of mothballs and grandma perfume.
This time--

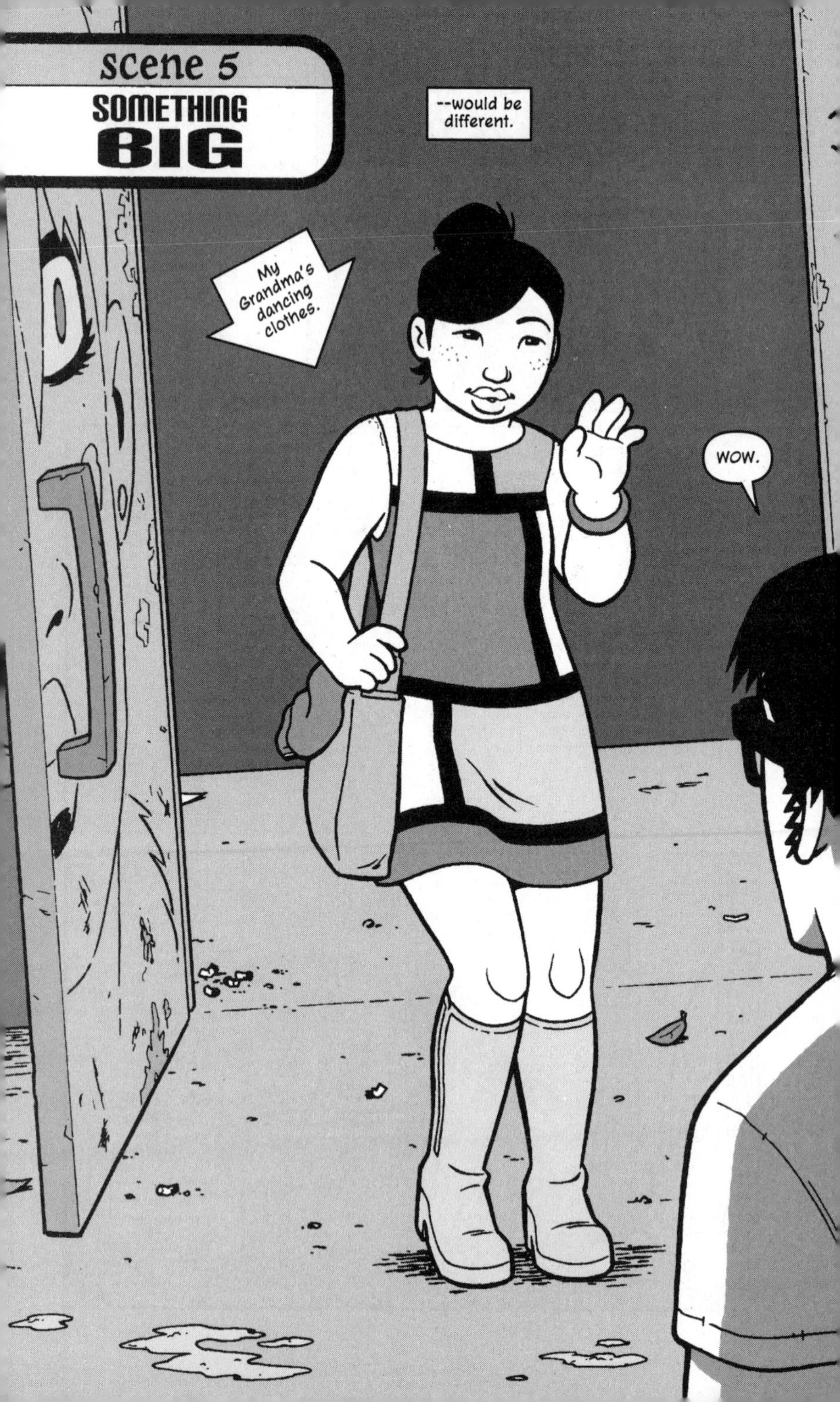
scene 5
SOMETHING
BIG
--would be different.
My Grandma's dancing clothes.
WOW.

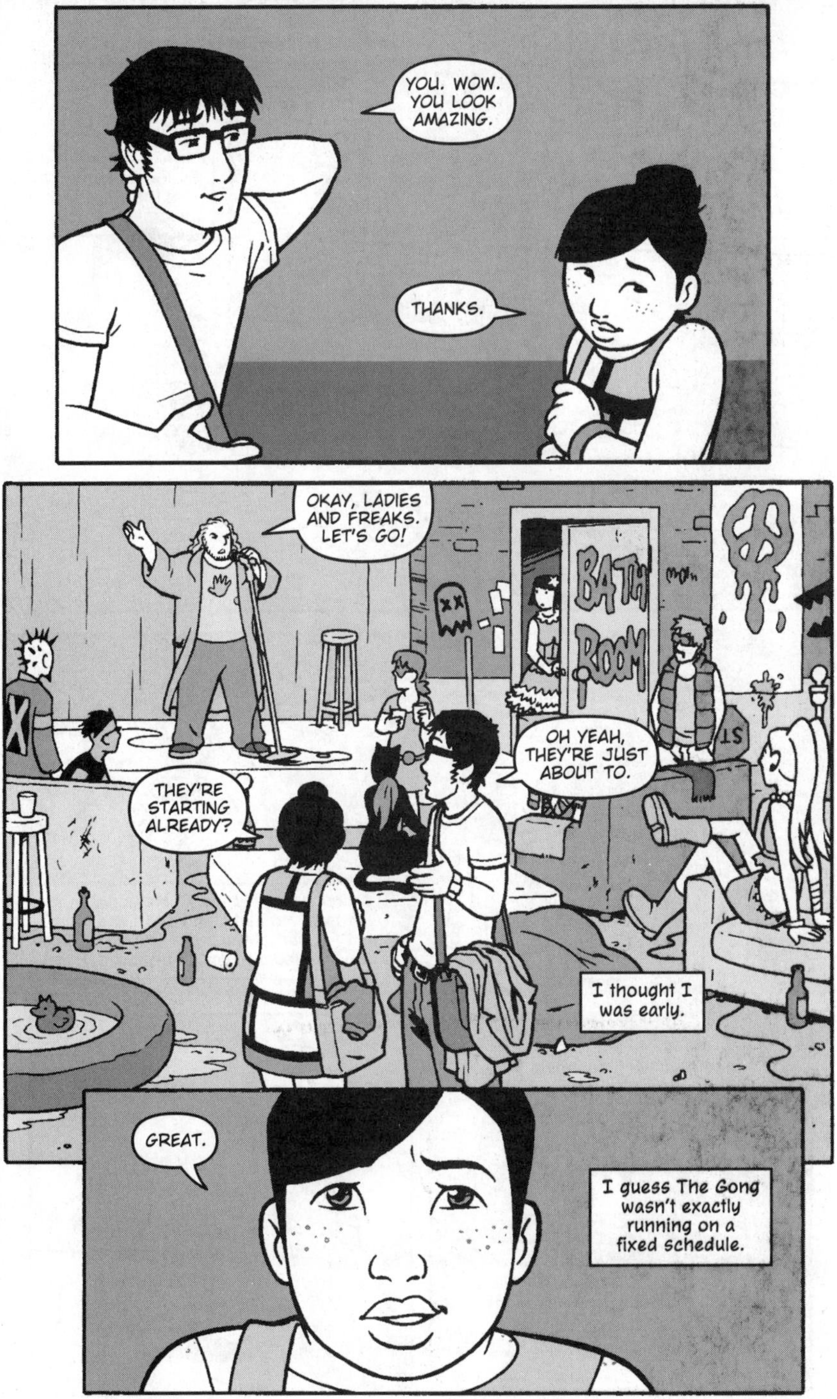

YOU. WOW. YOU LOOK AMAZING.
THANKS.
OKAY, LADIES AND FREAKS. LET'S GO!
BATH ROOM
THEY'RE STARTING ALREADY?
OH YEAH, THEY'RE JUST ABOUT TO.
I thought I was early.
GREAT.
I guess The Gong wasn't exactly running on a fixed schedule.

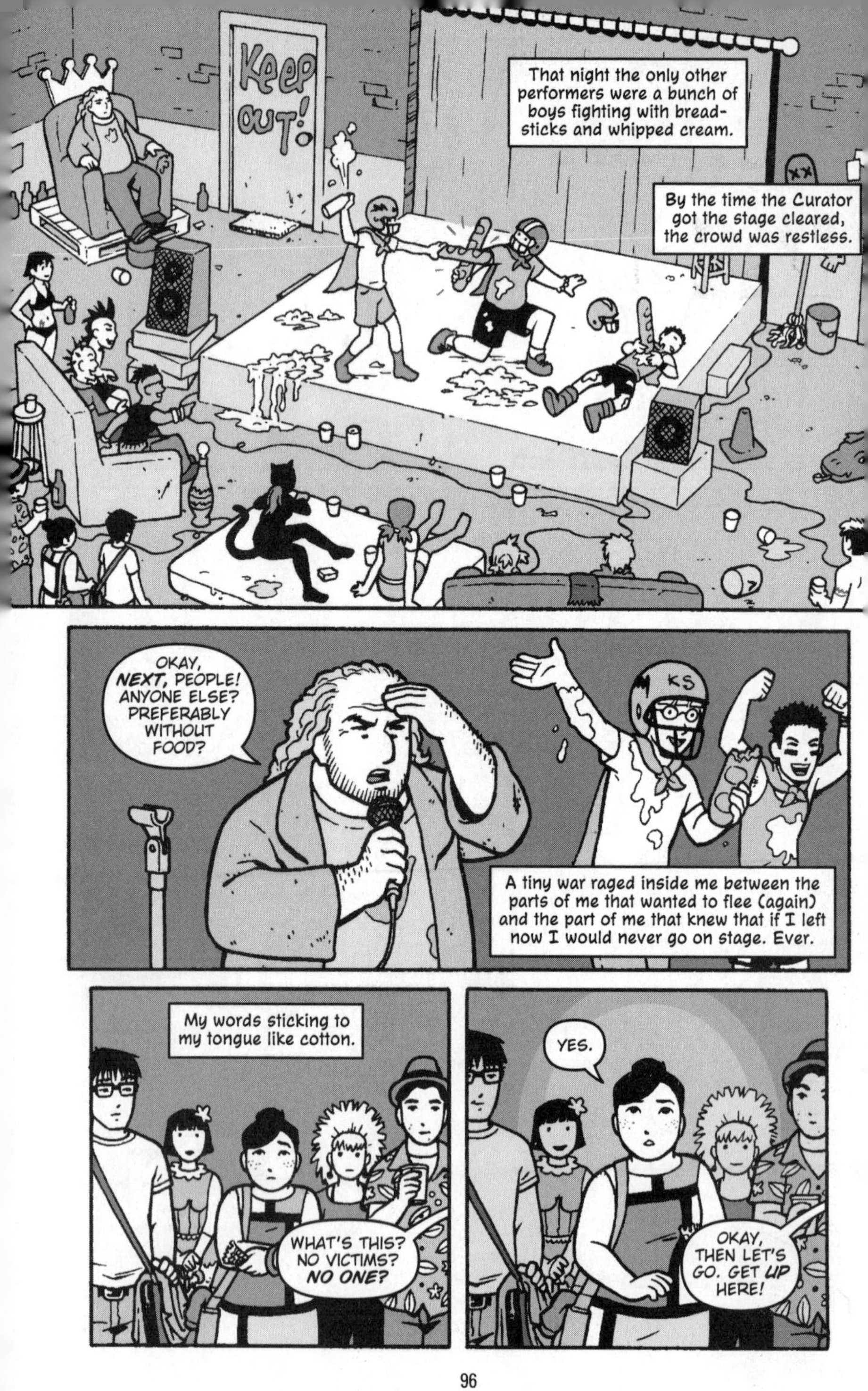
KEEP OUT!
That night the only other performers were a bunch of boys fighting with bread-sticks and whipped cream.
By the time the Curator got the stage cleared, the crowd was restless.
OKAY, NEXT, PEOPLE! ANYONE ELSE? PREFERABLY WITHOUT FOOD?
KS
A tiny war raged inside me between the parts of me that wanted to flee (again) and the part of me that knew that if I left now I would never go on stage. Ever.
My words sticking to my tongue like cotton.
WHAT'S THIS? NO VICTIMS? NO ONE?
YES.
OKAY, THEN LET'S GO. GET UP HERE!

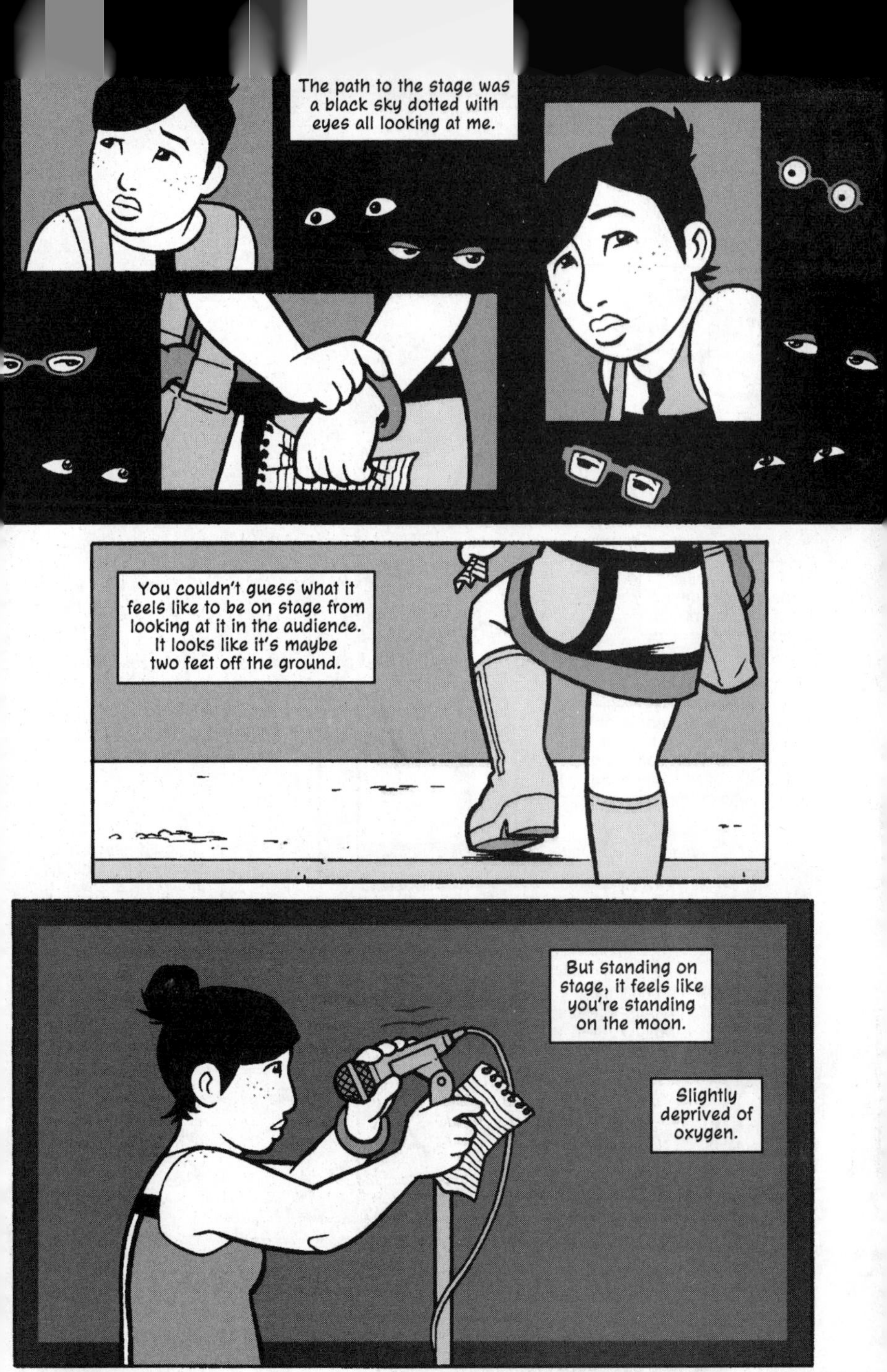
The path to the stage was a black sky dotted with eyes all looking at me.
You couldn't guess what it feels like to be on stage from looking at it in the audience. It looks like it's maybe two feet off the ground.
But standing on stage, it feels like you're standing on the moon.
Slightly deprived of oxygen.

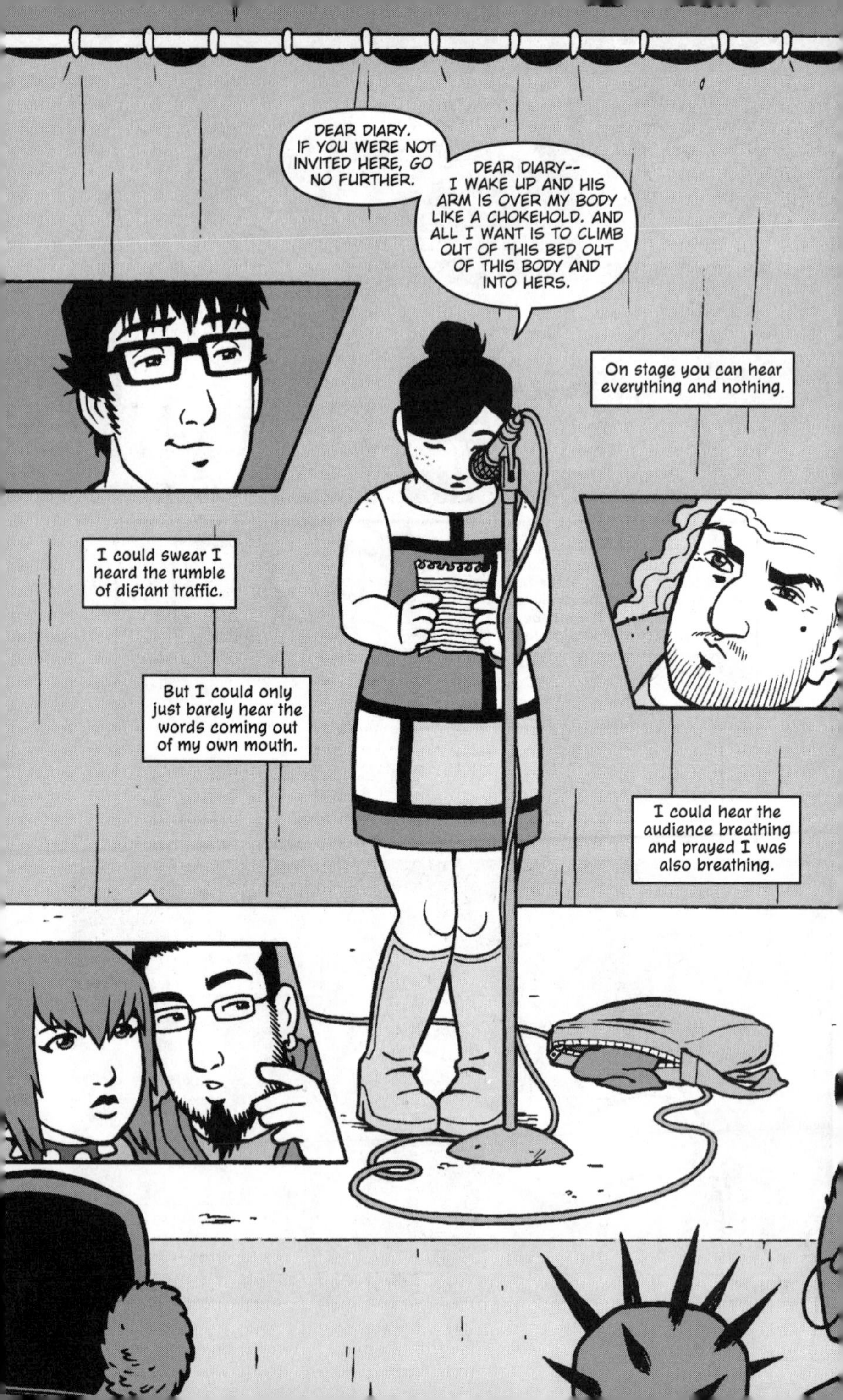
DEAR DIARY. IF YOU WERE NOT INVITED HERE, GO NO FURTHER.
DEAR DIARY-- I WAKE UP AND HIS ARM IS OVER MY BODY LIKE A CHOKEHOLD. AND ALL I WANT IS TO CLIMB OUT OF THIS BED OUT OF THIS BODY AND INTO HERS.
On stage you can hear everything and nothing.
I could swear I heard the rumble of distant traffic.
But I could only just barely hear the words coming out of my own mouth.
I could hear the audience breathing and prayed I was also breathing.

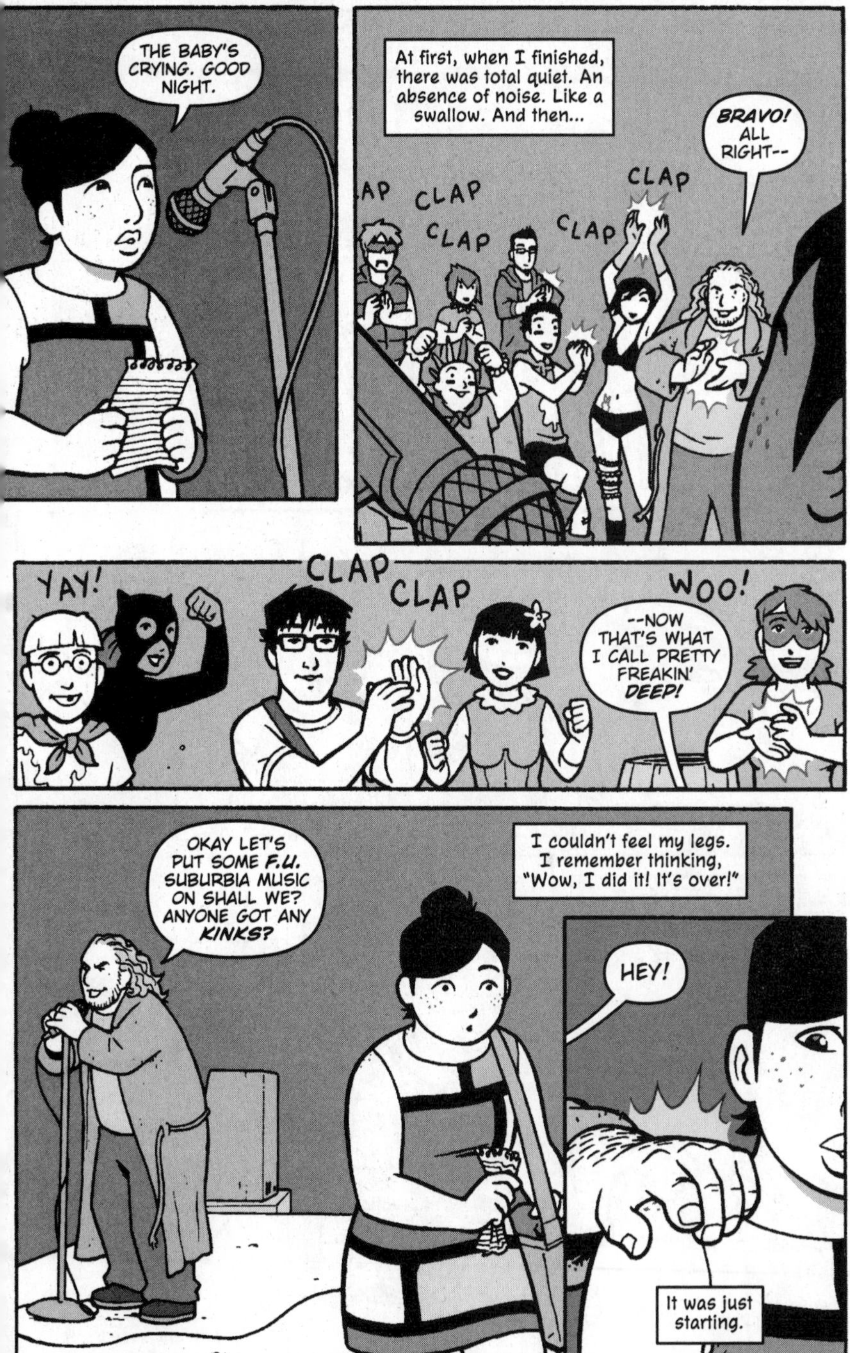
THE BABY'S CRYING. GOOD NIGHT.
At first, when I finished, there was total quiet. An absence of noise. Like a swallow. And then...
AP CLAP
CLAP
CLAP
CLAP
BRAVO! ALL RIGHT--
YAY!
CLAP
CLAP
WOO!
--NOW THAT'S WHAT I CALL PRETTY FREAKIN' DEEP!
OKAY LET'S PUT SOME F.U. SUBURBIA MUSIC ON SHALL WE? ANYONE GOT ANY KINKS?
I couldn't feel my legs. I remember thinking, "Wow, I did it! It's over!"
HEY!
It was just starting.

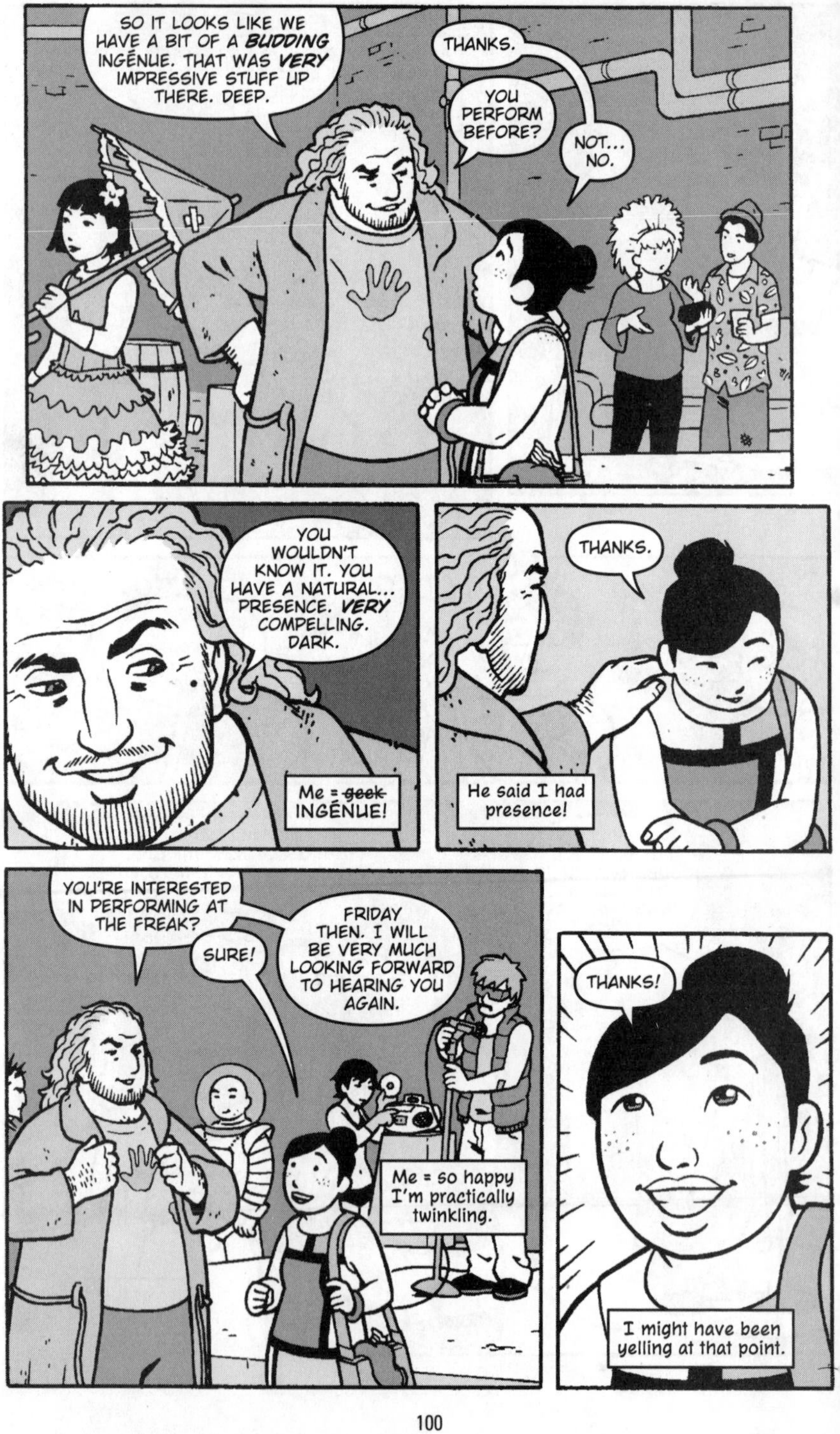
SO IT LOOKS LIKE WE HAVE A BIT OF A *BUDDING* INGÉNUE. THAT WAS *VERY* IMPRESSIVE STUFF UP THERE. DEEP.
THANKS.
YOU PERFORM BEFORE?
NOT... NO.
YOU WOULDN'T KNOW IT. YOU HAVE A NATURAL... PRESENCE. *VERY* COMPELLING. DARK.
Me = ~~geek~~ INGÉNUE!
THANKS.
He said I had presence!
YOU'RE INTERESTED IN PERFORMING AT THE FREAK?
SURE!
FRIDAY THEN. I WILL BE VERY MUCH LOOKING FORWARD TO HEARING YOU AGAIN.
Me = so happy I'm practically twinkling.
THANKS!
I might have been yelling at that point.

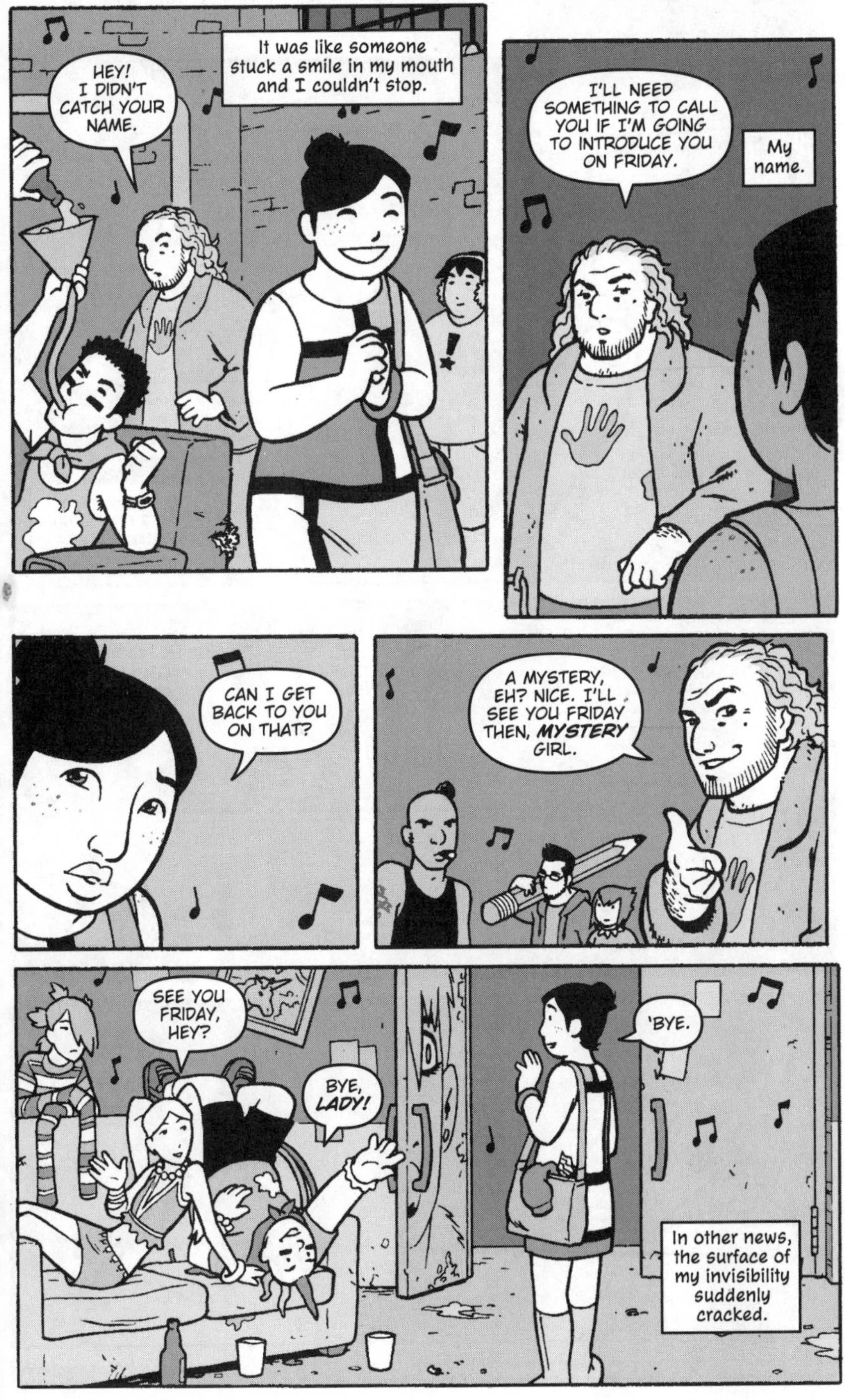
HEY! I DIDN'T CATCH YOUR NAME.
It was like someone stuck a smile in my mouth and I couldn't stop.
I'LL NEED SOMETHING TO CALL YOU IF I'M GOING TO INTRODUCE YOU ON FRIDAY.
My name.
CAN I GET BACK TO YOU ON THAT?
A MYSTERY, EH? NICE. I'LL SEE YOU FRIDAY THEN, *MYSTERY* GIRL.
SEE YOU FRIDAY, HEY?
BYE, *LADY!*
'BYE.
In other news, the surface of my invisibility suddenly cracked.

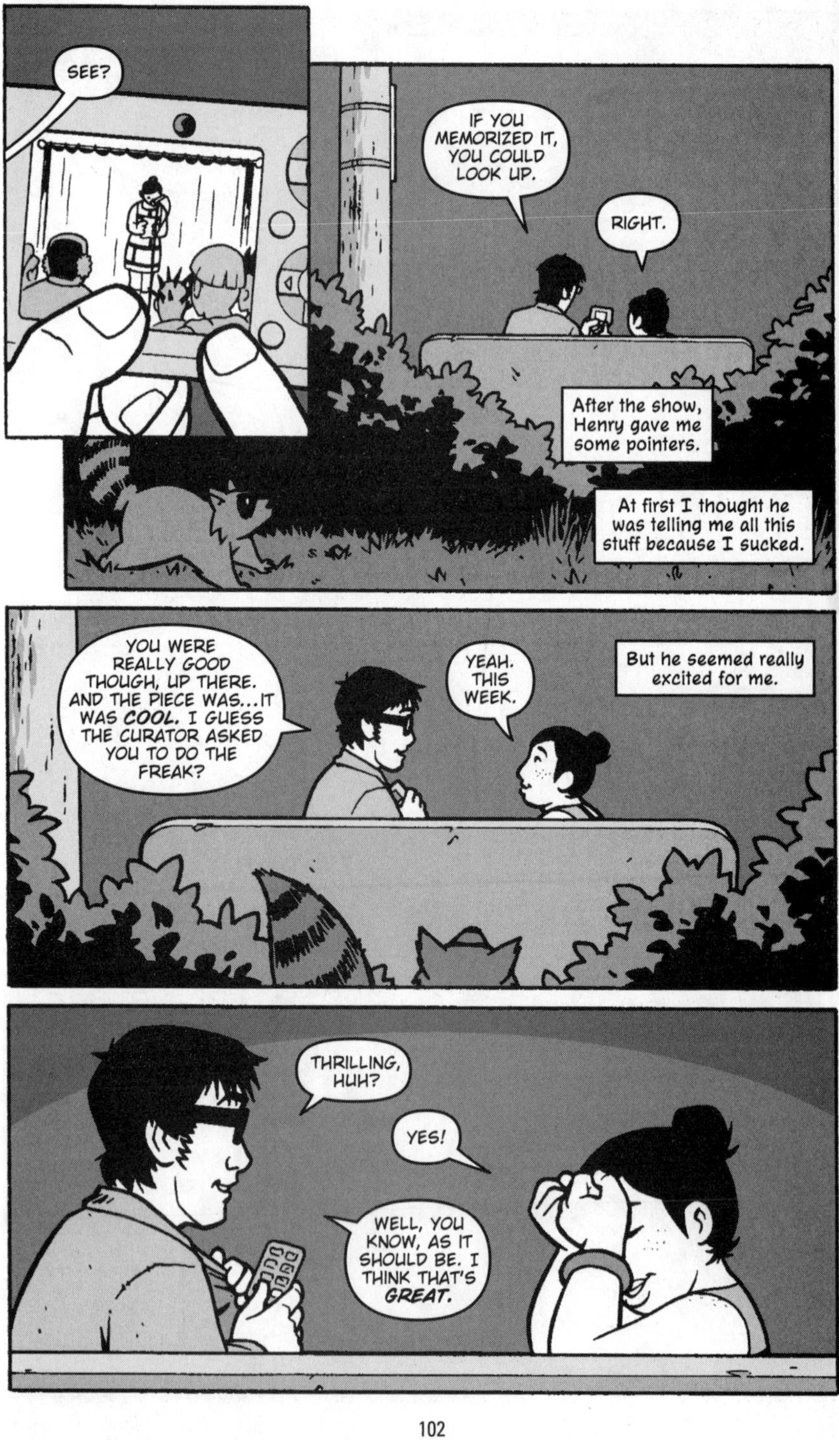
SEE?
IF YOU MEMORIZED IT, YOU COULD LOOK UP.
RIGHT.
After the show, Henry gave me some pointers.
At first I thought he was telling me all this stuff because I sucked.
YOU WERE REALLY GOOD THOUGH, UP THERE. AND THE PIECE WAS...IT WAS COOL. I GUESS THE CURATOR ASKED YOU TO DO THE FREAK?
YEAH. THIS WEEK.
But he seemed really excited for me.
THRILLING, HUH?
YES!
WELL, YOU KNOW, AS IT SHOULD BE. I THINK THAT'S GREAT.

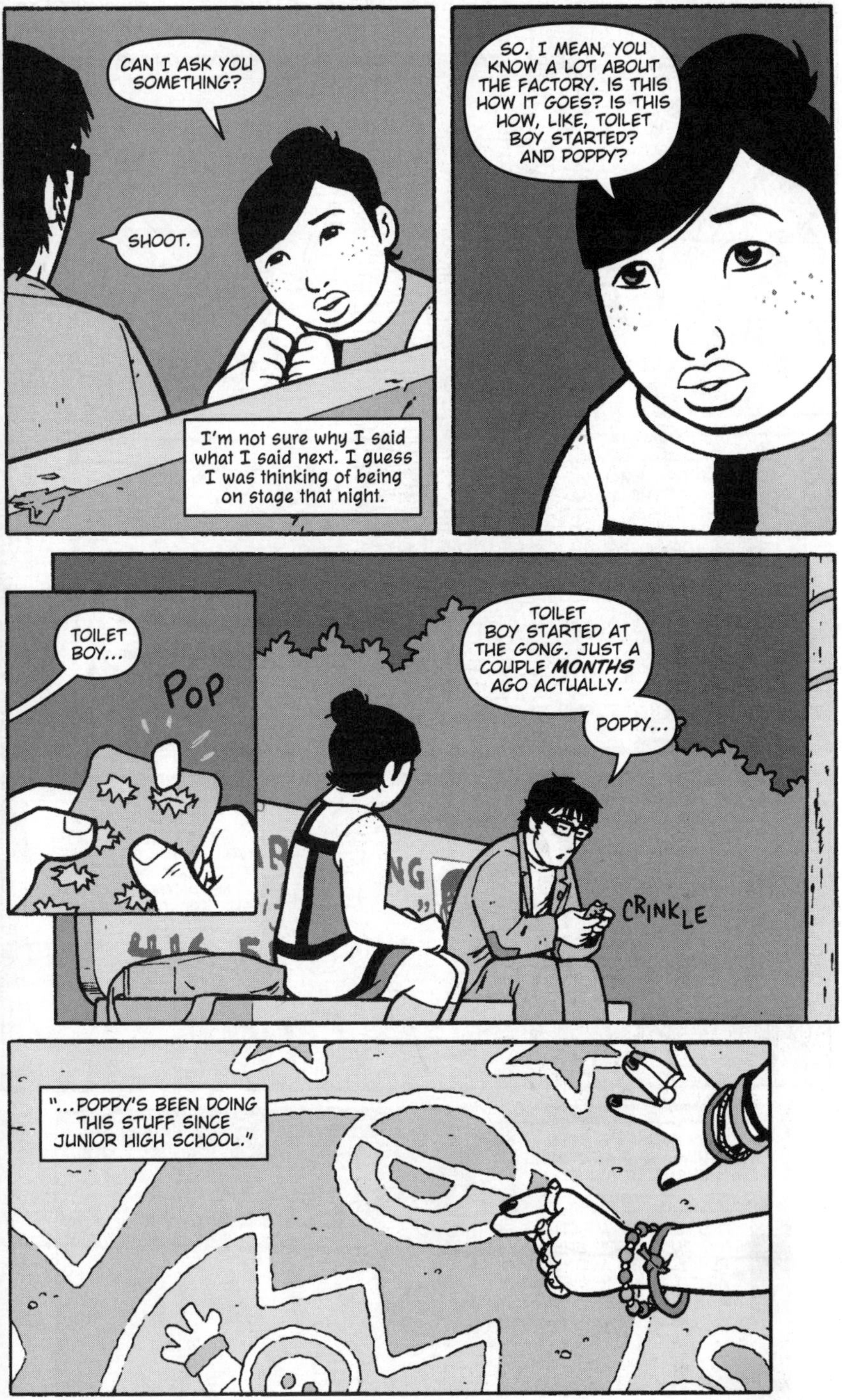
CAN I ASK YOU SOMETHING?
SHOOT.
I'm not sure why I said what I said next. I guess I was thinking of being on stage that night.
SO. I MEAN, YOU KNOW A LOT ABOUT THE FACTORY. IS THIS HOW IT GOES? IS THIS HOW, LIKE, TOILET BOY STARTED? AND POPPY?
TOILET BOY...
POP
TOILET BOY STARTED AT THE GONG. JUST A COUPLE MONTHS AGO ACTUALLY.
POPPY...
CRINKLE
"...POPPY'S BEEN DOING THIS STUFF SINCE JUNIOR HIGH SCHOOL."

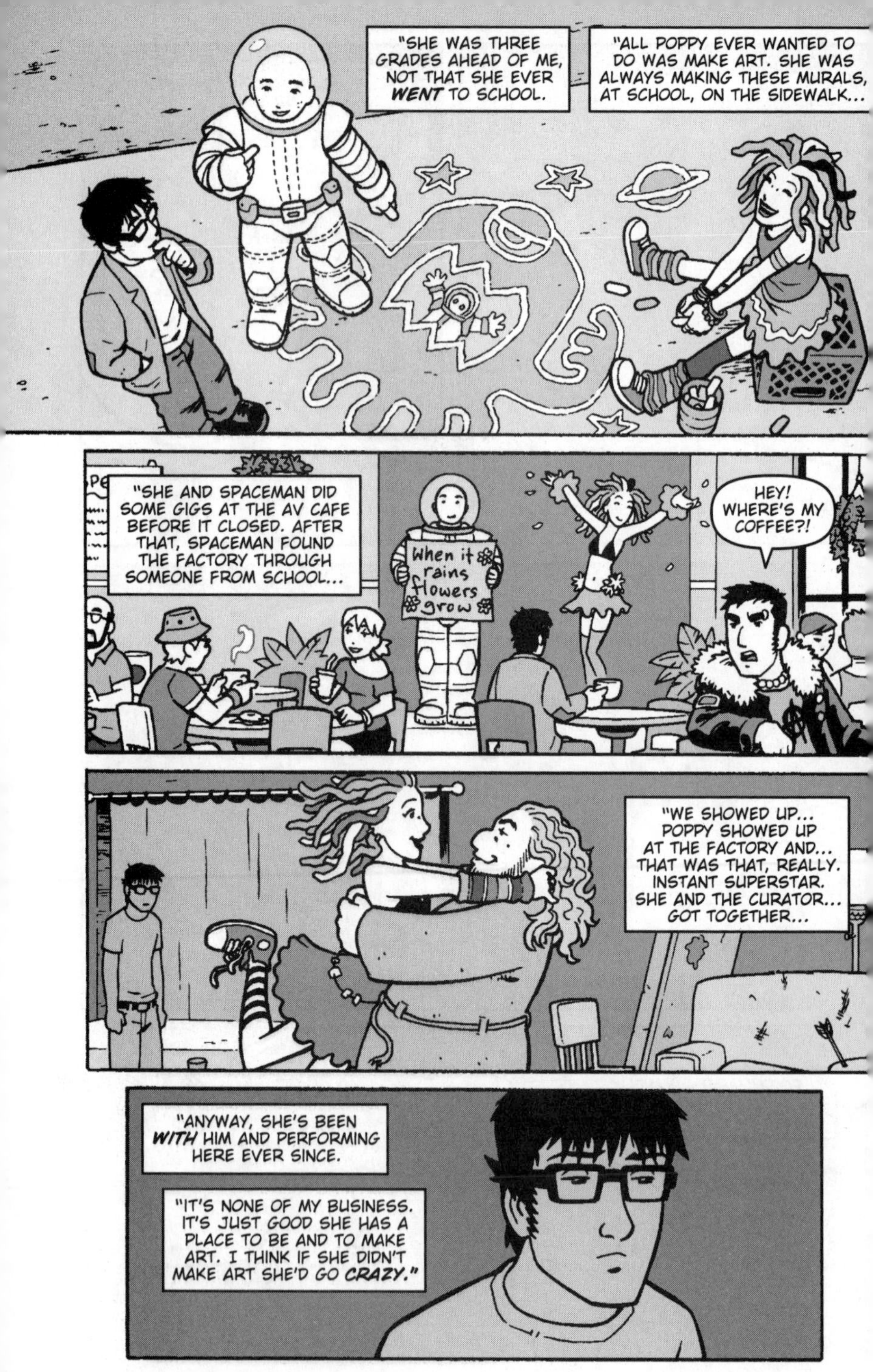
"SHE WAS THREE GRADES AHEAD OF ME, NOT THAT SHE EVER *WENT* TO SCHOOL.
"ALL POPPY EVER WANTED TO DO WAS MAKE ART. SHE WAS ALWAYS MAKING THESE MURALS, AT SCHOOL, ON THE SIDEWALK...
"SHE AND SPACEMAN DID SOME GIGS AT THE AV CAFE BEFORE IT CLOSED. AFTER THAT, SPACEMAN FOUND THE FACTORY THROUGH SOMEONE FROM SCHOOL...
When it rains flowers grow
HEY! WHERE'S MY COFFEE?!
"WE SHOWED UP... POPPY SHOWED UP AT THE FACTORY AND... THAT WAS THAT, REALLY. INSTANT SUPERSTAR. SHE AND THE CURATOR... GOT TOGETHER...
"ANYWAY, SHE'S BEEN *WITH* HIM AND PERFORMING HERE EVER SINCE.
"IT'S NONE OF MY BUSINESS. IT'S JUST GOOD SHE HAS A PLACE TO BE AND TO MAKE ART. I THINK IF SHE DIDN'T MAKE ART SHE'D GO *CRAZY*."

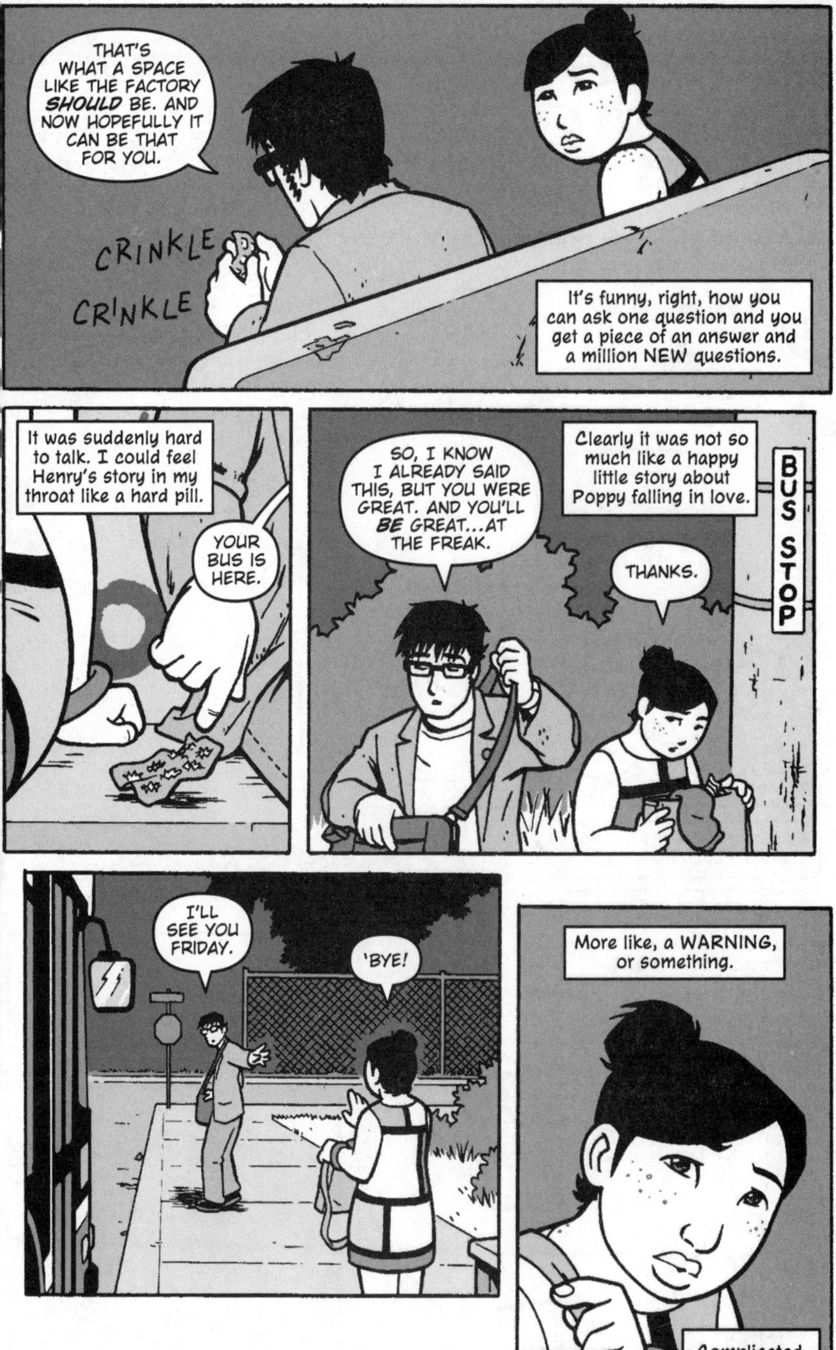
THAT'S WHAT A SPACE LIKE THE FACTORY *SHOULD* BE. AND NOW HOPEFULLY IT CAN BE THAT FOR YOU.
CRINKLE
CRINKLE
It's funny, right, how you can ask one question and you get a piece of an answer and a million NEW questions.
It was suddenly hard to talk. I could feel Henry's story in my throat like a hard pill.
YOUR BUS IS HERE.
SO, I KNOW I ALREADY SAID THIS, BUT YOU WERE GREAT. AND YOU'LL *BE* GREAT...AT THE FREAK.
Clearly it was not so much like a happy little story about Poppy falling in love.
BUS STOP
THANKS.
I'LL SEE YOU FRIDAY.
'BYE!
More like, a WARNING, or something.
Complicated.

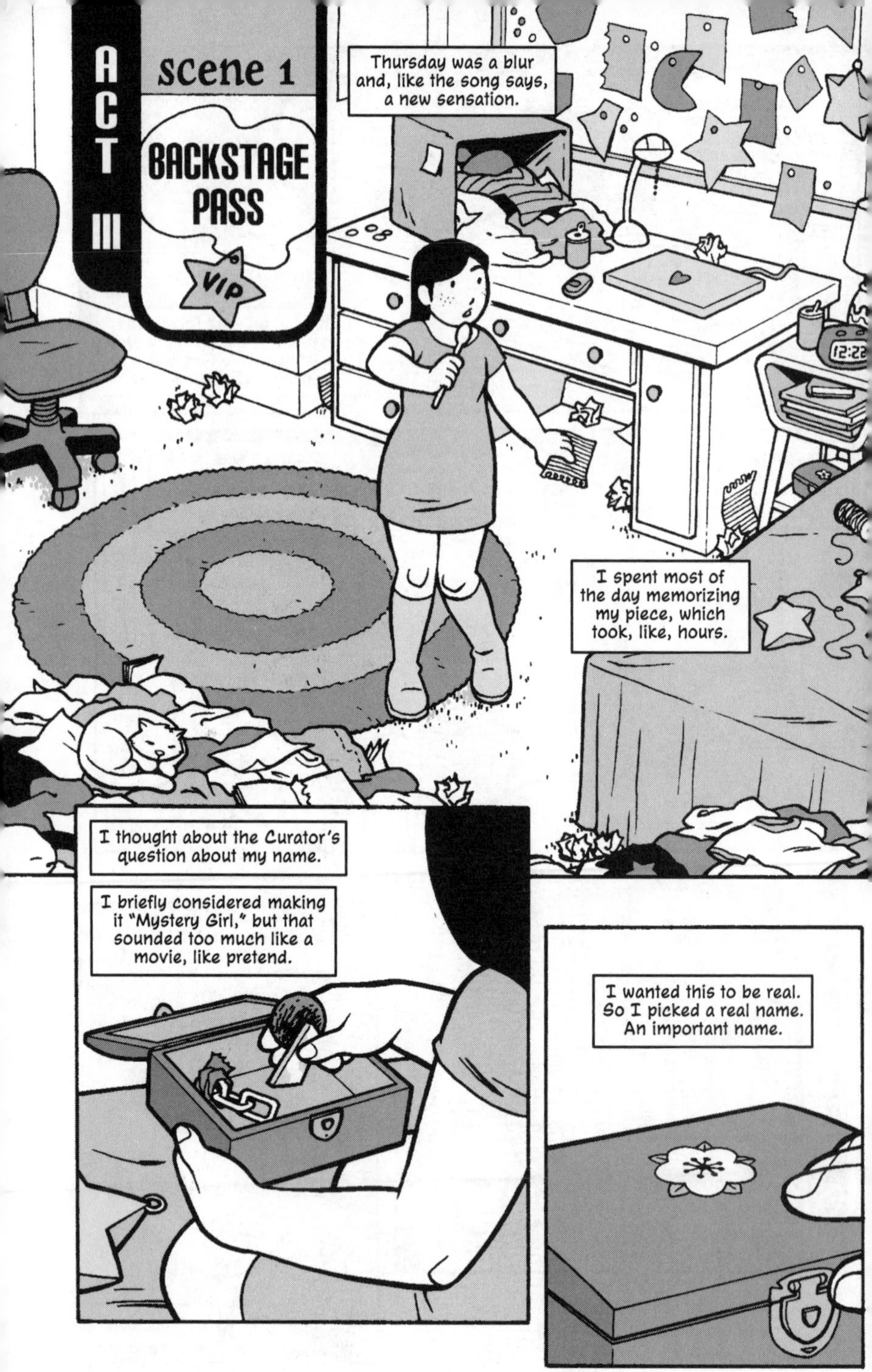
ACT III
scene 1
BACKSTAGE PASS
VIP
Thursday was a blur and, like the song says, a new sensation.
12:22
I spent most of the day memorizing my piece, which took, like, hours.
I thought about the Curator's question about my name.
I briefly considered making it "Mystery Girl," but that sounded too much like a movie, like pretend.
I wanted this to be real. So I picked a real name. An important name.

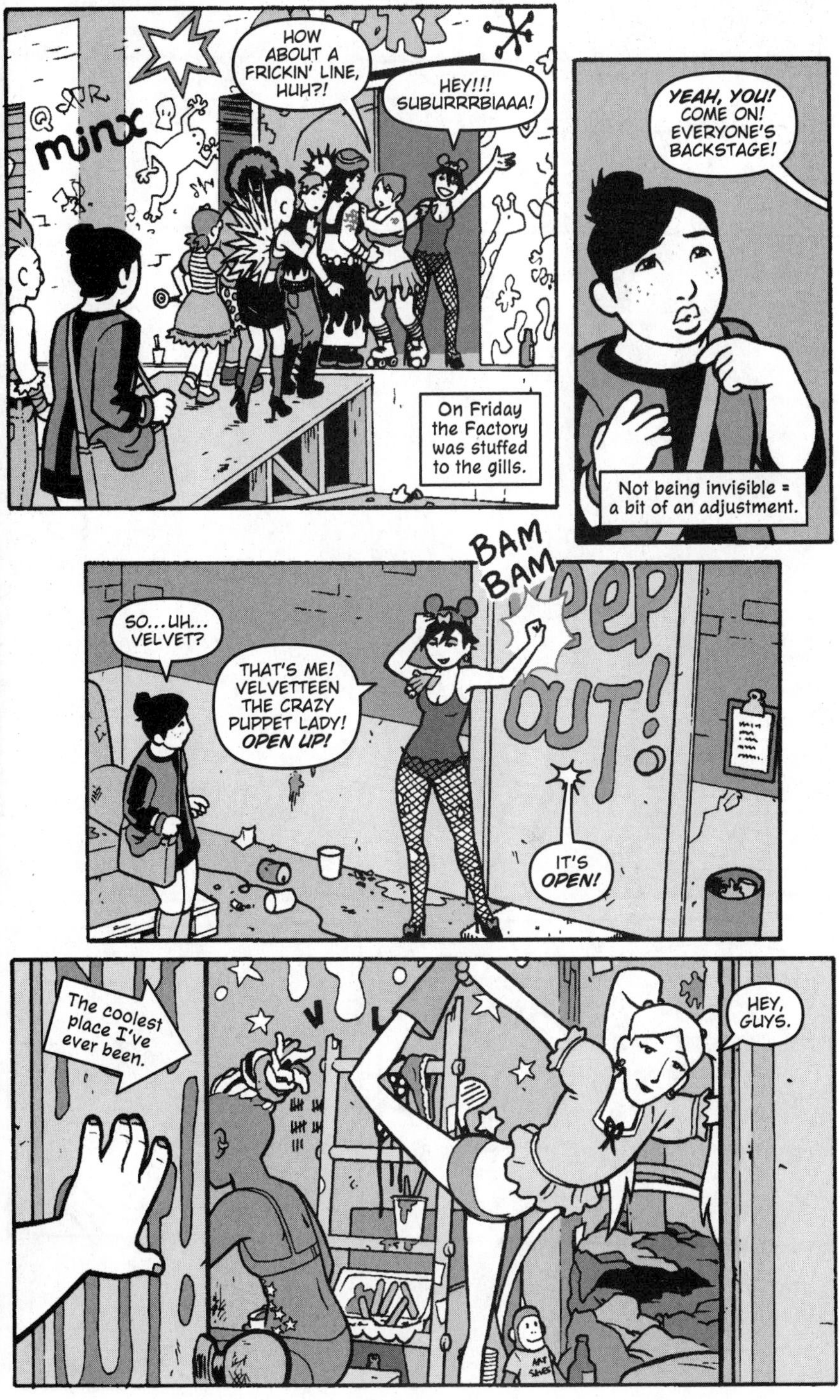
HOW ABOUT A FRICKIN' LINE, HUH?!
HEY!!! SUBURRRBIAAA!
minx
On Friday the Factory was stuffed to the gills.
YEAH, YOU! COME ON! EVERYONE'S BACKSTAGE!
Not being invisible = a bit of an adjustment.
BAM BAM
SO...UH... VELVET?
THAT'S ME! VELVETTEEN THE CRAZY PUPPET LADY! OPEN UP!
IT'S OPEN!
The coolest place I've ever been.
HEY, GUYS.

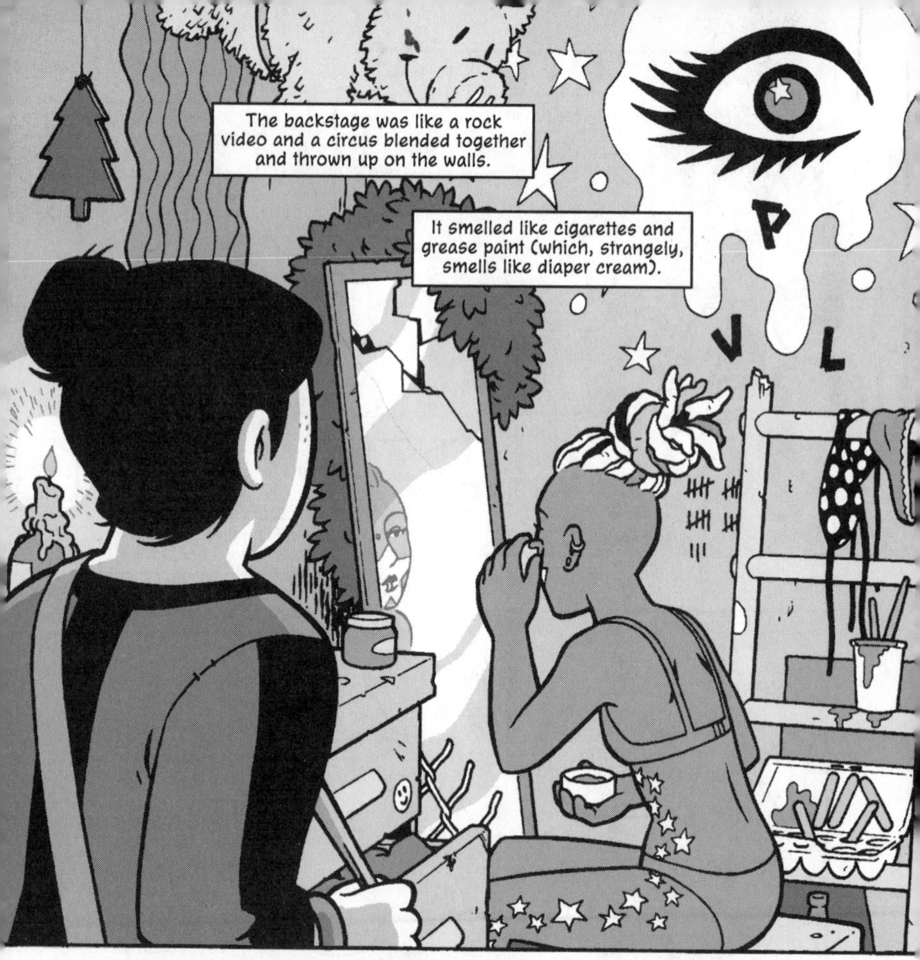
The backstage was like a rock video and a circus blended together and thrown up on the walls.
It smelled like cigarettes and grease paint (which, strangely, smells like diaper cream).
VPL

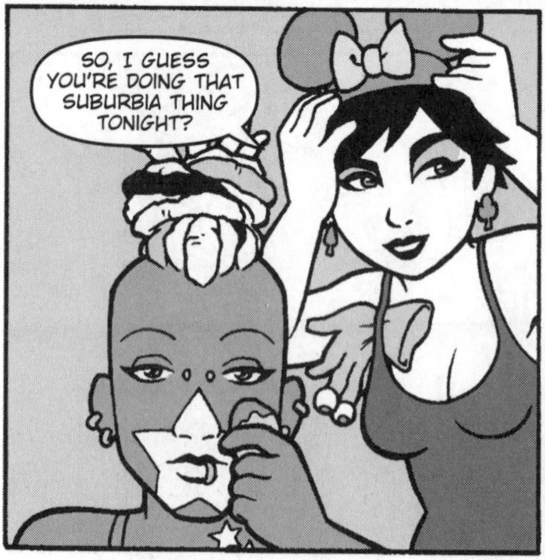
SO, I GUESS YOU'RE DOING THAT SUBURBIA THING TONIGHT?

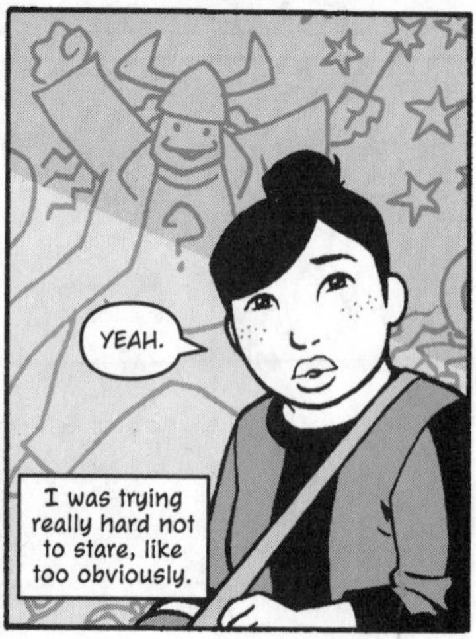
YEAH.
I was trying really hard not to stare, like too obviously.

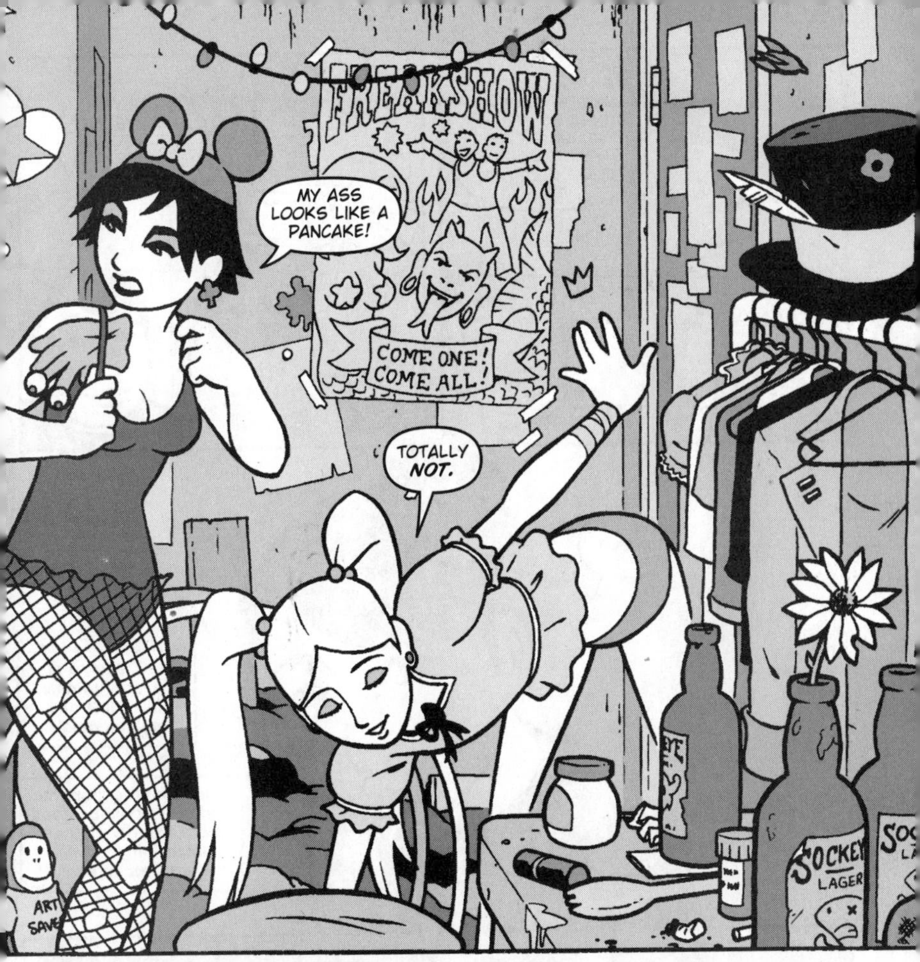
FREAKSHOW
MY ASS LOOKS LIKE A PANCAKE!
COME ONE! COME ALL!
TOTALLY NOT.
SOCKEYE LAGER
ART SAVE

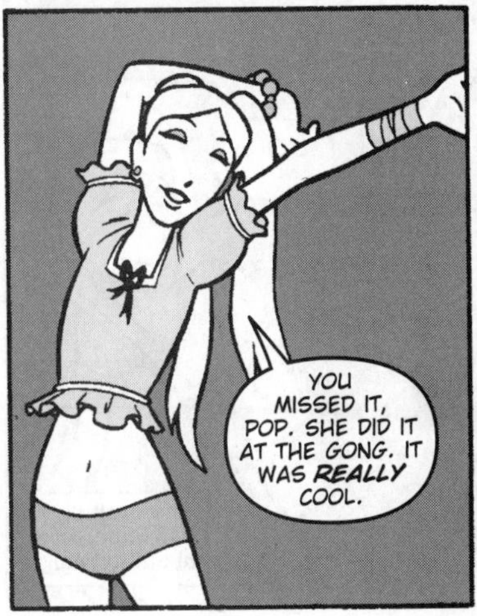
YOU MISSED IT, POP. SHE DID IT AT THE GONG. IT WAS REALLY COOL.

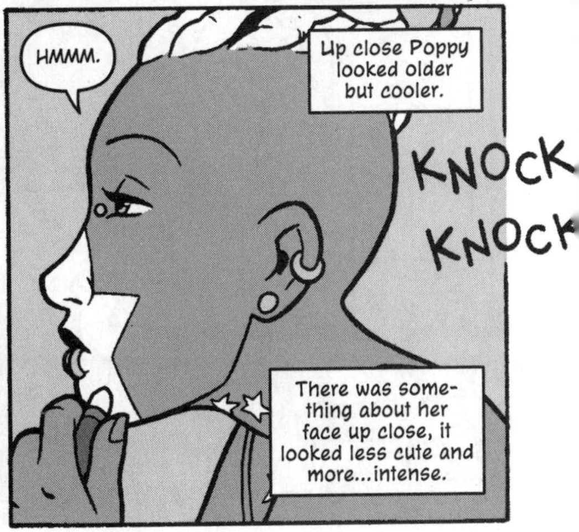
HMMM.
Up close Poppy looked older but cooler.
KNOCK
KNOCK
There was some-thing about her face up close, it looked less cute and more...intense.

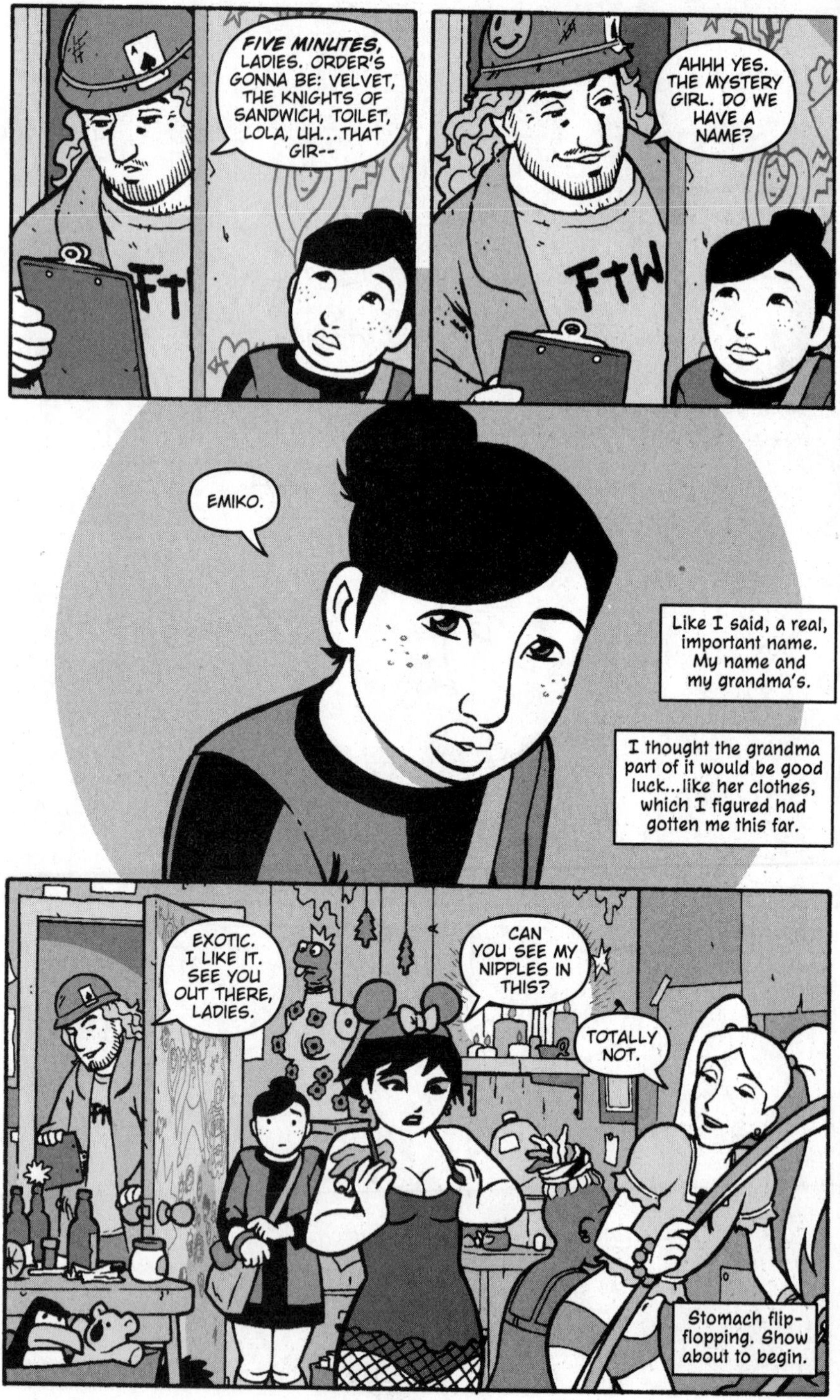
FIVE MINUTES, LADIES. ORDER'S GONNA BE: VELVET, THE KNIGHTS OF SANDWICH, TOILET, LOLA, UH...THAT GIR--
AHHH YES. THE MYSTERY GIRL. DO WE HAVE A NAME?
EMIKO.
Like I said, a real, important name. My name and my grandma's.
I thought the grandma part of it would be good luck...like her clothes, which I figured had gotten me this far.
EXOTIC. I LIKE IT. SEE YOU OUT THERE, LADIES.
CAN YOU SEE MY NIPPLES IN THIS?
TOTALLY NOT.
Stomach flip-flopping. Show about to begin.

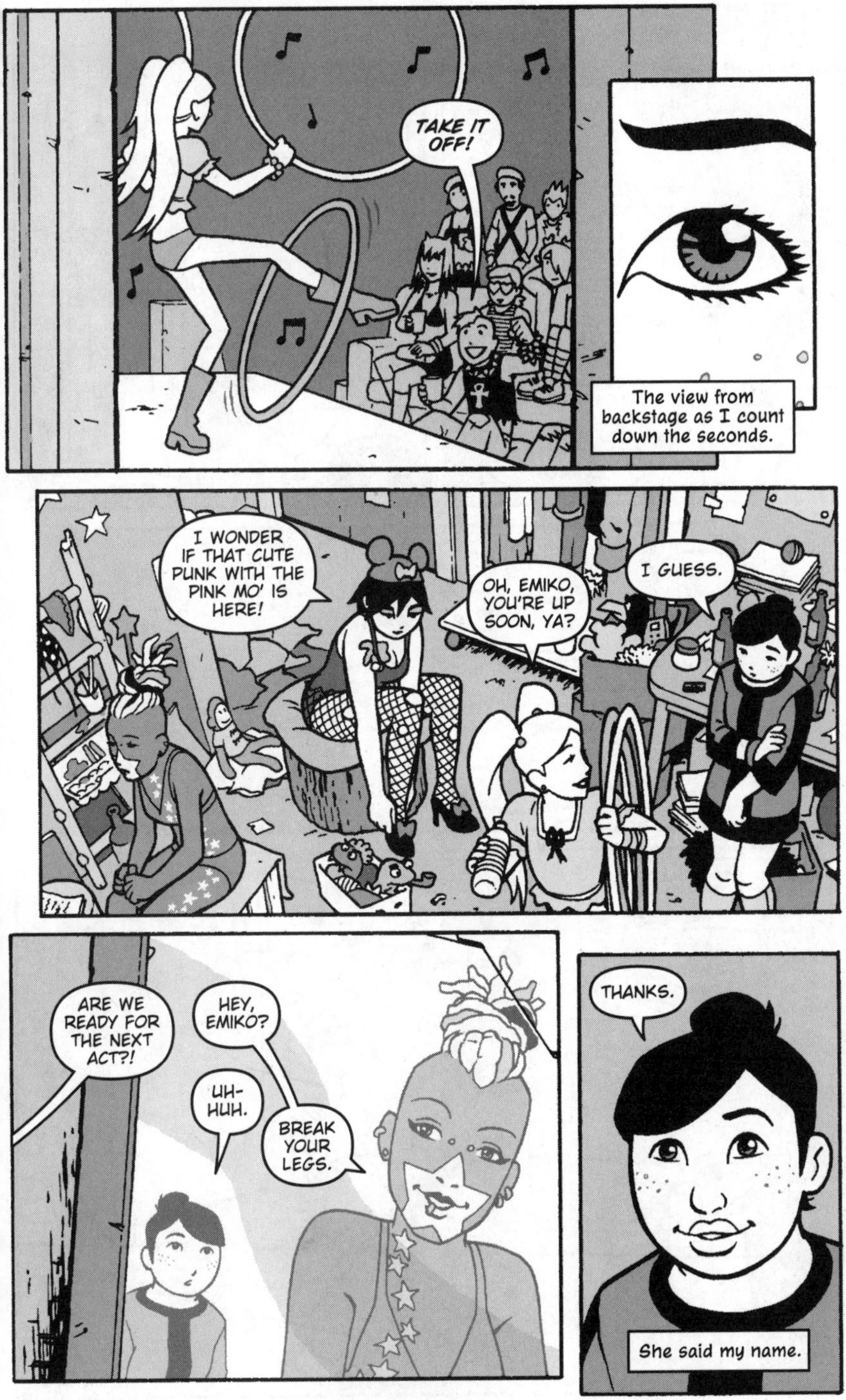
TAKE IT OFF!
The view from backstage as I count down the seconds.
I WONDER IF THAT CUTE PUNK WITH THE PINK MO' IS HERE!
OH, EMIKO, YOU'RE UP SOON, YA?
I GUESS.
ARE WE READY FOR THE NEXT ACT?!
HEY, EMIKO?
UH-HUH.
BREAK YOUR LEGS.
THANKS.
She said my name.

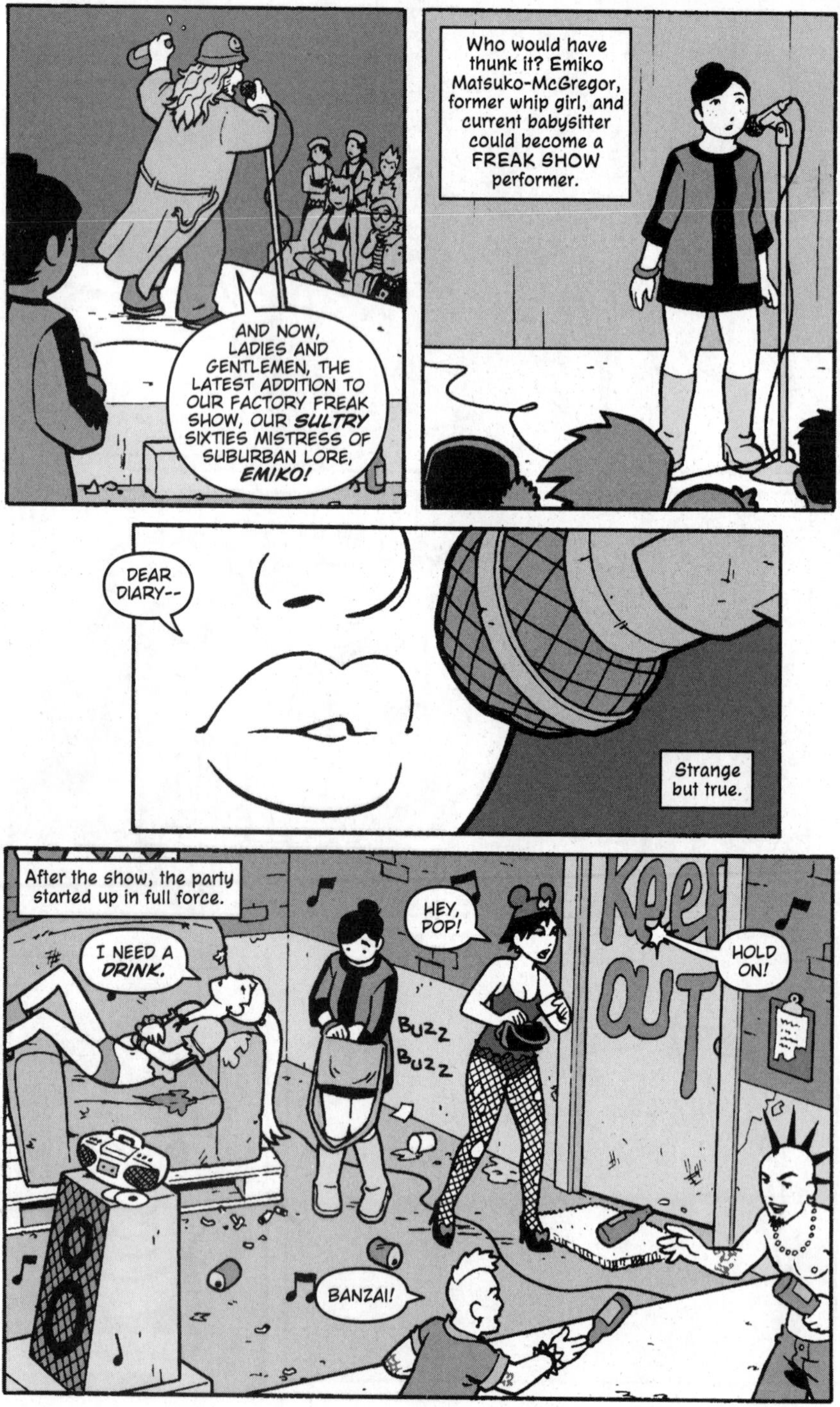
Who would have thunk it? Emiko Matsuko-McGregor, former whip girl, and current babysitter could become a FREAK SHOW performer.
AND NOW, LADIES AND GENTLEMEN, THE LATEST ADDITION TO OUR FACTORY FREAK SHOW, OUR SULTRY SIXTIES MISTRESS OF SUBURBAN LORE, EMIKO!
DEAR DIARY--
Strange but true.
After the show, the party started up in full force.
I NEED A DRINK.
HEY, POP!
HOLD ON!
BUZZ
BUZZ
BANZAI!

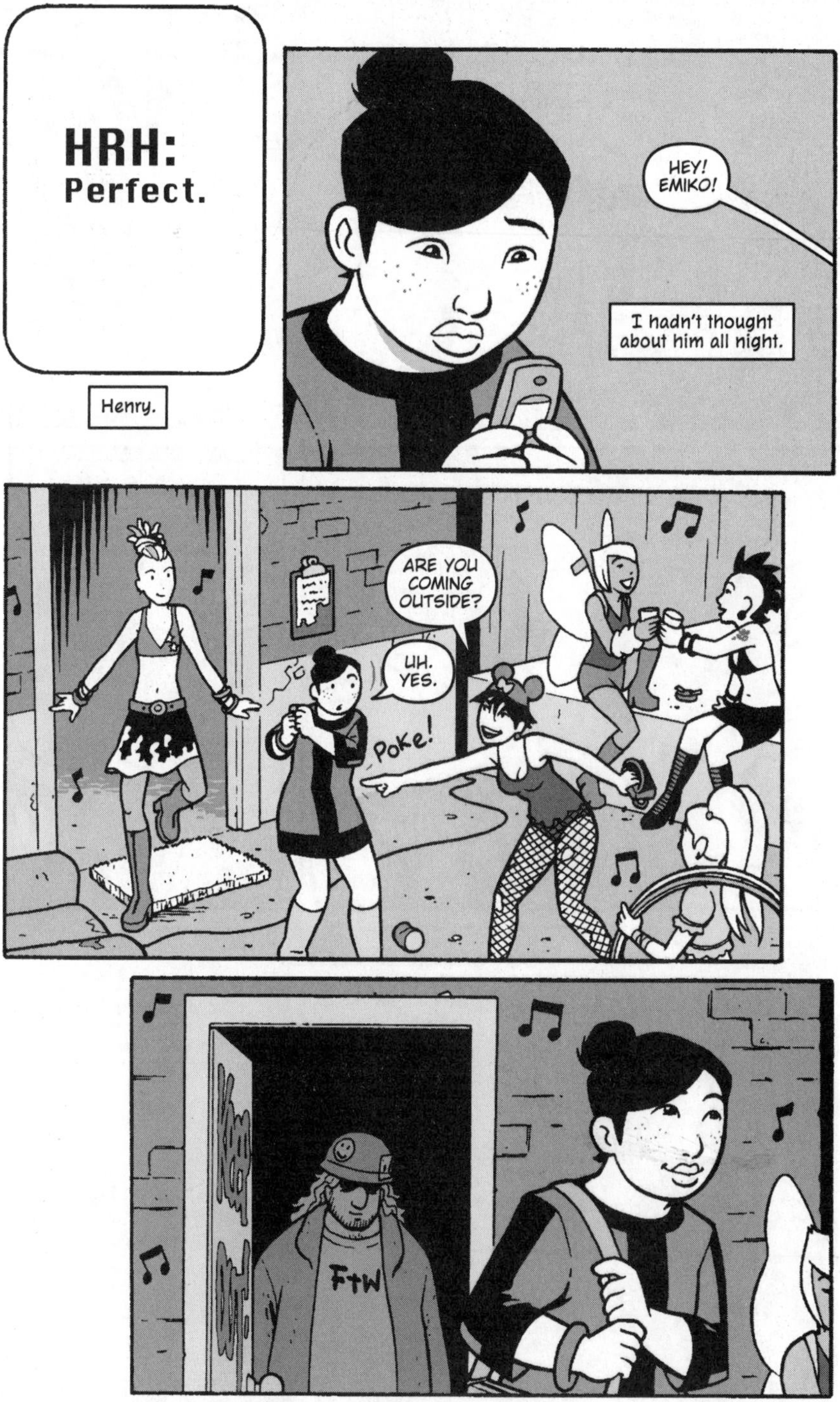

HRH:
Perfect.
Henry.
HEY! EMIKO!
I hadn't thought about him all night.
ARE YOU COMING OUTSIDE?
UH. YES.
Poke!
FTW

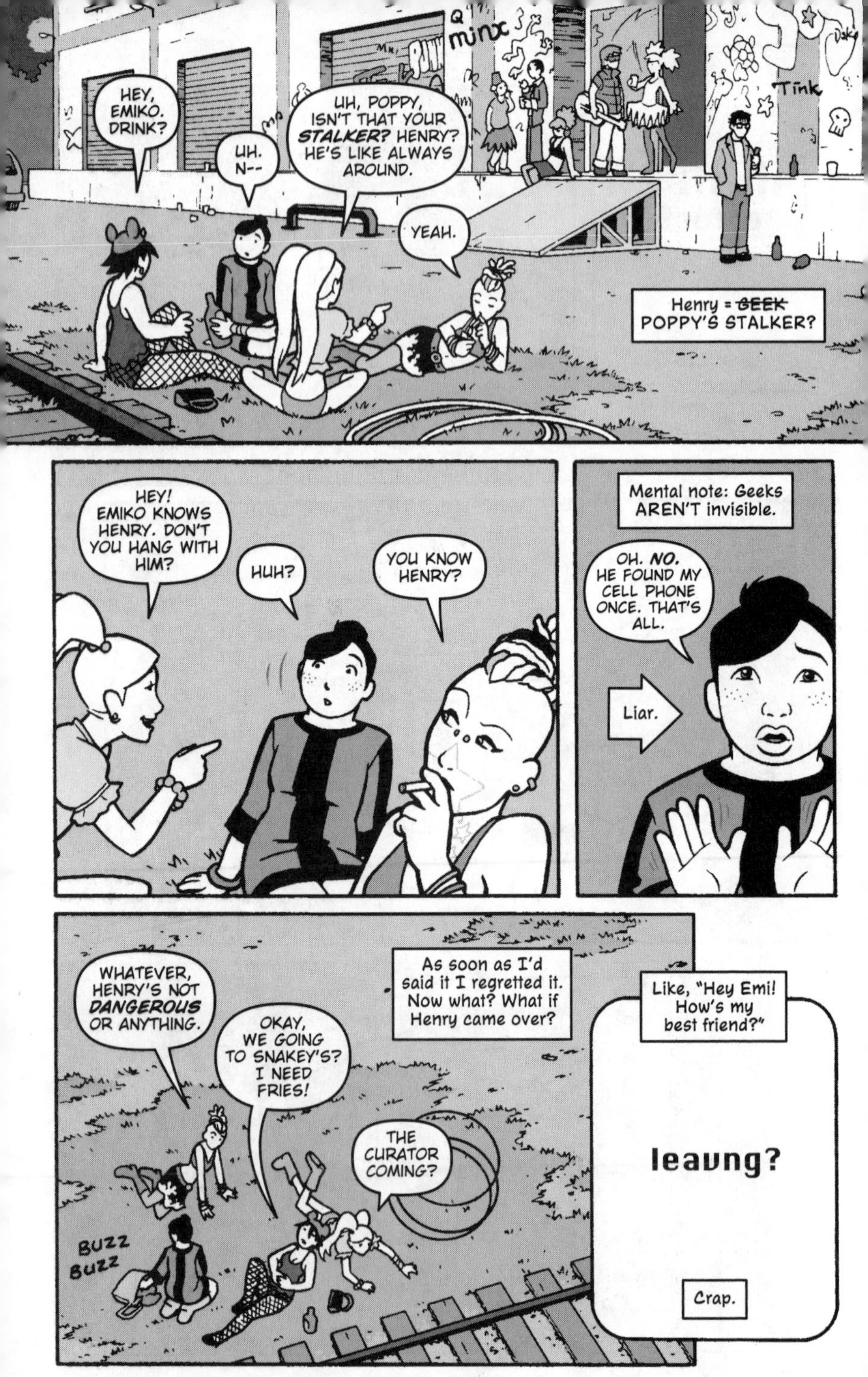

HEY, EMIKO. DRINK?
UH. N--
UH, POPPY, ISN'T THAT YOUR STALKER? HENRY? HE'S LIKE ALWAYS AROUND.
YEAH.
Henry = ~~GEEK~~ POPPY'S STALKER?
HEY! EMIKO KNOWS HENRY. DON'T YOU HANG WITH HIM?
HUH?
YOU KNOW HENRY?
Mental note: Geeks AREN'T invisible.
OH. NO. HE FOUND MY CELL PHONE ONCE. THAT'S ALL.
Liar.
WHATEVER, HENRY'S NOT DANGEROUS OR ANYTHING.
OKAY, WE GOING TO SNAKEY'S? I NEED FRIES!
As soon as I'd said it I regretted it. Now what? What if Henry came over?
Like, "Hey Emi! How's my best friend?"
THE CURATOR COMING?
BUZZ BUZZ
leavng?
Crap.

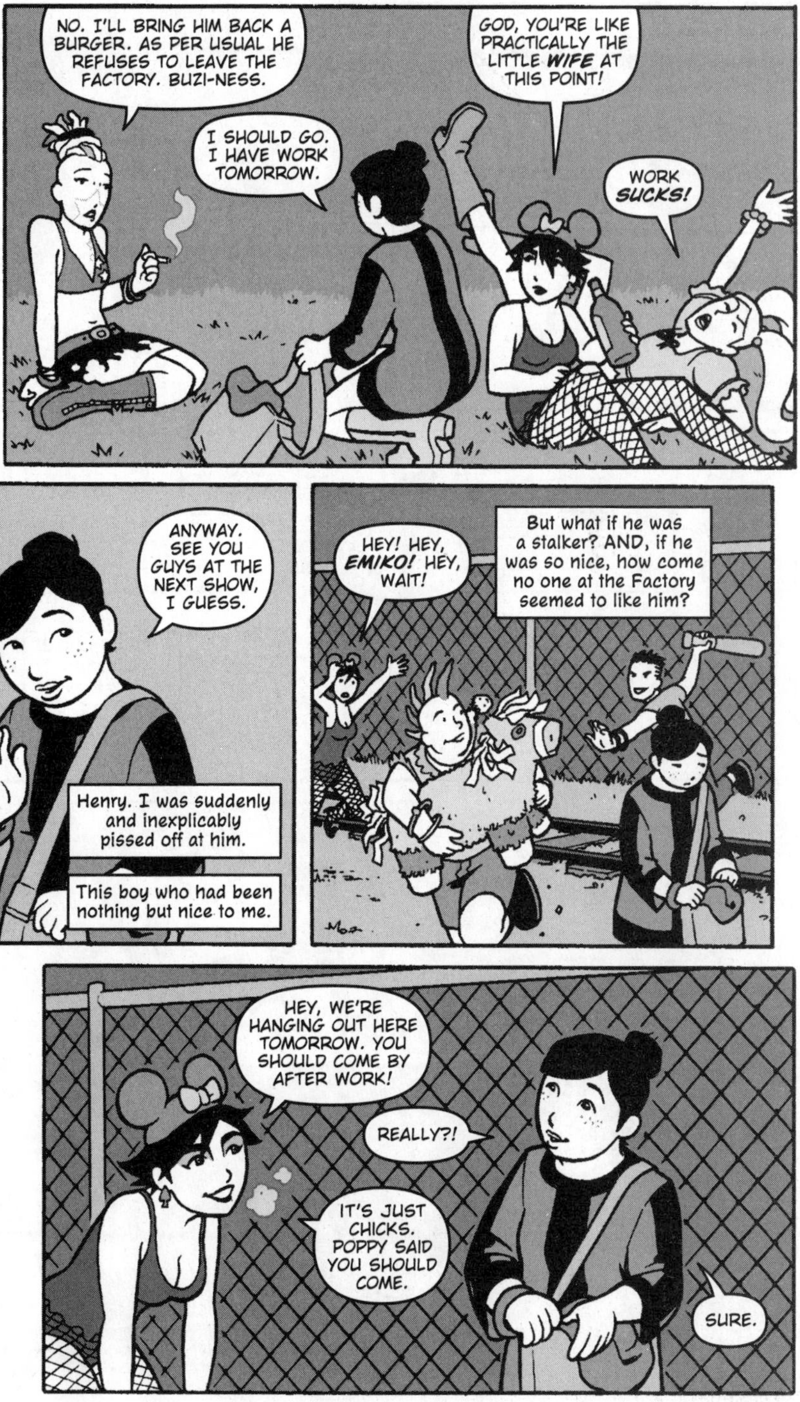
NO. I'LL BRING HIM BACK A BURGER. AS PER USUAL HE REFUSES TO LEAVE THE FACTORY. BUZI-NESS.
I SHOULD GO. I HAVE WORK TOMORROW.
GOD, YOU'RE LIKE PRACTICALLY THE LITTLE WIFE AT THIS POINT!
WORK SUCKS!
ANYWAY. SEE YOU GUYS AT THE NEXT SHOW, I GUESS.
Henry. I was suddenly and inexplicably pissed off at him.
This boy who had been nothing but nice to me.
HEY! HEY, EMIKO! HEY, WAIT!
But what if he was a stalker? AND, if he was so nice, how come no one at the Factory seemed to like him?
HEY, WE'RE HANGING OUT HERE TOMORROW. YOU SHOULD COME BY AFTER WORK!
REALLY?!
IT'S JUST CHICKS. POPPY SAID YOU SHOULD COME.
SURE.

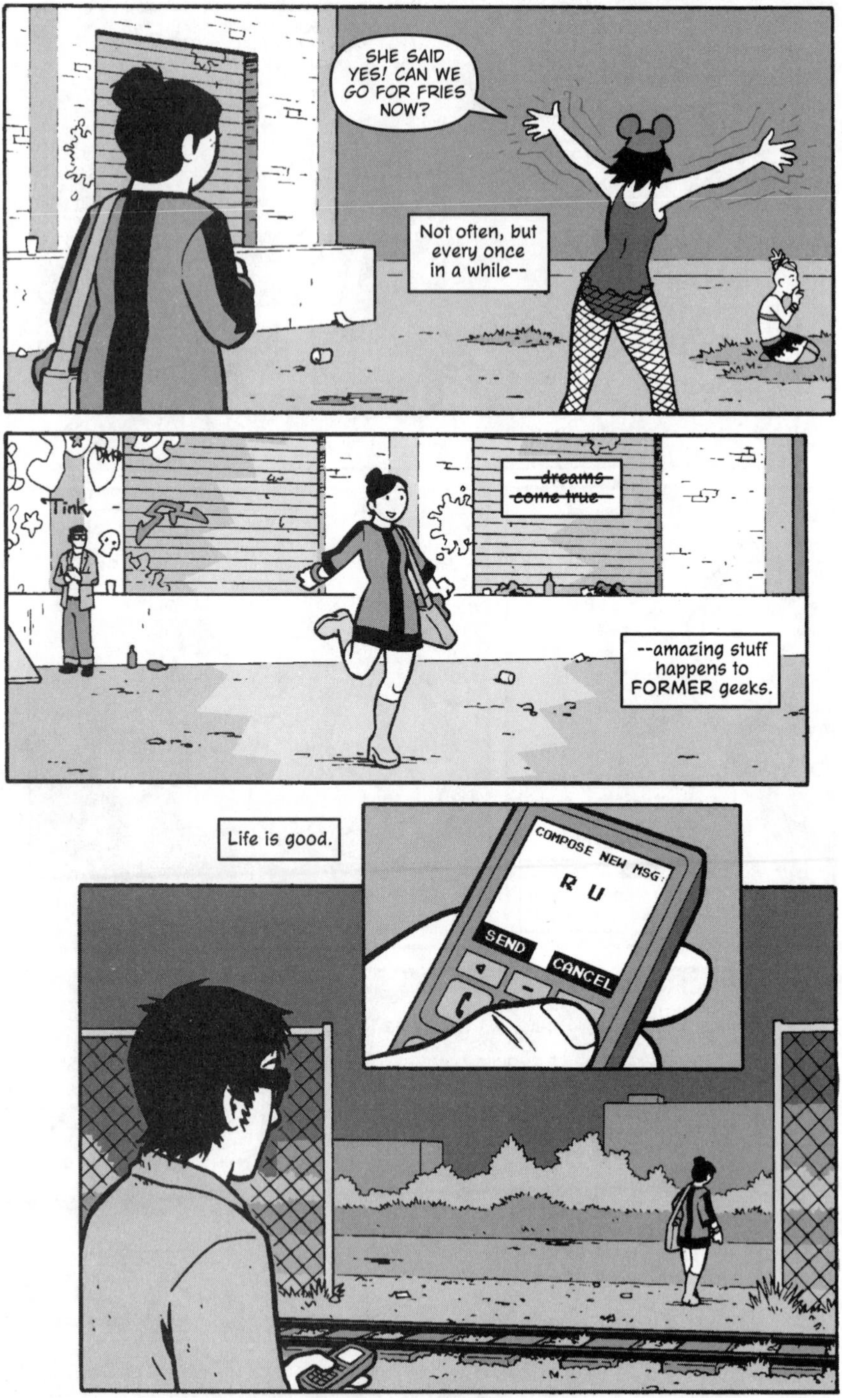
SHE SAID YES! CAN WE GO FOR FRIES NOW?
Not often, but every once in a while--
Tink
~~dreams come true~~
--amazing stuff happens to FORMER geeks.
Life is good.
COMPOSE NEW MSG:
R U
SEND
CANCEL

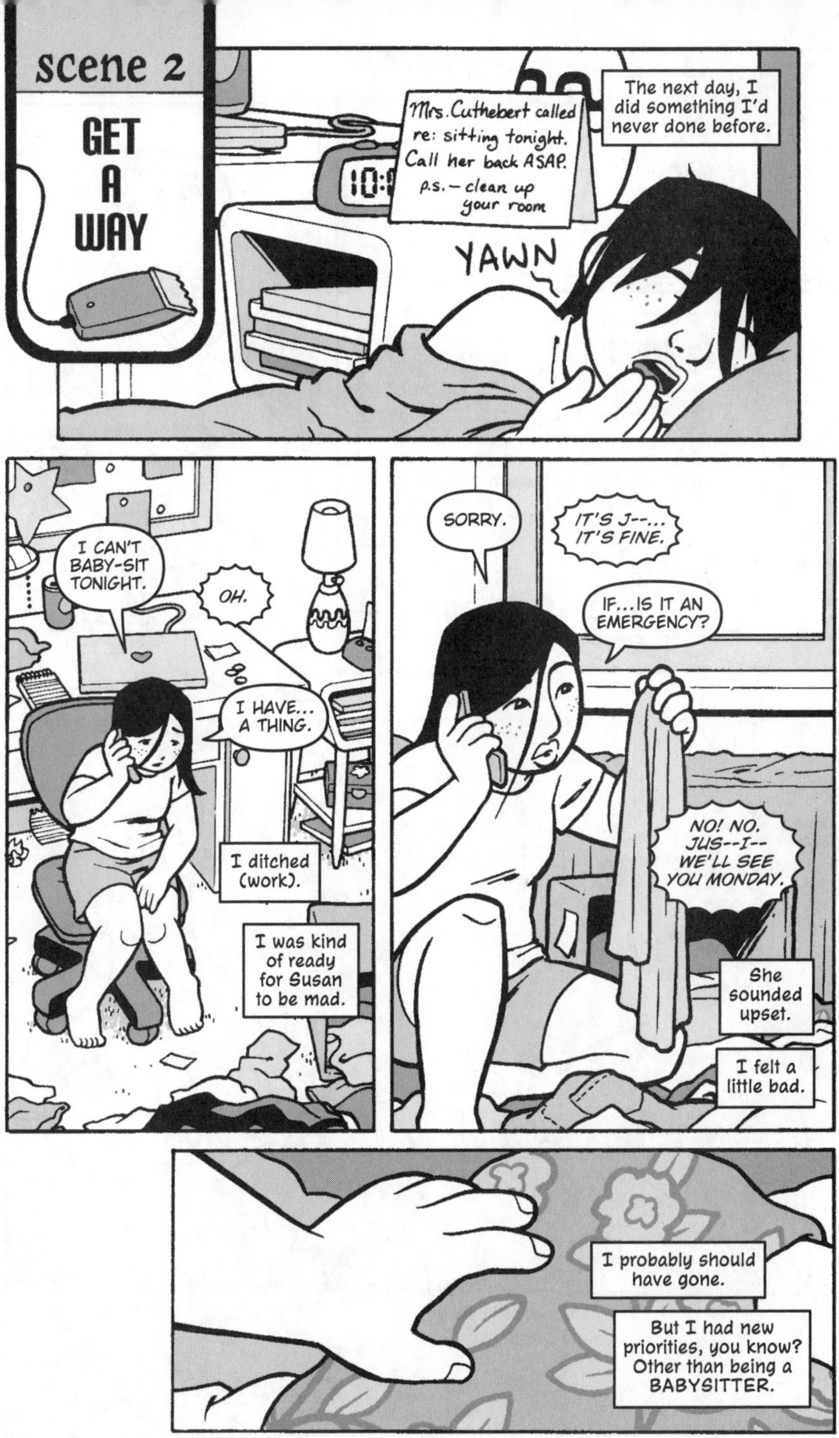
scene 2
GET A WAY
Mrs. Cuthebert called re: sitting tonight. Call her back ASAP. p.s. — clean up your room
10:
The next day, I did something I'd never done before.
YAWN
I CAN'T BABY-SIT TONIGHT.
OH.
I HAVE... A THING.
I ditched (work).
I was kind of ready for Susan to be mad.
SORRY.
IT'S J--... IT'S FINE.
IF...IS IT AN EMERGENCY?
NO! NO. JUS--I-- WE'LL SEE YOU MONDAY.
She sounded upset.
I felt a little bad.
I probably should have gone.
But I had new priorities, you know? Other than being a BABYSITTER.

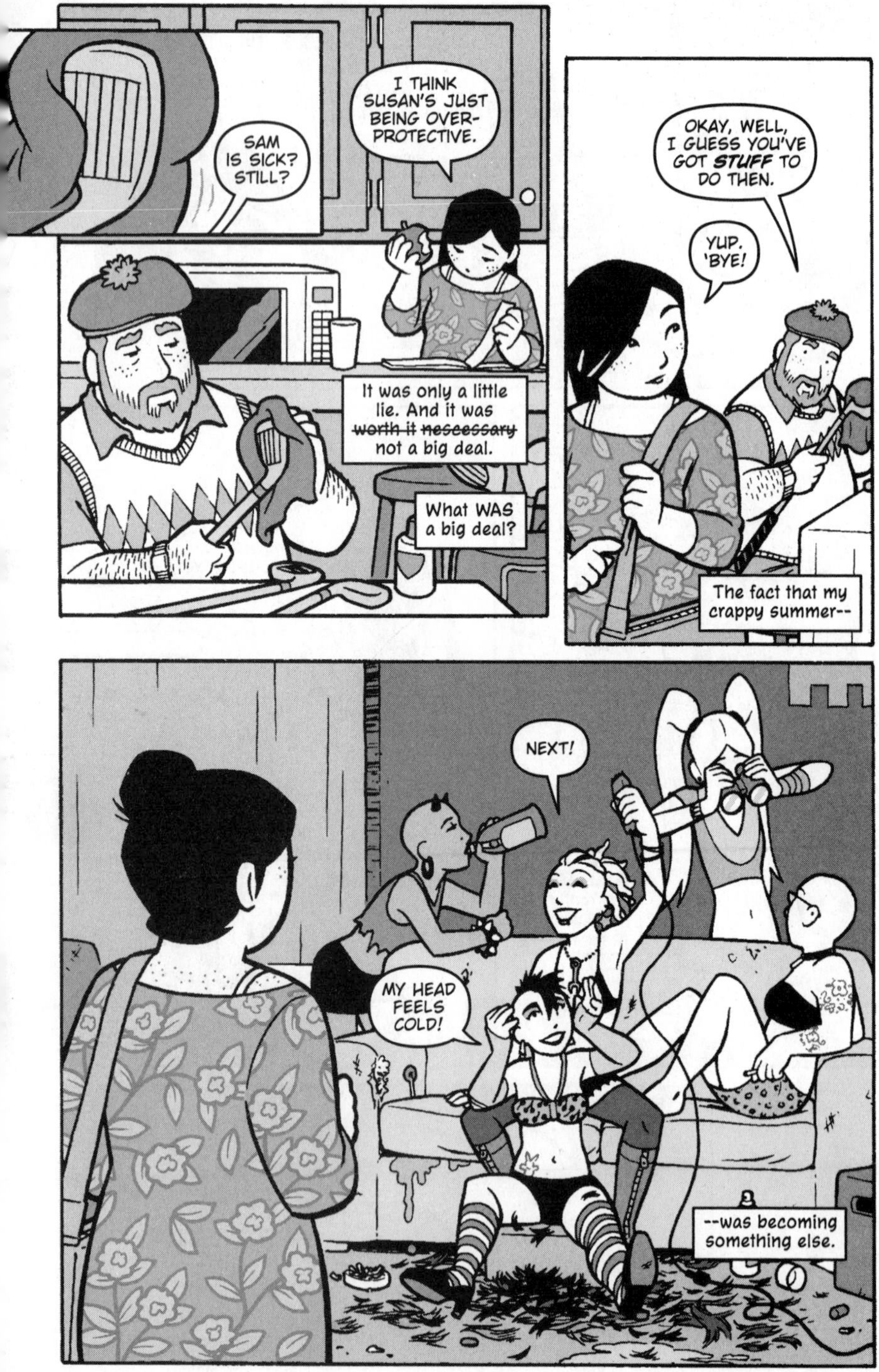
SAM IS SICK? STILL?
I THINK SUSAN'S JUST BEING OVER-PROTECTIVE.
It was only a little lie. And it was ~~worth it~~ ~~neseessary~~ not a big deal.
What WAS a big deal?
OKAY, WELL, I GUESS YOU'VE GOT **STUFF** TO DO THEN.
YUP. 'BYE!
The fact that my crappy summer--
NEXT!
MY HEAD FEELS COLD!
--was becoming something else.

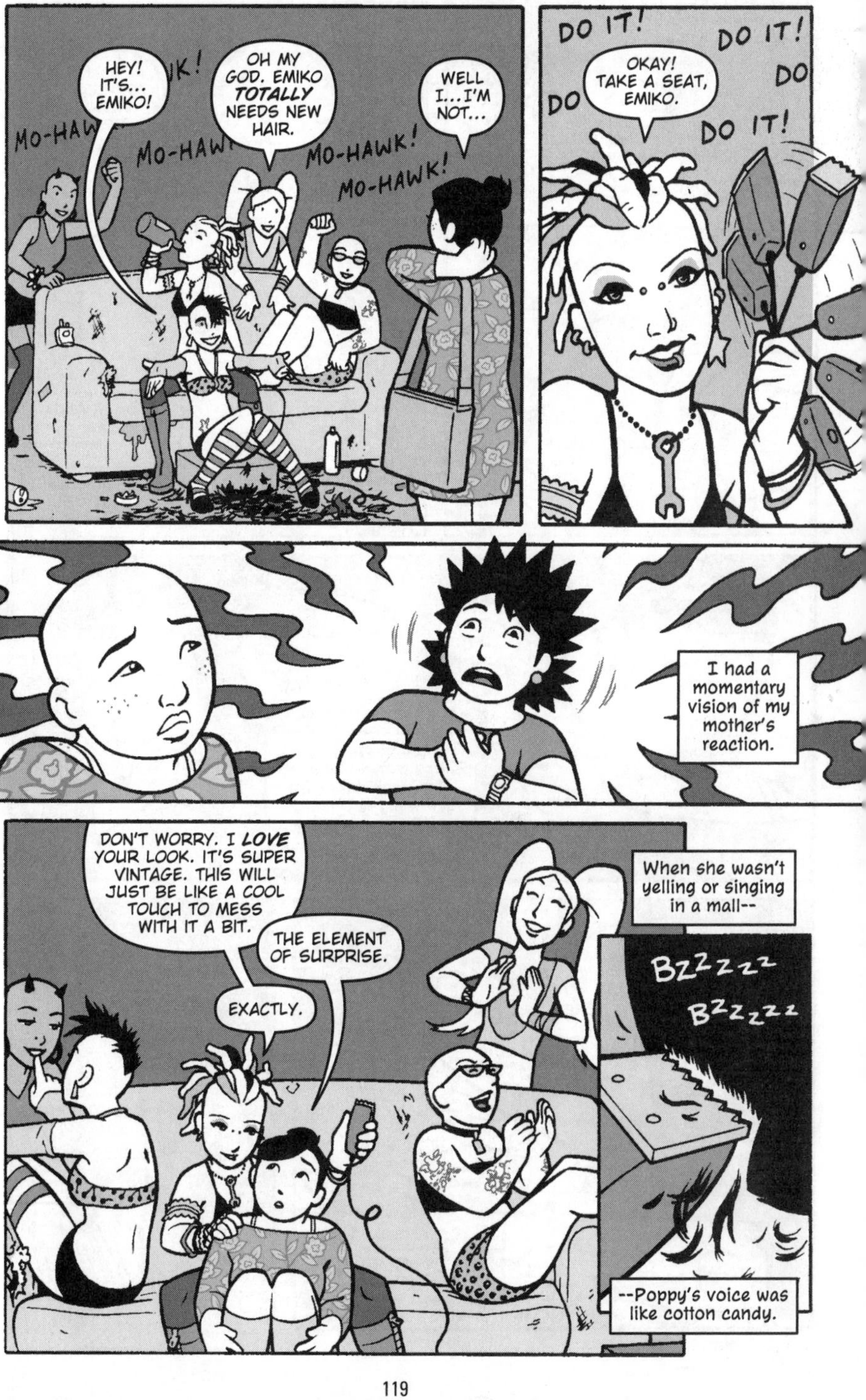
MO-HAWK!
MO-HAWK!
MO-HAWK!
MO-HAWK!
HEY! IT'S... EMIKO!
OH MY GOD. EMIKO **TOTALLY** NEEDS NEW HAIR.
WELL I...I'M NOT...
DO IT!
DO IT!
DO
DO
DO IT!
OKAY! TAKE A SEAT, EMIKO.
I had a momentary vision of my mother's reaction.
DON'T WORRY. I **LOVE** YOUR LOOK. IT'S SUPER VINTAGE. THIS WILL JUST BE LIKE A COOL TOUCH TO MESS WITH IT A BIT.
THE ELEMENT OF SURPRISE.
EXACTLY.
When she wasn't yelling or singing in a mall--
BZZzzzz
BZZzzzz
--Poppy's voice was like cotton candy.

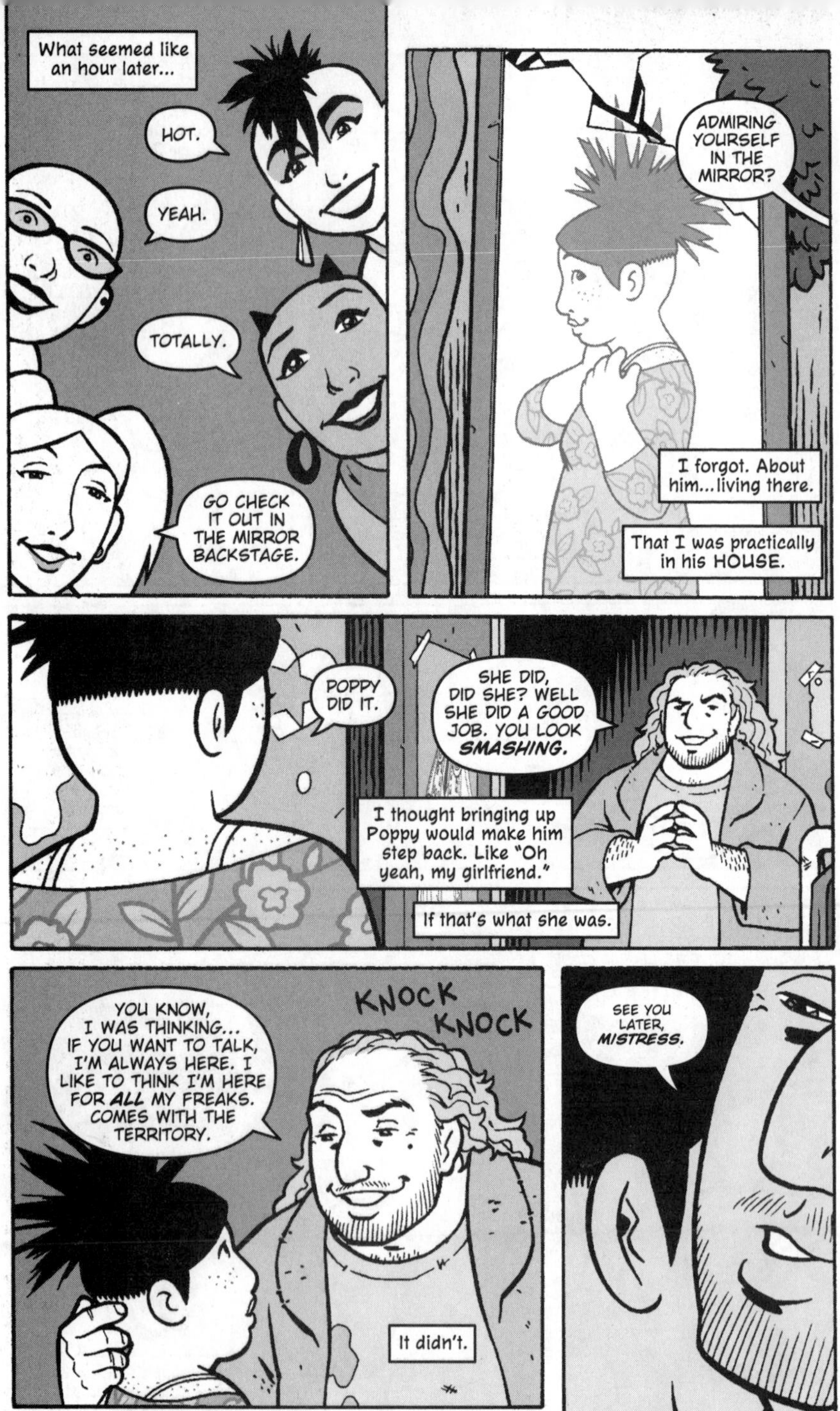
What seemed like an hour later...
HOT.
YEAH.
TOTALLY.
GO CHECK IT OUT IN THE MIRROR BACKSTAGE.
ADMIRING YOURSELF IN THE MIRROR?
I forgot. About him...living there.
That I was practically in his HOUSE.
POPPY DID IT.
SHE DID, DID SHE? WELL SHE DID A GOOD JOB. YOU LOOK SMASHING.
I thought bringing up Poppy would make him step back. Like "Oh yeah, my girlfriend."
If that's what she was.
YOU KNOW, I WAS THINKING... IF YOU WANT TO TALK, I'M ALWAYS HERE. I LIKE TO THINK I'M HERE FOR ALL MY FREAKS. COMES WITH THE TERRITORY.
KNOCK KNOCK
It didn't.
SEE YOU LATER, MISTRESS.

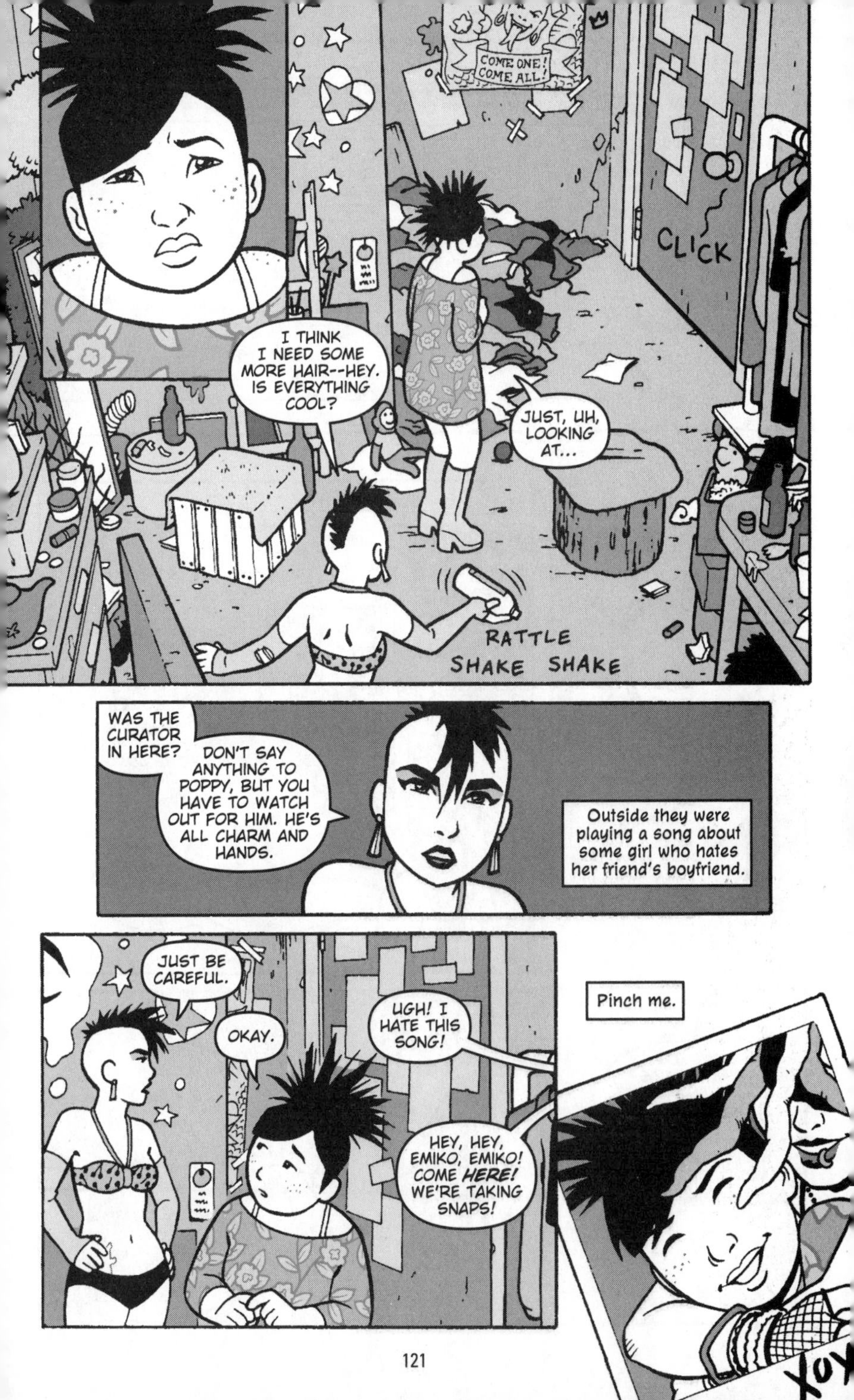
COME ONE! COME ALL!
I THINK I NEED SOME MORE HAIR--HEY. IS EVERYTHING COOL?
JUST, UH, LOOKING AT...
CLICK
RATTLE
SHAKE SHAKE
WAS THE CURATOR IN HERE?
DON'T SAY ANYTHING TO POPPY, BUT YOU HAVE TO WATCH OUT FOR HIM. HE'S ALL CHARM AND HANDS.
Outside they were playing a song about some girl who hates her friend's boyfriend.
JUST BE CAREFUL.
OKAY.
UGH! I HATE THIS SONG!
HEY, HEY, EMIKO, EMIKO! COME *HERE!* WE'RE TAKING SNAPS!
Pinch me.

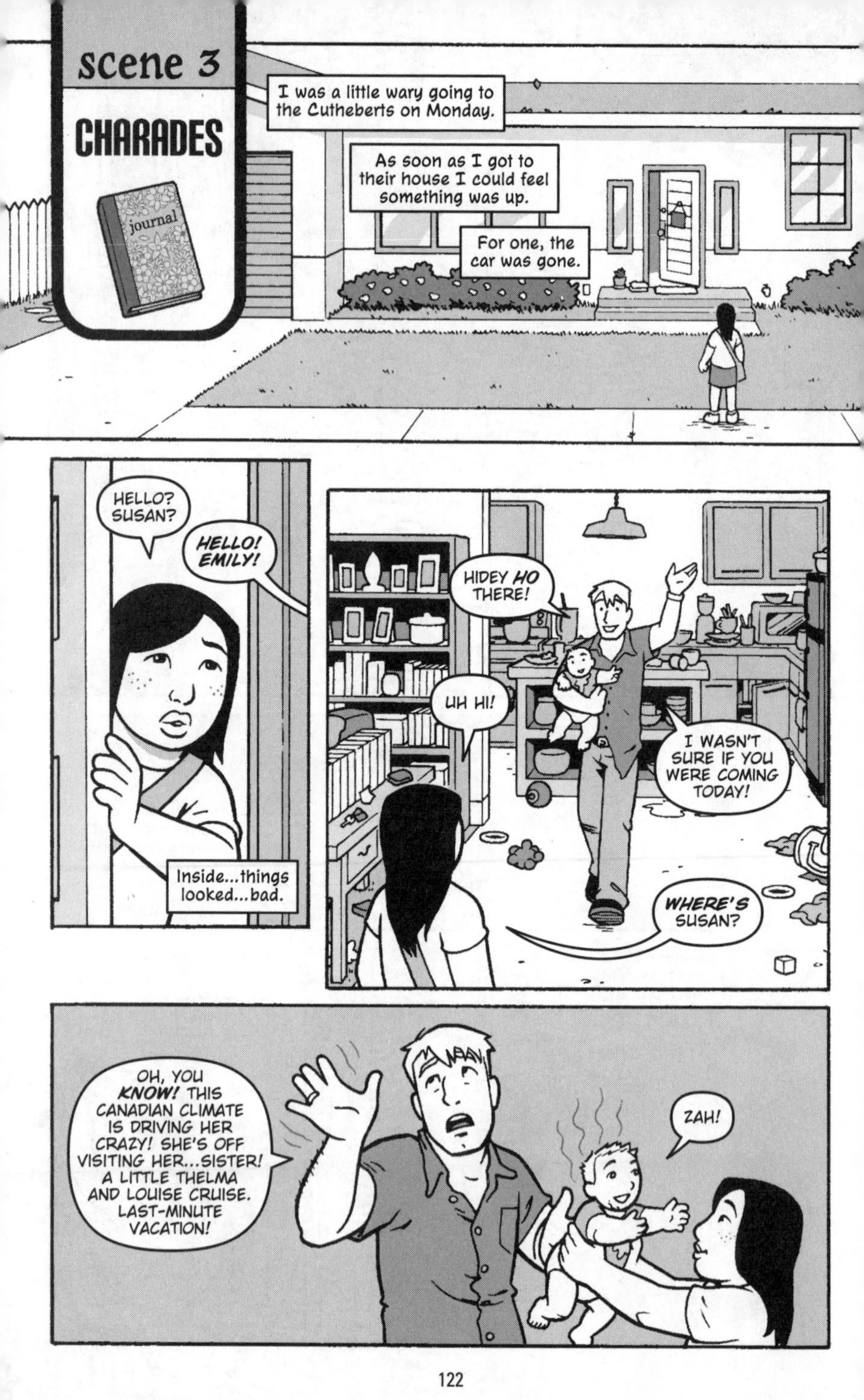
scene 3
CHARADES
journal
I was a little wary going to the Cutheberts on Monday.
As soon as I got to their house I could feel something was up.
For one, the car was gone.
HELLO? SUSAN?
HELLO! EMILY!
Inside...things looked...bad.
HIDEY HO THERE!
UH HI!
I WASN'T SURE IF YOU WERE COMING TODAY!
WHERE'S SUSAN?
OH, YOU KNOW! THIS CANADIAN CLIMATE IS DRIVING HER CRAZY! SHE'S OFF VISITING HER...SISTER! A LITTLE THELMA AND LOUISE CRUISE. LAST-MINUTE VACATION!
ZAH!

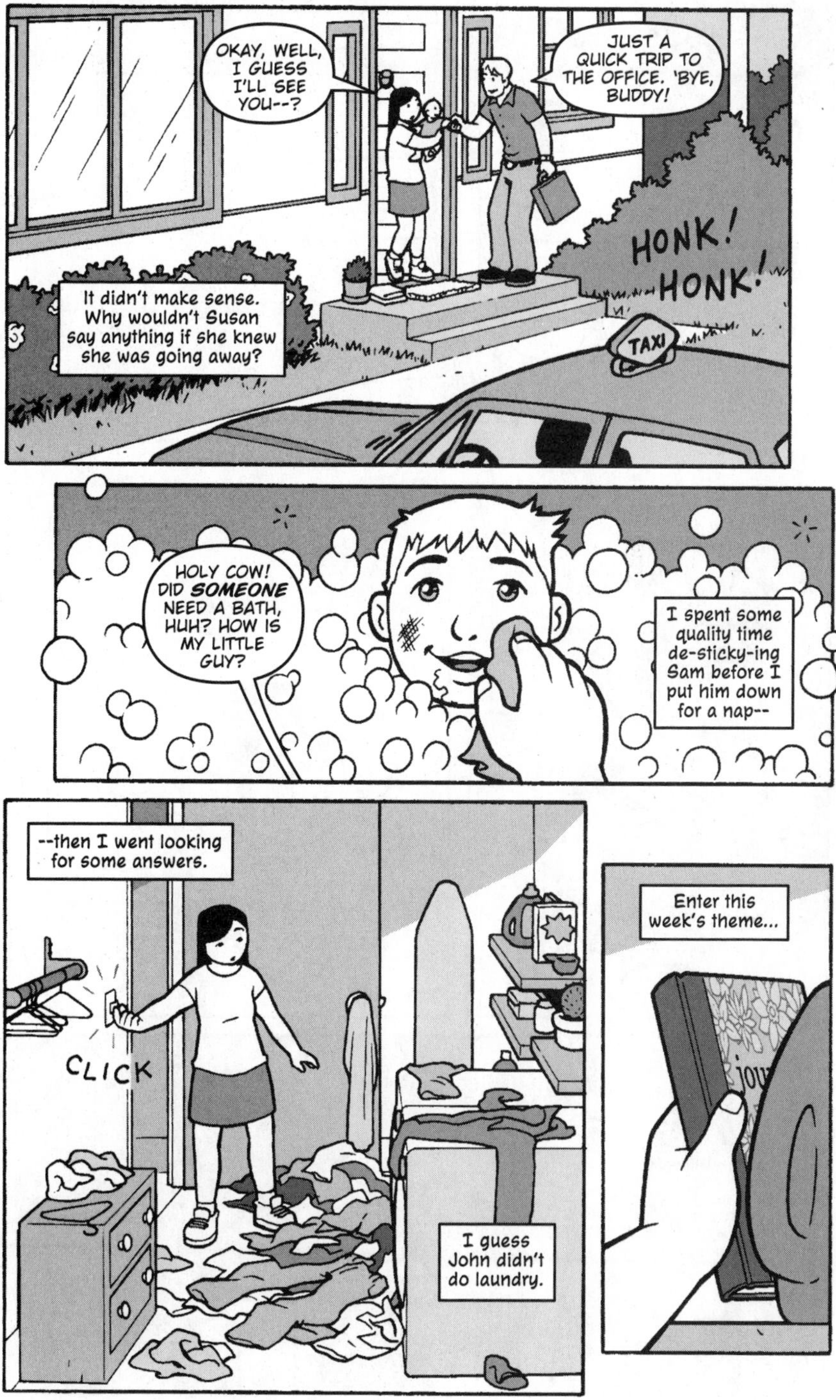
OKAY, WELL, I GUESS I'LL SEE YOU--?
JUST A QUICK TRIP TO THE OFFICE. 'BYE, BUDDY!
HONK! HONK!
TAXI
It didn't make sense. Why wouldn't Susan say anything if she knew she was going away?
HOLY COW! DID SOMEONE NEED A BATH, HUH? HOW IS MY LITTLE GUY?
I spent some quality time de-sticky-ing Sam before I put him down for a nap--
--then I went looking for some answers.
CLICK
I guess John didn't do laundry.
Enter this week's theme...

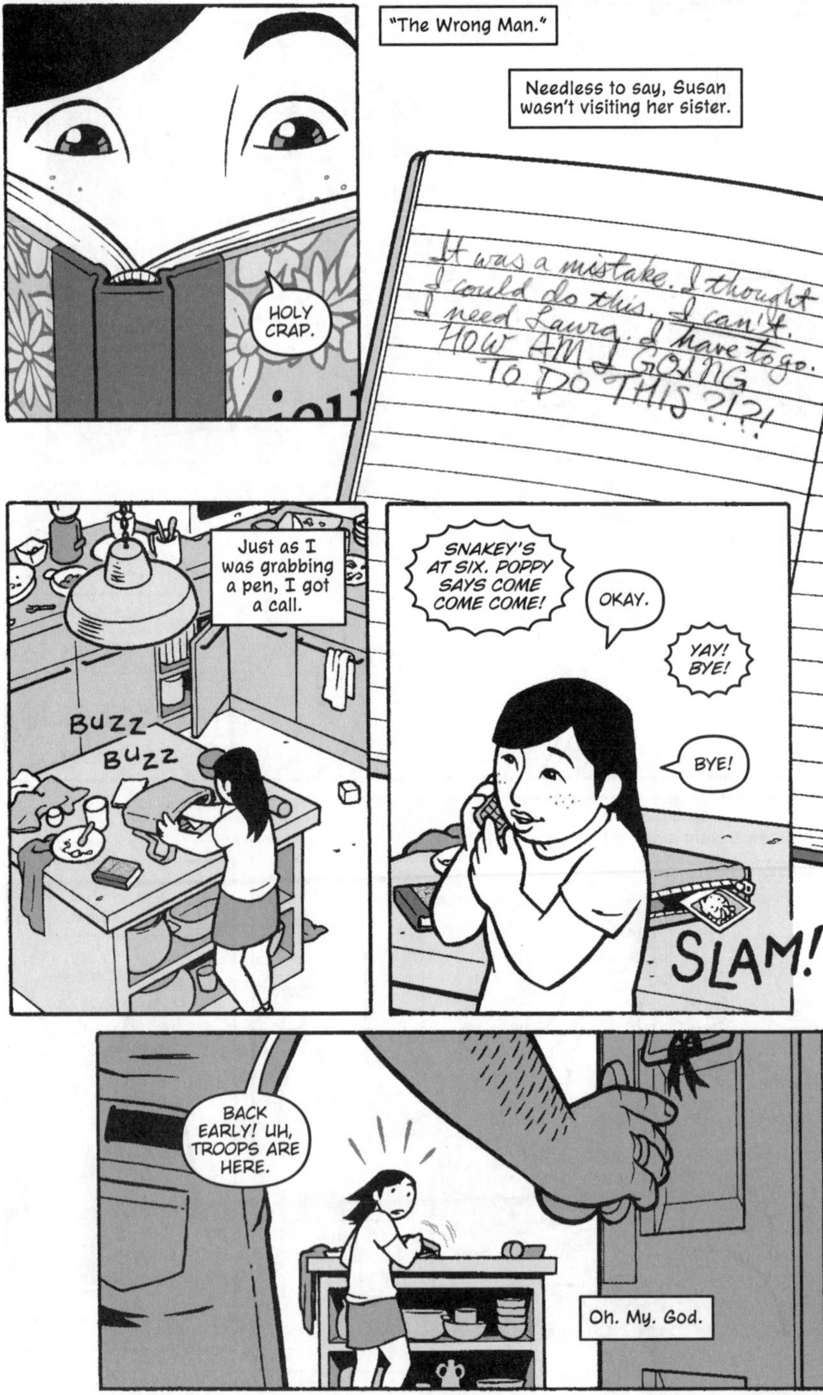

"The Wrong Man."
Needless to say, Susan wasn't visiting her sister.
HOLY CRAP.
It was a mistake. I thought I could do this. I can't. I need Laura. I have to go. HOW AM I GOING TO DO THIS?!?!
Just as I was grabbing a pen, I got a call.
BUZZ
BUZZ
SNAKEY'S AT SIX. POPPY SAYS COME COME COME!
OKAY.
YAY! BYE!
BYE!
SLAM!
BACK EARLY! UH, TROOPS ARE HERE.
Oh. My. God.

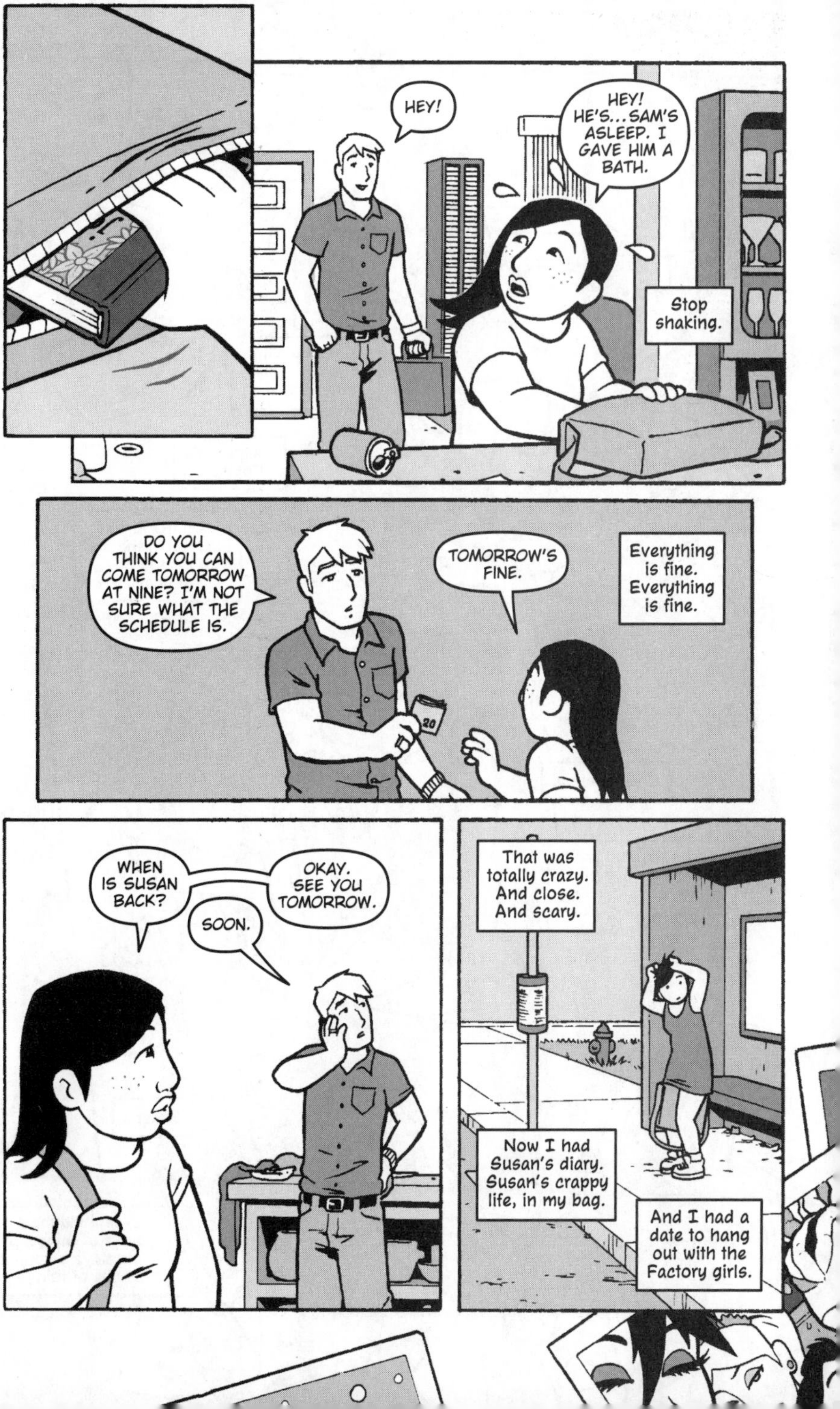
HEY!
HEY! HE'S...SAM'S ASLEEP. I GAVE HIM A BATH.
Stop shaking.
DO YOU THINK YOU CAN COME TOMORROW AT NINE? I'M NOT SURE WHAT THE SCHEDULE IS.
TOMORROW'S FINE.
Everything is fine. Everything is fine.
20
WHEN IS SUSAN BACK?
SOON.
OKAY. SEE YOU TOMORROW.
That was totally crazy. And close. And scary.
Now I had Susan's diary. Susan's crappy life, in my bag.
And I had a date to hang out with the Factory girls.

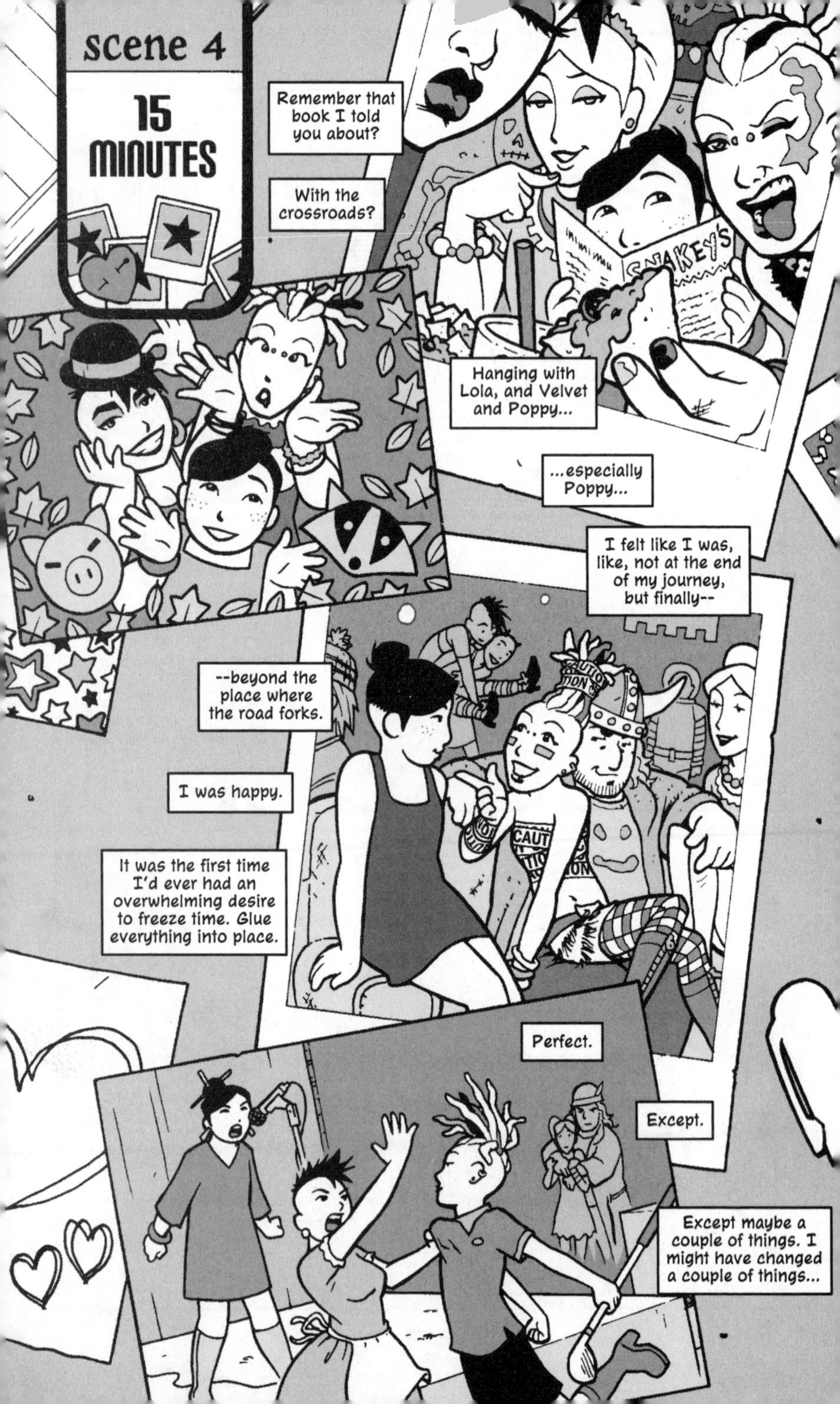
scene 4
15 MINUTES
Remember that book I told you about?
With the crossroads?
SNAKEY'S
Hanging with Lola, and Velvet and Poppy...
...especially Poppy...
I felt like I was, like, not at the end of my journey, but finally--
--beyond the place where the road forks.
I was happy.
It was the first time I'd ever had an overwhelming desire to freeze time. Glue everything into place.
Perfect.
Except.
Except maybe a couple of things. I might have changed a couple of things...

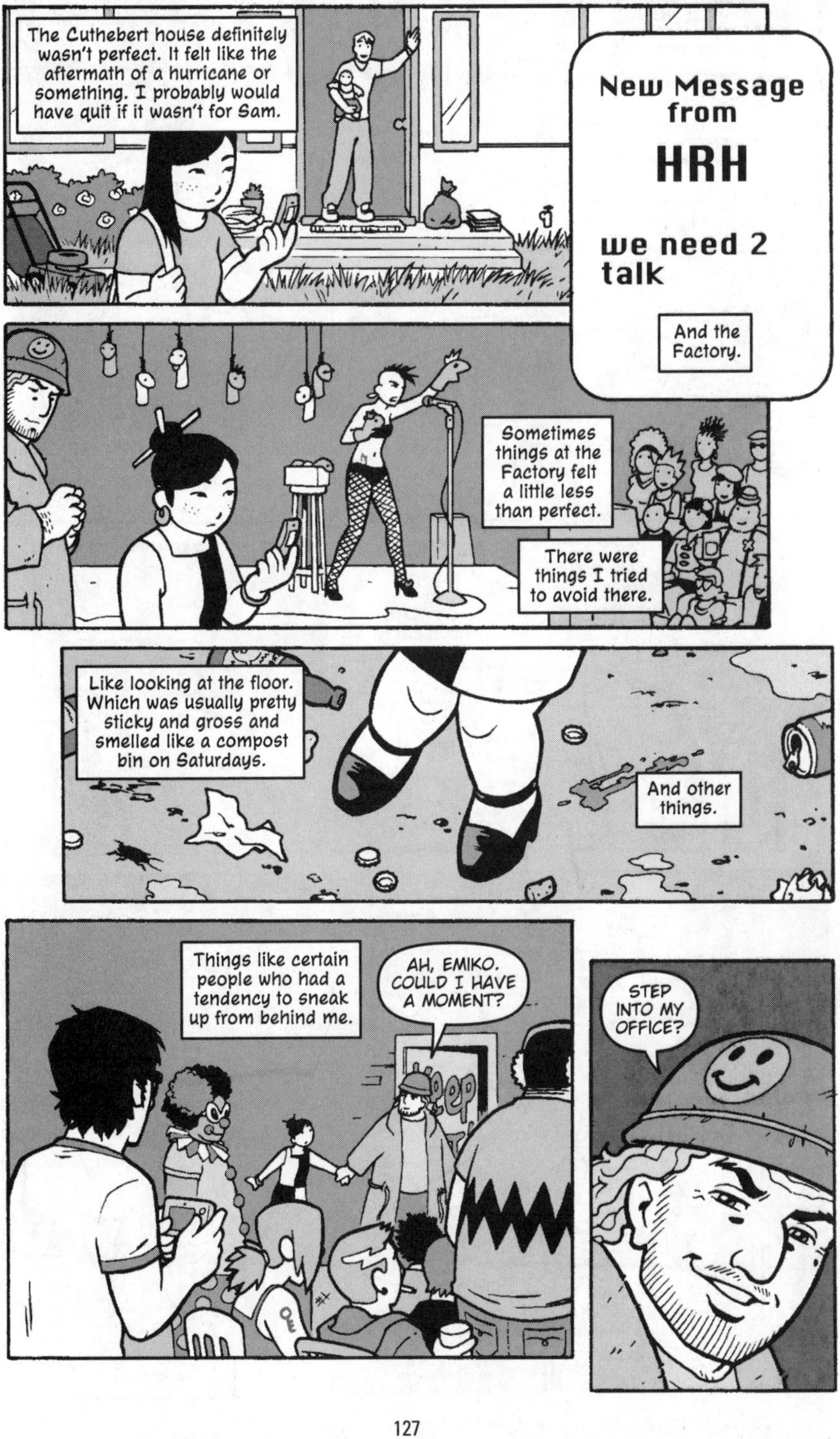
The Cuthebert house definitely wasn't perfect. It felt like the aftermath of a hurricane or something. I probably would have quit if it wasn't for Sam.
New Message from
HRH
we need 2 talk
And the Factory.
Sometimes things at the Factory felt a little less than perfect.
There were things I tried to avoid there.
Like looking at the floor. Which was usually pretty sticky and gross and smelled like a compost bin on Saturdays.
And other things.
Things like certain people who had a tendency to sneak up from behind me.
AH, EMIKO. COULD I HAVE A MOMENT?
STEP INTO MY OFFICE?

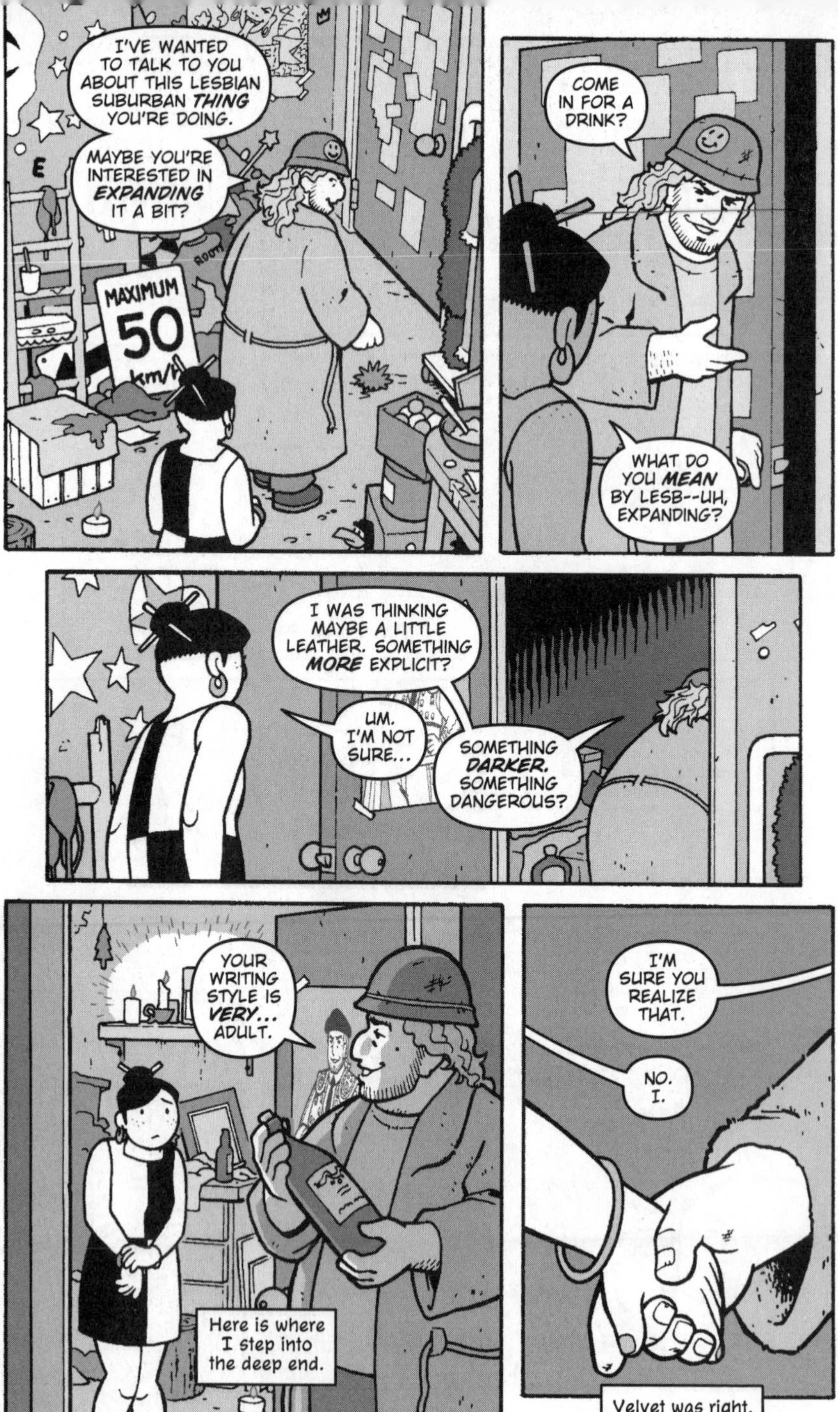
I'VE WANTED TO TALK TO YOU ABOUT THIS LESBIAN SUBURBAN THING YOU'RE DOING.
MAYBE YOU'RE INTERESTED IN EXPANDING IT A BIT?
MAXIMUM 50 km/h
COME IN FOR A DRINK?
WHAT DO YOU MEAN BY LESB--UH, EXPANDING?
I WAS THINKING MAYBE A LITTLE LEATHER. SOMETHING MORE EXPLICIT?
UM. I'M NOT SURE...
SOMETHING DARKER. SOMETHING DANGEROUS?
YOUR WRITING STYLE IS VERY... ADULT.
Here is where I step into the deep end.
I'M SURE YOU REALIZE THAT.
NO. I.
Velvet was right.

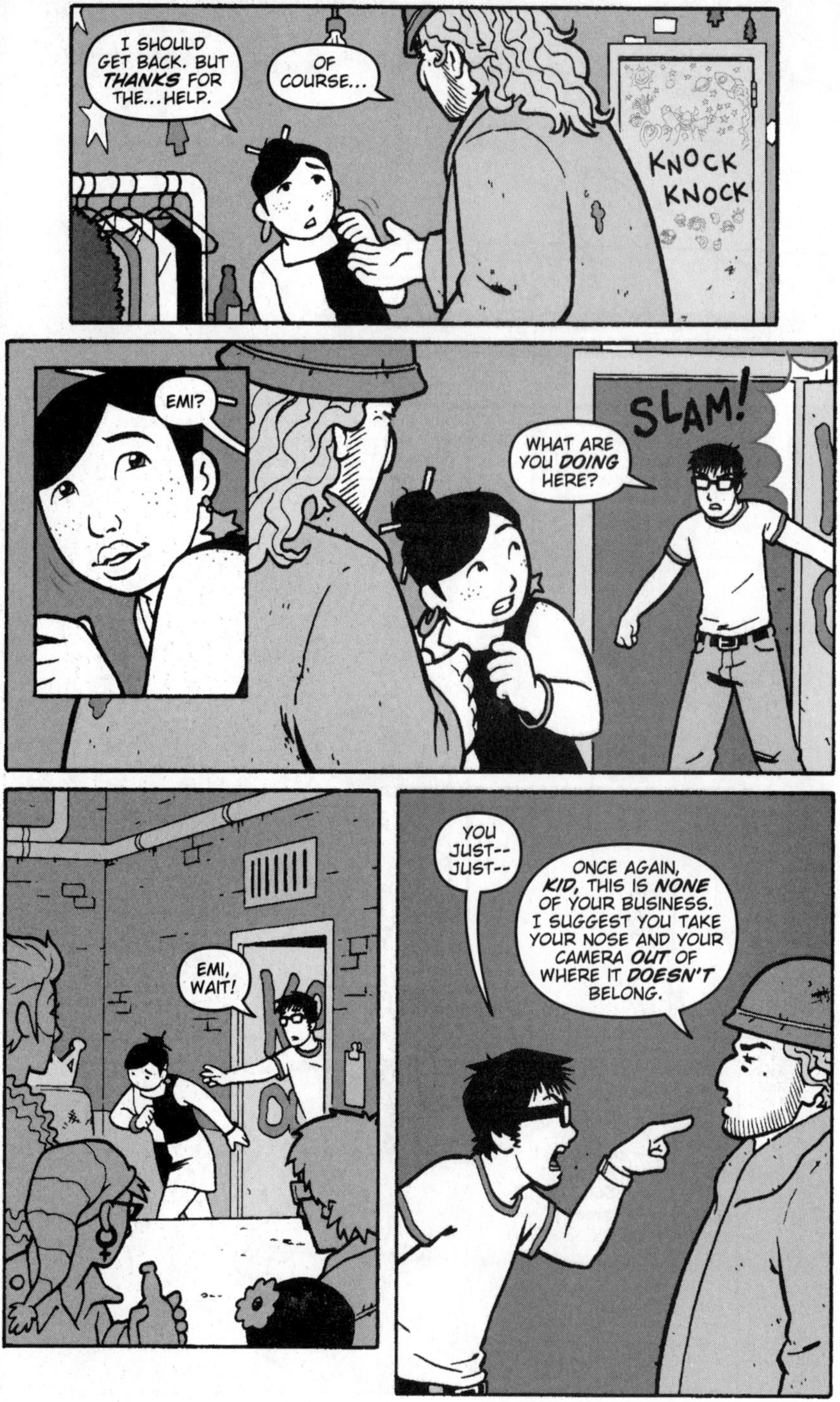
I SHOULD GET BACK. BUT THANKS FOR THE...HELP.
OF COURSE...
KNOCK KNOCK
EMI?
SLAM!
WHAT ARE YOU DOING HERE?
EMI, WAIT!
YOU JUST-- JUST--
ONCE AGAIN, KID, THIS IS NONE OF YOUR BUSINESS. I SUGGEST YOU TAKE YOUR NOSE AND YOUR CAMERA OUT OF WHERE IT DOESN'T BELONG.

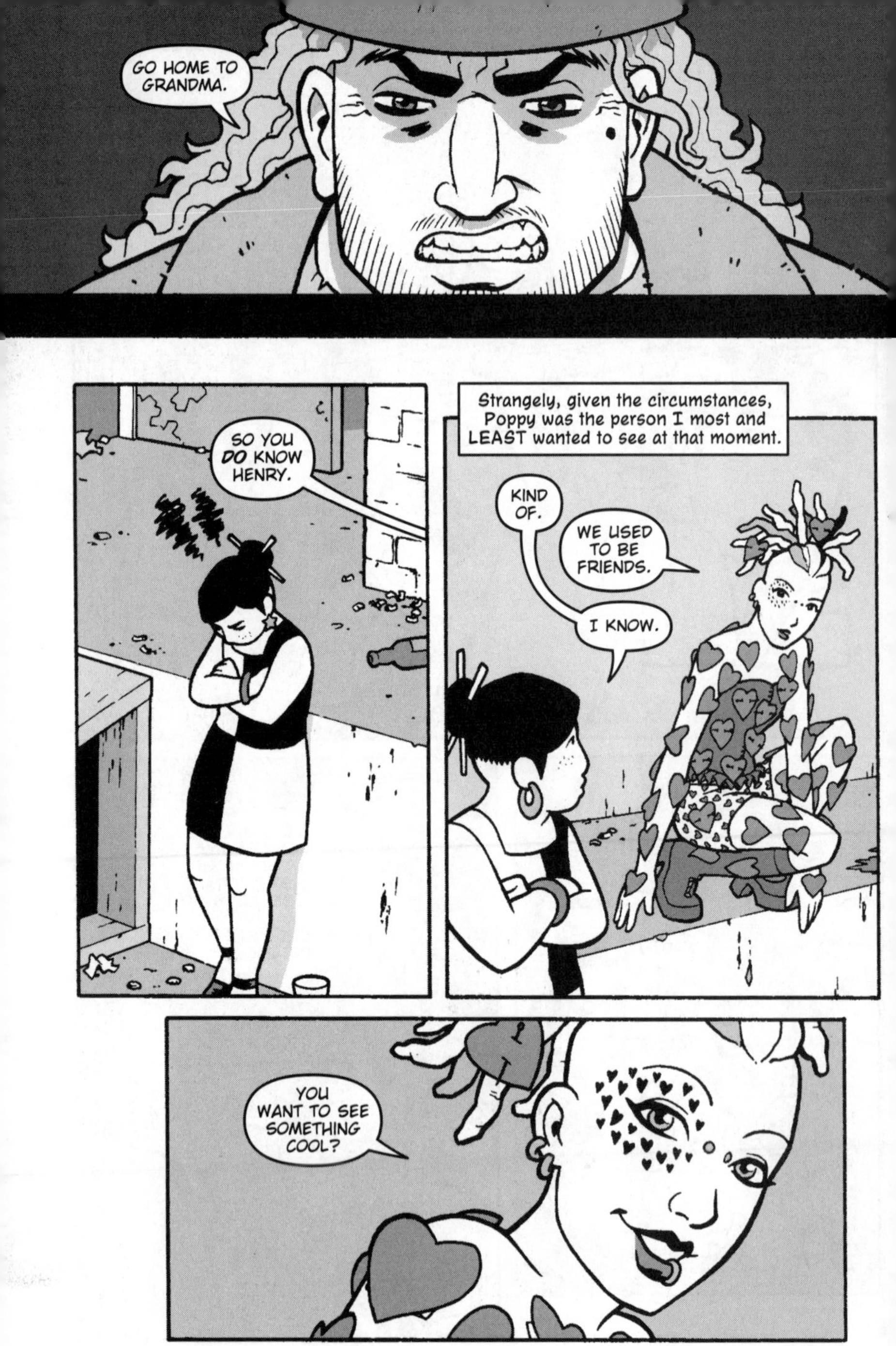
GO HOME TO GRANDMA.
SO YOU DO KNOW HENRY.
Strangely, given the circumstances, Poppy was the person I most and LEAST wanted to see at that moment.
KIND OF.
WE USED TO BE FRIENDS.
I KNOW.
YOU WANT TO SEE SOMETHING COOL?

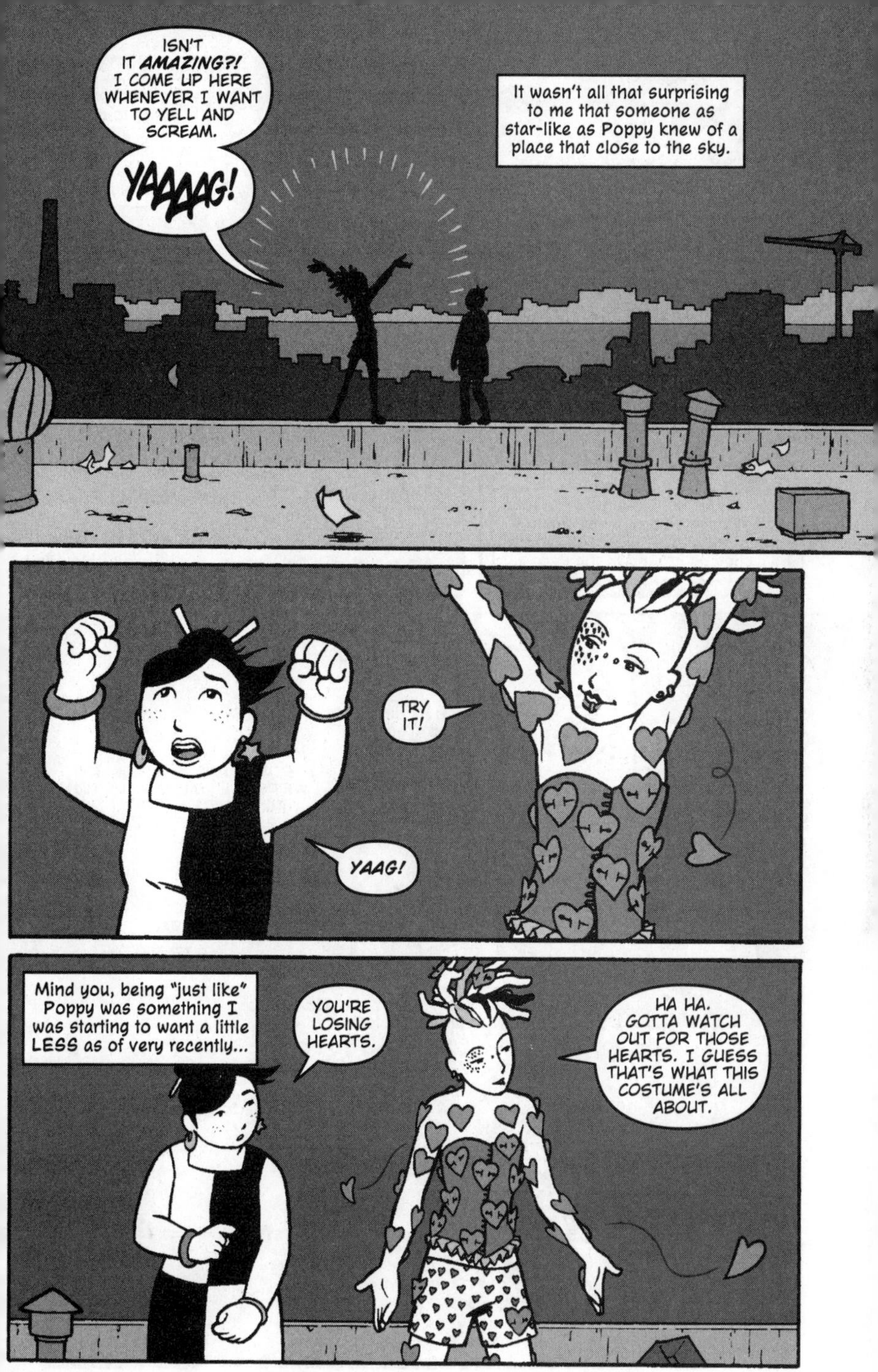

ISN'T IT AMAZING?! I COME UP HERE WHENEVER I WANT TO YELL AND SCREAM.
YAAAAG!
It wasn't all that surprising to me that someone as star-like as Poppy knew of a place that close to the sky.
TRY IT!
YAAG!
Mind you, being "just like" Poppy was something I was starting to want a little LESS as of very recently...
YOU'RE LOSING HEARTS.
HA HA. GOTTA WATCH OUT FOR THOSE HEARTS. I GUESS THAT'S WHAT THIS COSTUME'S ALL ABOUT.

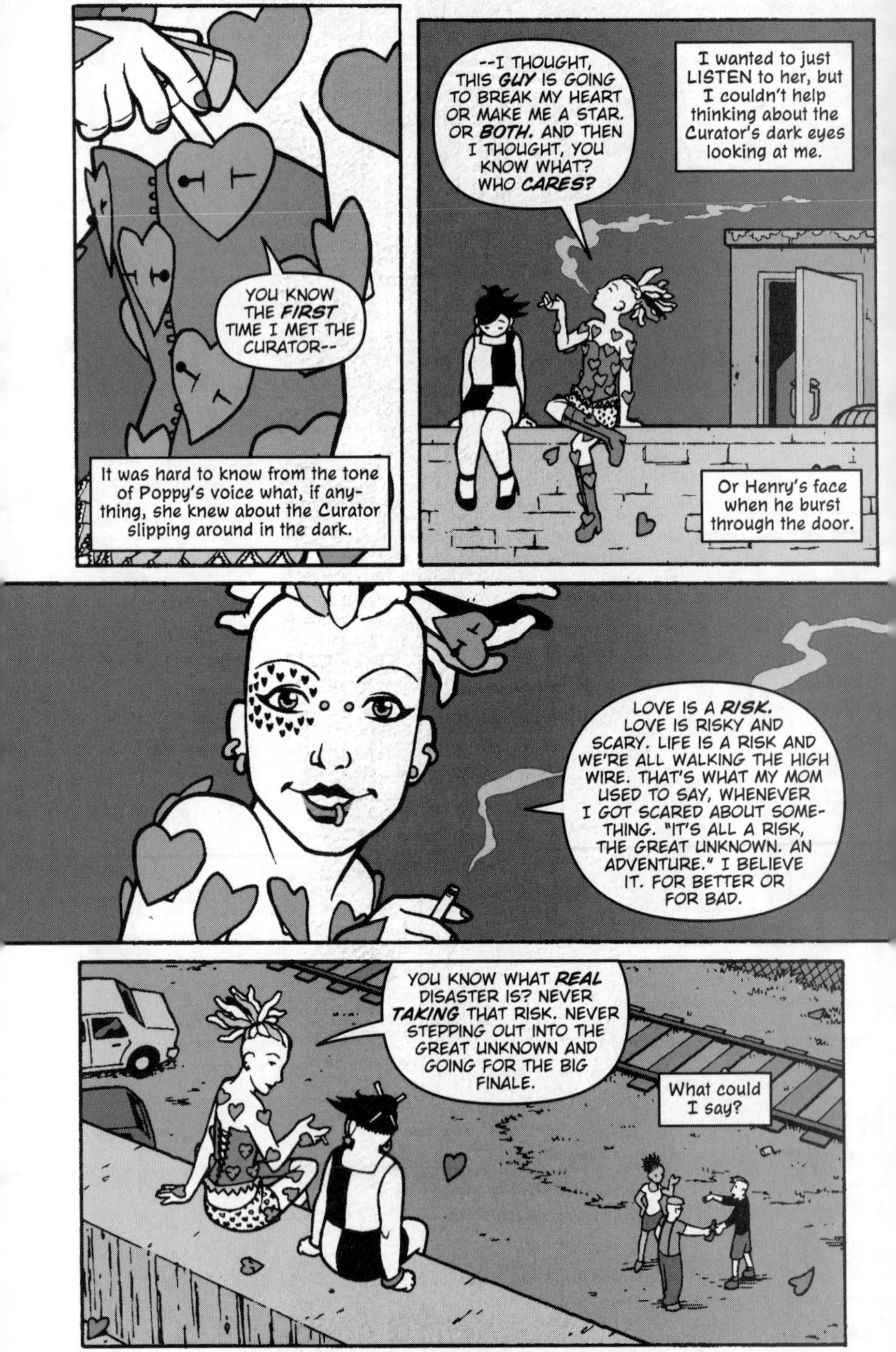
YOU KNOW THE FIRST TIME I MET THE CURATOR--
It was hard to know from the tone of Poppy's voice what, if anything, she knew about the Curator slipping around in the dark.
--I THOUGHT, THIS GUY IS GOING TO BREAK MY HEART OR MAKE ME A STAR. OR BOTH. AND THEN I THOUGHT, YOU KNOW WHAT? WHO CARES?
I wanted to just LISTEN to her, but I couldn't help thinking about the Curator's dark eyes looking at me.
Or Henry's face when he burst through the door.
LOVE IS A RISK. LOVE IS RISKY AND SCARY. LIFE IS A RISK AND WE'RE ALL WALKING THE HIGH WIRE. THAT'S WHAT MY MOM USED TO SAY, WHENEVER I GOT SCARED ABOUT SOMETHING. "IT'S ALL A RISK, THE GREAT UNKNOWN. AN ADVENTURE." I BELIEVE IT. FOR BETTER OR FOR BAD.
YOU KNOW WHAT REAL DISASTER IS? NEVER TAKING THAT RISK. NEVER STEPPING OUT INTO THE GREAT UNKNOWN AND GOING FOR THE BIG FINALE.
What could I say?

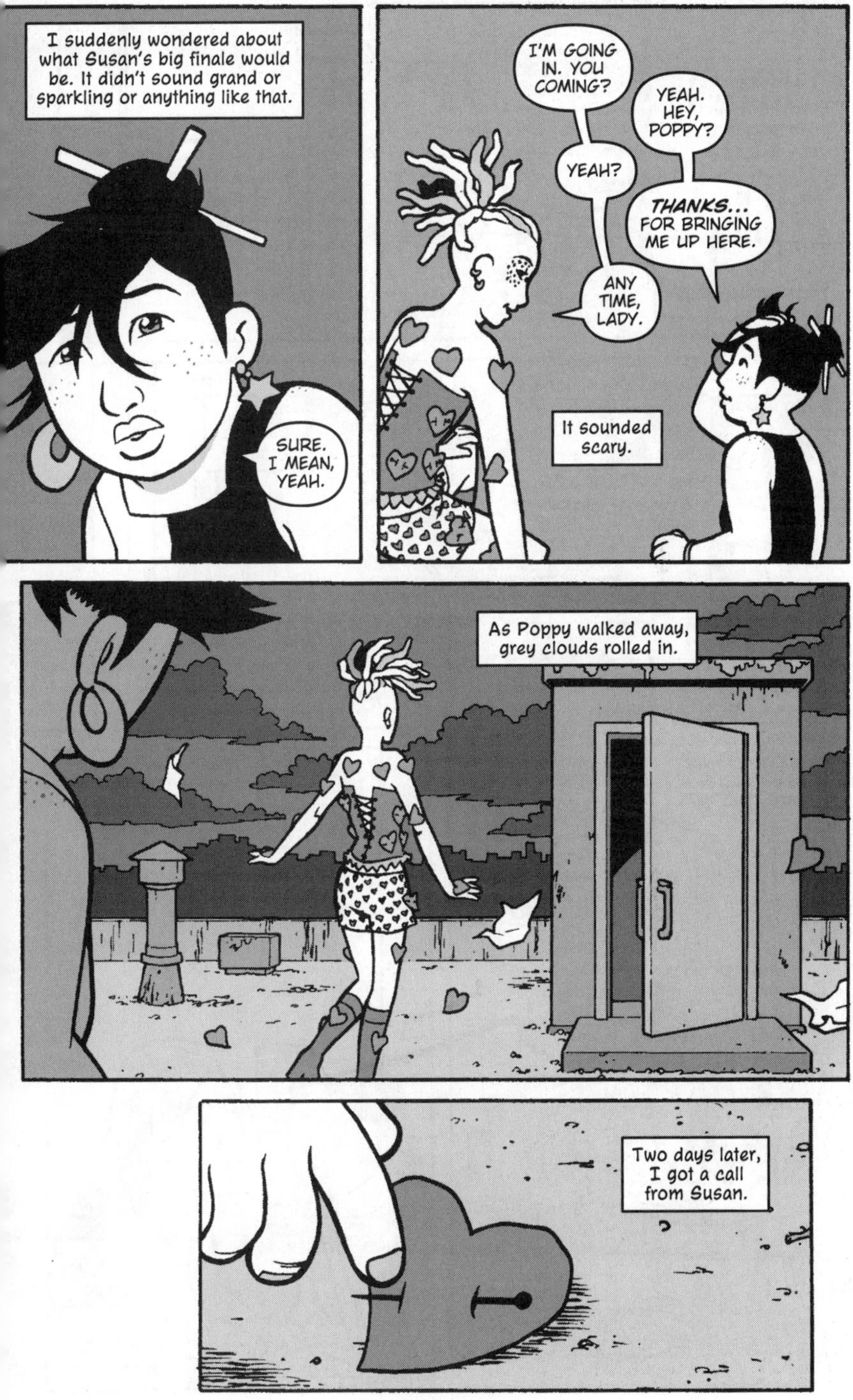
I suddenly wondered about what Susan's big finale would be. It didn't sound grand or sparkling or anything like that.
SURE. I MEAN, YEAH.
I'M GOING IN. YOU COMING?
YEAH. HEY, POPPY?
YEAH?
THANKS... FOR BRINGING ME UP HERE.
ANY TIME, LADY.
It sounded scary.
As Poppy walked away, grey clouds rolled in.
Two days later, I got a call from Susan.

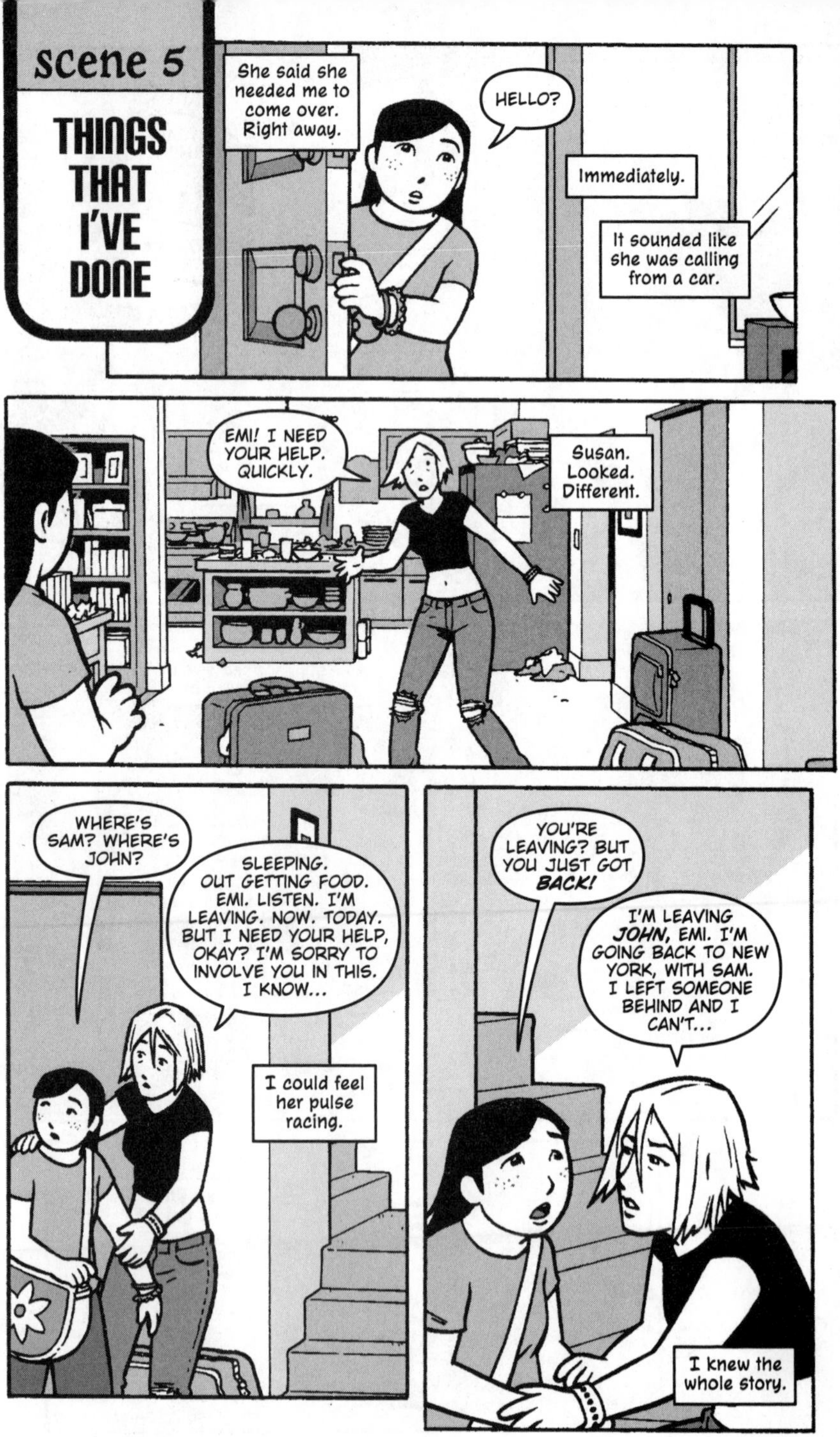
scene 5
THINGS THAT I'VE DONE
She said she needed me to come over. Right away.
HELLO?
Immediately.
It sounded like she was calling from a car.
EMI! I NEED YOUR HELP. QUICKLY.
Susan. Looked. Different.
WHERE'S SAM? WHERE'S JOHN?
SLEEPING. OUT GETTING FOOD. EMI. LISTEN. I'M LEAVING. NOW. TODAY. BUT I NEED YOUR HELP, OKAY? I'M SORRY TO INVOLVE YOU IN THIS. I KNOW...
I could feel her pulse racing.
YOU'RE LEAVING? BUT YOU JUST GOT *BACK!*
I'M LEAVING *JOHN,* EMI. I'M GOING BACK TO NEW YORK, WITH SAM. I LEFT SOMEONE BEHIND AND I CAN'T...
I knew the whole story.

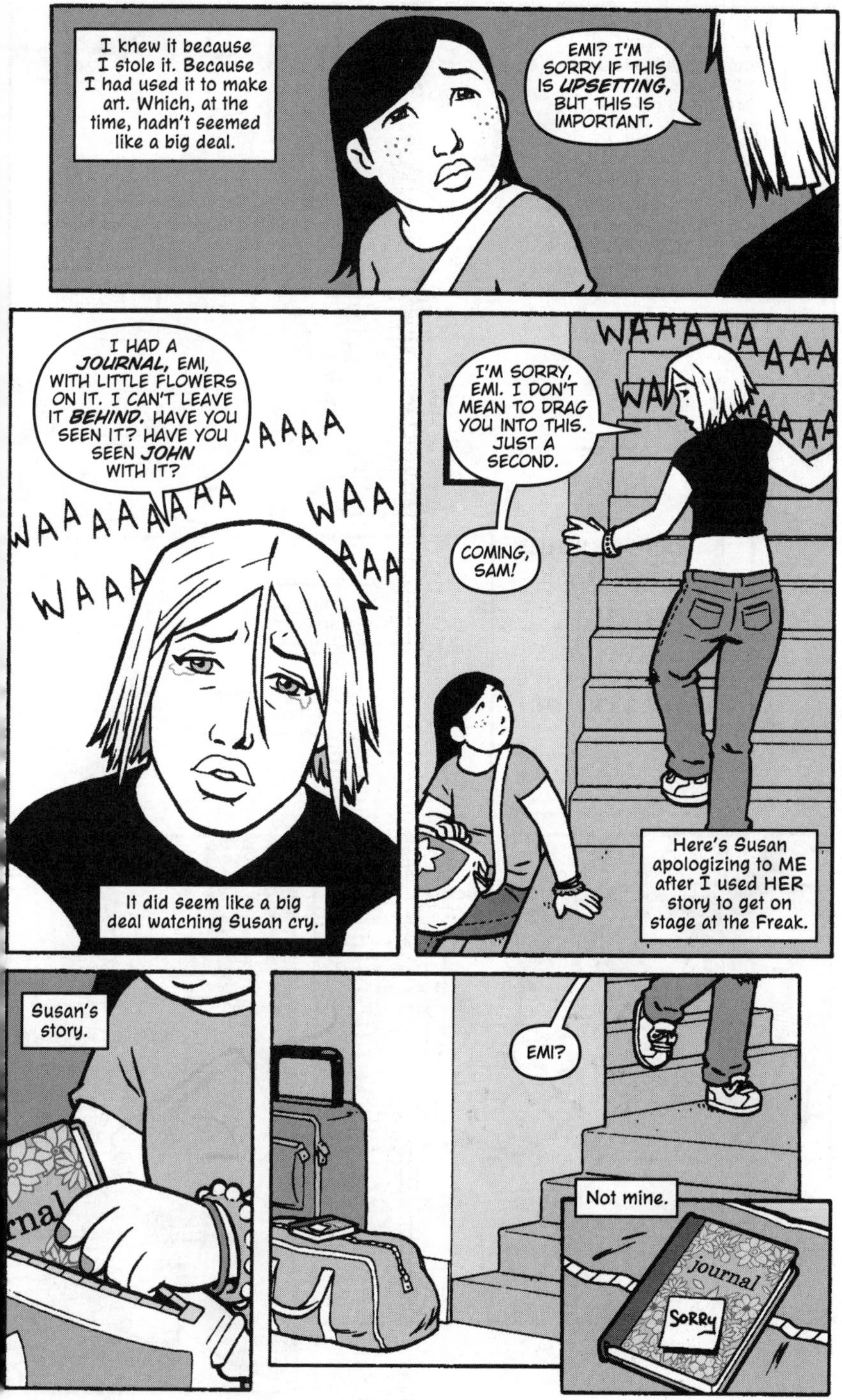

I knew it because I stole it. Because I had used it to make art. Which, at the time, hadn't seemed like a big deal.
EMI? I'M SORRY IF THIS IS *UPSETTING,* BUT THIS IS IMPORTANT.
I HAD A *JOURNAL,* EMI, WITH LITTLE FLOWERS ON IT. I CAN'T LEAVE IT *BEHIND.* HAVE YOU SEEN IT? HAVE YOU SEEN *JOHN* WITH IT?
WAAAAAAAAA
WAAAAAAA
WAA
It did seem like a big deal watching Susan cry.
WAAAAAAAAA
I'M SORRY, EMI. I DON'T MEAN TO DRAG YOU INTO THIS. JUST A SECOND.
COMING, SAM!
Here's Susan apologizing to ME after I used HER story to get on stage at the Freak.
Susan's story.
journal
EMI?
Not mine.
journal
SORRY

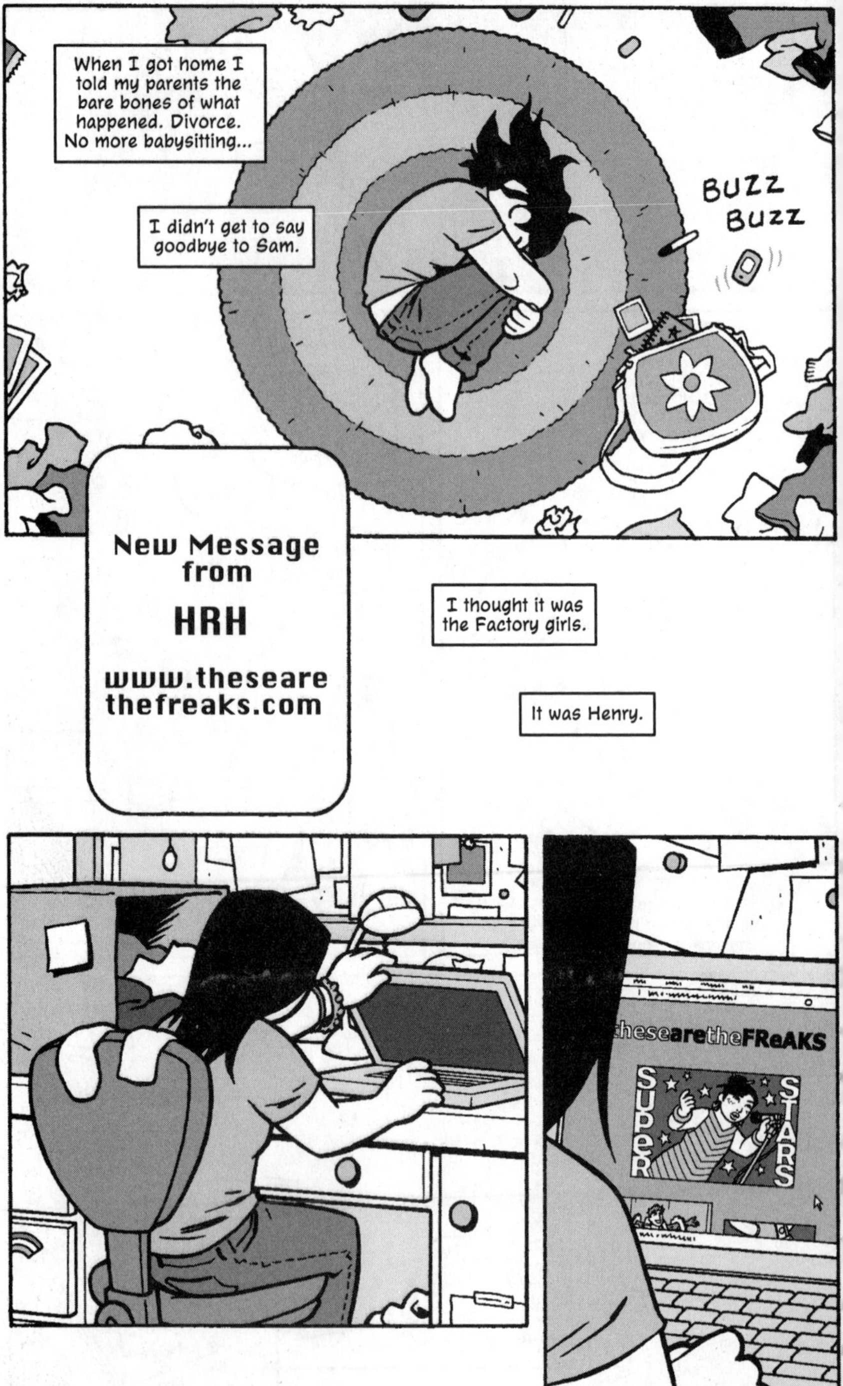
When I got home I told my parents the bare bones of what happened. Divorce. No more babysitting...
I didn't get to say goodbye to Sam.
BUZZ BUZZ
New Message from
HRH
www.thesearethefreaks.com
I thought it was the Factory girls.
It was Henry.
thesearetheFREAKS
SUPER STARS

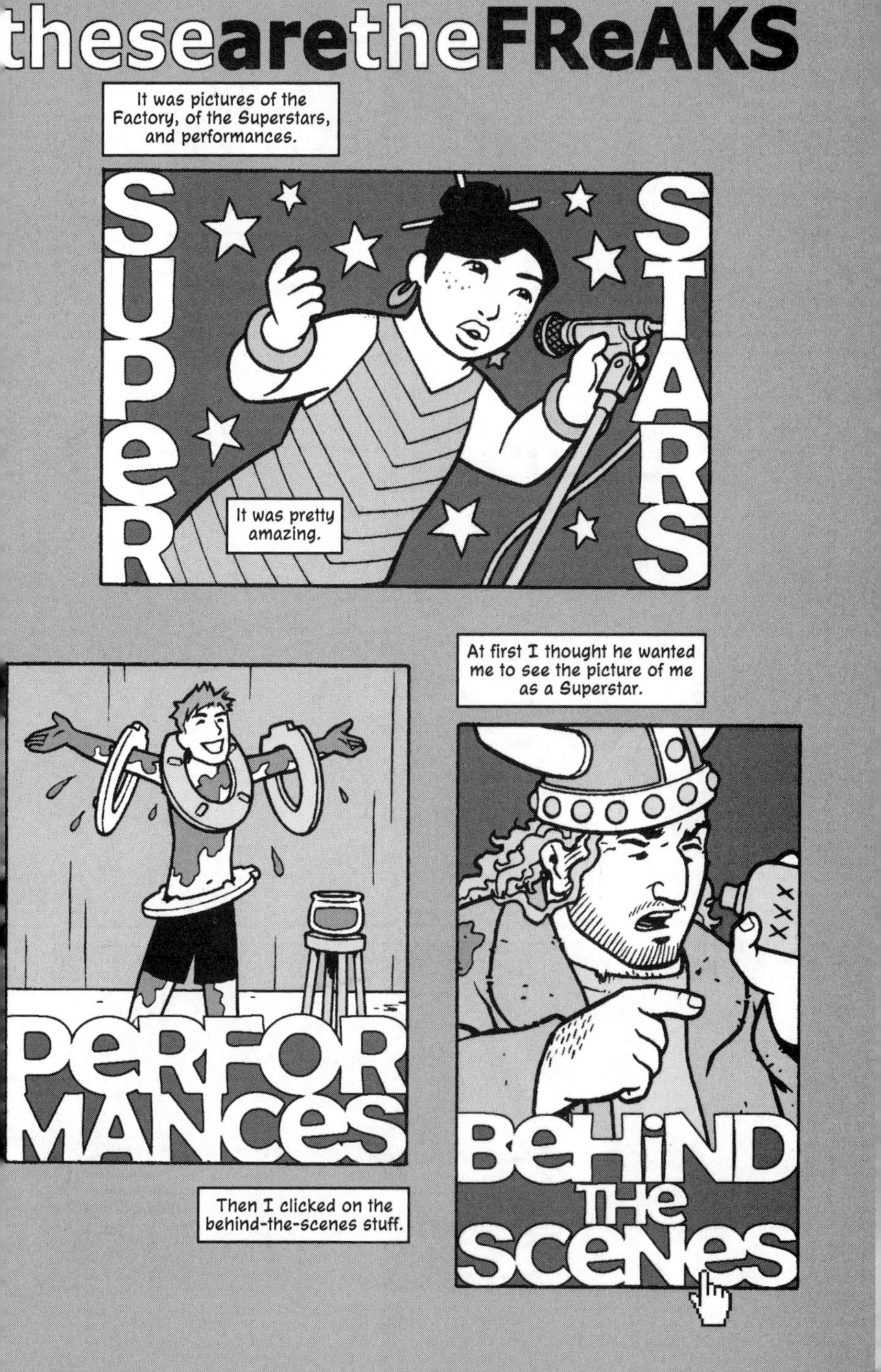
theseareTheFReAKS
It was pictures of the Factory, of the Superstars, and performances.
SUPeR
STARS
It was pretty amazing.
PeRFORMANCeS
Then I clicked on the behind-the-scenes stuff.
At first I thought he wanted me to see the picture of me as a Superstar.
BeHiND THe SCeNeS

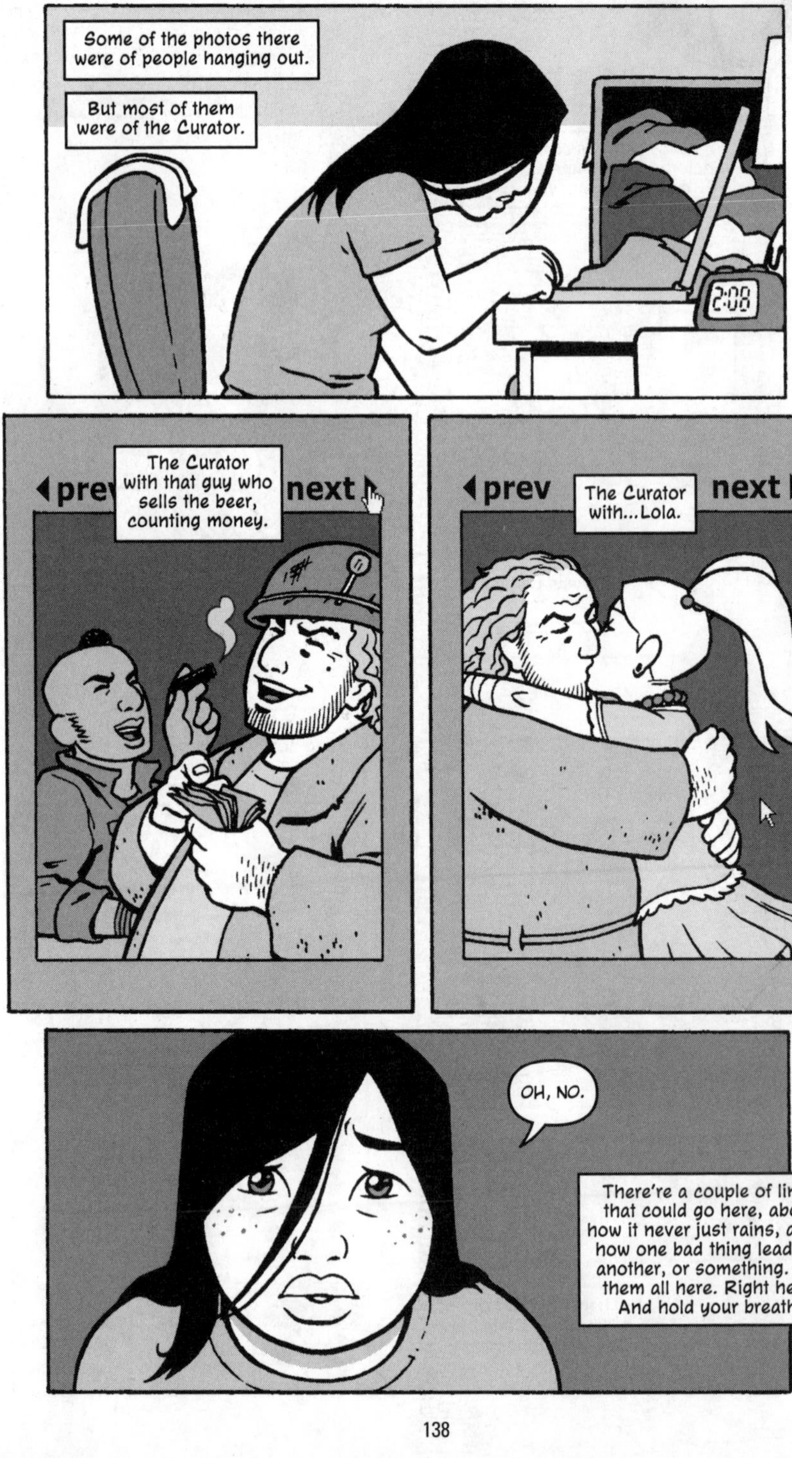
Some of the photos there were of people hanging out.
But most of them were of the Curator.
2:08
prev
The Curator with that guy who sells the beer, counting money.
next
prev
The Curator with...Lola.
next
OH, NO.
There're a couple of lines that could go here, about how it never just rains, about how one bad thing leads to another, or something. Put them all here. Right here. And hold your breath.

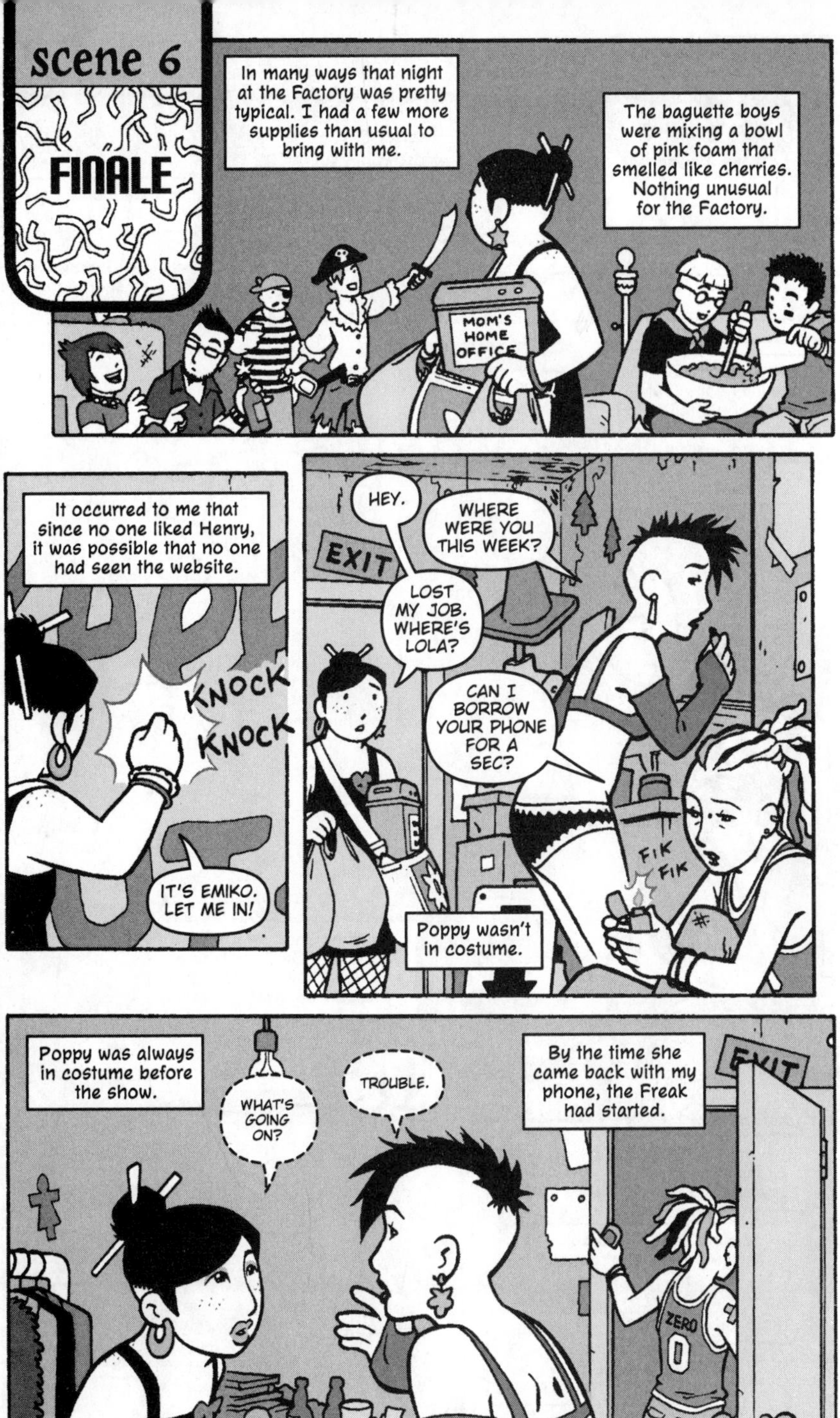
scene 6
FINALE
In many ways that night at the Factory was pretty typical. I had a few more supplies than usual to bring with me.
The baguette boys were mixing a bowl of pink foam that smelled like cherries. Nothing unusual for the Factory.
MOM'S HOME OFFICE
It occurred to me that since no one liked Henry, it was possible that no one had seen the website.
KNOCK KNOCK
IT'S EMIKO. LET ME IN!
EXIT
HEY.
WHERE WERE YOU THIS WEEK?
LOST MY JOB. WHERE'S LOLA?
CAN I BORROW YOUR PHONE FOR A SEC?
FIK FIK
Poppy wasn't in costume.
Poppy was always in costume before the show.
WHAT'S GOING ON?
TROUBLE.
By the time she came back with my phone, the Freak had started.
ZERO
0

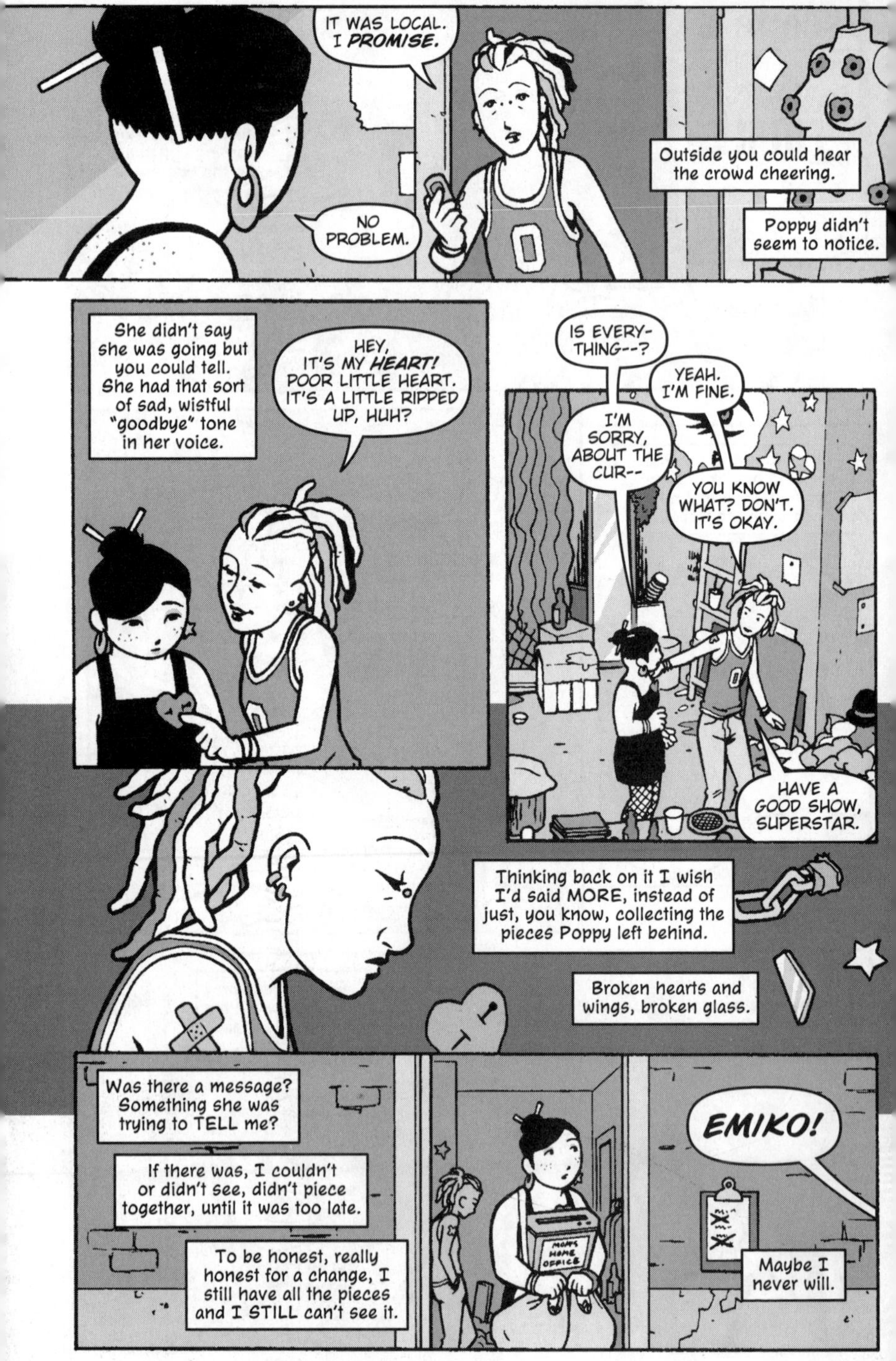
IT WAS LOCAL. I PROMISE.
NO PROBLEM.
Outside you could hear the crowd cheering.
Poppy didn't seem to notice.
She didn't say she was going but you could tell. She had that sort of sad, wistful "goodbye" tone in her voice.
HEY, IT'S MY HEART! POOR LITTLE HEART. IT'S A LITTLE RIPPED UP, HUH?
IS EVERY-THING--?
YEAH. I'M FINE.
I'M SORRY, ABOUT THE CUR--
YOU KNOW WHAT? DON'T. IT'S OKAY.
HAVE A GOOD SHOW, SUPERSTAR.
Thinking back on it I wish I'd said MORE, instead of just, you know, collecting the pieces Poppy left behind.
Broken hearts and wings, broken glass.
Was there a message? Something she was trying to TELL me?
If there was, I couldn't or didn't see, didn't piece together, until it was too late.
To be honest, really honest for a change, I still have all the pieces and I STILL can't see it.
EMIKO!
Maybe I never will.

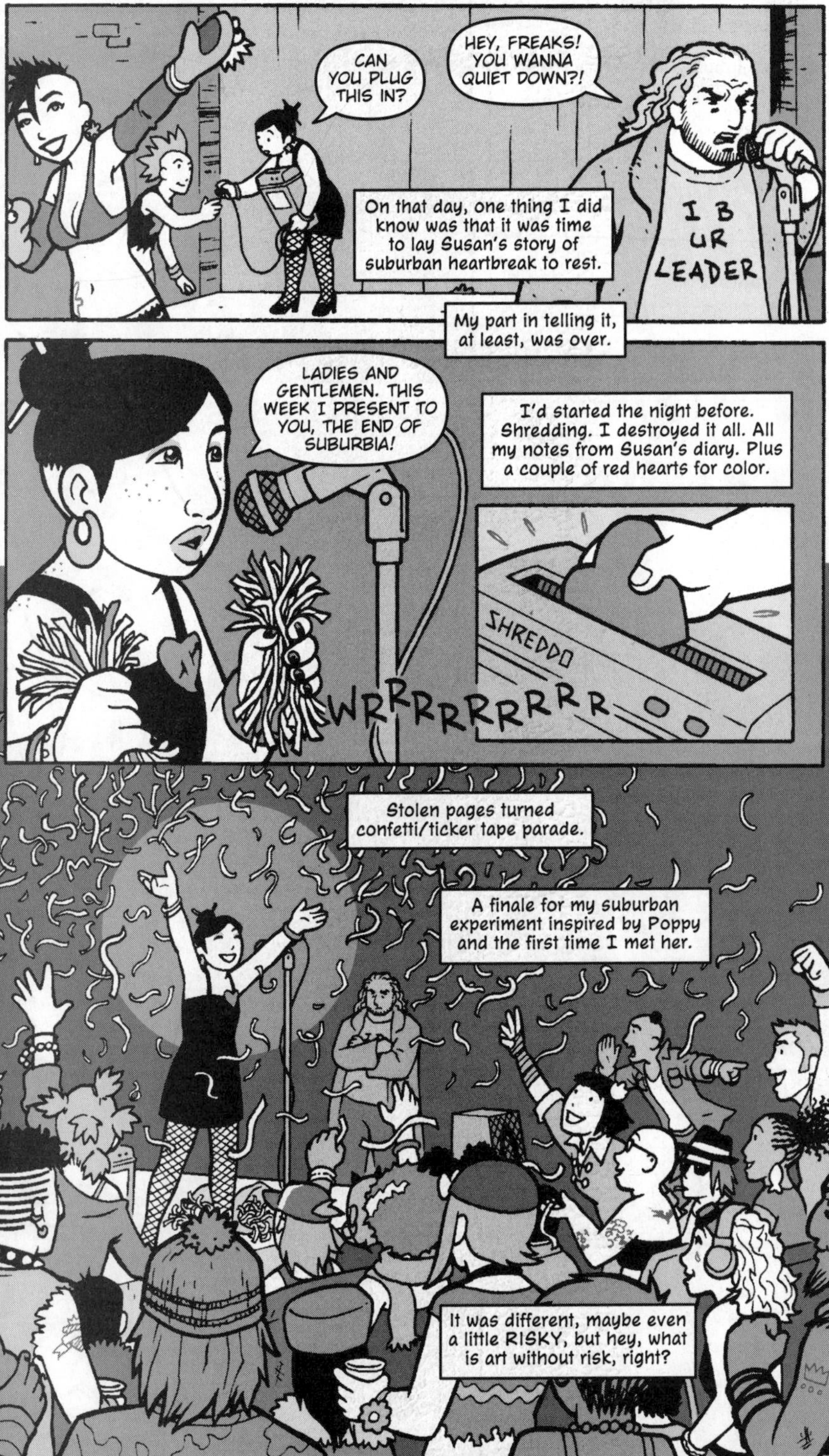

CAN YOU PLUG THIS IN?
HEY, FREAKS! YOU WANNA QUIET DOWN?!
I B UR LEADER
On that day, one thing I did know was that it was time to lay Susan's story of suburban heartbreak to rest.
My part in telling it, at least, was over.
LADIES AND GENTLEMEN. THIS WEEK I PRESENT TO YOU, THE END OF SUBURBIA!
I'd started the night before. Shredding. I destroyed it all. All my notes from Susan's diary. Plus a couple of red hearts for color.
SHREDDO
WRRRRRRRRRR
Stolen pages turned confetti/ticker tape parade.
A finale for my suburban experiment inspired by Poppy and the first time I met her.
It was different, maybe even a little RISKY, but hey, what is art without risk, right?

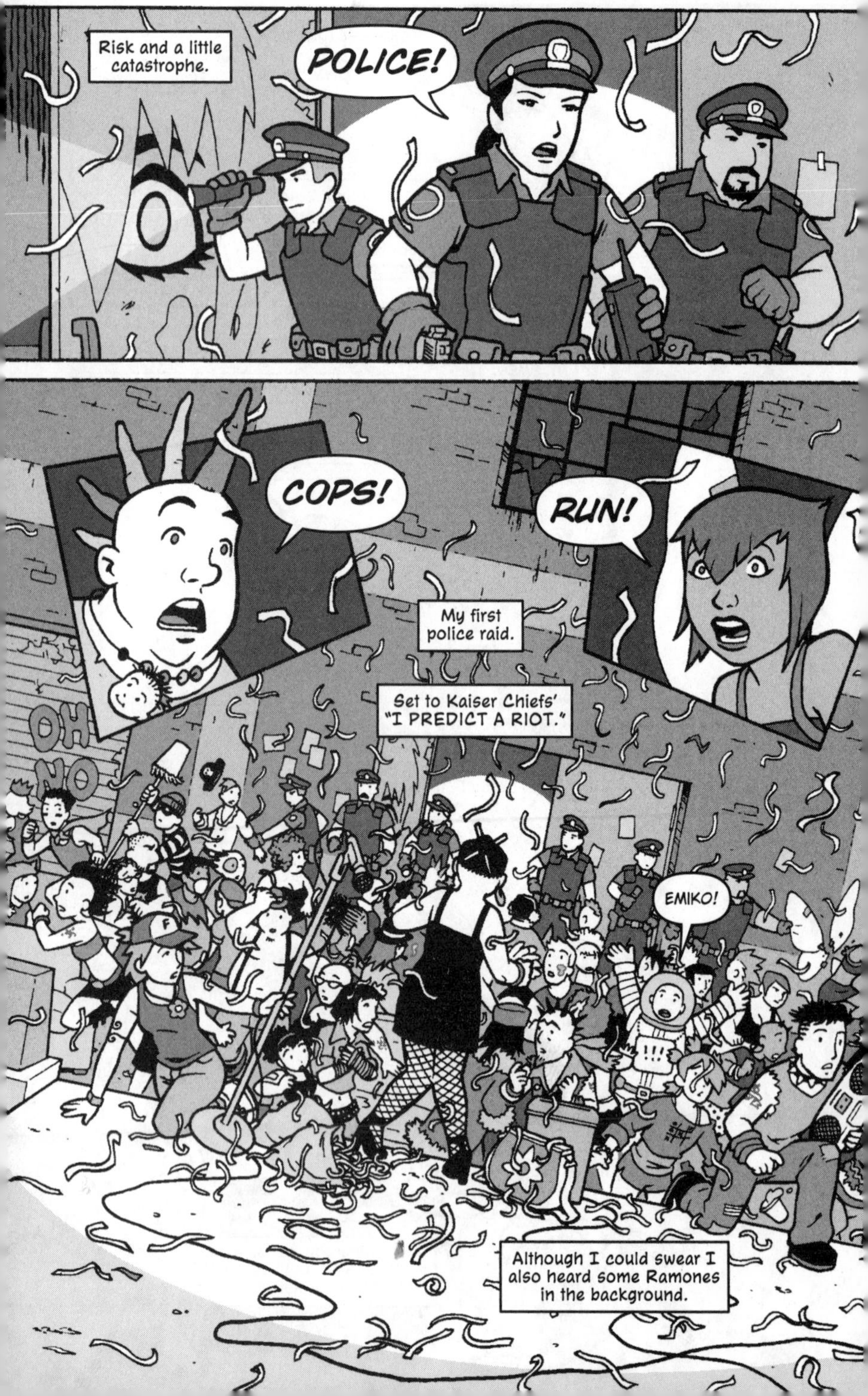
Risk and a little catastrophe.
POLICE!
COPS!
RUN!
My first police raid.
Set to Kaiser Chiefs' "I PREDICT A RIOT."
OH NO
EMIKO!
!!!
Although I could swear I also heard some Ramones in the background.

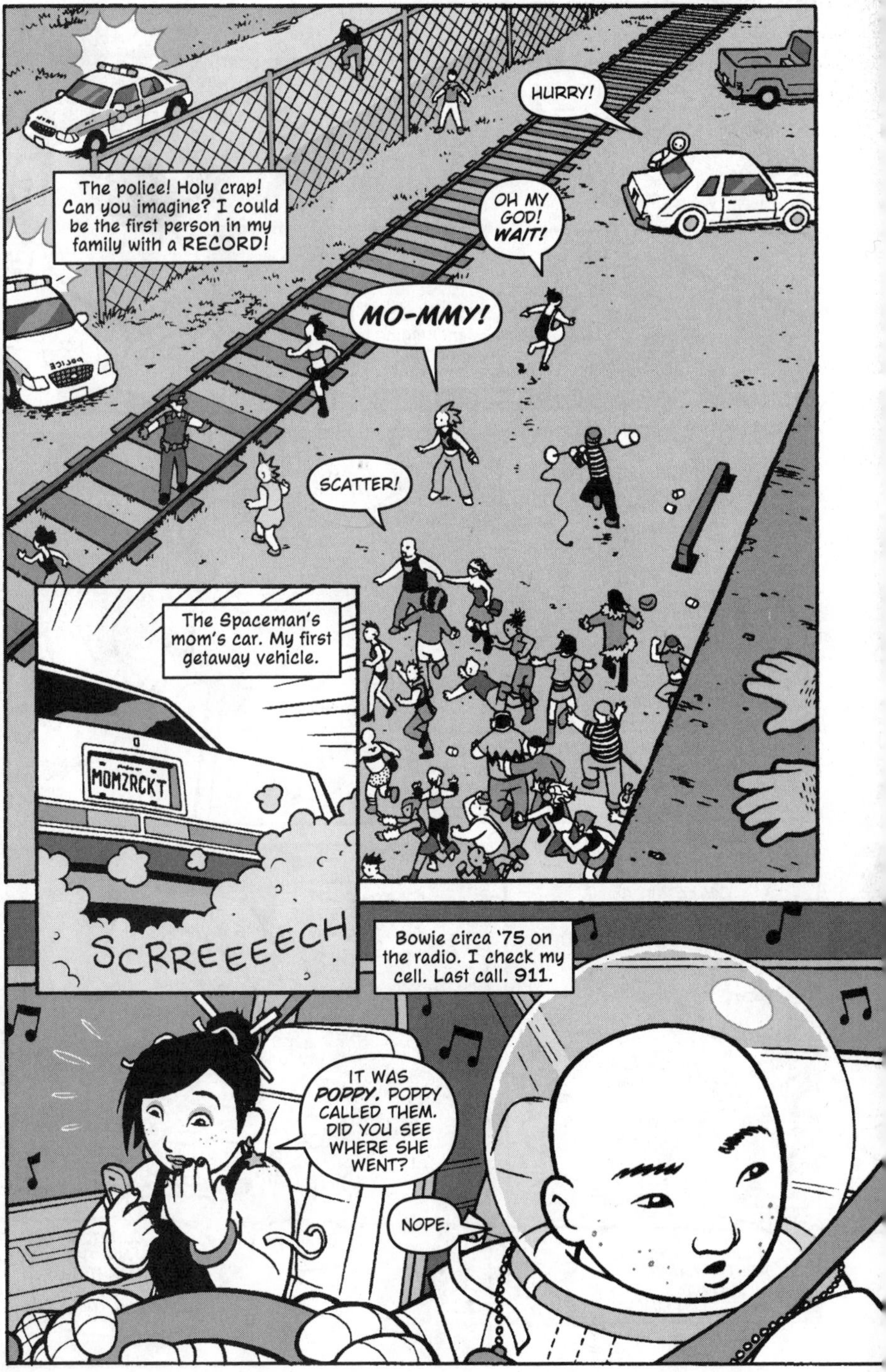
HURRY!
The police! Holy crap! Can you imagine? I could be the first person in my family with a RECORD!
OH MY GOD! WAIT!
MO-MMY!
SCATTER!
The Spaceman's mom's car. My first getaway vehicle.
MOMZRCKT
SCRREEEEECH
Bowie circa '75 on the radio. I check my cell. Last call. 911.
IT WAS POPPY. POPPY CALLED THEM. DID YOU SEE WHERE SHE WENT?
NOPE.

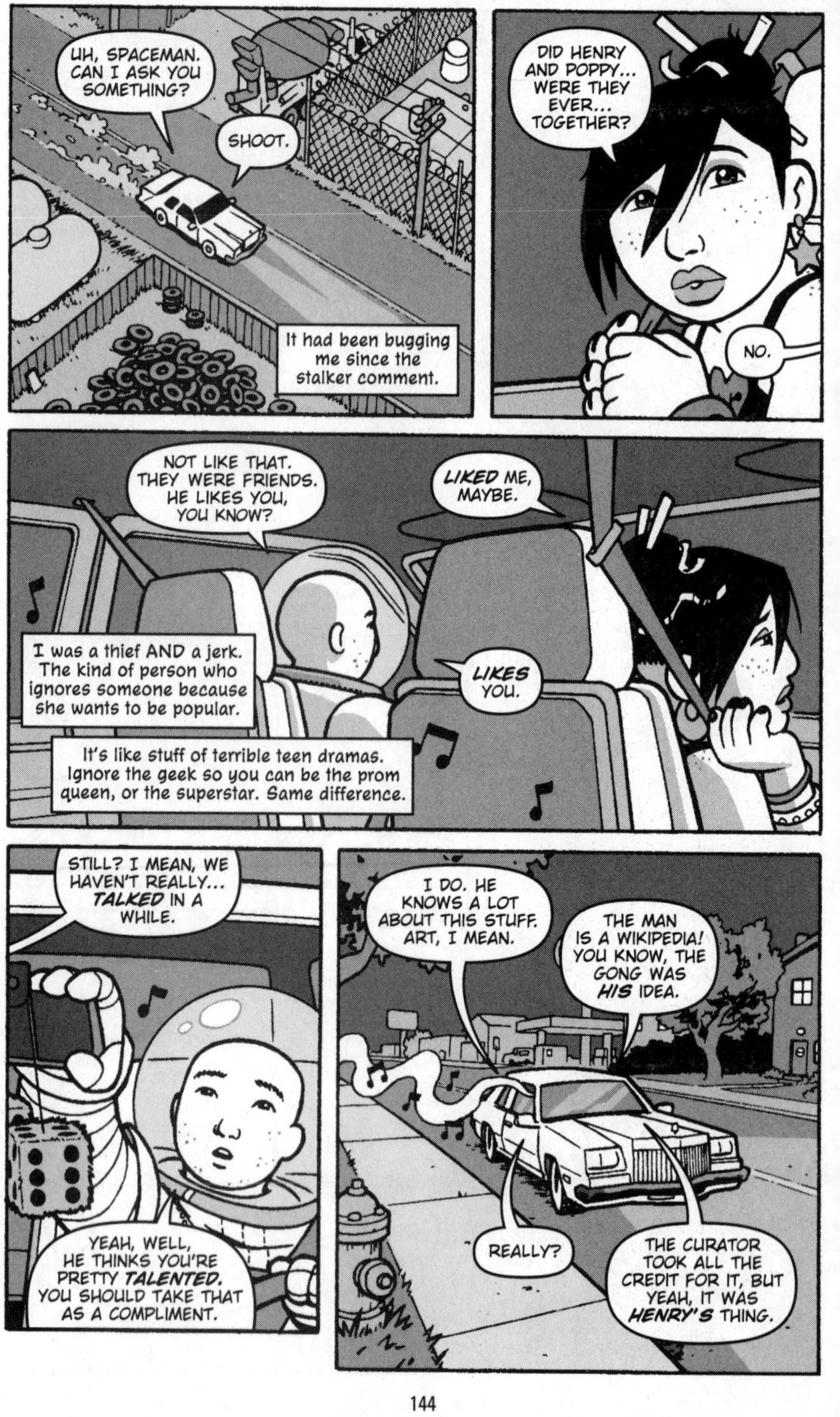
UH, SPACEMAN. CAN I ASK YOU SOMETHING?
SHOOT.
It had been bugging me since the stalker comment.
DID HENRY AND POPPY... WERE THEY EVER... TOGETHER?
NO.
NOT LIKE THAT. THEY WERE FRIENDS. HE LIKES YOU, YOU KNOW?
LIKED ME, MAYBE.
LIKES YOU.
I was a thief AND a jerk. The kind of person who ignores someone because she wants to be popular.
It's like stuff of terrible teen dramas. Ignore the geek so you can be the prom queen, or the superstar. Same difference.
STILL? I MEAN, WE HAVEN'T REALLY... TALKED IN A WHILE.
YEAH, WELL, HE THINKS YOU'RE PRETTY TALENTED. YOU SHOULD TAKE THAT AS A COMPLIMENT.
I DO. HE KNOWS A LOT ABOUT THIS STUFF. ART, I MEAN.
THE MAN IS A WIKIPEDIA! YOU KNOW, THE GONG WAS HIS IDEA.
REALLY?
THE CURATOR TOOK ALL THE CREDIT FOR IT, BUT YEAH, IT WAS HENRY'S THING.

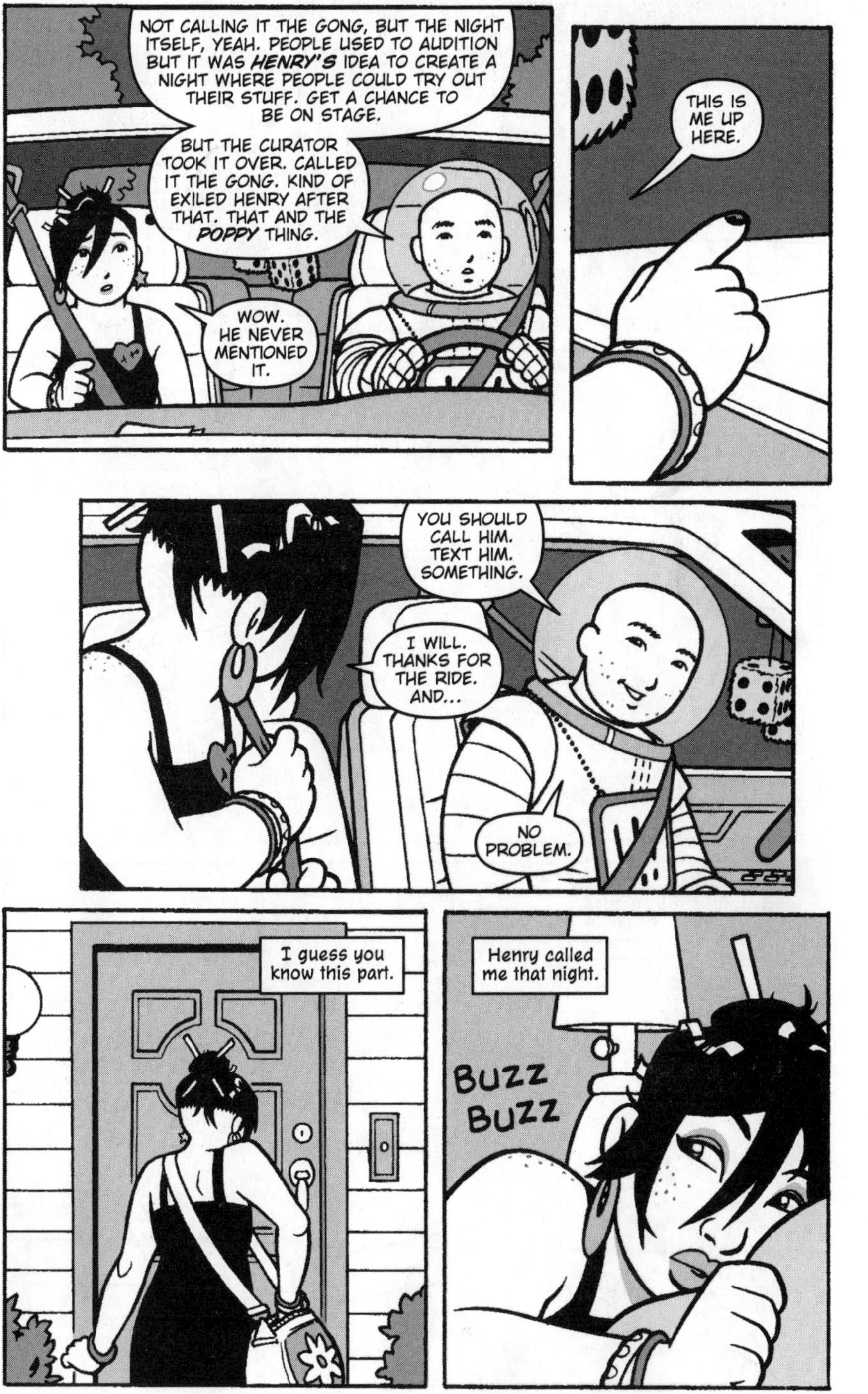
NOT CALLING IT THE GONG, BUT THE NIGHT ITSELF, YEAH. PEOPLE USED TO AUDITION BUT IT WAS HENRY'S IDEA TO CREATE A NIGHT WHERE PEOPLE COULD TRY OUT THEIR STUFF. GET A CHANCE TO BE ON STAGE.
BUT THE CURATOR TOOK IT OVER. CALLED IT THE GONG. KIND OF EXILED HENRY AFTER THAT. THAT AND THE POPPY THING.
WOW. HE NEVER MENTIONED IT.
THIS IS ME UP HERE.
YOU SHOULD CALL HIM. TEXT HIM. SOMETHING.
I WILL. THANKS FOR THE RIDE. AND...
NO PROBLEM.
I guess you know this part.
Henry called me that night.
BUZZ BUZZ

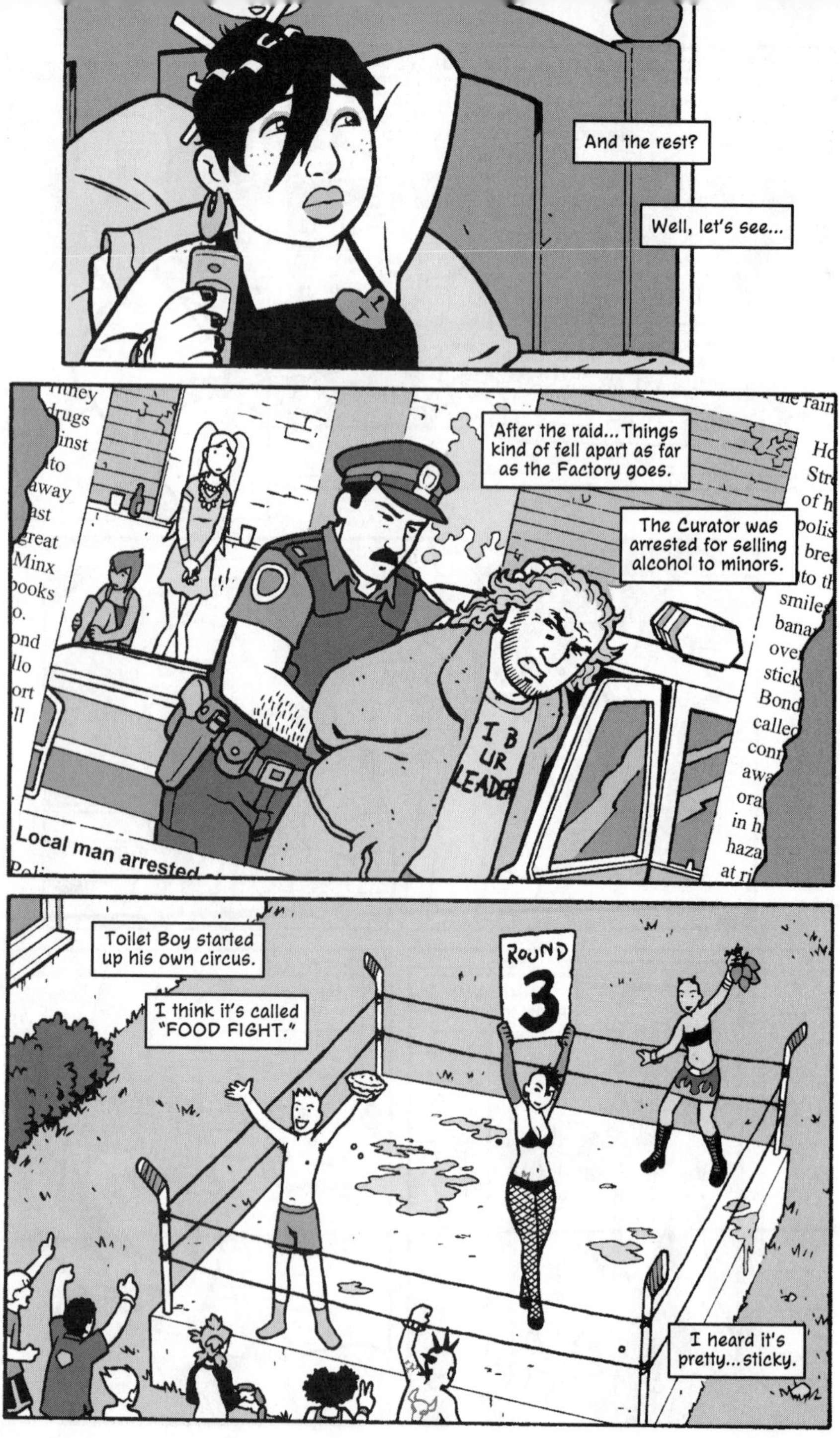
And the rest?
Well, let's see...
After the raid... Things kind of fell apart as far as the Factory goes.
The Curator was arrested for selling alcohol to minors.
I B UR LEADER
Local man arrested
Toilet Boy started up his own circus.
I think it's called "FOOD FIGHT."
ROUND 3
I heard it's pretty... sticky.

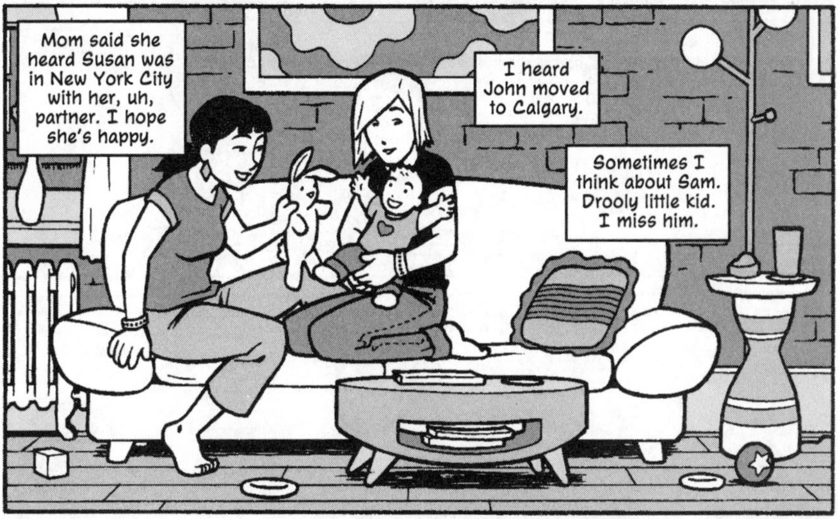
Mom said she heard Susan was in New York City with her, uh, partner. I hope she's happy.
I heard John moved to Calgary.
Sometimes I think about Sam. Drooly little kid. I miss him.

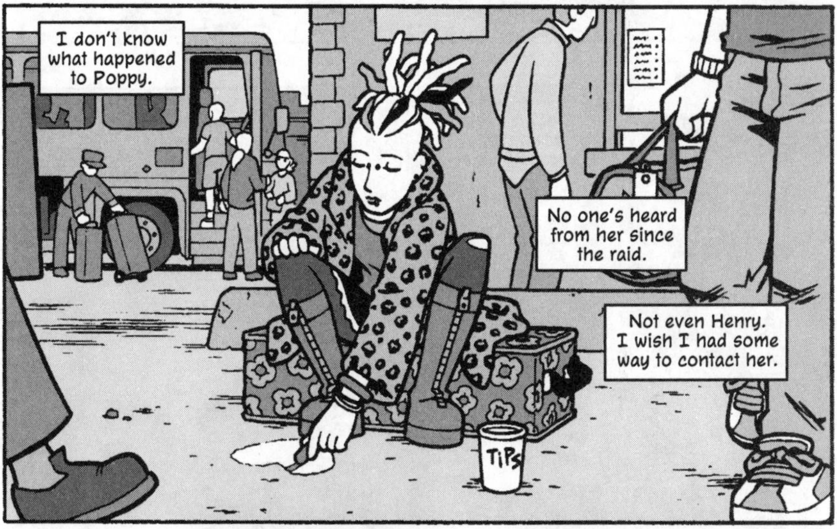
I don't know what happened to Poppy.
No one's heard from her since the raid.
Not even Henry. I wish I had some way to contact her.
TIPS

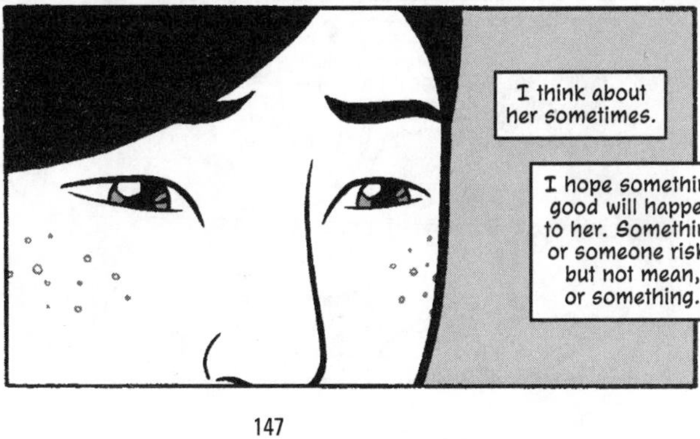
I think about her sometimes.
I hope something good will happen to her. Something or someone risky but not mean, or something.

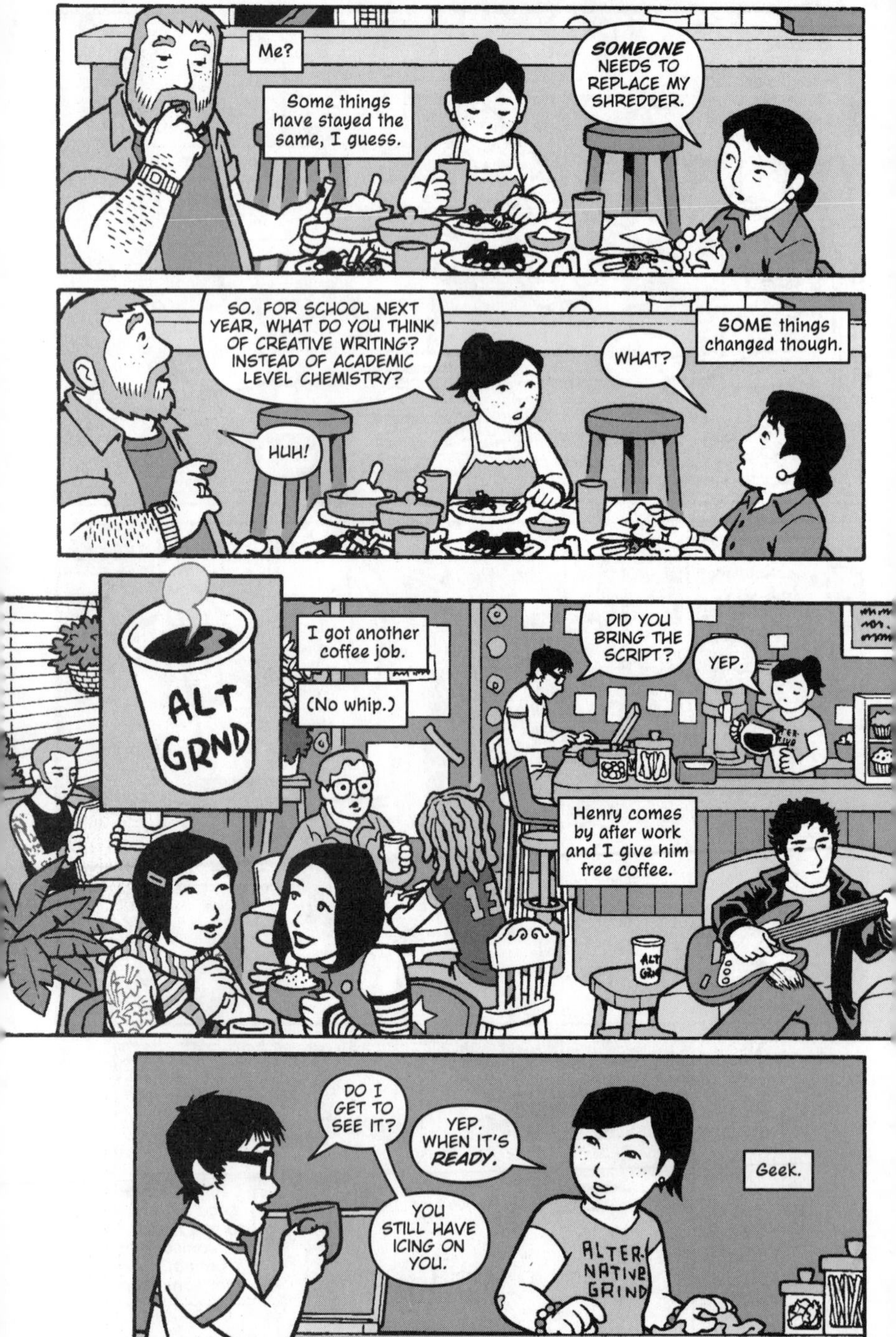
Me?
Some things have stayed the same, I guess.
SOMEONE NEEDS TO REPLACE MY SHREDDER.
SO. FOR SCHOOL NEXT YEAR, WHAT DO YOU THINK OF CREATIVE WRITING? INSTEAD OF ACADEMIC LEVEL CHEMISTRY?
WHAT?
SOME things changed though.
HUH!
ALT GRND
I got another coffee job.
(No whip.)
DID YOU BRING THE SCRIPT?
YEP.
Henry comes by after work and I give him free coffee.
DO I GET TO SEE IT?
YEP. WHEN IT'S READY.
YOU STILL HAVE ICING ON YOU.
Geek.
ALTER-NATIVE GRIND

As far as art goes...

I decided to re-retire Grandma Emiko's clothes.

Not to say I won't use them again, but--

★ GRANDMA ★
EMIKO'S STUFF
DO NOT
★ THROW
OUT!

THANKS, GRAM.

--right now I need to work on finding my own style.

I told Henry the truth about the diary stuff. He said it's a good story and that I should make it my own.

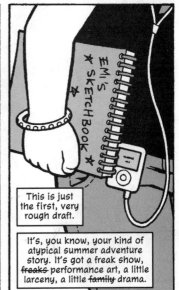

EMI'S ★SKETCHBOOK★

This is just the first, very rough draft.

It's, you know, your kind of atypical summer adventure story. It's got a freak show, ~~freaks~~ performance art, a little larceny, a little ~~family~~ drama.

I guess it's a story about love, although it's difficult to say what love is in this story.

I guess it's a story about how love isn't always what it makes itself out to be, if that makes sense.

It's a story about how true love is hard to find.

Mostly it's a story about me and how I became a Superstar, for a little while.

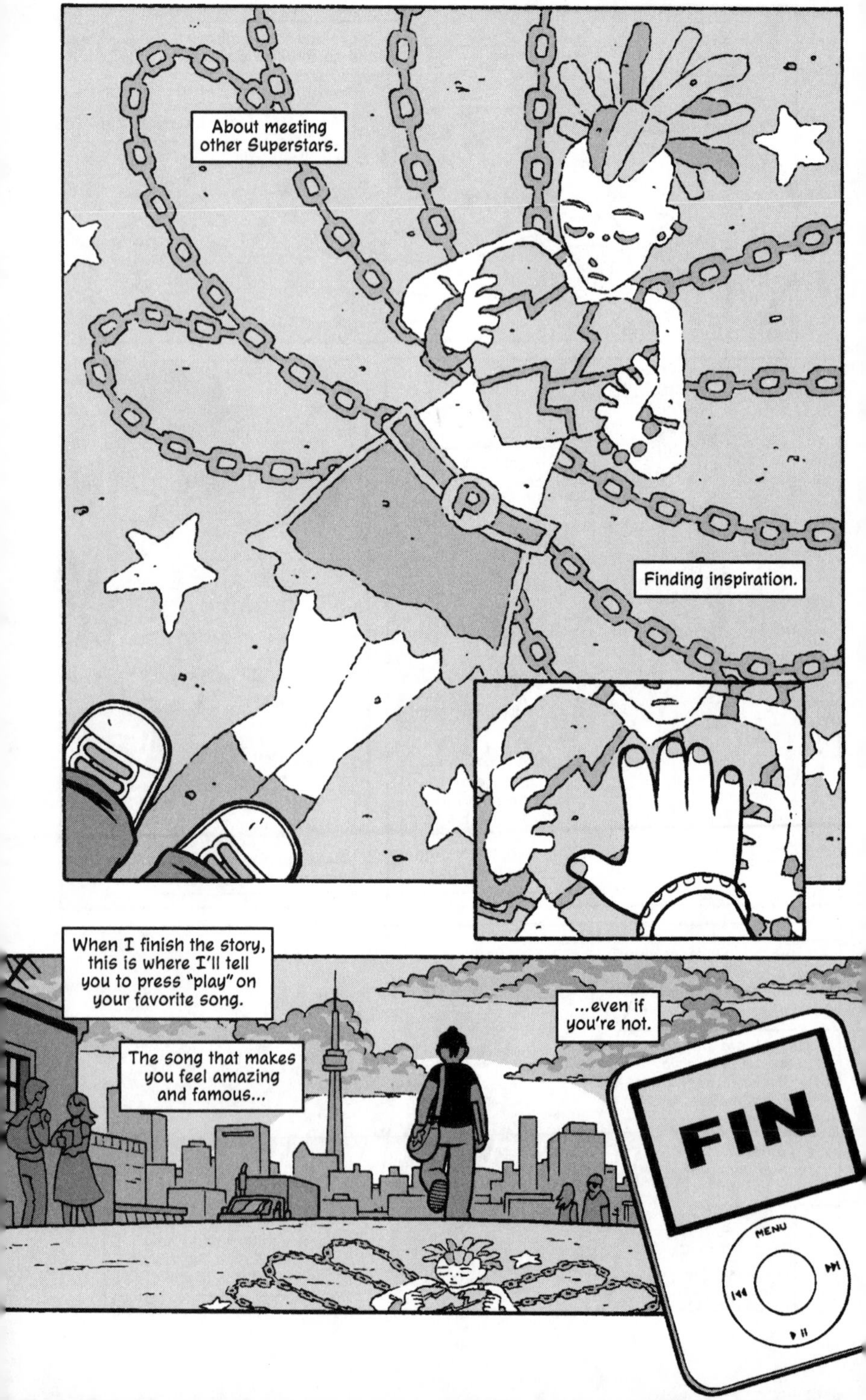
About meeting other Superstars.
Finding inspiration.
When I finish the story, this is where I'll tell you to press "play" on your favorite song.
The song that makes you feel amazing and famous...
...even if you're not.
FIN
MENU

MARIKO TAMAKI

Mariko is a Toronto writer, performer and playwright. She loves writing about hanging out and collaborating with amazing freaks and nerds who make art. Her previous work includes two collections of creative nonfiction and a graphic novel, *Skim*, about the trials of high school love (created with her cousin Jillian). When Mariko is not sitting in front of her computer she is usually zipping around the city on her scooter, Edie. Check out her website at www.marikotamaki.com.

STEVE ROLSTON

At the other end of Canada, Steve can be found drawing comics and whatnot in Vancouver. He made his first big splash as the premier artist on the Eisner Award-winning spy comic *Queen & Country*. His other credits include *The Escapists, Degrassi: Extra Credit, Pounded,* and his "slacker noir" graphic novel *One Bad Day*. You can spot him online at www.steverolston.com.

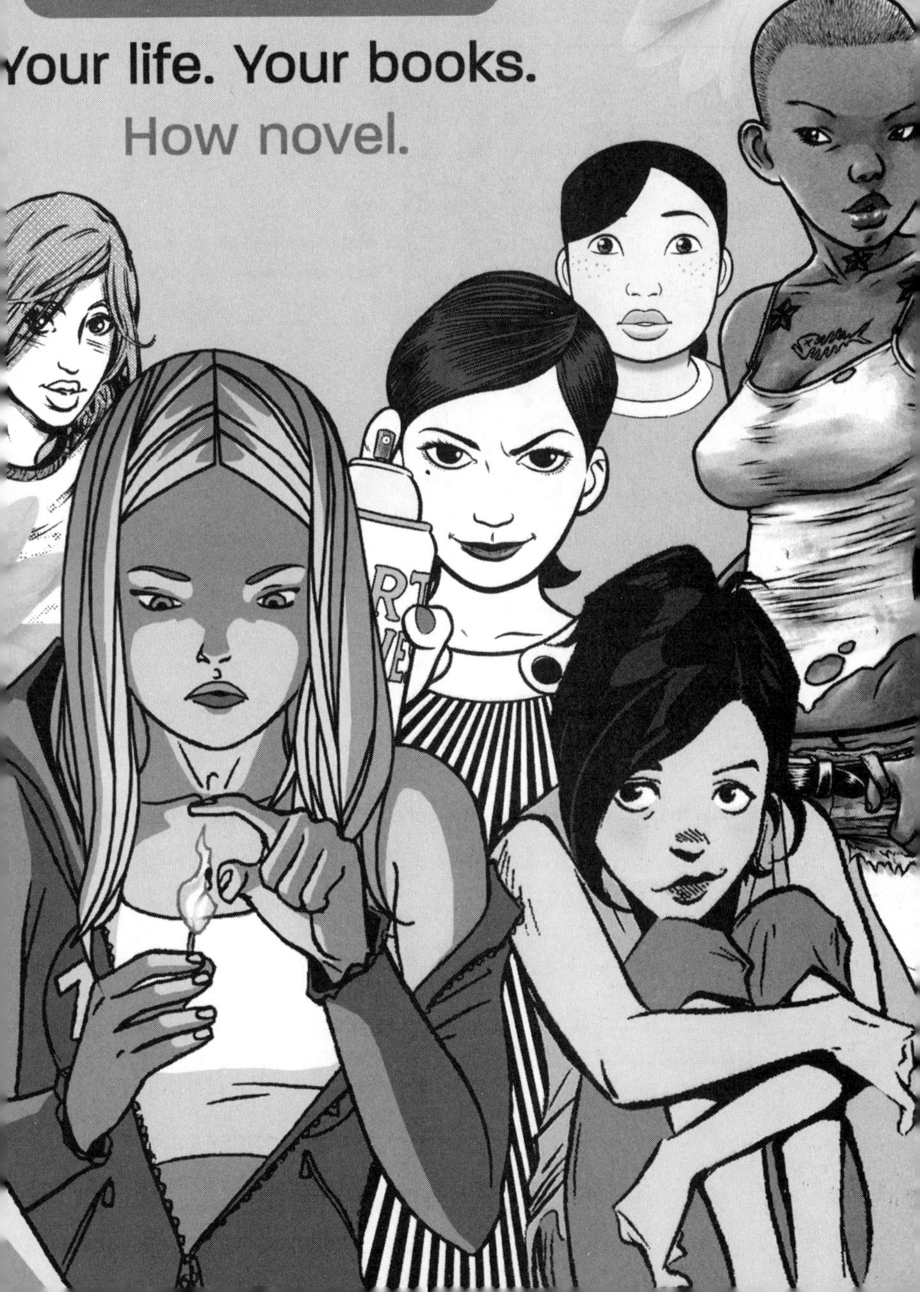

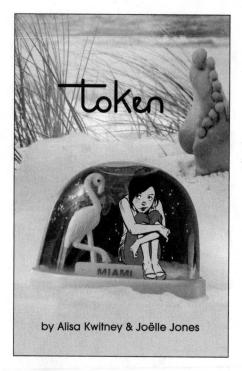

token

by Alisa Kwitney & Joëlle Jones

Written by noted comics author
and novelist ALISA KWITNEY

Can a Jewish "girl out of time" and a Spanish old soul survive culture clashes and

criminal records to find true love in the sun-drenched, sequined miasma that was

South Beach in the Big '80s?

By ALISA KWITNEY & JOËLLE JONES
AVAILABLE IN OCTOBER ■ Read on.
But please note: The following pages are not sequential.

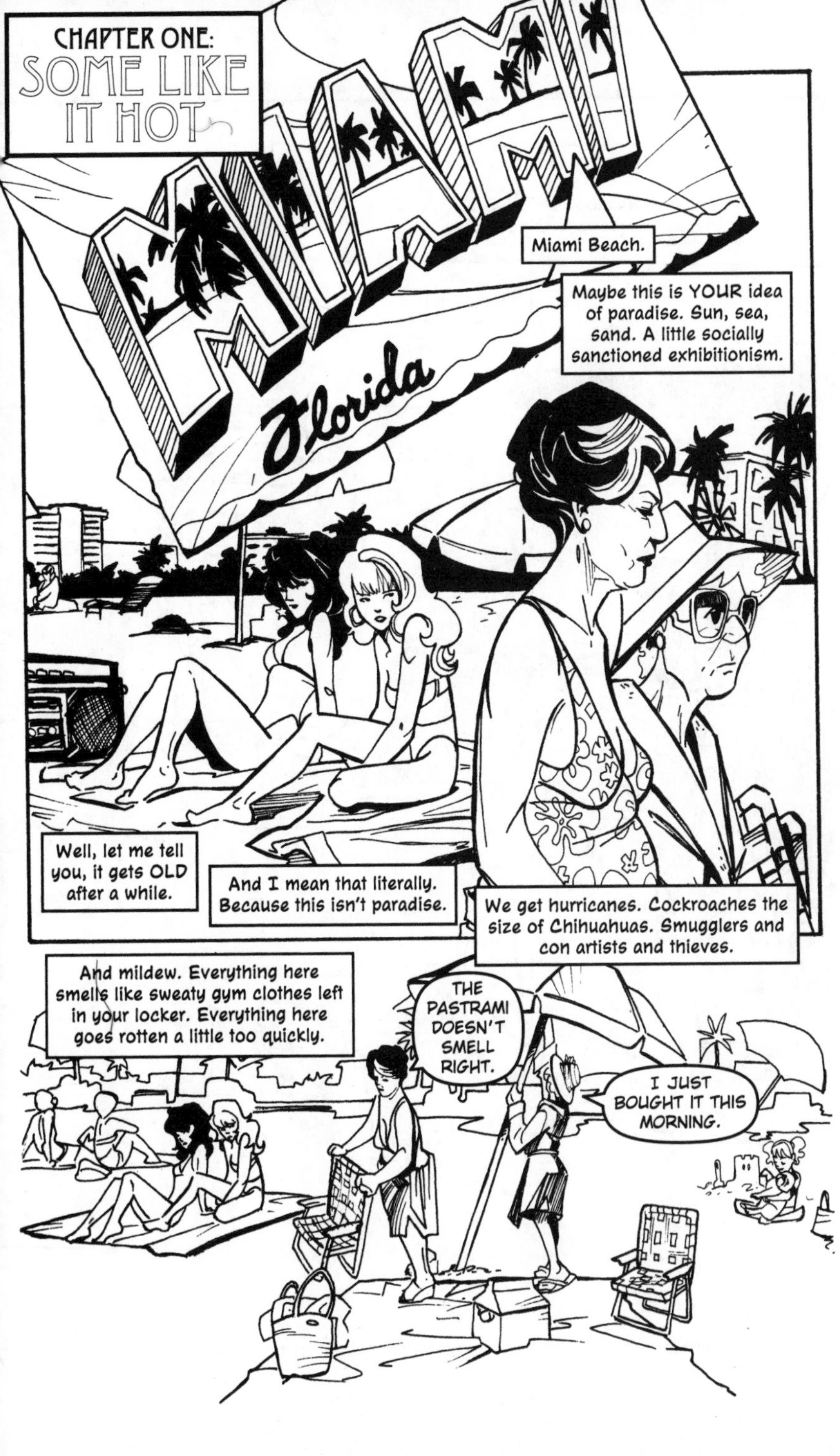
CHAPTER ONE:
SOME LIKE IT HOT
MIAMI
Florida
Miami Beach.
Maybe this is YOUR idea of paradise. Sun, sea, sand. A little socially sanctioned exhibitionism.
Well, let me tell you, it gets OLD after a while.
And I mean that literally. Because this isn't paradise.
We get hurricanes. Cockroaches the size of Chihuahuas. Smugglers and con artists and thieves.
And mildew. Everything here smells like sweaty gym clothes left in your locker. Everything here goes rotten a little too quickly.
THE PASTRAMI DOESN'T SMELL RIGHT.
I JUST BOUGHT IT THIS MORNING.

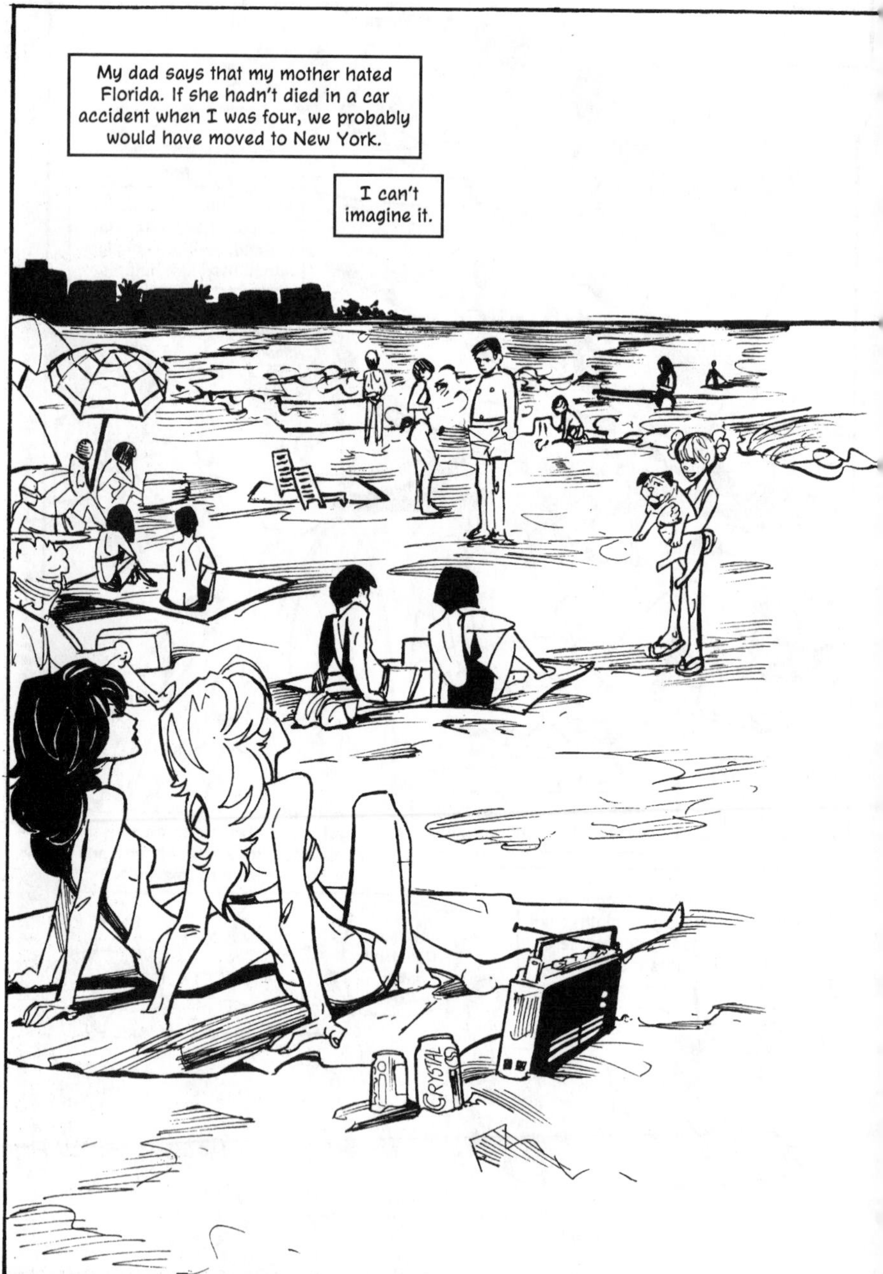

My dad says that my mother hated Florida. If she hadn't died in a car accident when I was four, we probably would have moved to New York.
I can't imagine it.
CRYSTAL

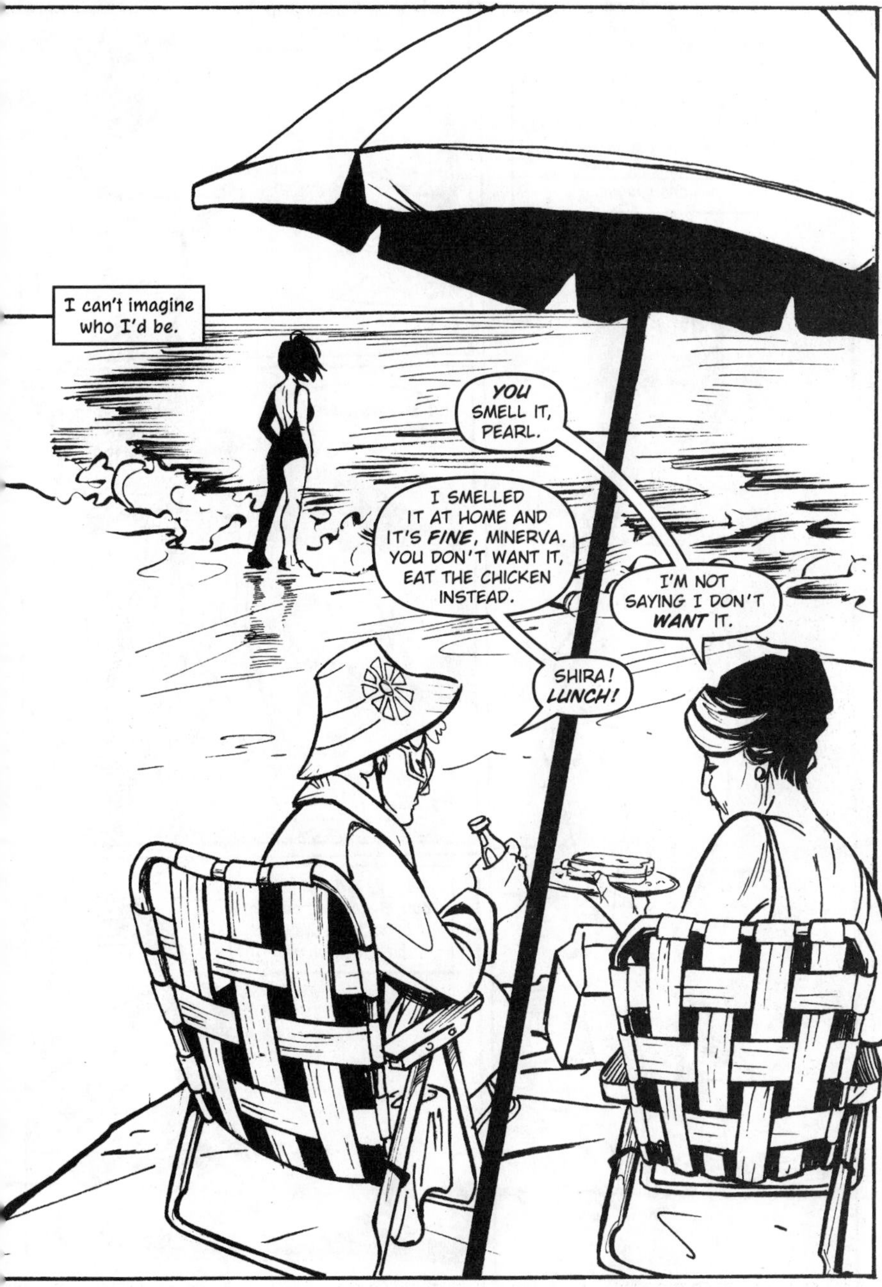
I can't imagine who I'd be.
YOU SMELL IT, PEARL.
I SMELLED IT AT HOME AND IT'S *FINE*, MINERVA. YOU DON'T WANT IT, EAT THE CHICKEN INSTEAD.
I'M NOT SAYING I DON'T *WANT* IT.
SHIRA! *LUNCH!*

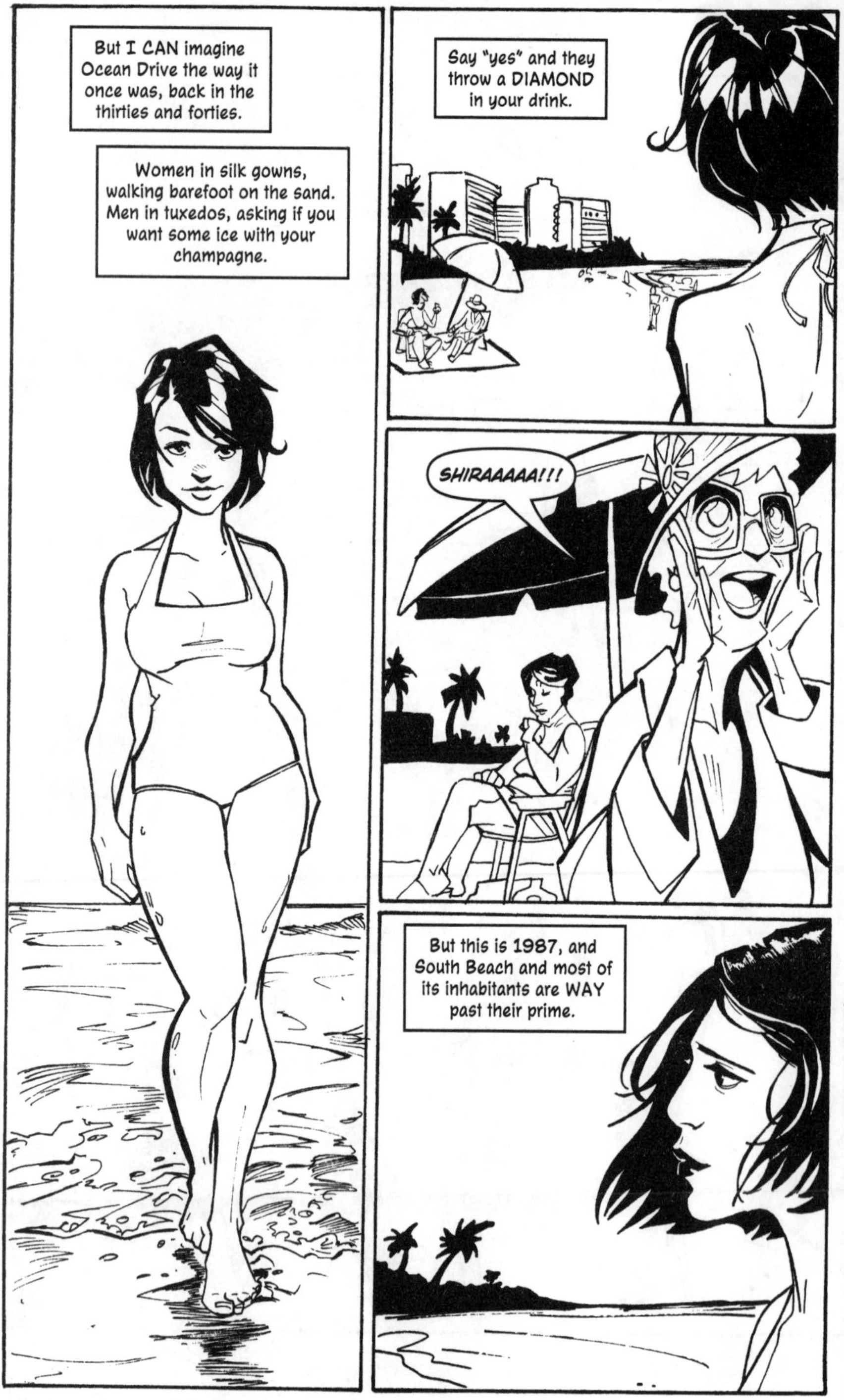
But I CAN imagine Ocean Drive the way it once was, back in the thirties and forties.
Women in silk gowns, walking barefoot on the sand. Men in tuxedos, asking if you want some ice with your champagne.
Say "yes" and they throw a DIAMOND in your drink.
SHIRAAAAA!!!
But this is 1987, and South Beach and most of its inhabitants are WAY past their prime.

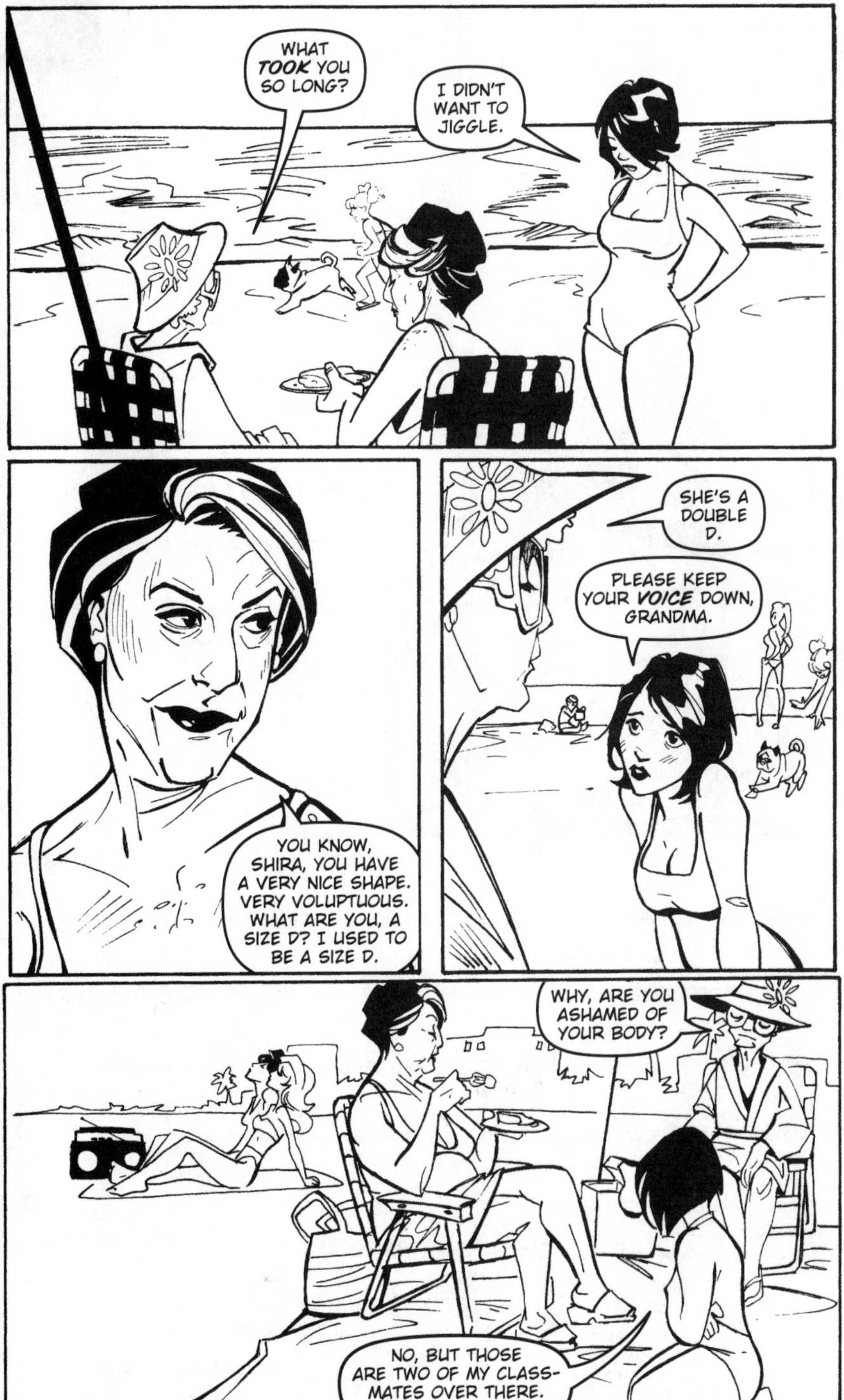
WHAT *TOOK* YOU SO LONG?
I DIDN'T WANT TO JIGGLE.
YOU KNOW, SHIRA, YOU HAVE A VERY NICE SHAPE. VERY VOLUPTUOUS. WHAT ARE YOU, A SIZE D? I USED TO BE A SIZE D.
SHE'S A DOUBLE D.
PLEASE KEEP YOUR *VOICE* DOWN, GRANDMA.
WHY, ARE YOU ASHAMED OF YOUR BODY?
NO, BUT THOSE ARE TWO OF MY CLASS-MATES OVER THERE.

By the highly acclaimed author of *Boy Proof* and *Beige*

JANES ♥ in LOVE

by CECIL CASTELLUCCI *and* JIM RUGG

Praise for The Plain Janes:

"Thought-provoking....absolutely engaging..."

— Booklist, Starred review

Starred review in Publishers Weekly

Washington Post Best of 2007 pick

Included in The New York Public Library's Books for the Teen Age 2008

The second title in the PLAIN JANES series finds the coolest clique of misfits playing cupid and becoming entangled in the affairs of the heart. P.L.A.I.N., People Loving Art In Neighborhoods, goes global once the art gang procures a spot in the Metro City Museum of Modern Art contest. And the girls will discover that in art and in love, general rules don't often apply.

By CECIL CASTELLUCCI & JIM RUGG
AVAILABLE NOW ■ Read on.

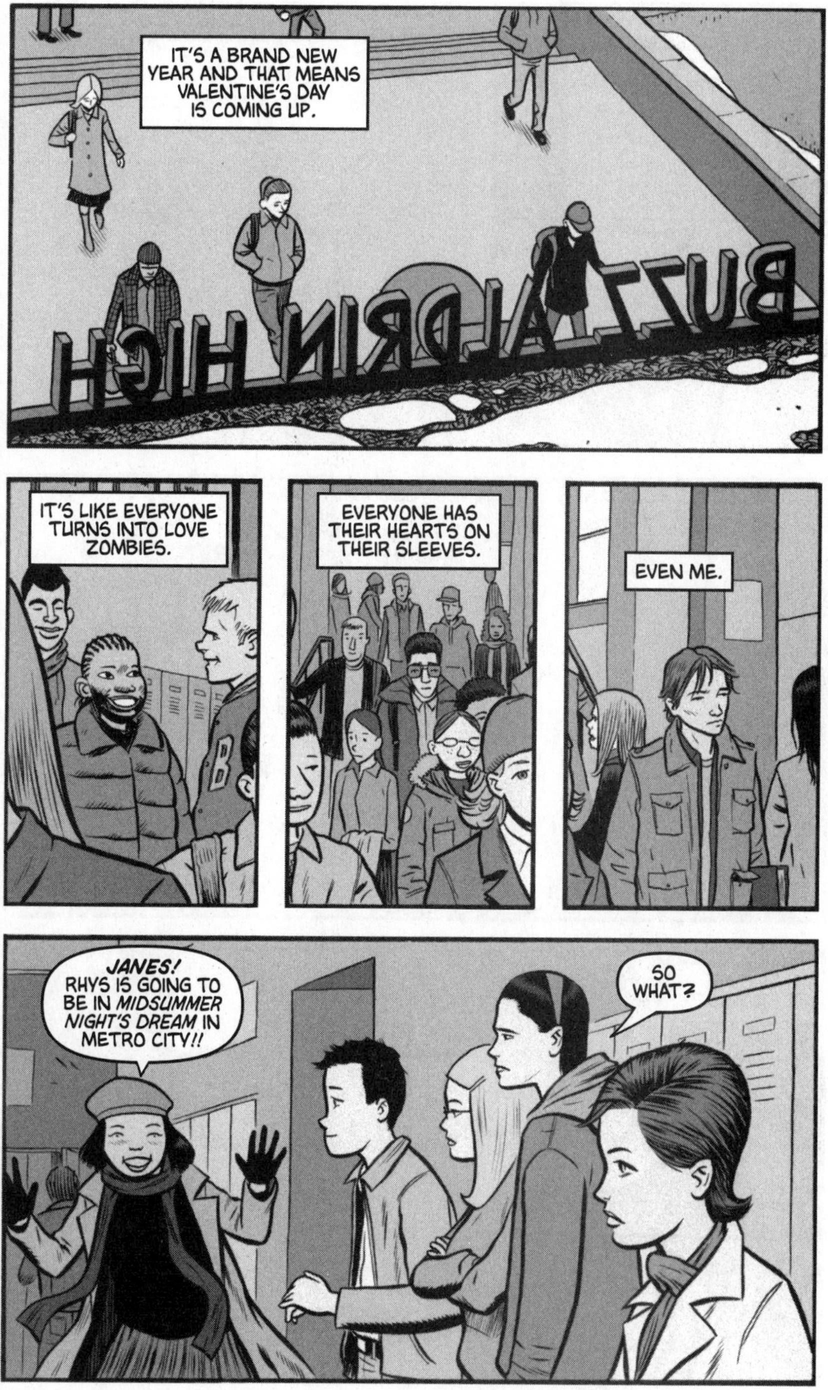
IT'S A BRAND NEW YEAR AND THAT MEANS VALENTINE'S DAY IS COMING UP.
IT'S LIKE EVERYONE TURNS INTO LOVE ZOMBIES.
EVERYONE HAS THEIR HEARTS ON THEIR SLEEVES.
EVEN ME.
JANES! RHYS IS GOING TO BE IN *MIDSUMMER NIGHT'S DREAM* IN METRO CITY!!
SO WHAT?

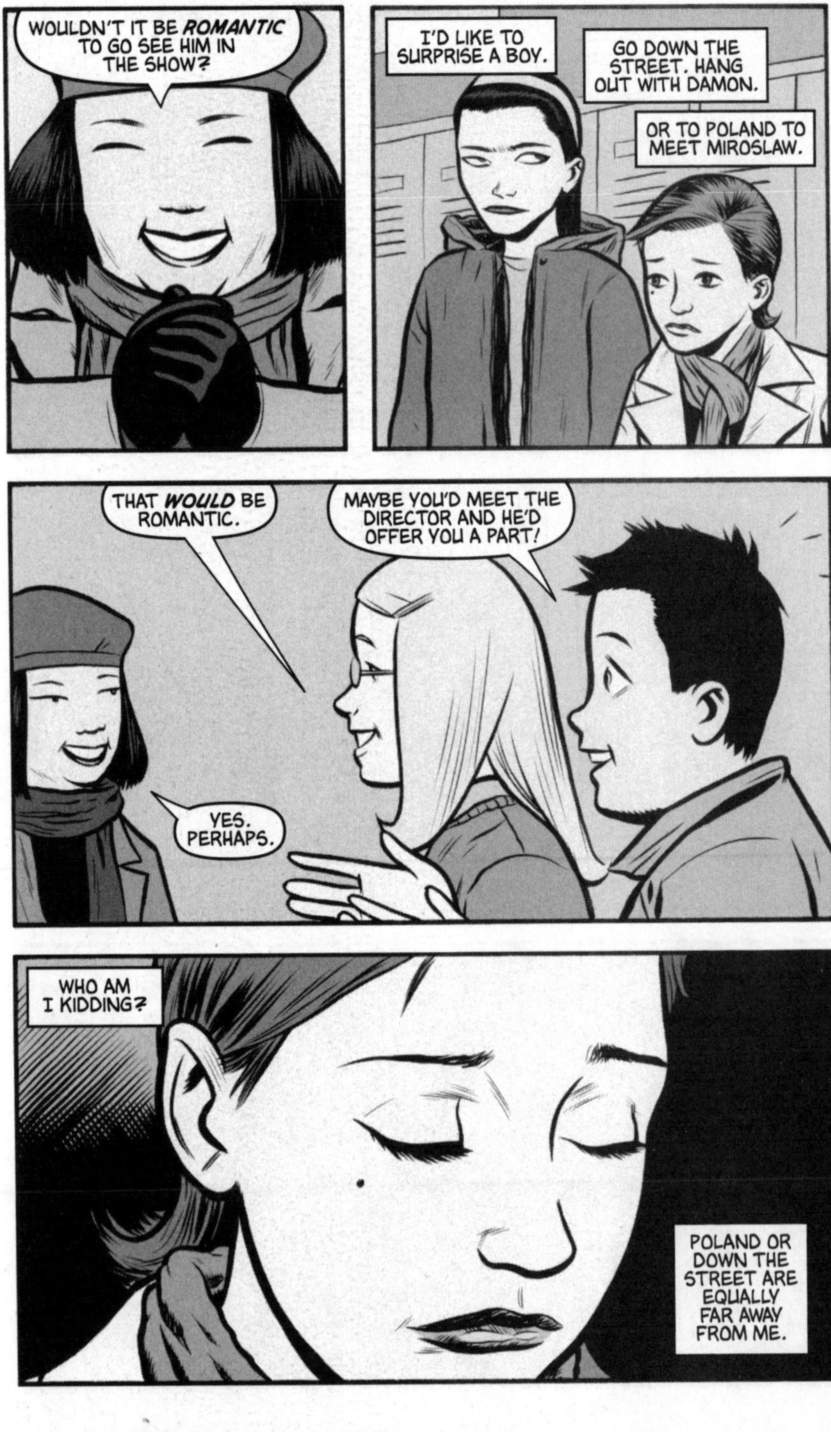
WOULDN'T IT BE ROMANTIC TO GO SEE HIM IN THE SHOW?
I'D LIKE TO SURPRISE A BOY.
GO DOWN THE STREET. HANG OUT WITH DAMON.
OR TO POLAND TO MEET MIROSLAW.
THAT WOULD BE ROMANTIC.
MAYBE YOU'D MEET THE DIRECTOR AND HE'D OFFER YOU A PART!
YES. PERHAPS.
WHO AM I KIDDING?
POLAND OR DOWN THE STREET ARE EQUALLY FAR AWAY FROM ME.

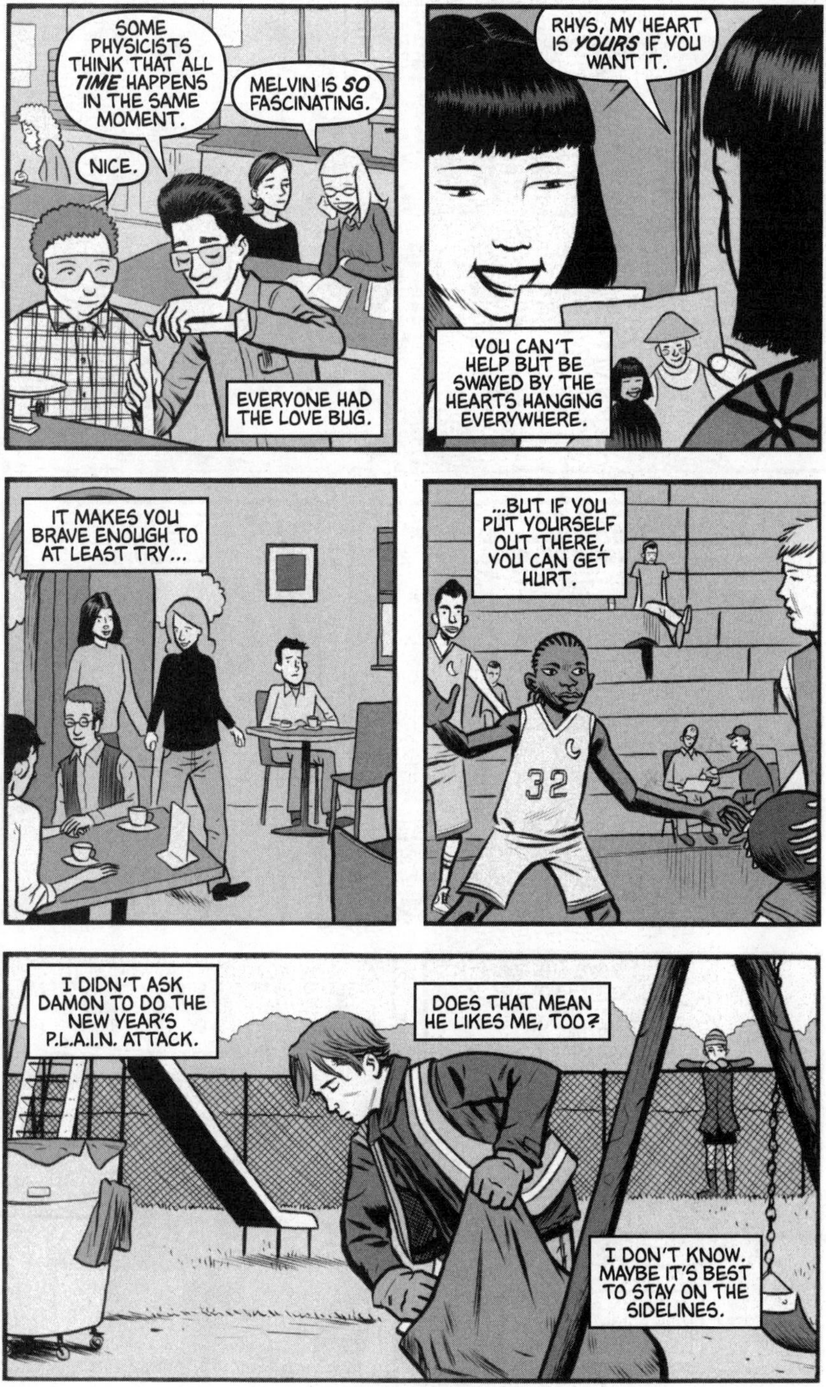
SOME PHYSICISTS THINK THAT ALL TIME HAPPENS IN THE SAME MOMENT.
MELVIN IS SO FASCINATING.
NICE.
EVERYONE HAD THE LOVE BUG.
RHYS, MY HEART IS YOURS IF YOU WANT IT.
YOU CAN'T HELP BUT BE SWAYED BY THE HEARTS HANGING EVERYWHERE.
IT MAKES YOU BRAVE ENOUGH TO AT LEAST TRY...
...BUT IF YOU PUT YOURSELF OUT THERE, YOU CAN GET HURT.
32
I DIDN'T ASK DAMON TO DO THE NEW YEAR'S P.L.A.I.N. ATTACK.
DOES THAT MEAN HE LIKES ME, TOO?
I DON'T KNOW. MAYBE IT'S BEST TO STAY ON THE SIDELINES.

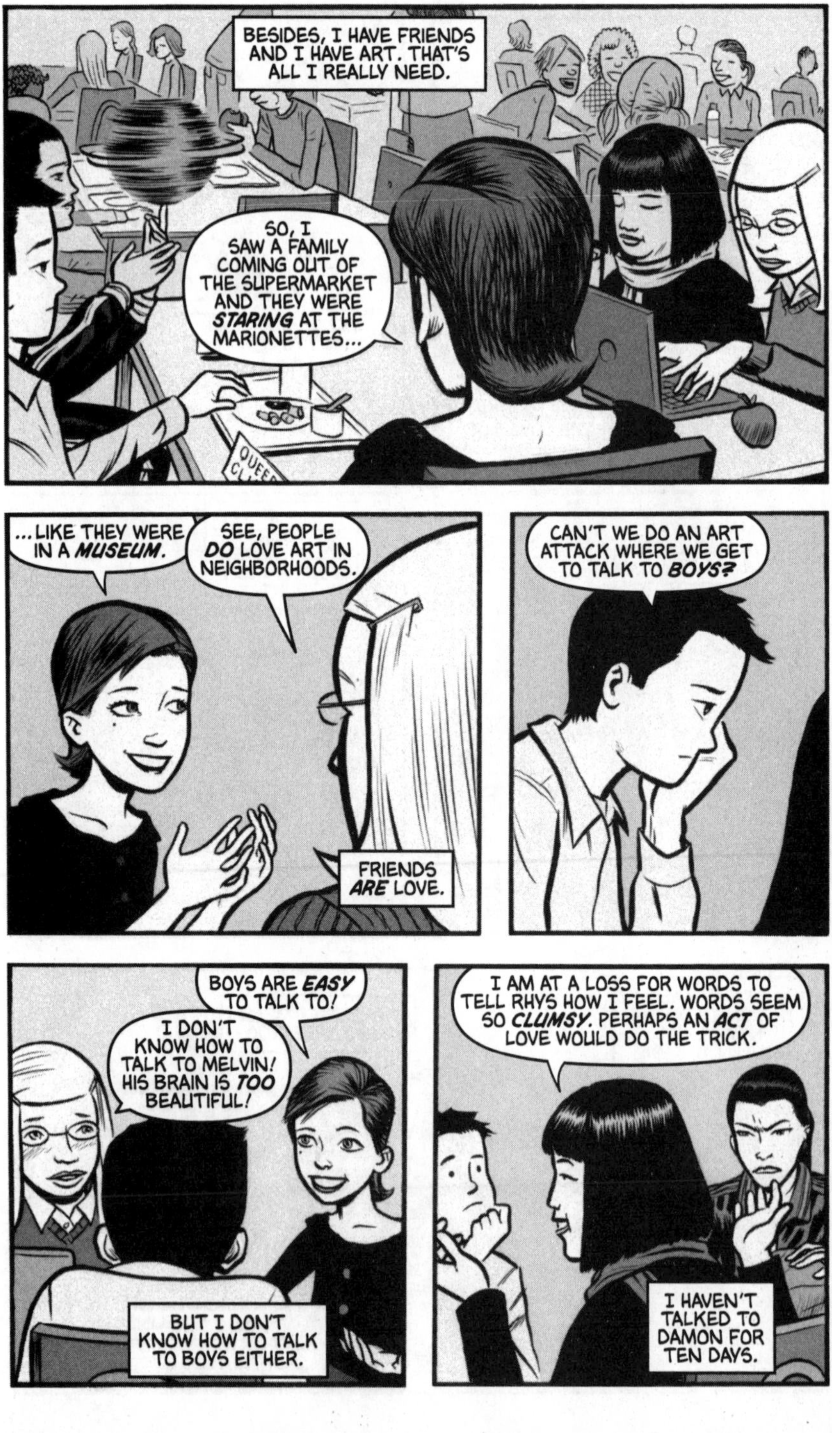
BESIDES, I HAVE FRIENDS AND I HAVE ART. THAT'S ALL I REALLY NEED.
SO, I SAW A FAMILY COMING OUT OF THE SUPERMARKET AND THEY WERE *STARING* AT THE MARIONETTES...
...LIKE THEY WERE IN A *MUSEUM*.
SEE, PEOPLE *DO* LOVE ART IN NEIGHBORHOODS.
FRIENDS *ARE* LOVE.
CAN'T WE DO AN ART ATTACK WHERE WE GET TO TALK TO *BOYS?*
BOYS ARE *EASY* TO TALK TO!
I DON'T KNOW HOW TO TALK TO MELVIN! HIS BRAIN IS *TOO* BEAUTIFUL!
BUT I DON'T KNOW HOW TO TALK TO BOYS EITHER.
I AM AT A LOSS FOR WORDS TO TELL RHYS HOW I FEEL. WORDS SEEM SO *CLUMSY*. PERHAPS AN *ACT* OF LOVE WOULD DO THE TRICK.
I HAVEN'T TALKED TO DAMON FOR TEN DAYS.

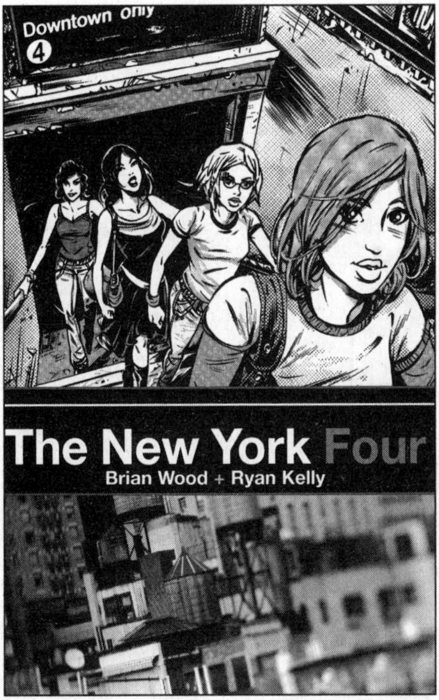
Downtown only
4
The New York Four
Brian Wood + Ryan Kelly

Written by multiple Eisner Award nominee/indie icon BRIAN WOOD

Experience New York City through the eyes of Riley, a shy, almost reclusive straight-A student who convinces three other NYU freshmen to join a research group to earn extra money.

As the girls become fast friends, two things complicate what should be the greatest time of Riley's life: connecting with her arty, estranged older sister and having a mysterious online crush on a guy known only as "sneakerfreak."

By BRIAN WOOD & RYAN KELLY

AVAILABLE NOW ■ Read on.

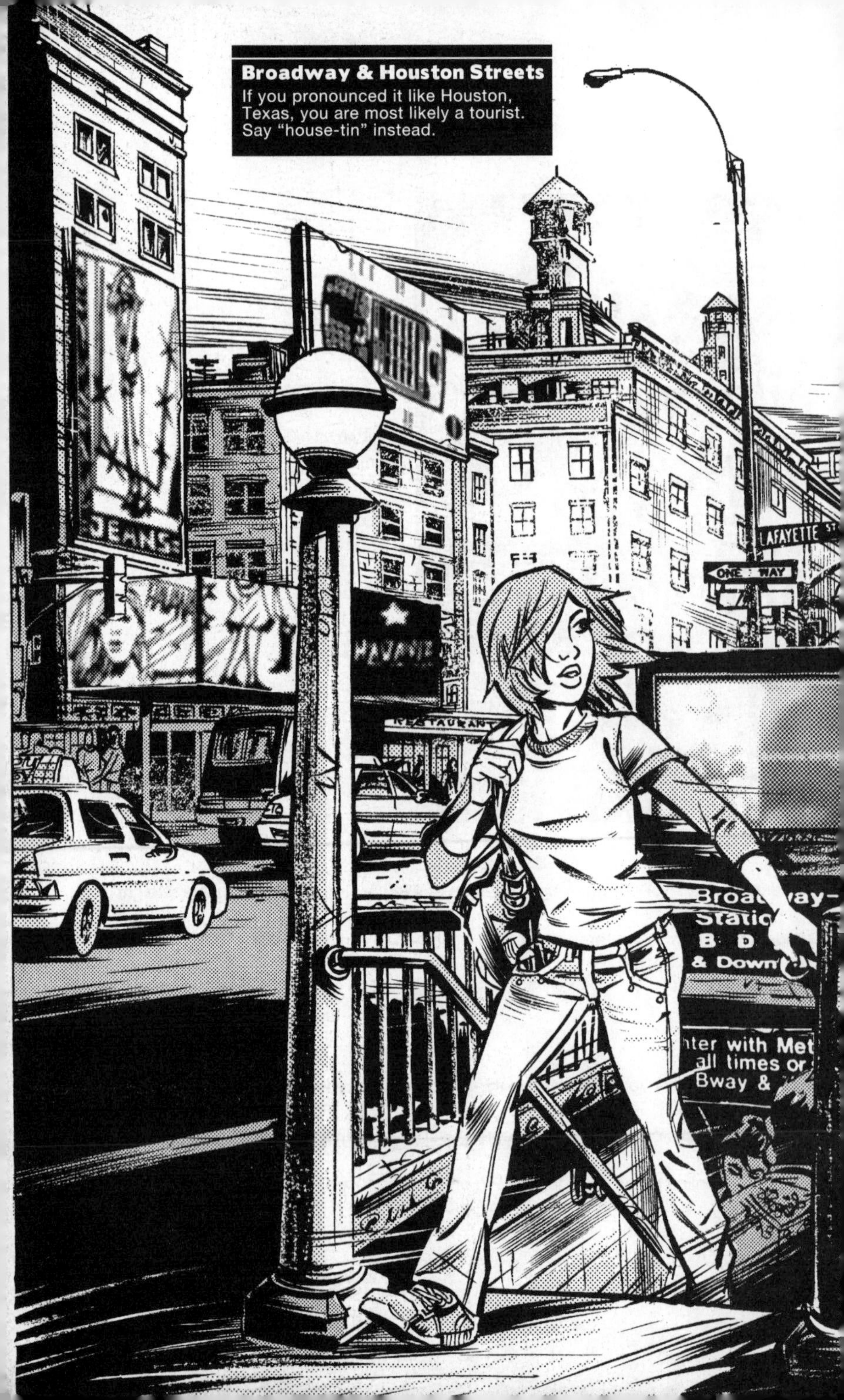
Broadway & Houston Streets
If you pronounced it like Houston, Texas, you are most likely a tourist. Say "house-tin" instead.
JEANS
LAFAYETTE ST
ONE WAY
RESTAURANT

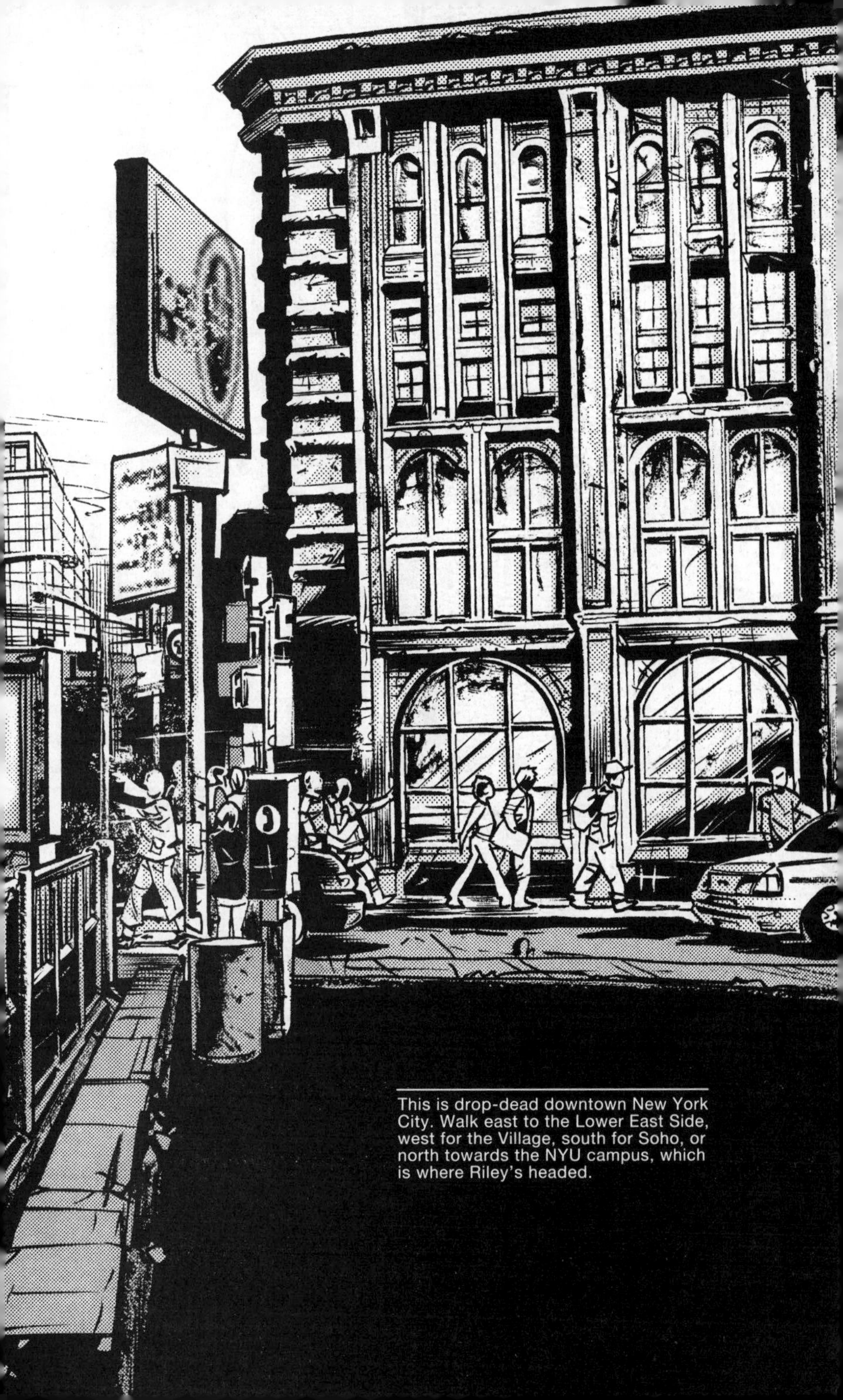
This is drop-dead downtown New York City. Walk east to the Lower East Side, west for the Village, south for Soho, or north towards the NYU campus, which is where Riley's headed.

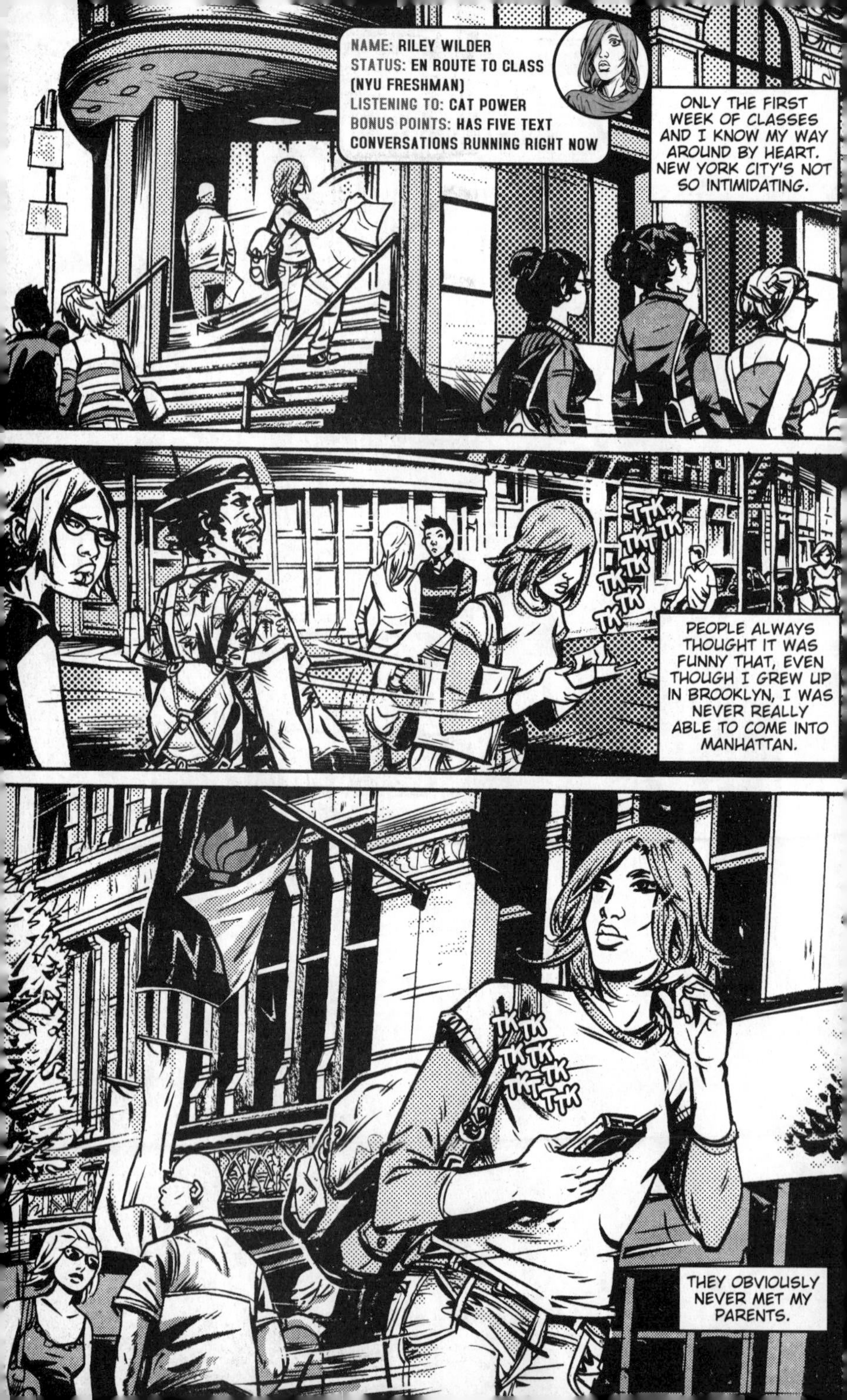
NAME: RILEY WILDER
STATUS: EN ROUTE TO CLASS (NYU FRESHMAN)
LISTENING TO: CAT POWER
BONUS POINTS: HAS FIVE TEXT CONVERSATIONS RUNNING RIGHT NOW
ONLY THE FIRST WEEK OF CLASSES AND I KNOW MY WAY AROUND BY HEART. NEW YORK CITY'S NOT SO INTIMIDATING.
TTK TK TK TK TK TK TK TK TK
PEOPLE ALWAYS THOUGHT IT WAS FUNNY THAT, EVEN THOUGH I GREW UP IN BROOKLYN, I WAS NEVER REALLY ABLE TO COME INTO MANHATTAN.
TK TK TK TK TKT TK TTK
THEY OBVIOUSLY NEVER MET MY PARENTS.

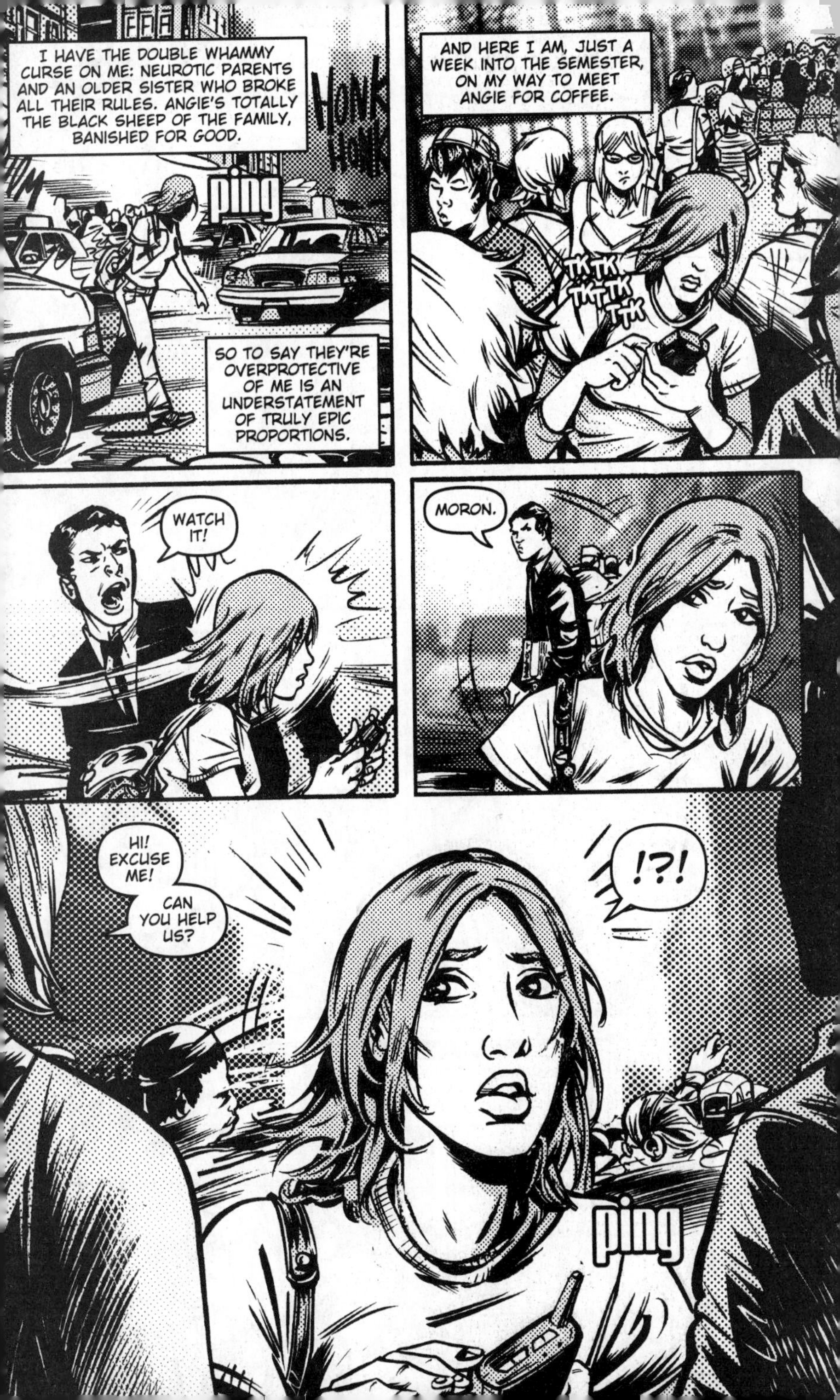
I HAVE THE DOUBLE WHAMMY CURSE ON ME: NEUROTIC PARENTS AND AN OLDER SISTER WHO BROKE ALL THEIR RULES. ANGIE'S TOTALLY THE BLACK SHEEP OF THE FAMILY, BANISHED FOR GOOD.
HONK
HONK
ping
SO TO SAY THEY'RE OVERPROTECTIVE OF ME IS AN UNDERSTATEMENT OF TRULY EPIC PROPORTIONS.
AND HERE I AM, JUST A WEEK INTO THE SEMESTER, ON MY WAY TO MEET ANGIE FOR COFFEE.
TK TK TK TK TK TK
WATCH IT!
MORON.
HI! EXCUSE ME!
CAN YOU HELP US?
!?!
ping

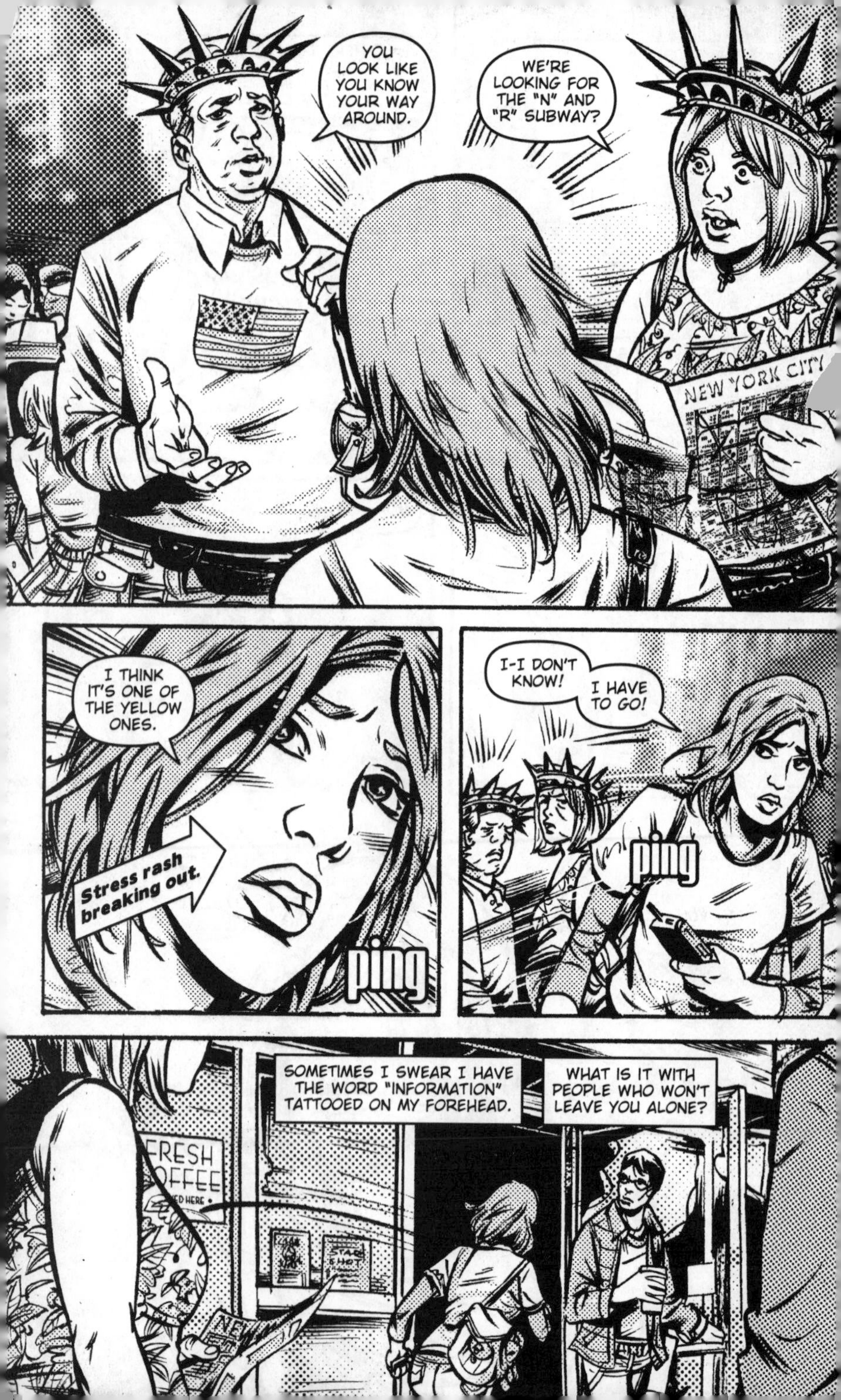
YOU LOOK LIKE YOU KNOW YOUR WAY AROUND.
WE'RE LOOKING FOR THE "N" AND "R" SUBWAY?
NEW YORK CITY
I THINK IT'S ONE OF THE YELLOW ONES.
Stress rash breaking out.
ping
I-I DON'T KNOW!
I HAVE TO GO!
ping
SOMETIMES I SWEAR I HAVE THE WORD "INFORMATION" TATTOOED ON MY FOREHEAD.
WHAT IS IT WITH PEOPLE WHO WON'T LEAVE YOU ALONE?
FRESH
OFFEE

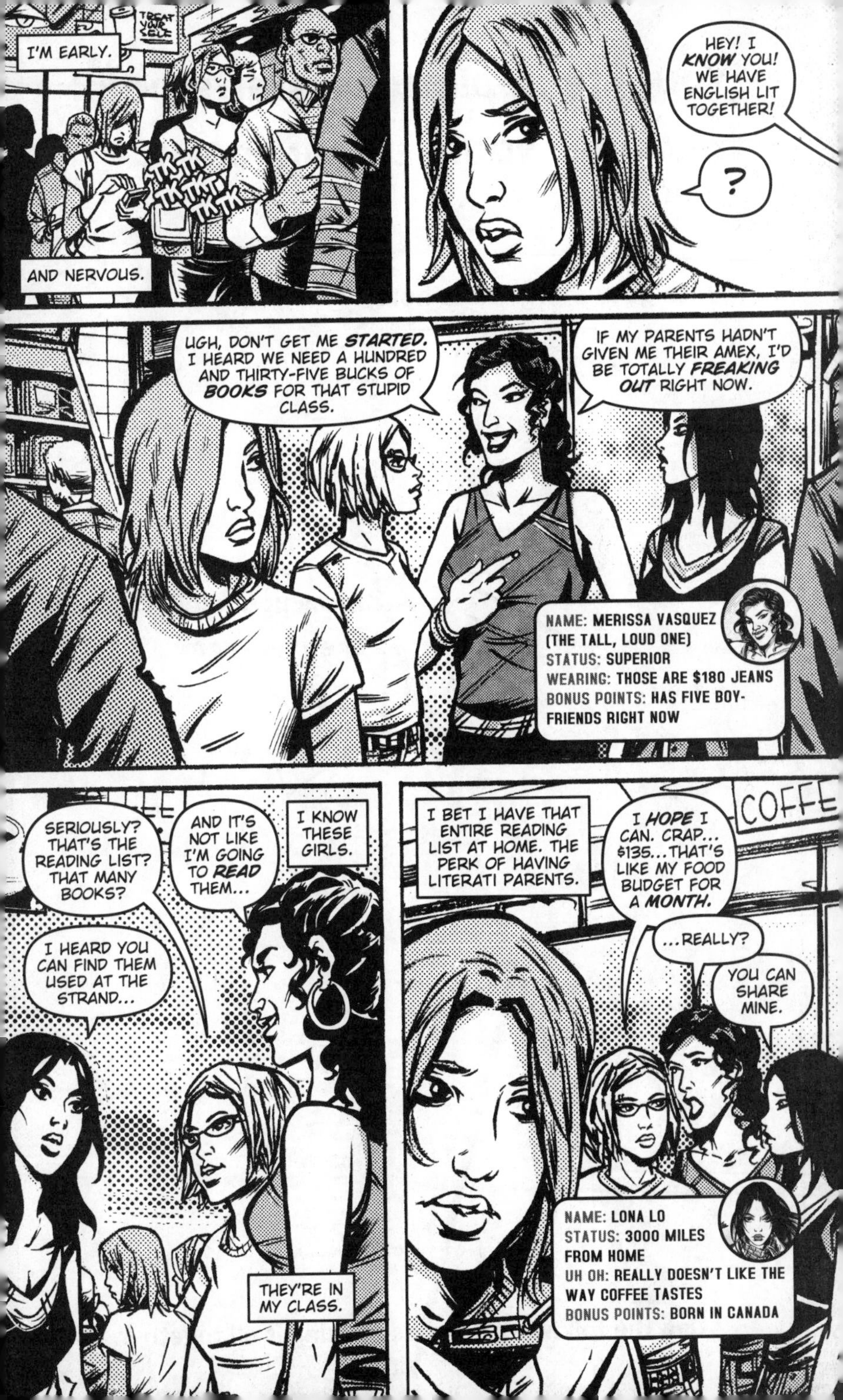
TREAT YOUR SELF
I'M EARLY.
TK TK TK TK TK TK
AND NERVOUS.
HEY! I KNOW YOU! WE HAVE ENGLISH LIT TOGETHER!
?
UGH, DON'T GET ME STARTED. I HEARD WE NEED A HUNDRED AND THIRTY-FIVE BUCKS OF BOOKS FOR THAT STUPID CLASS.
IF MY PARENTS HADN'T GIVEN ME THEIR AMEX, I'D BE TOTALLY FREAKING OUT RIGHT NOW.
NAME: MERISSA VASQUEZ (THE TALL, LOUD ONE)
STATUS: SUPERIOR
WEARING: THOSE ARE $180 JEANS
BONUS POINTS: HAS FIVE BOY-FRIENDS RIGHT NOW
SERIOUSLY? THAT'S THE READING LIST? THAT MANY BOOKS?
AND IT'S NOT LIKE I'M GOING TO READ THEM...
I KNOW THESE GIRLS.
I HEARD YOU CAN FIND THEM USED AT THE STRAND...
THEY'RE IN MY CLASS.
COFFE
I BET I HAVE THAT ENTIRE READING LIST AT HOME. THE PERK OF HAVING LITERATI PARENTS.
I HOPE I CAN. CRAP... $135...THAT'S LIKE MY FOOD BUDGET FOR A MONTH.
...REALLY?
YOU CAN SHARE MINE.
NAME: LONA LO
STATUS: 3000 MILES FROM HOME
UH OH: REALLY DOESN'T LIKE THE WAY COFFEE TASTES
BONUS POINTS: BORN IN CANADA

Your life in pictures starts here!

~A DO-IT YOURSELF MINI COMIC~

Write your story ideas here:

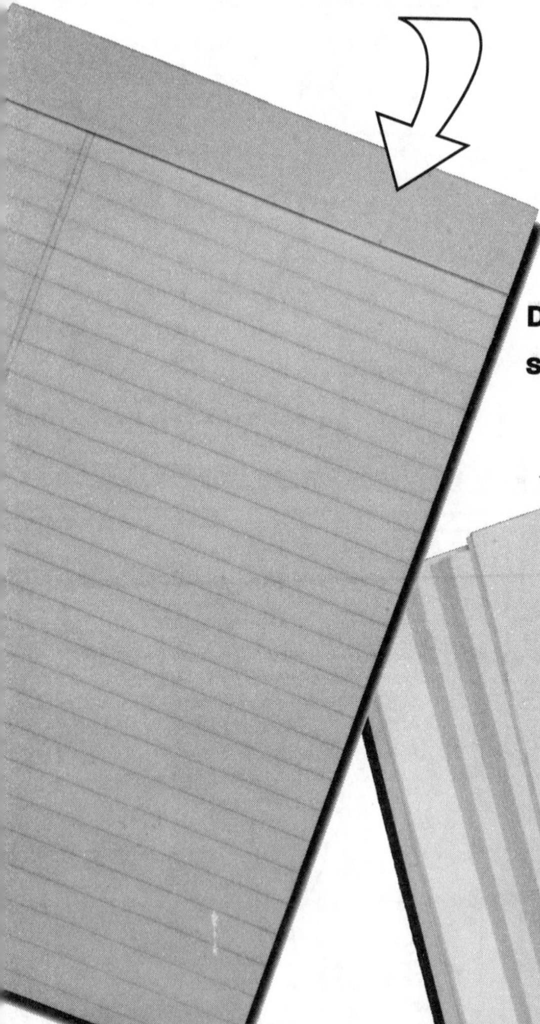

Draw your main character sketches here:

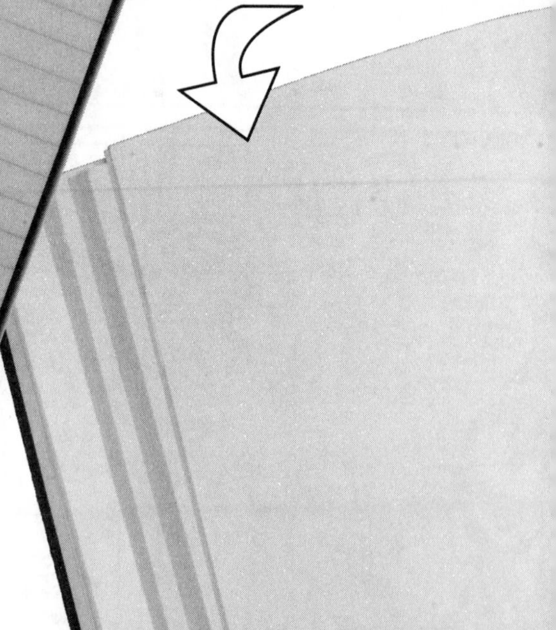

Use the following 3 pages to bring it all together.

TITLE: BY:

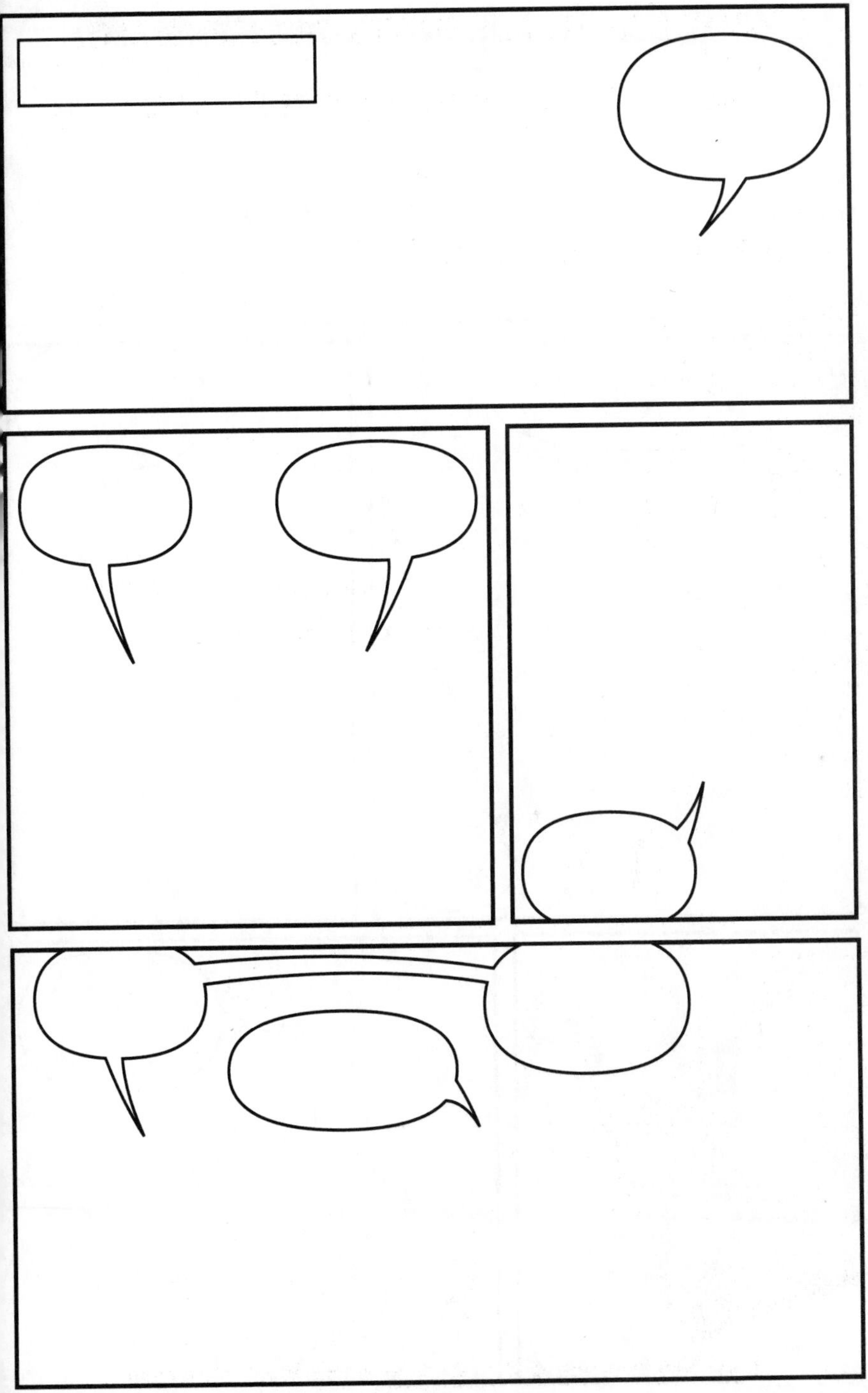

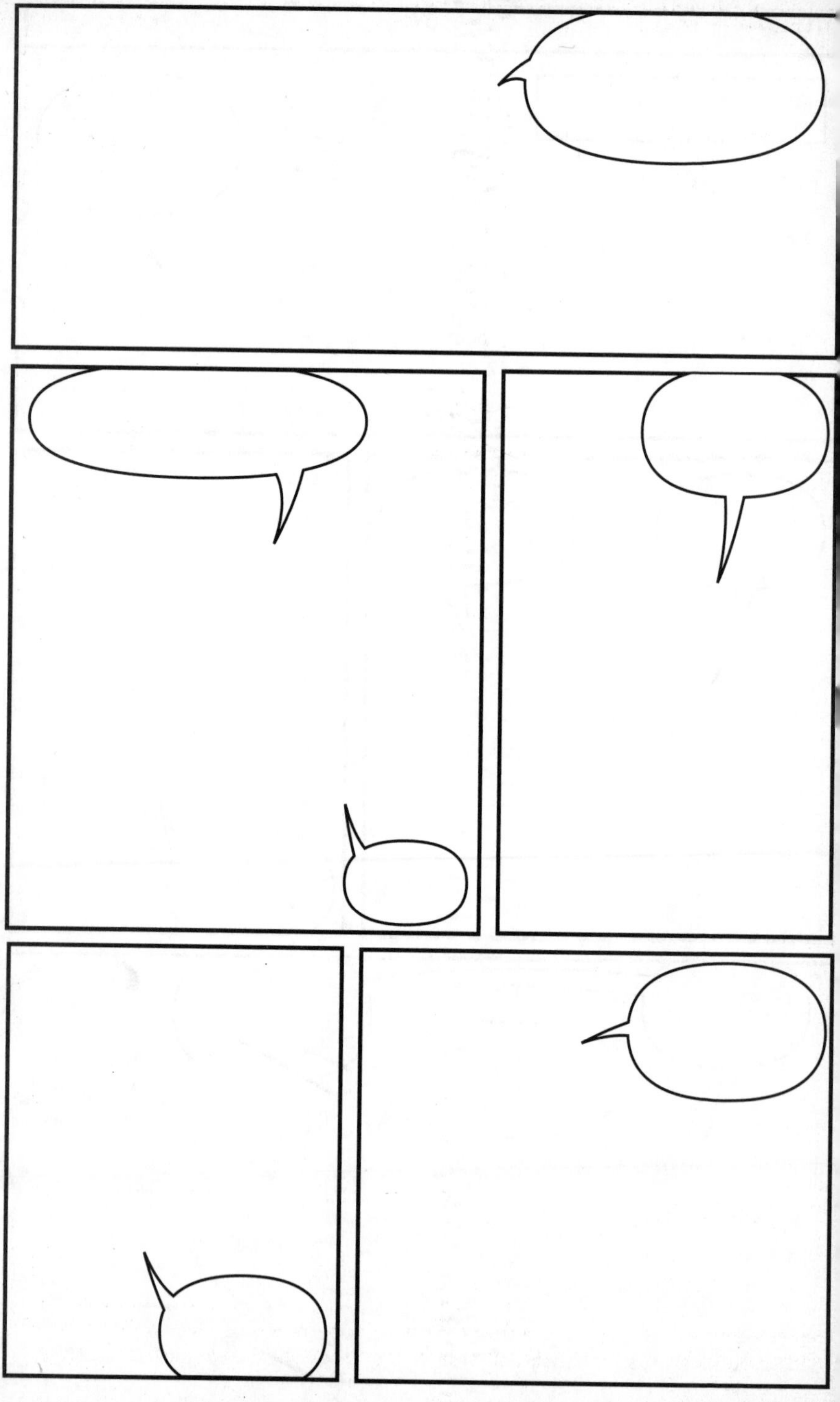

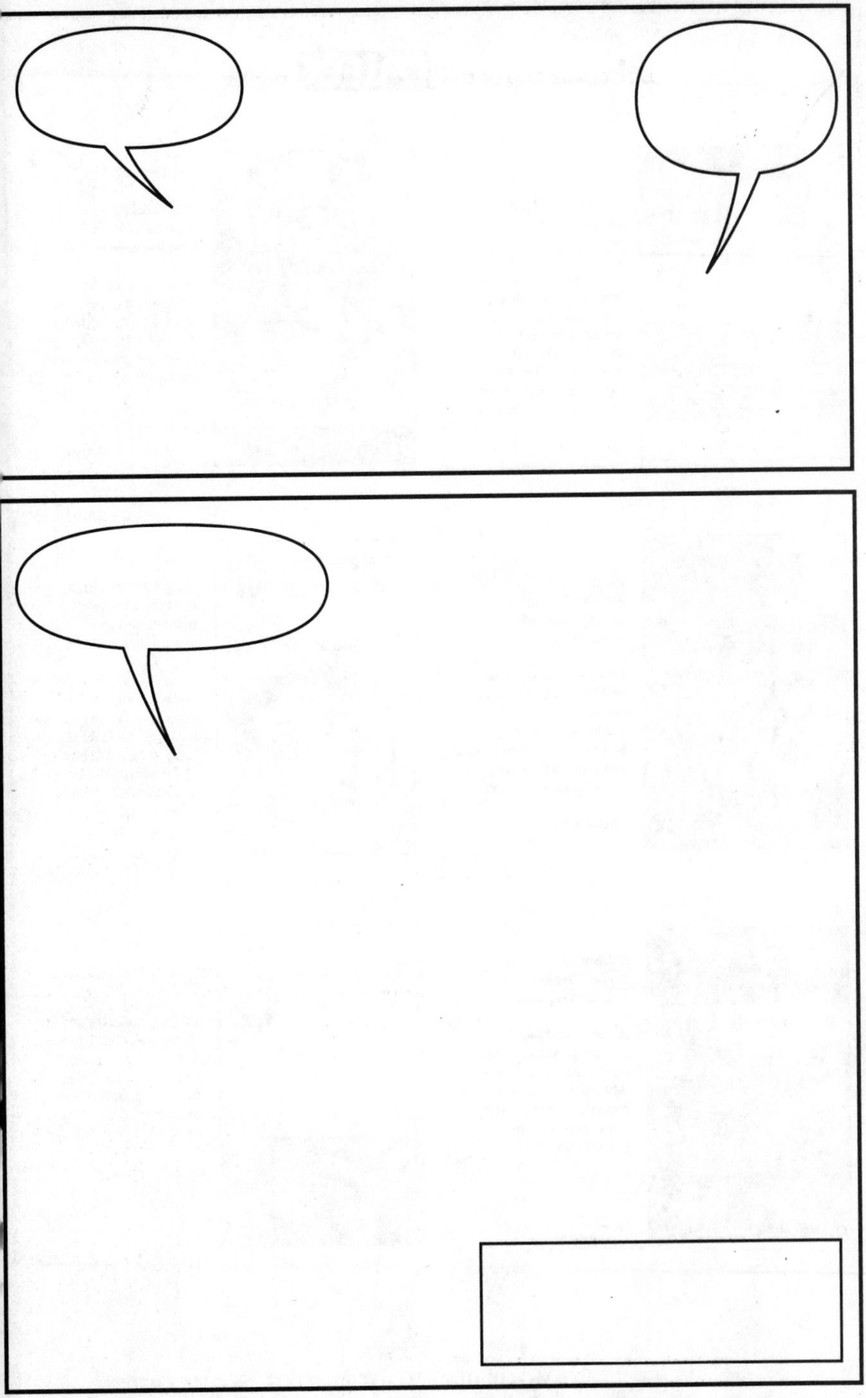

CHECK OUT STORYTELLING TIPS FROM TOP WRITERS AND ARTISTS AT MINXBOOKS.NET

Don't miss any of the minx books:

THE PLAIN JANES
By Cecil Castellucci
and Jim Rugg

Four girls named Jane are anything but ordinary once they form a secret art gang called P.L.A.I.N. — People Loving Art In Neighborhoods. But can art attacks really save the hell that is high school?

GOOD AS LILY
By Derek Kirk Kim
and Jesse Hamm

What would you do if versions of yourself at 6, 29 and 70 suddenly appear and wreak havoc on your already awkward existence?

RE-GIFTERS
By Mike Carey,
Sonny Liew and
Marc Hempel

It's love, Korean-American style when a tenacious martial artist falls for a California surfer boy and learns that in romance and recycled gifts, what goes around comes around.

YALSA Winner

CONFESSIONS OF A BLABBERMOUTH
By Mike and Louise Carey
and Aaron Alexovich

When Tasha's mom brings home a creepy boyfriend and his deadpan daughter, a dysfunctional family is headed for a complete meltdown. By the father-daughter writing team.

CLUBBING
By Andi Watson
and Josh Howard

A spoiled, rebellious Londoner takes on the stuffy English countryside when she solves a murder mystery on the 19th hole of her grandparents' golf course.

KIMMIE66
By Aaron Alexovich

This high-velocity, virtual reality ghost story follows a tech-savvy teenager on a dangerous quest to save her best friend, the world's first all-digital girl.

Your life. Your books. *How novel.*

minxbooks.net